Language Acquisition and Development

Language Acquisition and Development

Studies of Learners of First and Other Languages

Edited by Brian Tomlinson

continuum

Continuum

The Tower Building	80 Maiden Lane
11 York Road	Suite 704
London SE1 7NX	New York, NY 10038

British Library Cataloguing-in-Publication Data
A catalogue record for this book is available from the British Library.

ISBN: 0-8264-8612-6 (HB)

Typeset by RefineCatch Limited, Bungay, Suffolk
Printed and bound in Great Britain by
Athenaeum Press Ltd, Gateshead, Tyne and Wear

Contents

List of Contributors

Jane Arnold, University of Seville

Javier Avila, University of Cordoba

Nola Bacha, The Lebanese American University, Byblos

Erlin Susanti Barnard, University of Wisconsin

Natalie Braber, Nottingham Trent University

Beatriz Centeno-Cortes, Colegio Montessori, Salamanca

Bao Dat, Assumption University, Bangkok

Carmen Fonseca, University of Huelva

Irma-Kaarina Ghosn, The Lebanese American University, Byblos

Agatha van Ginkel, Leeds Metropolitan University

Catherine von Knorring, Leeds Metropolitan University

James Lantolf, The Pennsylvania State University

Hitomi Masuhara, Leeds Metropolitan University

Luke Prodromou, Freelance

Ivor Timmis, Leeds Metropolitan University

Brian Tomlinson, Leeds Metropolitan University

Introduction: Some similarities and differences between L1 and L2 acquisition and development

Brian Tomlinson

1 Introduction

This is a book which aims to investigate and connect some of those aspects of L1 and L2 language acquisition which might be of interest and value to applied linguists and to language teaching practitioners. To some extent this has been done already by Foster-Cohen (1993, 1999) and it is done regularly in the journals *Applied Psycholinguistics* (Cambridge University Press), *Language Acquisition* (Lawrence Erlbaum Associates) and *Bilingualism: Language and Cognition* (Cambridge University Press). However their emphasis is often on theory per se and what this book is trying to do, wherever possible, is to relate theories of language acquisition and development to its practice.

The literature on both L1 and L2 language acquisition is vast and in this Introduction I do not intend to review it all. Neither am I going to just restrict the Introduction to those particular aspects of language acquisition focused on by contributors to this book. What I am going to do is to draw attention to some similarities and differences between L1 and L2 acquisition which interest me and which are of potential relevance for language learning. In doing so I intend to challenge some commonly held assumptions.

2 The difference between language acquisition and language development

In the *Longman Dictionary of Language Teaching and Applied Linguistics* (Richards *et al* 1992) language acquisition is defined as 'the learning and development of a person's language' (p. 197). Language development is not defined. Ellis (1994), in his introductory overview of second language acquisition makes no overt distinction between language acquisition and language development, neither do, for example, Larsen-Freeman and Long (1991) nor any of the major dictionaries I have consulted. In Ellis (1994) in the references from A to C 'language acquisition' is used 19 times in titles of articles or books and 'language development' is used twice, and in Larsen-Freeman and Long (1991) in the references A to C 'language acquisition' is used 23 times and 'language development' is used six times. There is no apparent differentiation in the use of the terms acquisition and development. However an Enfamil website implies a distinction by saying:

A child's language development is more than just learning to say; 'Mama' or 'Dada.' It also includes developing the ability to see and understand what is said and to speak to others. He eventually develops the ability to see and understand the use of written language and to write and read. We call this language-related learning 'emergent literacy.'

(http://www.enfamil.com/guides/childdevelopment/language.html)

For the purposes of this book I am going to make a distinction between 'acquisition' as the initial stage of gaining basic communicative competence in a language and 'development' as the subsequent stage of gaining the ability to use the language successfully in a wide range of media and genre for a wide variety of purposes. Acquisition in this distinction is viewed as gaining mastery of an efficient restricted code which makes use of a limited repertoire to achieve effective communication, whilst development is seen as a process of gaining mastery of an elaborated code capable of achieving effective communication in a wide variety of situations. Acquisition can be gained informally from motivated and meaningful exposure and also from formal instruction; development is typically gained both as a result of instruction and of an aptitude and inclination to learn from experience. All normal native speakers achieve acquisition in childhood but many of them fail to achieve effective development. Many non-native speakers fail to achieve acquisition but some do achieve effective development. All learners, whether of an L1 or an L2, become users of the language when they gain acquisition. This means that there is no such thing as an advanced learner and that some L2 users are more communicatively competent than the majority of L1 users (see Cook 2004 for a similar argument). The problem, of course, is in deciding when L2 learners stop acquiring a language and start developing their ability to use it. I would say that L2 learners who are at what is conventionally referred to as an intermediate level are ready to move towards being users of the L2. Many suffer from what is often referred to as an 'intermediate plateau' and many of these never really go on to develop their communicative proficiency because of a lack of need, motivation or aptitude. Or because they continue to be taught as learners needing to acquire language, rather than as developers needing to develop their ability to understand and use language effectively in a wide range of genres. Or it could be that at the early levels of acquisition they are forced by their coursebook and teachers to focus almost exclusively on low level language decoding and encoding skills and are not given a chance to transfer high level skills they have already developed in their L1.The same points apply, of course, to native speakers who have acquired their L1. Some go on to develop a high level of communicative proficiency but many do not.

3 Is L1 acquisition superior in quantity and quality to L2 acquisition?

Birdsong (1999b: 1) reflects many people's view that:

The facts of adult second language acquisition (L2A) contrast sharply with those of first language acquisition (L1A). Whereas the attainment of full linguistic competence is the birthright of all normal children, adults vary widely in their ultimate level of attainment, and linguistic competence comparable to that of natives is seldom attested.

Interestingly no evidence is provided to support the 'facts' and the terms 'full linguistic competence' and 'level of attainment' are not defined. Obviously most L1 acquirers are at a huge advantage in terms of exposure, motivation, opportunities for use and availability of feedback on the effectiveness of their outcomes. And obviously most of these acquirers develop much greater lexical, grammatical and pragmatic competence than learners of the same language as an L2. But is this necessarily so? Are L1 acquirers always more fluent, accurate, appropriate and effective users of the language than their L2 counterparts? As Cook (2002: 3) says, some L2 users 'use the second language as skilfully as a monolingual native speaker, like Nabokov writing whole novels in English'. All children acquire their L1 effortlessly and effectively if they have both sufficient exposure to the language and opportunities to use it at home, at school and in the playground. But what percentage of them go on to develop the ability to be fluent and accurate in speech and writing in a range of genres and discourse contexts? And how many of them manage to develop the ability to match their use of language appropriately to a range of social contexts? And, above all, how many go on to develop the ability to achieve their intended effect consistently in speech and writing in a wide range of discourse contexts? Acquisition is natural and inevitable given the appropriate conditions but development requires tuition. My stance is that L1 acquirers are at a great advantage over their L2 counterparts but that L2 learners could be helped much more than they currently are if L2 curriculum developers, materials developers and teachers learned and applied more about what we know makes L1 acquisition so effective. I would also claim that to some extent L2 users receiving instruction are at an advantage in relation to the development of the skills required for consistently appropriate and effective use of the language and that curriculum developers, materials developers and teachers should learn and apply more about what can make L2 development so effective.

I am defining language acquisition as the gradual gaining of the linguistic, socio-linguistic and pragma-linguistic systems of a language. It requires motivated and meaningful exposure to the language in use, opportunities to use the language and feedback on the outcomes of this use. It is helped by other people (e.g. parents, siblings, peers and teachers) deliberately providing these opportunities as well as providing useful information about how the language is used. It results in varying degrees of ability to use the language receptively and productively in fluent, accurate, appropriate and effective ways. Acquirers can become fluent, accurate, appropriate and effective to differing degrees in different skills, media, genre and fields. For example, some acquirers are better listeners than readers, write emails better than they use the telephone, are more accurate in writing than in speech, are more fluent when talking in group discussion than in delivering a talk and are more accurate, fluent, appropriate and effective when talking about football than when talking about art.

Language development is the deliberate optimizing of communication skills already gained. It builds on from acquisition and requires conscious attention, frequent demanding use, self-reflection and informed feedback in order to construct large syntactical, lexical and strategic repertoires from which to select for potential effect. It results in the ability to use the language with a high frequency of success in a number of skills, media, genres and/or fields. For example, some developers become very effective conference presenters, intensive readers, story writers and instructors.

When L1 acquisition is effective it is typically because the learners:

- need to acquire the language in order to satisfy their wants;
- receive massive exposure to the language in use;
- are helped to achieve comprehensible intake by peers, siblings, parents and teachers using appropriate language to them in contexts which support understanding;
- frequently need to use the language to get what they want, to express their individuality as well as their membership of groups and to learn about the world around them;
- are given outcome feedback which lets them know how effective their language use is in relation to their achievement of intent.

However, L2 acquisition is often ineffective because the conditions for natural acquisition listed above are not provided for the learners.

L2 development can be effective because the learners:

- are motivated instrumentally by a need for development in relation to their education and/or careers;
- are motivated integratively by a desire to be able to understand and use the language at a higher level;
- receive instruction in how to understand and use the language at a higher level;
- receive information about the language which increases their ability to monitor and repair in planned discourse;
- receive feedback on their attempts to understand and use the language at a higher level;
- are often helped to reflect on their use of language and to make discoveries for themselves.

L1 development is often ineffective because the learners are not helped to achieve the conditions listed above for effective development.

Before moving on I would just like to list a few points for you to consider in relation to claims about the superiority of L1 acquisition:

- Most L2 acquirers have no real need to acquire the language.
- Most L2 acquirers receive very little comprehensible exposure to the language in use.
- Many L2 acquirers understandably stop acquiring (and therefore never develop) once they are able to do what they need to do with the language (i.e. their L2 fossilizes).
- Most L2 acquirers never need to attain native-like levels of language use.
- L2 acquirers are typically judged to be failing because they have not attained native-like levels of language use (even though they might be able to communicate effectively).
- Many L1 users exhibit 'grammatical deviance' and often suffer from 'performance variation' (Brown 1996).
- Some L2 users are able to understand and use the language at a much higher level of complexity than the 'average' native speaker (e.g. How many 'average' native speakers would pass the Cambridge Proficiency Examination?).
- Many L2 users are more proficient at using a regional or international variety of the language than many native speakers are at using their native variety of the language. For example, Prodromou (2005) has shown that proficient users of English as an international language are more 'grammatically correct' than many native speakers and differ from them mainly in their reluctance to use creative idiomaticity.
- Many L1 acquirers never develop beyond the use of a restricted code which is very efficient when used with their family and friends in relation to topics they are familiar with but which is ineffective when used in other social situations (e.g. Bernstein 1971).
- Many L1 acquirers never develop the ability to read and write effectively and some never develop the ability at all (e.g. there are surprisingly large percentages of adult illiterates in the UK and in the USA).

4 Critical period hypothesis

Birdsong (1999b: 1) says that 'CPH states that there is a limited developmental period during which it is possible to acquire a language, be it L1 or L2, to normal, native-like levels.' This significant claim has been generally accepted in the field and most of the disagreements have been about the actual age after which learners are no longer able to acquire a language to 'normal, native-like levels', and as to whether this ability suddenly stops at the end of a 'critical period' or is more gradual in offset and more varied in end-state attainment towards the end of a 'sensitive period' (see Long 1990). A lot of evidence has been provided to demonstrate the validity of the claims for a critical (or at least a sensitive) period for effective language learning (e.g. Lenneberg 1967; Patkowski 1980; Scovel 1988; Long 1990; Hurford 1991; Pinker 1997; Eubank and Gregg 1999) and many reasons have been suggested for this phenomenon. Lenneberg (1967) claims that the end of the critical period is marked by 'termination of a state of organisational plasticity linked with lateralisation of function' (p. 176) and many other researchers have made similar claims for the loss of neural plasticity around the onset of puberty. For example, Weber-Fox and Neville (1996) agree with Lenneberg 'that puberty may mark a significant point in language learning capacity and neural reorganisational capabilities' (p. 36). Other reasons put forward have included that:

- cognitive maturity is disadvantageous for language learning because the adult's 'greater available memory allows for extracting more of the input' but faces them with 'a more difficult problem of analyzing everything at once' (Newport 1991: 126);
- after childhood, unnecessary neural circuitry and the language learning faculty are dismantled (Pinker 1997);
- if the language learning faculty is not used after puberty it will be lost (e.g. Bever 1981);
- the successful childhood learning of the L1 inhibits the adult learning of an L2 because such learning is difficult to undo (e.g. Elman *et al* 1996).

However, considerable counter-evidence has recently cast doubt on the critical and sensitive period hypotheses. Birdsong (1992, 1999a, 1999b) has claimed to demonstrate that adults can and often do achieve 'native-like attainment' in an L2. Similar claims have been made, for example, by Mayberry (1993) in relation to late acquirers of American Sign Language, by Van Wuijtswinkel (1994) in relation to Dutch late acquirers of English, by White and Genesse (1996) in relation to French Canadian late acquirers of English and by Cranshaw (1997) in relation to French and Chinese late acquirers of English. Coppieters (1987: 90), however, has claimed that even 'native-like L2 users' language differs in important respects from the language of natives' and Ioup (2006: 432) concludes that 'child and adult language acquisition are fundamentally different, thus supporting the maturational constraint version of the critical period hypothesis that argues for a modular language acquisition mechanism available to child learners only'.

My own views on the critical period debate are:

- Much of the research on the critical period hypothesis has focused mainly on neural processing and seems to have neglected such crucial factors as motivation, exposure and opportunities for use as determiners of success in L2 learning (although Birdsong (1992) does briefly mention such 'exogenous factors' as 'variations in the amount and type of input', 'motivation' and 'attitude toward assimilating within the foreign culture' (pp. 8–9)).
- Much of the research on the critical period hypothesis has focused on the attainment of native-like levels of proficiency for L2 learners and yet this is not the objective for most L2 learners.
- There is sufficient doubt about claims that the ability to acquire a foreign

language to a high level disappears after puberty for us not to base important language planning decisions on them. Instead we should be looking at how to transfer some of the benefits enjoyed by young learners to adult learners (e.g. the ability to play with language without worrying about loss of face) and to transfer some of the benefits enjoyed by adult learners to young learners (e.g. being allowed to make decisions for themselves).

- Much of the research on the critical period hypothesis has made use of such instruments as grammaticality judgement tasks (e.g. Johnson and Newport 1989; Birdsong 1992). While such instruments might help the researchers to achieve reliability I have doubts about their validity as measures of communicative proficiency (see Brown *et al* 1996: 54–5) for a criticism of grammaticality judgement tasks). What I would like to see are more experiments which look at what adults typically can and can not do in the L2 and which look for ways in which the learning process could be manipulated in order to help adult learners to be able to do more.
- Much of the research on the critical period hypothesis which has claimed native-like success for L2 adult learners has done so for learners who have acquired the language through immersion in it rather than from learning about it (e.g. Birdsong 1992). One of the exceptions is the research of Bongaerts (1999), but his classroom learners of English were living in Holland, where at least 'partial immersion' in English can be fairly easily achieved. It would be interesting to compare how native-like a proficiency adult participants on 'immersion courses' (e.g. English through Literature, Drama or Motor Mechanics) achieve in comparison with those on conventional language instruction courses.

5 Some facilitators of L1 acquisition which could facilitate the acquisition of an L2

The following are well attested facilitators of L1 acquisition which it might be worth experimenting with when applied to the teaching of an L2:

- Motherese is often used to 'facilitate the teaching of new words to children and assist their comprehension' (de Boysson-Bardies 1999: 88).
- Mothers present new words in sentences, place greater emphasis on the new words and place them at the end of sentences (e.g. in 89 per cent of the examples reported by Aslin (1993), who mentions that this happens even in Turkish in which it is ungrammatical to place a noun at the end of a sentence).
- Children first learn to communicate through gestures and tone of voice (Peccei 1999).
- According to Nelson (1973), in the first 50 words acquired by children the biggest group involves naming things (ball; dog; juice) – 60 per cent, then actions/events (give; put; up); then modifiers (dirty, more; allgone); and then personal/social (yes; hi; bye-bye) – only 8 per cent. The first objects

named by children tend to be small and easily handled (shoe/sock v nappy/panty) + things that move, make a noise, change, etc. (car/ball/clock).

- Nelson (1973: 2) also reports that mistakes are made because of the rule systems that children build for themselves and which 'provide an insight into the kinds of "educated guesses" that they are making about the way their language works'. These mistakes can be categorized as overextensions (e.g. duck = bird and water; ball = anything round; at = hat, scarf, ribbon, hairbrush; bean = pea) or underextensions (e.g. white = snow). They can also be caused by knowing a word but finding it difficult (e.g. finger = thumb), using a related word to an unknown one in the hope of achieving communication and eliciting the more appropriate word (e.g. cat for guinea pig) and trying to communicate a more complex proposition than is evidenced (e.g. 'biscuit' as a comment on its location as well as naming an object).
- Rescoria (1980) also comments on the sort of overextension which is accepted as normal in L1 acquisition but which is typically considered erroneous in L2 acquisition (e.g. a word covering its category, as in apple = any fruit; a word standing for something physically or functionally analogous, as in cat = soft scarf and hat = hairbrush; a word standing for a whole sentence, as in 'Dolly' standing for 'Dolly's not in her bed.')

Obviously children acquiring an L1 naturally from exposure and need are very different from teenagers and adults learning a language from instruction, and some of the above observations do not easily lead to suggestions for application. However some of them could lead to direct applications (e.g. placing new words at the end of exemplar sentences) whilst others could lead to indirect applications (e.g. applying Nelson's observations (1973) to finding out what objects are particularly salient to a particular group of L2 beginners and then teaching words that refer to them first; applying Nelson's (1973) and Rescoria's (1980) observations about rule building by helping L2 learners to follow a process of experience + hypothesis + trial + revision).

6 Connections between L1 and L2 acquisition and development in this book

Many of the chapters in this book touch on one or more of the issues raised above and some of them raise other important issues related to the connection between acquiring and developing an L1 and acquiring and developing another language.

One chapter which directly relates phenomena in L1 with equivalents in L2 is Chapter 4 – The Roles of Audio-Visual Mental Aids in the Development of First and Other Language Proficiency by Brian Tomlinson and Javier Avila. This chapter describes the main roles and characteristics of visual imaging and of inner speech in L1 acquisition and development and then compares this situation to what research has revealed about the very different situation in L2 acquisition and development. Other chapters which take this approach to some extent are:

- Chapter 1 – The Role of Proto-Reading Activities in the Acquisition and Development of Effective Reading Skills by Hitomi Masuhara (in which she reports on typical proto-reading activities in the L1 and suggests ways of applying them to the teaching of reading skills in the L2).
- Chapter 9 – The Value of Recasts During Meaning Focused communication 1 by Brian Tomlinson (in which he refers to the literature on recasting in L1 acquisition but then focuses mainly on the value of recasting in L2 acquisition).
- Chapter 12 – The Value of Comprehension in the Early Stages of the Acquisition and Development of Bahasa Indonesian by Non-Native Speakers by Erlin Susanti Barnard (in which she reports on a large-scale experiment which made use of an L1-like comprehension approach to the teaching of Bahasa Indonesian to L2 beginners).
- Chapter 13 – Enhancing the language learning process for reticent learners of Vietnamese and of English in Vietnam by Bao Dat (in which he compares similar phenomena in L1 and L2 acquisition).
- Chapter 14 – A 'Sort of' Puzzle for English as a lingua franca by Luke Prodromou (in which he makes use of corpora to compare L1 use of English with SUE use of English (i.e. the use of English by successful users of English as another language).

One chapter which deals primarily with a phenomenon in L1 but implies connections with L2 is Chapter 3 – The Processing of Past Tense Verbs for L1 Learners of English by Natalie Braber. In this chapter Braber uses neuro-linguistic evidence to come to conclusions about how L1 learners typically process past tense verbs and, in doing so, implies questions about the value of this knowledge for the teaching of English as an L2. Agatha van Ginkel, in Chapter 2 – The Transfer of Reading from the Language of Wider Communication to the First Language looks at the problems of developing reading skills in the L1 having first learned to read in an L2.

The other chapters deal primarily with a phenomenon in L2 but suggest or imply connections with L1. For example, Chapter 16 – A Blind Learner in EFL Mainstream Courses: A Case Study at The Lebanese American University by Nola Bacha reports on a successful integration of a blind learner into a mainstream EFL class and in doing so makes reference to characteristics of blind learners which are contributory factors to the successful acquisition and development of their L1. Other chapters dealing with an L2 phenomenon are:

- Chapter 6 – Internalization and language acquisition by Jim Lantolf and Beatriz Centeno-Cortes investigates the role of private speech in learning Spanish as an L2 and in doing so refers to the literature on private speech in L1 acquisition too.

- Chapter 7 – Affect in L2 Teacher Talk by Jane Arnold and Carmen Fonseca reports on the effects which positive affect in teacher talk has on L2 learners and, in doing so, refers to affective characteristics of L1 input.
- Chapter 8 – The Attitudes of Language Learners Towards Target Varieties of the Language by Ivor Timmis looks at what L2 learners report as their attitudes towards target varieties of English and, in doing so, implies parallels with L1 acquisition.
- Chapter 11 – Output Like Input: Influence of Children's Literature on Young L2 Learners' Written Expression by Irma-Kaarina Ghosn focuses on L2 learners but also makes reference to the effect of literature on L1 learners' ability to write.
- Chapter 15 – Perceptions of Culture By British Students Learning French – Catherine von Knorring reports on the attitudes of groups of university undergraduate L2 learners towards the target culture.

The main objective of this book is not to assert correspondences between L1 and L2 acquisition and development but to stimulate thought about possible connections and their potential applications. This is one way that it differs from many books on language acquisition. Instead of concluding that 'more research needs to be done' before applying research findings to practice, it takes the position that the best way of finding out whether the findings are valuable is to apply them and find out.

References

Aslin, R. N. (1993), 'Segmentation of fluent speech into words: learning models and the role of maternal input', in B. de Boysson-Bardies, S. de Schonen, P. Juscyk and B. Bernstein (1971), *Class, Codes and Control: Vol.1 Theoretical Studies Towards a Sociology of Language*. London: Routledge and Kegan Paul.

Bernstein, B. (1971), *Class, Codes and Control*. London: Routledge and Kegan Paul.

Bever, T. G. (1981), 'Normal acquisition processes explaining the critical period for language learning', in K. C. Diller (ed.), *Individual Differences and Universals in Language Learning Aptitude*. Rowley, MA: Newbury House, pp. 176–98.

Birdsong, D. (1992), 'Ultimate attainment in second language acquisition'. *Studies in Second Language Acquisition*, 16, 169–82.

Birdsong, D. (ed.) (1999a), *Second Language Acquisition and the Critical Period Hypothesis*. Mahwah, NJ: Lawrence Erlbaum.

Birdsong, D. (1999b), 'Introduction: whys and why nots of the critical period hypothesis for second language acquisition', in D. Birdsong (ed.), *Second Language Acquisition and the Critical Period Hypothesis*. Mahwah, NJ: Lawrence Erlbaum, pp. 1–22.

Bongaerts, T. (1999), 'Ultimate attainment in L2 pronunciation: The case of very advanced late L2 learners', in D. Birdsong (ed.), *Second Language Acquisition and the Critical Period Hypothesis*. Mahwah, NJ: Lawrence Erlbaum, pp. 133–59.

Brown, G. (1996), 'Language learning, competence and performance', in G. Brown, K. Malmkjaer and J. Williams, *Performance and Competence in Second Language Acquisition*. Cambridge: Cambridge University Press.

Brown, G., Malmkjaer, K. and Williams, J. (1996), *Performance and Competence in Second Language Acquisition.* Cambridge: Cambridge University Press.

Cook, V. J. (2002), *Portraits of the L2 User.* Clevedon: Multilingual Matters.

Cook, V. J. (2004), *The L2 User Perspective.* Clevedon: Multilingual Matters.

Coppieters, R. (1987), 'Competence differences between native and near-native speakers'. *Language,* 63/3, 544–73.

Cranshaw, A. (1997), 'A Study of Anglophone Native and Near-Native Linguistic and Metalinguistic Performance' (unpublished doctoral dissertation, Universite de Montreal).

De Boysson-Bardies, B. (1999), *How Language Comes to Children: From Birth to Two Years.* Cambridge, MA: MIT Press.

Ellis, R. (1994), *The Study of Second Language Acquisition.* Oxford: Oxford University Press.

Elman, J. L. (1993), 'Learning and development in neural networks: The importance of starting small'. *Cognition,* 48, 71–99.

Elman, J. L., Bates, E. A., Johnson, M. H., Karmiloff-Smith, A., Parisi, D. and Plunkett, K. (1996), *Rethinking Innateness: A Connectionist Perspective on Development.* Cambridge, MA: MIT Press.

Eubank, L. and Gregg, K. (1999), 'Critical periods and (second) language acquisition; Divide and Impera', in D. Birdsong (ed.), *Second Language Acquisition and the Critical Period Hypothesis.* Mahwah, NJ: Lawrence Erlbaum Associates, pp. 65–99.

Foster-Cohen, S. H. (1993), 'Directions of influence in first and second language acquisition research'. *Second Language Research,* 9, 140–52.

Foster-Cohen, S. H. (1999, 'SLA and first language acquisition', in W. Grabe (ed.) (1999), *Annual Review of Applied Linguistics,* 19, pp. 3–21.

Hurford, J. R. (1991), 'The evolution of the critical period for language acquisition'. *Cognition,* 40, 159–201.

Ioup, G. (2006), 'Age in second language development', in E. Henkel (ed.), *Handbook of Research in Second Language Teaching and Learning.* Mahwah, NJ: Lawrence Erlbaum Associates, pp. 419–35.

Johnson, J. S. and Newport, E. L. (1989), 'Critical period effects in second language learning: the influence of maturational state on the acquisition of English as a second language'. *Cognitive Psychology,* 21, 60–99.

Larsen-Freeman, D. and Long, M. (1991), *An Introduction to Second Language Acquisition.* London: Longman.

Lenneburg, E. (1967), *Biological Foundations of Language.* New York: Wiley.

Long, M. H. (1990), 'Maturational constraints on language development'. *Studies in Second Language Acquisition,* 12, 251–85.

Mayberry, R. (1993), 'First-language acquisition after childhood differs from second-language acquisition; the case of American Sign Language'. *Journal of Speech and Hearing Research,* 36, 1258–70.

Nelson, K. (1973), 'Structure and strategy in learning to talk'. *Monograph of the Society for Research in Child Development,* 38, no. 149.

Newport, E. (1991), 'Contrasting conceptions of the critical period for language', in S. Carey and R. Gelman (eds), *The Epigenesis of Mind: Essays on Biology and Cognition.* Hillsdale, NJ: Lawrence Erlbaum Associates.

Patkowski, M. S. (1980), 'The sensitive period for the acquisition of syntax in a second language'. *Language Learning,* 30, 449–72.

Peccei, J. S. (1999), *Child Language* (2nd edn). London: Routledge.

Pinker, S. (1997), *How the Mind Works.* New York: Norton.

Prodromou, L. (2005), 'You See, It's Sort of Tricky for the L2 User: Idiomaticity in ELF'. (unpublished PhD thesis, University of Nottingham).

Rescoria, L. (1980), 'The role of universals in the acquisition of gerunds', in E. Van Wuijtswinkel (1994), 'Critical Period Effects on the Acquisition of Grammatical Competence in a Second Language' (unpublished BA thesis, Katholieke Universiteit, Nijmegen, Netherlands).

Richards, J. Platt, J. and Platt, H. (1992), *Longman Dictionary of Language Teaching and Applied Linguistics*. Harlow: Longman.

Scovel, T. (1988), *A Time to Speak; A Psycholinguitic Inquiry into the Critical Period for Human Speech*. Rowley, MA: Newbury House.

Van Wuijtswinkel, K. (1994), 'Critical Period Effects on the Acquisition of Grammatical Competence in a Second Language' (unpublished BA thesis, Nijmegen University).

Weber-Fox, C. M. and Neville, H. J. (1996), 'Maturational constraints on functional specializations for language processing: ERP evidence in bilingual speakers'. *Journal of Cognitive Neuroscience*, 8, 231–56.

White, L. and Genesse, F. (1996), 'How native is near-native? The issue of ultimate attainment in adult second language acquisition'. *Second Language Research*, 12, 238–65.

Part 1

CRITICAL REVIEWS OF THE LITERATURE

1 The role of proto-reading activities in the acquisition and development of effective reading skills

Hitomi Masuhara

1 Introduction

'. . .reading seems to mean almost invariably a slow and laborious decoding process, which often results in poor comprehension and in low self-esteem regardless of the ages, levels, and nationalities', reported Masuhara (2003) in her survey of L2 English reading research literature from the 1980s to 1990s. What she noted was the striking resemblance among the characteristics of L2 English learners' reading behaviour.

What is even more striking is the fact that this hesitant and tortuous way of reading, in fact, also applies to poor L1 English beginner/elementary readers. The surprise does not stop there: such L1 English literacy problems are not unusual but very common. For example, according to the 12th edition of the Report Card on American Education published by the American Legislative Exchange Council (ALEC) in 2006, 70 per cent of public school students in the eighth grade taking the reading portion of the National Assessment of Education Progress (NAEP) exam in 2003 performed below the 'proficiency' level. Chapman *et al* (2001) report similar L1 literacy problems in New Zealand. The Education Secretary in England advised the national curriculum to be amended in March 2006, based on the data that one in five 11-year-olds still leave primary school without reaching the necessary standard in English (reported in *The Guardian*, 21 March 2006).

How does L1 English reading acquisition occur? What are the difficulties of reading acquisition? Are there convergent elements between L1 and L2 reading acquisition? How can L1 and L2 reading acquisition be facilitated? What are the unique elements of L2 reading acquisition? How can L2 reading acquisition be nurtured? This chapter aims to review current literature in reading acquisition research in L1 and L2 in order to apply its findings to the development of principles and procedures for the teaching and learning of reading in L2.

2 How does L1 English reading acquisition occur?

2.1 What kinds of ability does reading involve?

According to 'Early Reading Strategy – The Report of the Expert Panel on Early Reading in Ontario, 2003' published by the Ministry of Education in Canada, nine skills are identified to be crucial in learning to read: oral language; world knowledge and experience; concepts about print; phonemic awareness; letter–sound relationships; vocabulary for reading; semantics, syntax and pragmatics; metacognition and comprehension strategies; and higher order thinking skills. This list helps us identify the kinds of skills required for a successful reading performance. In the L1 context, however, children normally come equipped with some level of skills already acquired during the initial five years of the L1 language acquisition phase before starting to learn to read in schools.

2.2 What kinds of skills has a 5-year-old pre-schooler acquired before reading acquisition starts in schools?

According to the 'Helping your pre-school child' published by the US Department of Education (2005), between their third and fourth birthdays, children are expected to:

- like silly humour, riddles and practical jokes;
- understand and follow spoken directions;
- use new words and longer sentences;
- be aware of rhyming sounds in words;
- possibly attempt to read;
- recognize print around them on signs or in logos;
- know that each alphabet letter has a name and identify at least ten alphabet letters, especially those in their own names; and
- 'write' or scribble messages.

Between their fourth and fifth birthdays, children are expected to:

- love to make rhymes, say nonsense words and tell jokes;
- know and use words that are important to school work, such as the names for colours, shapes and numbers;
- know and use words that are important to daily life, such as street names and addresses;
- know how books are held and read and follow print from left to right and from top to bottom of a page when listening to stories read aloud;
- recognize the shapes and names of all letters of the alphabet and know the sounds of some letters;
- write some letters, particularly those in his own name.

It seems that L1 children establish the foundations for many of the nine reading skills identified by the Canadian Ministry of Education. Let us now look at each reading skill and see what healthy L1 children in normal to privileged environments could achieve before they begin the formal learning of reading. Do note that there are considerable individual differences due to natural developmental variability, environment (Hart and Risley 1995) and disabilities (Perfetti and Sandak 2000; Shaywitz *et al* 2000; Tallal 2000).

Oral language

L1 children come to reading with considerable oral language experience. Through listening and speaking with their families, peers and teachers, children build the vocabulary, semantic knowledge (i.e. awareness of meaning) and syntactic knowledge (i.e. awareness of structure) that form a foundation for reading and writing. Children who are proficient in oral language have a solid beginning for reading.

World knowledge and experience

Children by the age of five are fairly self-reliant and coordinated. They are able to play with their peers and actively seek new experience. They develop their growing language abilities not only through their direct physical experience but also indirectly through books, games, songs, riddles and listening to stories.

Concepts about print

Children know how books are held and read and follow print from left to right and from top to bottom of a page when listening to stories read aloud. Children who have been read to may understand that the symbols on the page represent spoken language or that they convey meaning.

Phonemic awareness

Phonemic awareness means understanding the system of sound. Languages are made up of sounds. In English there are about 44 speech sounds. By spending approximately the first five years of their lives associating aural-oral verbal codes with non-verbal experience in natural communication, L1 learners acquire both the segmental and suprasegmental phonological systems of English. Children who have phonemic awareness are able to identify and manipulate the individual sounds in oral language. For example, they can divide a spoken word 'ship' into three distinct sounds: sh + i + p. Phonemic awareness prepares children for recoding the written codes in print into spoken language, either aloud or with their inner voice. Without this ability, children struggle and continue to have reading difficulties. This point will be further discussed in the next section 'What are the difficulties of reading acquisition?'.

Letter–sound relationships

Building on the foundation of phonemic awareness and concepts about print, children need to understand ways of connecting the sounds they hear with the print on the page in order to make meaning. By five, healthy children are expected to recognize the shapes and names of all letters of the alphabet and know the sounds of some letters. In the English writing system, one letter may not necessarily represent one single sound. This inconsistent spelling–sound relationship could cause some problems in L1 English reading acquisition. This point will also be further discussed in the next section 'What are the difficulties of reading acquisition?'.

Vocabulary for reading

Children need a broad vocabulary of words that they understand and can use correctly to label their knowledge and experiences. The breadth and depth of a child's vocabulary provide the foundation for successful reading. Nation and Waring (1997) estimated that L1 learners have already learned approximately 4,000–5,000 aural/oral words before they formally begin reading instruction in schools. Note here that, in L1 vocabulary acquisition, the signifying codes and the signified objects or phenomena are likely to have a direct and strong link in the minds of the L1 children. Furthermore, the words are learned in context, with associations of other verbal and non-verbal experience. Nation and Waring (*ibid.*) think that roughly 1,000 new word families are added every year to L1 children's vocabulary.

Oral vocabulary refers to words that are used in speaking or recognized in listening. Reading vocabulary refers to words that are recognized or used in print. Even children who have a very extensive oral vocabulary may have great difficulty reading words in print if they have a small reading vocabulary. The reading vocabulary – often referred to as sight vocabulary – is determined mainly by how many times a child has seen those words in print. Children who read a lot have a large pool of words they recognize immediately on sight; children who do little reading have a limited sight vocabulary.

Semantics, syntax and pragmatics

Reading involves the deciphering of phrases and sentences, which depends on both the words and how those words are organized. Syntax refers to the structure of a language and the ways that words are combined to form phrases, clauses and sentences. Syntax includes classes of words (such as noun, verb and adjective) and their functions (such as subject and object). Beginning readers may not need to be able to define noun or verb, but they need to understand that a word (like 'rain') can represent a thing or an action, depending on the context.

Parallel to cognitive learning of conceptual relationships, L1 learners are supplied with plenty of opportunities to learn the grammar systems intuitively. An example of this is the cause and effect relationship (e.g. making a mess causes mother to get upset) and the linguistic system of cohesion. Another one is the argument–predicate relationship (e.g. a dog barks) and the linguistic relationship of subject and verb.

Pragmatics involves understanding how the context influences the way sentences convey information. A sentence can have different purposes depending on the situation or context in which it is used. It can be a mere statement or affirmation, but it can also be a warning, a promise, a threat, or something else. Readers with pragmatic knowledge and skills are able to decipher these different intents from the context. L1 children come to recognize pragmatic values attached to linguistic systems. Prosodic features mark old and new information. The children learn to differentiate implicit messages from the intonation, tone and pitch. Thus the intensity of a mother's nagging would signal to a child how far (s)he can continue ignoring her order.

Lastly, some pre-schoolers may have had considerable opportunities for proto-reading experience – that is – listening to bedtime stories and shared reading. In such moments, they are likely to be relaxed and securely focused on the content of their favourite stories, whilst enjoying the rhythmical language sparking off various sensations in the mind. Most of the vocabulary in the text is likely to be known and the unknown can either be inferred, explained either visually or verbally in interaction with a parent, or just be ignored until the pre-schoolers' needs and wants arise. If L1 pre-schoolers are privileged enough to have plenty of such proto-reading experience, it is likely that reading is associated with pleasure and positive emotional associations.

In sum, L1 children seem to have more or less developed seven out of the nine fundamental skills before reading instruction begins at school.

2.3 What else do L1 children need to learn for reading acquisition?

According to the Canadian Ministry of Education, two more skills are necessary for successful reading:

Metacognition and comprehension strategies

Good readers plan and monitor their reading at a metacognitive level. What they are doing is thinking about good ways of making sense of the text. When they run into difficulty, they evaluate their reading to determine the best strategy for improving their understanding of the text. Metacognitive strategies include, for example, deconstructing long words, connecting text with prior experiences, guessing meanings of unfamiliar words, identifying main ideas, drawing inferences from the text and synthesizing information. Readers can use a variety of strategies to decode and understand text and to know when and why to apply particular strategies. Their understanding of the text extends beyond the literal.

Higher-order thinking skills

Good readers are not passive. They not only understand most of what they have read but they are able to relate it to their previous knowledge, evaluate the relevance of new information, analyse and evaluate the information, formulate opinions and substantiate their thinking. The development of higher-order thinking skills is said to be essential throughout the primary grades.

3 What are the difficulties of reading acquisition?

'. . . Written language must stand on the shoulder of oral language . . .' explains Tallal (2003) from the perspectives of neuroscience in her interview for Children of the Code, a Social Education Project. Thousands of years of evolution have genetically programmed the human brain to acquire spoken languages. Babies are known to recognize some significant speech sounds even before birth and children tune in to spoken language in their environment.

Reading acquisition certainly does not happen naturally argues Wren (2002). He claims that reading is one of the most unnatural things that humans do. The staggering pictures at the beginning of this chapter of both adults and children struggling to read are an eloquent testimony of how reading is a difficult artifact to acquire. In the previous section, we have looked at idealistic transitions from language to reading acquisition. In this section, we will look at the causes of L1 reading problems.

According to the literature, there seem to be three main causes for reading difficulties: phonemic awareness deficiency; inconsistency between the sound and spelling in English orthography; and confusions in reading pedagogy.

3.1 Phonemic awareness deficiency

Phonemic awareness seems to be the most fundamental building block for healthy reading ability. In every language, the spoken system existed before the writing system developed. Writing systems are in fact coded spoken language. In reading, the brain has to be able to identify written symbols and automatically activate corresponding phonological sounds.

Tallal (2003) calls the brain an 'experience-dependent learning machine'. She describes how the brain is programmed to process the sensory world, turn that into the phonological representations and turn those into syllables, words, phrases and ultimately allow us to develop a written code which is the orthography or letters that go with those sounds.

Research on human infant speech perception demonstrates such a process. Babies in the uterus are reported to become able to assimilate some speech sounds after about 20 weeks of pregnancy (Snyder 2005). By 10 months, research shows that babies are already able to segment the speech stream and recognize their names and their interested topics (Jusczyk 1997; Pruden *et al* 2006).

Tallal (2003) describes how some infants suffer from a temporal spectral processing problem (i.e. difficulty in tracking acoustic frequency changes occurring over time). They cannot organize complex auditory signals or extract the phonemes of the language from the incoming sounds. This is the ability critical for language 'since speech is a series of rapidly successive acoustic changes that have to be tracked, encoded, and represented'. 'Their brain just needs more time between events to integrate them and track them.' Tallal (2000) reports there is a high coincidence of these children with early language developmental delays eventually developing difficulty in oral performance, reading, writing and particularly spelling.

Approximately 3–6 per cent of all school-aged children are reported to have developmental reading disabilities, or dyslexia (Frost and Emery 1995). Dyslexia is a neurocognitive deficit that is specifically related to the reading and spelling processes. Typically, children classified as dyslexic are reported to be bright and capable in other intellectual domains. Current research indicates that the vast majority of children with dyslexia have phonological core deficits. The severity of the phonological deficits varies across individuals, and children with these deficits have been shown to make significantly less progress in basic word reading skills compared to children with equivalent IQs. Neurobiological studies of dyslexia on brain activation patterns provide evidence of an imperfectly functioning system for segmenting words into their phonologic constituents (Burton *et al* 2000; Shaywitz *et al* 2000).

3.2 Inconsistency between sound and spelling in English

When reading instruction begins in schools, L1 children spend a lot of time and energy on orthographic learning. First, they have to learn how to identify, pronounce and write alphabet letters. It would be relatively easy to learn about phonemes if one letter (grapheme: smallest meaningful unit of script) consistently maps onto one and the same sound (phoneme: smallest meaningful unit of sound), or if one phoneme consistently maps to one and the same letter. In English, however, the correspondence between grapheme and phoneme is not straightforward. For example, grapheme 'a' can be pronounced as /æ/ as in 'bat', /ei/ as in 'cake', or could be /ə/ as in 'can' in a certain phonetic environment.

Secondly, English-speaking children have to learn how to associate individual letters in clusters (i.e. syllables and words). Again, the grapheme/phoneme relationship is very complicated. For example, 'ough' in English is pronounced differently in 'through', 'bough', 'though', 'thought' and 'tough'. Some irregular words completely elude apparent phonemic sense as in 'yacht'! In English, the words 'cow' and 'bough' rhyme as do 'true' and 'through', although one would not expect it from appearances.

Davis (2005) reports a comparative study which shows that after one year of instruction, English children show the lowest percentage of correct word reading on a scale in comparison to other European countries; with only 30–40 per cent correct words compared to German, Greek and Finnish, which achieve close to 100 per cent. It is interesting that by around 12 years of age English children are reported to catch up with their European peers, and the differences disappear. It has been recognized that English children apparently learn to read more slowly due to the nature of the inconsistent orthography.

3.3 Confusion in reading pedagogy

Experts do not seem to agree how reading should be taught. Take, for example, the phonics versus the whole language approach debate which got so heated that it was described as 'reading wars' (Pearson 2004). Phonics is a bottom-up approach that starts with learning about the components of words and moves towards reading as a whole. Lessons may involve sounding out first letters followed by combinations of letters, emphasis on sight vocabulary, 'basal/basic' readers with numerous skills exercises. Proponents maintain that children are better able to decode words on their own only after learning how to decipher letters, sounds and letter groupings (Armbruster *et al* 2001). Recent research findings on the vital importance of phonological processing (see 3.1 above) seem to support the bottom-up approach using explicit and mechanical acoustic segmentation exercises.

The whole-language approach, on the other hand, is a holistic top-down method. It often incorporates oral/silent reading of authentic literature rather than basal readers, and may involve integrated thematic studies and the extended use of writing. Whole language is not a systemized approach, but rather a philosophy that assumes that reading and general language competencies are acquired through integrated use instead of through learning separate and finite skills such as phonics and word attack. Supporters of whole-language instruction assert that children learn to read similar to the way they learn to speak. Just as their desire to communicate orally prompted them to master vocabulary and learn to put whole sentences together, children will be so motivated to learn to communicate in the written form (Coles 2000). Proponents argue that the phonics/skills approach does nothing to teach children the meaning of words or expose them to the varied use of words.

Many teachers today use a blended approach. But what kinds of mix may be most effective remains controversial. Experts agree that at-risk readers need an individual diagnosis of their problems. Imagine a particular child with some language impairment that causes reading difficulty. She is a healthy, happy and intelligent child. What kinds of interventions would suit her? Should she be placed in a reading remediation class and work on her weakness through phonics? Or should the teacher focus on her strengths and appeal to her intelligence and affect by reading her literature? Or maybe what she really needs is strengthening her aural/oral ability so that she has a stronger phonological base in her brain to graft the reading skills on to. But schools are expected to teach L1 children how to read, not how to talk!

4 Are there convergent elements between L1 and L2 reading acquisition?

Let us now consider how language and reading are typically learned in L2. We will take the case of Japanese EFL learners as an example.

Most Japanese EFL learners start English language learning at the age of 12–13 when they enter public junior high school as the final part of compulsory education. Since society functions almost exclusively in Japanese, the classroom is the main, if not only, source of English learning. Motivated by the societal awareness of the importance of English as an international lingua franca, some students seek extra tuition with private tutors or at night schools. The effect of such extra learning, however, tends to be insignificant when analysed statistically (Masuhara *et al* 1996).

When L2 language learning begins in junior high school, L2 learners are expected to learn orthographic, phonological and morphosyntactic systems of L2 verbal codes almost at the same time within a very short period of time.

To illustrate how quickly L2 learners are expected to acquire the new language, we will make a very rough comparison of the amount of time spent for language acquisition in L1 and L2. L1 pre-schoolers, calculating on a very crude assumption that they are exposed to English for eight hours per day, are estimated to have 14,600 hours of exposure to their native language in five years. And this does not count the orthographic learning which takes place after schooling begins.

Japanese EFL learners, on the other hand, spend six years learning English at secondary school according to the recommendation of the Course of Study published by the Ministry of Education. The approximate total hours of English classes based on the curriculum specification amounts to 609–783 hours. Compared to L1 pre-schoolers, the physical amount of time given for L2 language acquisition seems very small.

Research on vocabulary size gives another indication of the stark difference between L1 and L2. Aitchison (2003) estimated that L1 English college graduates with Bachelor of Education degrees are able to recognize at least 50,000 word families (i.e. sing, singing, sung are counted as one). Nation and Waring (1997) made a conservative estimate of L1 English university students as having a vocabulary size of around 20,000 word families. In comparison, many adult foreign learners of English, according to Nation and Waring (1997), have a vocabulary size of much less than 5,000 word families in spite of having studied English for several years. Large numbers of second language learners do achieve vocabulary sizes that are like those of educated native speakers, but they are not the norm.

The comparison of the quality of L1 language acquisition of pre-schoolers and L2 formal language learning makes us realize a far more sobering difference. In L1, toddlers are surrounded by the language in real contexts, get personal attention, have plenty of proficient users around to help them negotiate meaning, etc. In the L2 formal learning context, many non-native EFL teachers prefer to lecture in Japanese to a large class about vocabulary or grammar knowledge of English. In the worst cases, audiotapes are probably the only source of authentic one-way input. Also frequent testing features heavily in the L2 instruction, which could nurture negative associations when learning L2 language and reading.

What is crucial here is that L2 reading instruction also begins simultaneously with L2 language learning. Or more accurately, no reading instruction per se is given but the learners are expected to read texts on some naive assumption that once we learn a language system (i.e. lexicon and syntax), we should be able to read well. In this way, L2 reading instruction is always accompanied by confusions between teaching language and teaching reading. In the former, the text is a language specimen that provides context for particular knowledge about the target language. In the latter, L2 learners should be, for example, getting the wanted information or enjoying personal engagement in interaction with the author. It seems that most of the reading classes try to kill two birds with one stone and fail to kill either.

Interestingly, the above descriptions of Japanese EFL scenes in secondary schools do not seem particularly unique to Japan. At the anecdotal level, the descriptions of Japanese EFL scenes seem also to resonate with the descriptions of EFL in, for example, China, Greece, Turkey, Venezuela, and Vietnam. Even in countries whose dominant national language is closer to English (e.g. French, German, Spanish), teachers appear to share similar problems of ineffective TEFL in their secondary education.

How do L2 learners cope and manage not only to acquire L2 but also to learn to read effectively in L2? Compared to how L1 learners begin their L1 reading instruction, when Japanese EFL learners start their L2 reading, they do not have L2 neural networks in their brain for:

- flexible and extensive aural/oral vocabulary;
- mastery of segmental and suprasegmental phonological systems;
- intuitive knowledge of English syntax.

In the first place, their L1 is sufficient for social survival. Therefore there is not really an internal necessity to acquire L2, despite their claimed wish to acquire English.

The Japanese EFL learners, however, do have:

- well-developed L1 language systems and ability to use them;
- world knowledge and experience;
- established cognitive control of their verbal and non-verbal facilities;
- motivation for external reasons to learn the L2 (e.g. instrumental motivation that English is a major subject in the exams, integrative motivation based on the view of English as the international lingua franca).

What seems to happen is that L2 learners soon learn to compensate for literacy stage and have reached a mature cognitive level with established L1 language neural circulatory.

- L1 literacy literature takes some elements for granted that are vital for L2 reading acquisition. For example, connection between the language codes and meaning (i.e. multi-dimensional mental representation) and pragmatic interpretation.
- Unlike L1, L2 language acquisition and reading acquisition start at the same time. There is no time for the L2 learners to establish the necessary phonological core ability. This is the reason why the reading behaviours of L2 learners are so similar to L1 unsuccessful readers. It does not help that traditionally there has always been confusion between teaching language and teaching reading.

7 How can L2 reading acquisition be nurtured?

Proposal 1 Separate language teaching and teaching reading. Develop aural/oral skills before introducing reading

Tomlinson (2001) offers extensive discussions and suggests ways of making a smooth transition from an aural/oral phase to skilful reading. Total Physical Response and Total Physical Response Plus (Tomlinson 1994) provide ample opportunity for aural learning. L1 reading acquisition literature recommends use of rhymes, songs and games. Similar approaches for L2 learners could be fun, provided that the content is made suitable for L2 learners' cognitive levels. Listening to stories and drama would be another effective avenue to explore.

Proposal 2 Phonological segmentation but also supra-segmental teaching (rhythm, intonation, chunking)

Supra-segmental phonological training needs explanation because L1 literature often does not go beyond the word level. Phonological recoding beyond word level reduces the demand on the limited capacity of our working memory during syntactical and semantic processing in reading a longer stretch of text. Working memory is the kind of memory which is used to coordinate and to cross-reference the new incoming sensory information with the relevant long-term information stored in our memory when solving a problem at hand. Working memory is known to be a limited resource: it can only actively handle small quantities of material at a time.

The comprehension process requires working memory to serve as a temporary verbatim store during linguistic decoding. Skilled readers are reported to encode connected discourse in phrasal units. Adams (1994: 856) explains that 'the language comprehension system is designed to work with whole, cohesive grammatical units – whole phrases' or sentences' worth of words – at once'. This seems to happen regardless of whether in listening or reading. The words are interpreted on line, but they are more fully digested when the phrase, clause, sentence or utterance is completed. It is during these end-of-sentence pauses that listeners or readers actively construct and reflect upon their interpretations.

Phonological processing seems to reduce the demand on working memory at least in three ways. First, phonological processing provides more economical and efficient ways of processing larger stretches of text by making use of existing robust sound-meaning neural routes established through experience. Secondly, phonological processing extends the longevity and holding capacity of its verbatim memory by voluntary rehearsals. Lastly, it helps the reader chunk the textual data into a length which is more or less comparable to the working memory capacity.

Furthermore, intonation, tone of voice, pitch and stress play a vital role in spoken language in marking pragmatic functions, conveying speaker's attitudes and intentions (Coulthard 1985; Carter and McCarthy 1995; Carter and McCarthy 1997; Carter *et al* 1995; Carter *et al* 1997). Note, however, written discourse provides no such clues except for punctuation marks and occasional visual markers such as capitalization. The segregation of phrasal and clausal units and inferring the pragmatic meaning from the text is left largely to the reader. Reading in this sense presumes syntactical and pragmatic sophistication on the part of readers. The question is whether L2 learners, even at an advanced level, possess the kind of auditory images similar to those of L1 skilled readers? If not, the reading pedagogy has to provide such intervention.

Proposal 3 Provide opportunity to connect language and multi-dimensional mental representation

One of the main criticisms against the phonic approach by the whole language proponents was that phonological recoding is one thing but comprehension of the text is quite another.

According to neuroscientists, mental representation is an individual, multi-dimensional and dynamic reality manufactured in the brain in the form of biological electricity running between the brain cells and creating networks combining external and internal information (Llinàs 1990).

In order to comprehend the word 'apple', for example, it seems that you need activation of three major neural networks. The first is perceptual processing: when you see the word 'apple', visual and phonological processing of linguistic codes takes place.

Through our experience, we have in our brains massive networks in relation to 'what apples are' with individual sensory, motor, cognitive and affective colouring. Those who like apples would have strong associations with emotional networks. Some of us may have stronger cognitive association, such as the nutrients of apples learned in a biology class or through reading some magazine articles. This second network is non-verbal and is likely to be

There are different approaches in how to make people aware of the differences and similarities, for example, the 'whole language approach', which teaches reading by observing others read, breaking down stories in letters and teaching word attack skills (Easthouse 1994). There is also the 'multi-strategy approach' with a global and analytical approach. It has both top-down and bottom-up approaches, with each approach being taught by a different teacher (Stringer and Faraclas 1987). Another approach is the first language only approach. It is a simplified multi-strategy approach using the first language only (Rempel 1998).

To summarize, there seem to be no studies available about the transfer of reading from LWC to the L1. The manuals, articles and methodologies that are there, suggest that reading is more or less the same activity in each language and that the transfer of reading can be taught by moving from items that are the same in languages to items that are different.

2.4 Transfer of reading from L1 to L2

There is no shortage of research about the transfer of reading skills and strategies from L1 to L2. Reviewing the literature on this topic might have merit as it might help to understand if and how transfer of reading across languages takes place.

The question whether or not reading is also a language activity is very important (Urquhart and Weir 1998). If reading is just a reading activity and not a language activity, then there are many variables that do not have to be taken into account and one can assume that reading is the same in all languages. Bernardt (1991) notes that reading in another language is influenced by a number of variables:

(1) Linguistic variables, including words, lexicon and syntax (Bernardt 1991).
(2) Literacy variables, including the literacy proficiency in the other language (Bernardt 1991). When someone has developed good reading behaviour in one language, he tends to use those L1 strategies on the L2 (Hulstijn 1991).
(3) World knowledge variables. Knowledge of the world of a text to be read also influences good reading behaviour. When the reader knows about the subject of the text, comprehension levels tend to be higher (Bernardt 1991).

Urquhart and Weir (1998) point out that these variables would not matter if reading was considered to be just a reading activity, but if reading is also considered a language activity, they would be very important. Making generalizing statements about L2 reading processes should be done with great care as they could be language dependent.

Observations from LWC–L1 transfer readers in Kenya suggest that there might be a difference in the success of reading transfer depending how much alike the LWC and the L1 are. For example, transfer of reading from a Bantu language to a Bantu language seems to be relatively easy, in some cases only a few hours practise is enough. However, when the LWC is linguistically quite different from the L1, weeks of training appear not to be enough to read the L1 fluently. These observations seem to suggest there might indeed be linguistic factors involved, as the only difference is the linguistic environment in which the transfer of reading takes place.

In L1–L2 transfer of reading, reading skills and strategies are often mentioned. The importance of skills and strategies for reading lies in the assumption that the difference between good and poor reading behaviour is the availability and use of certain skills and strategies. For many years, there has been the belief that reading consists of a number of skills. However, researchers have not been able to come up with conclusive evidence of unique reading skills and a possible hierarchy (Rosenshine 1980; Alderson 1990). One of the problems was that the terms 'reading skills' and 'reading strategies' have been used in an inconsistent manner. It was hard to distinguish the two, and researches have referred to the same 'item' as a skill and as a strategy (Williams and Moran 1989), which makes it difficult to compare studies.

Despite the above limitations, skills and strategies are still assumed. There is some evidence that academic and linguistic skills do transfer to L2, even in the case where the L1 and L2 has different writing systems (Cummins 1991; Au 1993; Ovando and Collier 1998; Ernst-Slavit and Mulhern 2003). However, some literature indicates that transfer of reading skills from one language to another might not always happen (e.g. Clarke 1998; Devine 1998). The success of transfer of reading skills seems to be related to language proficiency. It is generally accepted that there is interaction between language proficiency and reading ability (e.g. Bossers 1991; Devine 1998; Walter 2004). A low language proficiency makes comprehension difficult. Slow reading is often related to low L2 language proficiency. An increase in knowledge of syntactic knowledge enhances the L2 reading. The LWC–L1 transfer readers do know their L1 language well, thus low language proficiency is not an issue. As said before, there seem to be other linguistic factors that play a role.

Another interesting thought comes from a study that compared L2 and L1 reading in advanced bilinguals (Segalowitz et al 1991). It found that in bilinguals L2 reading was about 30 per cent slower than L1 reading. Nor were the bilinguals able to perform their reading tasks as easily as in their L1. This might indicate that the transfer from LWC to L1 is a different process than from the L1 to the L2. If an LWC reader would not read as well as an L1 reader would, then the transfer of skills and strategies might be different as they might not have developed the same range of flexibility in the use of skills and strategies as an L1 reader has. Segalowitz et al (1991) concluded that the slow reading in L2 might be associated with poorer lower level skills such as word recognition. They suggest that in order to improve reading, the focus should be on word recognition skills that do not use the context.

A new area of research is that of the effect of the L2 on the L1. There is an indication that the L2 has an influence on, for example, collocations and free expression in L1. One study suggests that L2 users process their L1 in a different way than monolingual L1 users do (Cook *et al* 2003). Even though this study did not investigate reading, it could be possible that it is also relevant to reading in L1. This could be a reason why in certain linguistic environments LWC–L1 transfer of reading is more difficult than in others. It could be possible that readers will initially use their knowledge of their L2 syntax on the L1 syntax, resulting in comprehension difficulties.

All these studies point to some possible causes of problems experienced in LWC to L1 transfer of reading. It seems to be that there are some linguistic variables involved. It could also be possible that L2 reading skills and strategies are not as easily transferable to the L1 when the L2 and L1 are linguistically quite different. The influence of the L2 on the L1 could hinder syntactic processing. Also recognition of words seem to be a good indicator of reading fluency. Word recognition is well studied in L1 reading. This would be the next topic to explore.

2.5 First language reading

Studies have shown that initial reading acquisition strongly relates to word recognition (Stanovich 1984). As the general reading ability increases, readers tend to rely less on word recognition and more on the context. In adults, word recognition seems to be a basis on which to predict reading comprehension abilities. Since word recognition is such an important factor in reading, it would be helpful to know how readers recognize words. What processes take place? Is there only one way or are there different ways readers recognize words?

New readers and LWC–L1 transfer readers have an auditory lexical memory (when they hear a word they recognize it) however, they do not have a visual lexical memory yet. This visual lexical memory has to be built up. There are five different ways a reader can gain access to a word (Ehri and Metsala 1998):

(1) decoding, associating a grapheme to sound;
(2) recognizing groups of letters and putting those together;
(3) recognizing the whole word;
(4) analogy to words that are already known;
(5) using the context to guess words.

The first four are often seen as lower level skills, while using the context is seen as a higher level skill. The first four ways will be explored and related to their usefulness for Sabaot reading.

Decoding

Decoding by associating sounds to letters is also referred to as phonological processing of words. One would presume that it would be a different process when a language has a transparent orthography, than when a language has an opaque orthography. In the latter case, a reader would not be able to rely on phonological information, while in the former case this could be a strategy readers could use. If this were the case, it would mean that readers of transparent orthographies would benefit from learning to read using phonological information. A few studies (e.g. Oney and Peter 1997) have been done to investigate this. Their study confirmed that readers of a transparent orthography use phonological decoding more than readers of an opaque orthography. The study also showed that with experience the reliance on phonological decoding decreased.

Recognizing groups of letters

The second way readers can process a word is by chunking groups of letters together. Several studies have been done to see how chunking letters would enhance reading (Levy and Lysynchuk 1997). This is the way Kiswahili reading is taught. It uses the ba, bo, bi, be, bu to teach the different sounds and make learners aware of syllables. Of special interest is to establish whether or not morphemes play a specific part in word recognition and if so what part it is. This question is of interest as the L1 in this study is agglutinative and often words are made up of many morphemes. If recognition of morphemes would accelerate the reading process then this would be something the readers of this language could take advantage of. Several studies indicate the morpheme recognition indeed influences word recognition (e.g. Davis 1994; Carlisle and Stone 2005). Readers at different levels make use of morpheme structures in words. Morphological awareness appears to be even a better predictor of reading than phonological awareness.

Of interest would be if morphemes are stored the same way in different languages. This topic has attracted many studies (e.g. Schreuder *et al* 1991). They discovered that it might depend on the language how the words are stored in the mental lexicon. Some languages are stored in morphemes while others are stored in words. This difference might be due to the different inflectional systems in the language. When a language has a more complex inflection it is possible that an amount of storage is saved by only storing stems and affixes of verbs and not storing all full forms, which would be much larger than a language with a more simple inflection. In the case of Sabaot and Kiswahili and English, it would be interesting to know how these languages are stored in the minds of the people, and if this would cause problems for reading?

Word recognition and word analogy

Whole word recognition is another way readers recognize words. Instead of putting parts together, they recognize the whole word at once. This can only take place when readers have a visual word lexicon, which means that some training and reinforcement of word recognition has taken place. Word recognition takes place with high frequency words and shorter words. In cases where languages are similar cognates help to build up the visual lexicon more quickly, for example 'supermarkt' (Dutch) and 'supermarket' (English) are easy to recognize. However, in the case of Kiswahili, English and Sabaot there are very few cognates and people will have to build up a completely new visual lexicon.

Other interesting facts on word recognition and reading fluency have come from eye movement studies. They have been able to show some facts about reading that were just guesses for a long time. Sophisticated computer programs have been able to show that fluent readers do not decode each word, they will only look at 20–30 per cent of the words in a text (Rayner 1981; Paulson 2005). This seems to indicate that decoding is indeed a part of the process, but its role is only limited.

The conclusions from studies of eye movement seem to suggest that different types of information are gathered from different regions during the fixation, the short period of time an eye stays focused on a certain amount of information in a text:

(1) A six to eight letter span is used for semantic identification.
(2) The effective vision during a fixation is about four characters to the left of the fixation and about 14–16 characters to the right of the fixation (Rayner and McConkie 1977; Rayner 1981; Rayner 1997). This is what a reader uses to make semantic interpretations of words.
(3) At least 20–30 per cent of the words are skipped (Rayner 1997). Factors that influence if a word is skipped are word length, word frequency and predictability.
(4) The fixation time depends on the word length, and on lexical, syntactical and discourse variables (Rayner 1997). For example, ambiguous words or ambiguous discourse parsing need a longer fixation.
(5) Poor readers do not fail to comprehend because they have a small perceptual span. Thus, an intervention to broaden the perceptual span to help poor readers to become better readers is not likely to achieve its goal.

To summarize, studies of word recognition show that there are different ways of processing words. How words are processed might depend on the language. In addition, eye movement studies have indicated several things that are language dependent that influence reading fluency. Next, reading and tone orthography will be looked at. An area of interest as the L1 in this case is a tonal language and tone is marked in the orthography.

2.6 Reading and tone orthography

Tone is a very common feature in African languages. A feature of tonal languages is that a difference in pitch conveys a different lexical or grammatical meaning. A language can have lexical tone, where tone is the only distinctive feature for meaning, or grammatical tone, where tone is responsible for conveying grammatical meaning such as tense, or both.

Reading and tone orthography is an area of research that is hardly explored, even though many languages in the world are tonal and reading tone is something many readers will have to deal with. The general assumption is that adding tone marks to an orthography will enhance the reading process as it decreases ambiguity (Bird 1999a). However, not many experimental studies have been undertaken to substantiate such a claim. Zero marking of tone does not seem to be a good solution as many homographs can appear in written language and reading becomes difficult (Bird 1999a). Most languages do have homographs, but when there are too many homographs reading will become cumbersome, as too much guessing will have to take place.

There are a few important points to elicit from the studies on tone, orthography and reading:

(1) A high tone density (surface marking) hinders reading fluency due to cognitive overload (Bird 1999b).
(2) A constant word visual enhances reading fluency (Bird 1999b).
(3) A deep tone orthography, e.g. Sabaot, makes reading the language initially more difficult as the reader will have to figure out which tone pattern applies to which mark and context.
(4) An appropriate tone pedagogy enhances the reading fluency (Bird 1999b).

3 Implications for LWC–L1 reading transfer

Understanding the linguistic environment, having seen some of the L1 reading that takes place after some training, and having gained some insights from the literature review, it becomes clearer what some of the problems in LWC–L1 transfer reading could be for the Sabaot people. As research in this area is still emerging, no real answers can be given. There are some indications of variables that could play a role in LWC–L1 transfer of reading:

(1) There are strong indications that reading is a reading and a language activity.
(2) Research has shown L1–L2 transfer of reading skills and strategies depends on a linguistic threshold. A linguistic threshold is not an issue in LWC–L1 transfer reading, but it seems that in LWC–L1 transfer reading other linguistic variables play a part. For example, the effect of the L2 on

the L1 might play a role in syntactic processing when reading in the L1, especially when the LWC and L1 are linguistically quite different.

(3) Reading ability in the L2 could play a role in LWC–L1 reading. Even when multilingual people are good readers in the L2, their L2 reading is still different from their L1 reading. When people cannot read their L1 and use their 'different developed' reading skills from L2 on the L1, it might not necessarily be the most appropriate skills and strategies to develop good reading behaviour in the L1. Especially, when the L2 and L1 are quite different linguistically.

(4) Word recognition plays an important role in reading:

    (a) Phonological decoding is helpful in transparent orthographies.

    (b) Morphological decoding is useful for languages where words consist of many morphemes.

    (c) Whole word recognition enhances reading fluency. It happens for high frequency words and short words. The Sabaot language has few short words, which tend to be high frequency words as well. But the longer words do not have a stable word visual, which might hinder rapid processing and thus delay reading.

    (d) Cognates enhance reading fluency. However, there are hardly any cognates between the LWCs and the L1. Thus, this is not something readers can make use of.

    (e) A fluent reader does not process all the words in a text. Being able to skip words enhances reading fluency. If words can be skipped depends on their length, frequency and predictability. As the L1 has long words, which change in appearance, it could be that readers do not skip many words, and fluent reading becomes difficult.

    (f) Reading fluency is also enhanced by a short fixation time. Fixation time depends on word length, syntax and ambiguous discourse. The L1 has long words, quite a different syntax from the LWCs and the tone orthography makes syntax initially ambiguous. All causes for reading to slow down.

(5) Tone orthography plays a role in reading. The tone orthography as it is used in the Sabaot language might initially require more time to process and thereby hinder fluency.

This list shows that there might be several variables that could impede LWC–L1 transfer reading in certain linguistic environments. There might be other variables that have not been mentioned in this chapter. It will require much more research to establish what exactly are the factors that hinder this process. Finding answers to these questions will open the world of education for millions of children, who now receive education in a foreign language because their own L1 teachers do not know how to read their L1. It will assist minority languages that are threatened with disappearing from this earth to revive and gain strength, and with that, knowledge, culture and identities will be saved. It will also help the Sabaot woman to feel good about herself, because she will be able to read her own language as well.

References

Alderson, J. C. (1990), 'Testing reading comprehension skills (Part one)', *Reading in a Foreign Language*, 6, 2, 425–38.

Au, K. H. (1993), *Literacy Instruction in Multicultural Settings*. Fort Worth, TX: Harcourt Brace Jovanovich.

Bernardt, E. B. (1991), 'A psychological perspective on second language literacy'. *Aila Review*, 8, 31–44.

Bird, S. (1999a), 'Strategies for representing tone in African writing systems: A critical review'. *Written Language and Literacy*, 2, 1–44.

Bird, S. (1999b), 'When marking tone reduces fluency: An orthography experiment in Cameroon'. *In Language and Speech* 42, 83–115.

Bossers, B. (1991), 'On thresholds, ceilings and Short short-circuits: the relation between L1 reading, L2 reading, and L2 knowledge'. *Aila Review*, 8, 45–60.

Carlisle, J. F. and Stone, C. A. (2005), 'Exploring the role of morphemes in word reading'. *Reading Research Quarterly*, 40, 428–49.

Clarke, M. A. (1998), 'The short circuit hypothesis of ESL reading–or when language competence interferes with reading performance', in P. L. Carrell, J. Devine and D. E. Eskey (eds), *Interactive Approaches to Second Language Reading*. Cambridge: Cambridge University Press, pp. 114–24.

Cook, V., Iarossi, E., Stellakis, N. and Tokumaru, Y. (2003), 'Effects of the L2 on the Syntactic Processing of L1', in V. Cook (ed.), *Effects of the Second Language on the First*. Clevedon: Multilingual Matters, pp. 193–213.

Cummins, J. (1991), 'Interdependence of first- and second-language proficiency in bilingual children', in E. Bialystok (ed.), *Language Processing in Bilingual Children*. Cambridge: Cambridge University Press, pp. 70–89.

Davis, P. M. (1994), *Literacy Acquisition, Retention and Usage: A case study of the Machiguenga of the Peruvian Amazon*. Texas: University of Texas at Austin.

Devine, J. (1998), 'The relationship between general language competence and second language reading proficiency: implications for teaching', in P. L. Carrell, J. Devine and D. E. Eskey (eds), *Interactive Approaches to Second Language Reading*. Cambridge: Cambridge University Press, pp. 260–77.

Durgunoglu, A. Y. and Hancin, B. J. (1992), 'An overview of cross-language transfer in bilingual reading', in B. J. Harris (ed.), *Cognitive Processing in Bilinguals*. Amsterdam: Elsevier Science Publishers B.V., pp. 391–407.

Easthouse, L. O. (1994), 'A whole language approach to transition literacy: A Peruvian Quechua trial'. *Notes on Literacy*, 20, 1–26.

Ehri, L. C. and Metsala, J. L. (1998), *Word Recognition in Beginning Literacy*. Mahwah, NJ: Lawrence Erlbaum Associates.

Ernst-Slavit, G. and Mulhern, M. (2003), 'Bilingual books: Promoting literacy and biliteracy in the second-language and mainstream classroom'. *Reading Online*, 7, (2). Available: www.readingonline.org/articles/art_index.asp?HREF=ernst-slavit/index.html.

Hulstijn, J. H. (1991), 'How is reading in a second language related to reading in a first language?'. *Aila Review*, 8, 5–14.

Hunter, G. G. (1994), *Reading Transfer: A Practical Guide to Making Transition Materials*. Tucson, AZ: Summer Institute of Linguistics.

Kutch Lojenga, C. (1989), 'Transition primers'. *Notes on Literacy*, 60, 31–5.

Larsen, I. (1989), 'A puzzling dissimilation process in Southern Nilotic'. *Fourth Nilo-Saharan Conference*, Bayreuth, Hamburg: Helmut Buske Verlag Hamburg.

Levy, B. A. and Lysynchuk, L. (1997), 'Beginning word recognition: Benefits of training by segmentation and whole word methods'. *Scientific Studies of Reading*, 1, 359–87.

Oney, B. and Peter, M. (1997), 'Phonological processing in printed word recognition: Effects of age and writing system'. *Scientific Studies of Reading*, 1, 65–83.

Ovando, C. J. and Collier, V. (1998), *Bilingual and ESL Classrooms: Teaching in Multicultural Contexts*. New York: McGraw-Hill.

Paulson, E. J. (2005), 'Viewing eye movements during reading through the lens of chaos theory: How reading is like the weather'. *Reading Research Quarterly*, 40, 338–58.

Rayner, K. (1981), 'Eye movement and the perceptual span in reading', in F. J. Pirozzolo and M. C. Wittrock (eds), *Neuropsychological and Cognitive Processes in Reading*. New York: Academic Press, pp. 145–65.

Rayner, K. (1997), 'Understanding eye movements in reading'. *Scientific Studies of Reading*, 1, 317–39.

Rayner, K. and McConkie, G. W. (1977), 'Perceptual processes in reading: The perceptual spans', in A. Reber and D. Scarborough (eds), *Toward a Psychology of Reading*. Hillsdale, NJ: Erlbaum, pp. 183–205.

Rempel, R. (1998), 'Transition primer manual for trainers and teachers: For developing and teaching mother tongue only transition primers based on the 4 basic elements'. *Notes on Literacy*, 24, 27–38.

Rosenshine, B. V. (1980), 'Skill hierarchies in reading comprehension', in R. J. Spiro, B. Bruce and W. Brewer (eds), *Theoretical Issues in Reading Comprehension*. Hillsdale, NJ: Erlbaum, pp. 535–54.

Schreuder, R., Grendel, M., Poulisse, N., Roelofs, A. and Voort, M. V. D. (1991), 'Lexical processing, morphological complexity and reading', in D. A. E. Balota, G. B. F. E. D'Arcais and K. E. Rayner (eds), *Comprehension Processes in Reading*. Hillsdale, NJ: Lawrence Erlbaum Associates, pp. 125–41.

Segalowitz, N., Poulsen, C. and Komoda, M. (1991), 'Lower level components of reading skill in higher level bilinguals: implications for reading instructions'. *Aila Review*, 8, 15–30.

Stanovich, K. E. (1984), 'Word recognition: changing perspectives', in R. Bar, M. L. Kamil, P. B. Mosenthal and P. D. Pearson (eds), *Handbook of Reading Research Vol. 2*. New York: Longman, pp. 418–52.

Stringer, M. D. and Faraclas, N. G. (1987), *Working Together for Literacy*, Wewak: Christian Books Melanesia Inc.

Urquhart, A. H. and Weir, C. (1998), *Reading in a Second Language, Process, Product and Practice*. Harlow: Pearson Education Limited.

Walter, C. (2004), 'Transfer of reading comprehension skills to L2 is linked to mental representations of text and to L2 working memory'. *Applied Linguistics*, 25, 315–39.

Williams, E. and Moran, C. (1989), 'Reading in a foreign language at intermediate and advanced levels with particular reference to English'. *Language Teaching*, 22, 217–28.

3 The processing of past tense verbs for L1 learners of English

Natalie Braber

1 Introduction

For many years a debate has raged in the linguistic and psychological worlds about the processing of past tense in language acquisition by L1 children and by L2 learners of English. It centres around two theories: the dual-route and the single mechanism theories. The dual-route model proposes that regular verbs are formed by a learned rule (addition of *-ed*) and for irregular verbs both present and past tense are stored in the lexicon (e.g. Ullman 1999). The more recent single mechanism model asserts that all verbs are processed in a single system, drawing simultaneously on semantic and phonological knowledge and affected by regularity, frequency and interaction of semantics which allow strong connections to be formed for all verbs (McClelland and Patterson 2002a, 2002b). These theories have now been extended to include adults with language impairments following brain trauma or stroke who seem to suffer from particular verb deficits. Dissociations have been found between different kinds of patients: those suffering from Alzheimer's disease and lesions in the posterior area of the brain were seen to perform at a lower level on irregular verbs, whereas those with anterior lesions, such as Broca's aphasia, had problems with regular verbs. Researchers supporting the dual-route model believe this is due to one of the routes being damaged by the brain trauma. However, examination of these features from the viewpoint of the single mechanism theory have established different answers.

2 Verb features and behaviour

All typical speakers, which include normally developing children, can communicate and receive an infinite number of messages using a finite set of resources, that is, language. This talent starts developing very quickly in children and is almost complete by the age of four (Pinker 1991: 530). Children tend to start using language to describe concrete and present situations and it is well established that children use language in a more abstract way and develop grammatical structures as they develop linguistic skills (Tomasello and Bates 2001: 7). Following the general learning trends of children allows us to follow children's development from the initial stages. One of the features of a child's language is the initial high occurrence of common nouns (Barrett 1996: 367). This proportion increases as the child's vocabulary grows from 0–100 words and then first levels and subsequently decreases after vocabulary growth reaches 200 words. The proportion of verbs in an infant's language follows at a slightly later stage. These initially rise in the 50–100 word stage, increasing until the word levels reach around 400–500 words and then even out. It is held (Hoff 2001:166) that this is the case mainly for languages like English which emphasize 'pointing and naming' for children. Western parents do not name actions and verbs in the same way as they do objects and nouns (Tomasello 1995: 123). Languages like Japanese and Korean do not follow the same trends (Hoff 2001: 157), in contrast to English, these languages are verb-final and children tend to hear more verbs per utterance than nouns (Merriman and Tomasello 1995: 11). It is the case that verbs are crucial in language, particularly where the organization of sentence structure is concerned. It is not known exactly which strategies children use to learn verbs and their argument structure (Kidd *et al* 2001: 1368).

Verbs are different from other parts of speech. Golinkoff quotes Frawley when making this point: 'A purely syntactic method for defining verbs is that any verb can be seen as "something that takes a subject or object" (Frawley 1992: 141 in Golinkoff *et al* 1995: 187). However, it seems that verbs are more complex to learn than other parts of speech and this adds to the fact that verbs (in English) appear later during lexical acquisition. This has raised the question of whether verbs are harder to learn than nouns (Golinkoff *et al* 1995: 195). This issue has been investigated by other researchers, such as Nelson, who argues that nouns are simpler to learn than verbs (although her reasoning only applies to very particular noun groups, such as nouns for names, objects and persons). She reasons that this is because nouns are less conceptually opaque than verbs, particularly in the case of object and person nouns. Verbs also tend to have more meanings than nouns. Finally, nouns are less 'linguistically defined' than verbs, which according to Nelson suggests that different aspects of verbs are stressed to different degrees in different languages, whereas nouns referring to objects require less linguistic context (Nelson 1995: 225).

3 Verb acquisition and usage

Tomasello has examined what the difficulties of verb learning could be, which he refers to as 'the packaging problem' (Tomasello 1995: 118). This applies to the different features of verbs that have to be taken into account when learning how to use them. Tomasello shows that different features will vary in importance depending on the specific verb being learnt: manner of motion ('to float'); instrument involved ('to hammer'); result achieved ('to empty'); action performed ('to wave'); causation (difference for example between 'die' and 'kill'); and verb pairs that depict the same event from different perspectives ('buy' versus 'sell'). It is also noteworthy in relation to

children's usage of verbs and other aspects of their language acquisition that
children are rarely corrected in their verb usage, but manage to acquire this
usage nevertheless (Braine and Brooks 1995: 358).

A very important aspect of verbs, both in connection with child language
acquisition as well as later language impairment is the fact that verbs have
different tenses. It has been noted that the acquisition of the past tense in
English reflects the learning of morphology as well as productive linguistic
rules for children (Plunkett and Juola 1999: 463), and it is the development
of grammar rules which has sparked a division among researchers. Pinker
states:

> Past tense inflection is an isolable subsystem in which grammatical mechanisms can
> be studied in detail, without complex interactions with the rest of language. It is
> computed independently of syntax, the subsystem that defines the form of phrases
> and sentences: The syntax of English forces its speakers to mark tense in every
> sentence, but no aspect of syntax works differently with regular and irregular verbs.
> (Pinker 1991: 531)

Irregular verbs are less frequent than regular verbs and irregular verbs have
become even less frequent throughout the history of English (Pinker 1991:
532). Less frequent irregular verbs (such as *abide-abode, chide-chid* and *gild-gilt*)
have become regular through the passage of time. Bybee and Slobin (1982)
discuss a study carried out by Kuczaj in 1977 which examined spontaneous
speech data from very young children which suggested that irregular verbs
are learned by rote memorization. They comment that 'chronological age is
a better predictor of success on irregular past forms than mean length of
utterance (MLU), while the reverse is true for the regular past-tense rule'
(Bybee and Slobin 1982: 266). Tomasello also argues that verbs tend to be
used initially as 'islands' by which he means that they tend to be used in the
forms ('sentence frames') in which they were initially heard and tend not to
transfer to other tenses and forms until much later (Tomasello and Bates
2001: 170).

Approximately 86 per cent of English verbs form the past tense using a
regular inflection (Plunkett and Nakisa 1997). The stem of the present tense
verb is transformed into the past tense by the addition of *-ed* to the written
form which can be one of three allophones in the phonological form. The
three allophones are dependent on the stem-final phoneme: the voiced allo-
phone [d] is added to stems ending in a voiced phoneme (e.g. *stabbed, loved,
raised*); the unvoiced [t] is used for stems ending with unvoiced phonemes
(e.g. *stopped, laughed, raced*); and for those stems already ending with an alveo-
lar stop, voiced or unvoiced, the syllable [Id] is added (e.g. *faded, hated*). The
past tense for the remaining 14 per cent of verbs is formed in a variety of
ways: no change (e.g. *hit → hit*); vowel change (e.g. *meet → met*); vowel change
and consonant addition (e.g. *leave → left*); consonant change (e.g. *send →
sent*); and a small number of high-frequency suppletive forms (e.g. *go →
went*). There thus exists a great difference between regular and irregular
verbs and Pinker comments that the two are different in almost every way:

'Whereas regulars are orderly and predictable, irregulars are chaotic and idiosyncratic' (Pinker 1999: 17).

Despite constituting only 14 per cent of all verbs, irregular verbs are among the most commonly used verbs in the English language. According to Pinker this is due to the fact that a verb has to be used frequently in order to be passed correctly from generation to generation. If a verb is not used frequently enough, only regular rules will be applied (Pinker 1999: 138). He writes that irregular forms are 'relics of history' and comments that irregular verbs form a closed class of items and that the last irregular verb to be added in our language was 'snuck', which was added in over a century ago (Pinker 1999: 18) and that regular past tense verbs 'have no history' (Pinker 1999: 213) as only the rule exists (according to the dual-route model which will be discussed below). In fact, it appears that irregulars are not completely irregular as they can be formed into groups of families. These form past tenses in a more consistent manner (e.g., *ring* → *rang*, *sing* → *sang*; *weep* → *wept*, *creep* → *crept*), and have been referred to as 'quasi-regulars' (McClelland and Patterson 2002a: 464). Although there are such families, there do not seem to be set rules for such forms and there are still many exceptions. Taatgen also writes about the difference between regular and irregular verbs when it comes to frequency:

> In the English past tense, regular verbs have a high *type-frequency*: most of the verbs are regular. However, although there are only a few irregular verbs, they tend to be used very often. As a consequence, the *token-frequency* of regular verbs, how often regular verbs occur in spoken or written speech, is actually much lower.
>
> (Taatgen and Anderson 2002: 125)

4 Children learning verbs

Within the speech of children first acquiring language, it seems that irregular verbs are more commonly learnt earlier than regular verbs (Bybee and Slobin 1982: 265). How is it that they spot the difference between regular and irregular and how does this relate to the ways they use to acquire language? Children are rarely corrected by parents for using incorrect tense forms and yet children learn to use them properly after a period of uncertainty. Baker (1979) suggests that children may be conservative learners and do not make generalizations about verb forms, only using them in formats they have heard used by other speakers. However, overgeneralization errors, which will be discussed in the next section, cast some doubt on this idea.

Another concept is that of preemption (Braine and Brooks 1995), which suggests that once a specific linguistic form has been learnt it usually stops other forms being used: 'According to the simplest and most widely accepted form of pre-emption, once a child has rote-learned an irregular form the erroneous regularized form drops out of the child's repertoire – the rote-learned irregular form is said to pre-empt the form generated by the rule'

(Braine and Brooks 1995: 360). However, this only works if verbs are accessed by a dual-route which deals independently with regular and irregular forms. Clark writes that children may learn the rule (add -*ed*) and then overgeneralize such forms to include irregular forms. The dual-route proposes that children learn to extract the rule for regular forms and have to learn irregular forms as they come across them and have to memorize the present and past tense forms independently (Clark 2003: 210). As children may initially not be aware of irregular verbs, overregularization errors may occur. Clark argues that the dual-route may look compelling in English but suggests that the flaws can be seen when it comes to examining other languages:

> 'Where does a French verb like *aller* 'to go' belong? Should it be stored as a stem (or set of stems) with rules for regular inflection for each tense, say, or should it be stored as a full set of inflected forms as an irregular verb? *Aller* is irregular only in the present tense; it is entirely regular in the imperfect, the future, the conditional, the perfect past, the historic past, and in its formation of the past participle'.
>
> (Clark 2003: 210)

Different research projects have shown that children's development of English verbs follows a particular path. It seems that initially children correctly inflect irregular past tense forms, then produce occasional overregularizations before mastering the correct forms. This has been referred to as a 'U-shaped sequence of development' (e.g. Marcus 1995; Taatgen and Anderson 2002). It is suggested that some rote learning must be in place, otherwise children could not develop forms such as '*go-went*' (Bybee and Slobin 1982: 266). Clark comments that this effect on verbs is greatest when children are between 2 and 3½ years old (Clark 2003: 211). The number of overregularizations differs in different research projects and has been calculated anywhere from 5 per cent (Marcus *et al* 1992) to 50 per cent (Kuczaj 1977; Maratsos 1993, 2000). It is clear that such errors decrease steadily as children progress. Pinker argues that these errors happen as children are not always capable of retrieving an irregular form and that the rule-based form will take over, producing a regular form. Furthermore, he comments that such errors also have to do with frequency, the more infrequent an irregular is, the more likely children are to make errors with it (Pinker 1994: 274). Pinker also notes that these errors are less likely to occur in irregulars that are part of a 'regular' group and those that have high frequency members (Pinker 1991: 532). He suggests it is partly to do with the fact that children's memory retrieval is less reliable than that of adults and as certain verb forms may still be unfamiliar, they will only have a weak memory trace for such forms (Pinker 2001: 7). On the other hand, Rumelhart and McClelland (1986) have noted that overregularizations may also go through specific stages, where initially we may only see addition of -*ed* (*goed*), later more complex forms may also appear where it seems that some concept of the irregular has been realized (e.g. *wented*). It seems that children do know particular restrictions placed on verbs when they produce overgeneralizations (Bavin and Kidd 2000).

5 The dual-route theory

The dual-route theory of verb processing considers how verbs are stored and accessed in the lexicon. Clark (2003) has asked how such verbs are stored and has said that what information children (and adults) use in producing inflected forms should have consequences for what they store about the forms of words in memory. Clark comments that the frequency of the verb, as well as the regularity, affect the way it is stored. Pinker (2001) points out that 'words and rules' are not solely used for verbs, but are applied on a much wider scale in language and Pinker and Ullman emphasize this point: 'The Words and Rules (WR) theory claims that the regular-irregular distinction is an epiphenomenon of the design of the human language faculty, in particular, the distinction between lexicon and grammar made in most traditional theories of language' (Pinker and Ullman 2002: 456).

The cornerstone of the dual-route theory of verb inflection is that the organization of language reflects the basic distinction between regular and irregular verbs (Ullman *et al* 1997; Pinker 1999). Theorists such as Clahsen (1999) and Pinker (1999) argue that there is a strict dichotomy between regular and irregular forms (Tomasello and Bates 2001: 7). According to this view the past and present tense forms of irregular verbs are stored in the lexicon, which is part of our memory. On the other hand, regular past tenses are formed by a rule-governed procedural system which applies not only to regular forms but also to novel verbs (evidence that has shown that this rule is productive in novel forms has been obtained by asking adults and children to produce past tense forms of non-words, such as 'moop' – see Tomasello and Bates 2001). This means that regular verbs are stored as stems with rules for adding the appropriate allomorph, whereas irregular verbs must have both forms in store. These forms have to be learnt and stored individually and cannot be constructed as part of a rule (Clark 2003: 210). Pinker and Ullman propose that this means that although irregulars are acquired and stored as all other words, they have a grammatical feature incorporated into their lexical entries, such as 'past tense' for the past tense forms (Pinker and Ullman 2002: 456).

It is assumed that when a past tense form is needed, both routes begin to operate simultaneously. If a matching verb is found in the lexicon, then the rule can be inhibited and the correct irregular form is retrieved from the lexicon. In the case of regular (and novel) verbs, no match can be found in the lexicon and therefore the rule is applied. Pinker is one of the supporters of the dual-route theory. He argues that once the rule has been learned, past tense forms for regular verbs do not have to exist in the lexicon as we have the rule to apply them. He writes: 'The category of regular forms is not a real category, but a virtual category: the list of forms that *would* be created if the rule were allowed to work its way through all the verbs in a person's vocabulary' (Pinker 1999: 313).

According to the dual route model, both types of verbs have advantages and disadvantages. Taatgen argues that the advantage of irregulars is their high frequency. On the other hand, regulars have the advantage of the rule. He points out: 'Concurrent with this trade-off is the trade-off between retrieval and the use of a rule. Retrieval is more efficient, since using a rule requires phonetic post-processing, but retrieval is possible only if an example is available from memory' (Taatgen and Anderson 2002: 151). Pinker adds that having two mechanisms doing the same thing would cause problems unless there was something mediating between them. If we can find an irregular, then the rule is blocked. However, if there is no form found in the lexicon, then the rule is applied. This results in forms like 'borked' and 'moshed' as these are non-words that do not have any forms in the lexicon (Pinker 1999: 19). Initially irregular verbs may be used correctly as these are the most common verbs encountered and these may be memorized. As more verbs are learned and a rule starts being applied, mistakes may be made as some irregulars may not yet have a stored form and an incorrect past tense form can be applied. However, as more examples are learned these over-generalizations slowly start to disappear and the final transition to adult-like language is made (Taatgen and Anderson 2002: 124). It has been suggested that a child's memory is more fallible than an adult's and thus more likely to make mistakes. This means that if an irregular form cannot be found, the vacuum is filled by using the regular route (Pinker 1994: 274).

6 Objections to the dual-route theory

Pinker has advocated some modification of the traditional words and rules theory: although the rule route still holds, he argues that memory is not a list of unrelated slots but is partly associative, features are linked to other features, as they are in the connectionist network accounts (Pinker 2001: 3 and Daugherty and Seidenberg 1992: 1). Ramscar argues that the dual-route theory is fallible and that it does not account for many irregular past tense verbs clustering with phonologically similar past tense verbs. Furthermore, he states that it is possible to create irregular nonce (non-word) verbs, if they are phonologically similar to real irregular verbs (for example creating 'splang' from 'spling' as this form is similar to both 'sing' and 'ring') (Ramscar 2002: 47). This means that the dual-route has to incorporate the lexicon not just containing a list of irregulars but also an associative memory component that can explain these irregularities.

McClelland and Seidenberg argue that the dual-route model does not adequately cover what happens in language. They write:

> The brain stores language in a way that systems of rules and lists of words can only approximate. The rules of language, such as the past tense, need not be explicitly represented. . . . For example, in the production of past-tense forms of verbs, the mechanism might simply adjust the connections among the neurons involved in forming past tenses when the network encounters the past-tense form of a word.
>
> (McClelland and Seidenberg 2000: 47)

7 The single mechanism theory

According to the dual-route theory rules are of crucial importance. However, there are other systems that deal with past tense processing without needing rules. Concepts such as parallel distributed processing and connectionism, as developed by Rumelhart and McClelland, suggest that people store associations between the sounds of stems and the sound of new past tense forms and generalize the associations to new words if they are similar. Rather than rules, memory is of major importance in this scheme. Rumelhart and McClelland propose:

> an alternative to explicit inaccessible rules. We suggest that lawful behavior and judgments may be produced by a mechanism in which there is no explicit representation of the rule. Instead, we suggest that the mechanisms that process language and make judgments of grammaticality are constructed in such a way that their performance is characterizable by rules, but that the rules themselves are not written in explicit form anywhere in the mechanism.
>
> (Rumelhart and McClelland 1986: 217)

This is the basis of the single mechanism theory.

This single mechanism model needs only one set of procedures for both regular and irregular verbs. It draws simultaneously on semantic and phonological knowledge and processes all types of verbs in the same route, without recourse to rules. Ramscar has suggested another factor of importance, not considered in the dual-route but part of the single mechanism theory, and this is the importance of semantics. Within the single mechanism, the system is affected by regularity, frequency and interaction from semantics. All processing can be accounted for by analogies that have been made in the memory, which means that rules are not needed (Ramscar 2002: 48).

Creating the first single mechanism model for learning the past tense, Rumelhart and McClelland suggest that the rules for past tense formation are not explicitly written down; we process language and make judgements without having rules for doing so (Rumelhart and McClelland 1986: 217). Their model consists of a simple pattern-associator network that learns the relationship between the phonological forms of the stems and past tenses of English words (McClelland and Patterson 2002b: 466) and rules are replaced with weighted connections which result in rule-like behaviours as the weight in these connections are adjusted (Ramscar 2002: 46). The question which arises from such assumptions is how children learn to use the past tense. According to the single mechanism theory this is done by using a network with 'weights' to adjust to learning. Taatgen describes the process in the following way:

> So in order to learn the past tense, the child has to hear a past tense form from a parent or other speaker, and has to determine what the stem is. Consequently the stem has to be selected for 'uptake', and if it is, it is fed into the network to determine the past tense again. Its performance is then compared to the past tense

initially heard, and weights are adjusted accordingly. When the child actually has to produce a past tense, the network is used without any learning, as there is no feedback to adjust its weights.

(Taatgen and Anderson 2002: 129)

Within Taatgen's explanation, U-shaped learning occurs due to the changes in vocabulary size. The network needs to be able to shift the weights to accommodate regularization and the new verbs it is encountering, but the time needed to integrate the different types of verbs causes the temporary U-shape which occurs in the speech of many children (Taatgen and Anderson 2002: 124).

Frequency affects regular and irregular verbs differently depending on which model is followed. Within the dual-route view, irregular past tense forms are retrieved from memory, which means they are expected to be sensitive to frequency, whereas regular past tense verbs should not be as they are formed by applying a rule. Within the single mechanism theory, both are processed in the same route and should therefore both show frequency effects. Not only this, but 'neighbourhood effects' are also to be expected and verbs may be strengthened by verbs sharing similar patterns, both for the regular and irregular. This has been shown in research to be the case in research conducted by Plunkett and Marchman (1991) as well as Rumelhart and McClelland (1986).

8 Objections to the single mechanism theory

Pinker argues that verbs must be learned by a rule as tense marking is not an innate ability children have, as some languages do not mark tense (Pinker 1999: 223). He has suggested that learning a rule seems a simpler suggestion than radically re-altering distributions and weights. Daugherty and Plunkett comment that: 'It would be important to determine whether a connectionist network can explain all of the relevant facts about the past tense or whether, as Pinker suggests, it will have to be supplemented by a rule' (Daugherty and Seidenberg 1992: 1). Those supporting the dual-route model believe that some rules have to be in place for verb usage to occur correctly. Ullman carried out a study of frequency and neighbourhood strength contrasts between regular and irregular verbs. He proposed that the results found in his study (Ullman 1999) are predicted by the dual-route in that irregular and regular verbs should show different results because of the different systems used to retrieve them (rule and storage) and that these results show the single mechanism theory is flawed as this would expect such effects also for consistent regular verbs, which was not the case in this study.

9 Adults with language impairments

People who suffer from brain trauma or disease can show particular problems with past tense processing for regular and irregular verbs. These have been researched in various projects which will be examined here in light of both theories. Ullman *et al* (1997) have reported a double dissociation for the past tense forms of regular and irregular verbs across different patient types. A group of patients with Alzheimer's disease and a group of posterior aphasics had poorer performance with irregular than regular verbs. In contrast, a group of patients with Parkinson's disease demonstrated a slight difference favouring irregular over regular verbs, while an anterior aphasic patient exhibited the same difference on a much larger scale. Ullman assumes that this double dissociation supported his theories that emphasize that grammar and lexicon are distinct components. Within these two patient groups, either the rule-route or the lexicon had been damaged impairing one verb type only. Ullman states that 'a majority of studies find AD [Alzheimer Disease] patients relatively unimpaired at processing the syntax of sentences, suggesting that grammar is largely unaffected' (Ullman *et al* 1997: 268). A different pattern is displayed by Parkinson's patients who show suppression of rule programming and therefore difficulties with generating rule-generated past tense forms (Ullman *et al* 1997: 272).

According to the single mechanism theory the double dissociation that can be found across the different patient groups reflects phonological and semantic influences on a single process. This dissociation is attributed to two different factors. First, the greater reliance on word meaning for irregular verbs (Joanisse and Seidenberg 1999) and secondly, the greater phonological complexity of the regular past tense (what this means will be discussed below). The single mechanism model predicts that poor performance with irregular verbs, especially for low frequency items, should be associated with semantic impairment, while the deficit for regular verbs reported in Broca's aphasic patients can be associated with a phonological impairment. This is opposed by Marslen-Wilson and Tyler who propose that:

> if regular and irregular forms are mentally represented and processed in fundamentally the same way, then both should be affected in similar ways by damage to the brain that disrupts morphological processing systems, and should show equivalent deficits in the appropriate experimental tests.
>
> (Marslen-Wilson and Tyler 1998: 429)

It will be argued below that in the case of the Broca's aphasia patients such errors are not due to morphological problems (as is also held by Tyler *et al* 2002: 13) but that for these patients all problems with regular past tense processing are due to phonological impairments.

Experimental studies have been carried out using the single-mechanism effects on patients. While it was found that these effects are similar to those described by Ullman, the explanation of the problems was very different. Patterson *et al* (2001) studied 11 patients with semantic dementia, a condition which gradually erodes the meaning for words, faces, objects and other non-verbal stimuli. The patients were asked to generate the past tense of regular, irregular and novel verbs in simple sentence frames and also to indicate the correct past tense in forced-choice recognition tasks. These patients had essentially normal performance in generating and recognizing the past tense forms of novel and regular verbs, but substantially reduced accuracy on the irregular past tense that was modulated by the frequency of the words and by the degree of the patients' semantic impairment.

Meanwhile, Bird *et al* (2003) investigated the link between poor regular verb performance and phonological impairment in ten patients with Broca's aphasia. These patients had disfluent and agrammatic speech typical of this type of aphasia but also showed impairments on the reading, repetition and production of regular verbs. The Bird study shows that rather than these problems being directly linked to regular verb past tense processing, it appears that this problem is mainly phonological. When people consider the phonological structure of past tense verbs, it seems that there are significant differences between regular and irregular verbs. On the whole, regular verbs contain complex consonantal clusters at the offset of the word (for example, stepped, walked, blinked) which occurs far less frequently in irregular verbs (thought, ran, saw). On a battery of general language testing, it was found that these patients performed poorly on phonological testing (rhyme production, rhyme judgement and tests of segmentation). If these patients suffer from a general phonological deficit, then we would expect them to perform at a lower level on such complex verb endings. To establish whether this was the case, the tests of verb reading, repetition and production were carried out again, but with regular and irregular past tense verbs that were matched exactly for phonological complexity (e.g. compare 'stepped' and 'slept', which both have CCVCC structure). Within these tests, the advantage for irregular verbs disappeared completely. To further examine whether regular verb difficulties could be motivated by the morphology, a further test was carried out. In this experiment regular stem and past tense pairing (e.g. press–pressed) were compared with non-verb word pairing that had a matching phonological contrast (e.g. chess–chest). The Broca patients were required to make same–different judgements to each spoken pair. In all cases, the patient's accuracy for the verb and non-verb pairing was almost identical – suggesting that their poor verb performance reflected their more general phonological impairment rather than a specific morphological deficit.

Two further studies have dealt with the problems with phonology by analysing the errors made within a large sample of testing (Braber *et al* 2005 and Lambon Ralph *et al* 2005). These experiments were carried out with ten (Braber *et al* 2005), and then eight (Lambon Ralph *et al* 2005), non-fluent Broca aphasia type patients. They all showed an initial advantage for irregular verbs, which disappeared when verbs were matched for phonological complexity. All patients had good comprehension and performed poorly on tasks which were phonologically based. These tests and errors were used to test the notion that a generalized phonological impairment was central to the patients' language impairment and to reveal some of the qualities of this deficit. The centrality of the patients' phonological impairment was reinforced by the fact that the majority of the errors found in all tests of reading, repetition and sentence completion were phonological in nature. In reading and repetition, there were a high number of inflectional omissions (final *d/t*) which would be expected in a dual-route theory. It is suggested, however, that such errors are a subset of a more general class of phonological errors which could arise due to this complex consonantal cluster. The errors made by these patients were made up from a combination of substitutions, deletions and additions, but with the majority of errors ending in a phonologically simplified version of the target word. However, errors were not only found at the end of words as would be predicted for such past tense errors if a morphological deficiency was the cause of problems, but also occurred equally across all parts of the word, leaving only the vowel spared.

The second study (Lambon Ralph *et al* 2005) examined what causes the difficulties in the past tense regular verbs for these patients. These tests included the repetition of words of varying complexity (ranging from 'lick' to 'blink') and words that varied in position of lexical stress. Although much more detailed research needs to be conducted on the relationship between morphological and phonological processing, the results of these tests can be seen as part of the explanation. For the problems these patients had with regular verb processing was directly linked to the extent which they showed problems with the tests of complexity and stress. Of the aphasia patients examined, those with the most consistent advantage for irregular verbs, and therefore poorest at regular verbs were also most adversely affected by phonological complexity and phonological atypicality (in the form of syllabic stress on second rather than first position). This evidence seems to suggest that previous morphological evidence for such errors can be explained in phonological terms. It seems that errors made by this group of patients can be linked to the complex phonological structure of regular verbs rather than the result of a damaged rule-route as predicted by the dual-route theory. These studies all point to the validity of the single mechanism theory which states the importance of frequency, regularity and interaction from semantics when all verb types are processed.

9 Conclusion

While the studies reported above have informed academic discourse, they provide no final answer to the question how the past tense is processed in language acquisition by children and learners of English. Answering this question will also help us to learn more about how language is processed in general. Meanwhile, the debate between the dual-route and the single mechanism will continue to spark controversy. Pinker describes the situation well: 'Both alternatives have been developed into famous, full-blown theories of the English past-tense system. Their clash is one of the most vigorous controversies in the modern study of the mind, echoing through psychology, linguistics, philosophy, computer science and neuroscience' (Pinker 1999: 96–7).

References

Baker, C. L. (1979), 'Syntactic theory and the projection problem'. *Linguistic Inquiry*, 10, 533–81.

Barrett, M. (1996), 'Early lexical development', in P. Fletcher and B. MacWhinney (eds), *The Handbook of Child Language*. Oxford: Blackwell Publishing, pp. 362–92.

Bavin, E. L. and Kidd, E. (2000), 'Learning new verbs: Beyond the input', in C. Davis, T. van Gelder and R. Wales (eds), *Cognitive Sciences in Australia*. Adelaide: Causal, 113–24.

Bird, H., Lambon, R., Matthew A., Seidenberg, M. S., McClellend, J. L. and Patterson, K. (2003), 'Deficits in phonology and past-tense morphology: What's the connection?'. *Journal of Memory and Language*, 48, (3), 502–26.

Braber, N., Patterson, K., Ellis, K., McClelland, J. L. and Lambon Ralph, M. A. (2005), 'The relationship between phonological and morphological deficits in Broca's aphasia: Further evidence from errors in verb inflection'. *Brain and Language*, 92, 278–87.

Braine, Martin D.S. and Brooks, P. (1995), 'Verb argument structure and the problem of avoiding an overgeneral grammar', in M. Tomasello and W.E. Merriman. (eds), *Beyond Names for Things: Young Children's Acquisition of Verbs*. Hove: Lawrence Erlbaum, pp. 353–76.

Bybee, J. L. and Slobin, D. I. (1982), 'Rules and schemas in the development and use of the English past tense'. *Language*, 58, 265–89.

Clahsen, H. (1999), 'Lexical entries and rules of language: A multidisciplinary study of German inflection'. *Behavioral and Brain Sciences*, 22, 991–1060.

Clark, E. V. (2003), *First Language Acquisition*. Cambridge: Cambridge University Press.

Daugherty, K. and Seidenberg, M.S. (1992), 'Rules or connections? The past tense revisited', in *Proceedings of Cognitive Science Society*. Hove: Lawrence Erlbaum, 1–6.

Golinkoff, R. M., Hirsh-Pasek, K., Mervis, C. B., Frawley, W. B. and Parillo, M. (1995), 'Lexical principles can be extended to the acquisition of verbs', in M. Tomasello and W. E. Merriman (eds), *Beyond Names for Things: Young Children's Acquisition of Verbs*. Hove: Lawrence Erlbaum, pp. 185–221.

Hoff, E. (2001), *Language Development* (2nd edn). Belmont: Wadsworth.

Joanisse, M. F. and Seidenberg, M. S. (1999), 'Impairment in verb morphology following brain injury: A connectionist model'. *Proceedings of the National Academy of Science*, 96, 7592–7.

Kidd, E., Bavin, E. L. and Rhodes, B. (2001), 'Two-year-olds' knowledge of verbs and argument structures', in M. Almgren *et al*, *Research on Child Language*. Somerville, MA: Cascadilla Press, pp. 1368–82.

Kuczaj, S.A. II (1977), 'The acquisition of regular and irregular past tense forms'. *Journal of Verbal Learning & Verbal Behavior*, 16, 589–600.

Lambon Ralph, M. A., Braber, N., McClelland, J. L. and Patterson, K. (2005), 'What underlies the neuropsychological pattern of irregular > regular past-tense verb production'. *Brain and Language*, 93, 106–19.

Maratsos, M. P. (1993), 'Artifactual overregularizations?', in E. V. Clark (ed.), *Proceedings of the 24th Annual Child Language Research Forum*. Stanford: CSLI, pp. 139–48.

Maratsos, M. P. (2000), 'More overregularizations after all: New Data and discussion of Marcus, Pinker, Ullman, Hollander, Rosen and Xu'. *Journal of Child Language*, 27, 183–212.

Marcus, G. F. (1995), 'The acquisition of the English past tense in children and multilayered connectionist networks'. *Cognition*, 56, 271–9.

Marcus, G. F., Pinker, S., Ullman, M., Hollander, M., Rosen, T. J. and Xu, F. (1992), 'Overregularization in language acquisition'. *Monographs of the Society for Research in Child Development*, 57.

Marslen-Wilson, W. and Tyler, L. K. (1998), 'Rules, representations and the English past tense'. *Trends in Cognitive Sciences*, 2, 428–35.

McClelland, J. L. and Patterson, K. (2002a), ' "Words *or* Rules" cannot exploit the regularity in exceptions'. *Trends in Cognitive Sciences*, 6, 464–5.

McClelland, J. L. and Patterson, K. (2002b), 'Rules or connections in past-tense inflections: what does the evidence rule out?' *Trends in Cognitive Sciences*, 6, 465–72.

McClelland, J. L. and Seidenberg, M. S. (2000), 'Language: Why do kids say *goed* and *brang*?'. *Science*, 287, 47–8.

Merriman, W. E. and Tomasello, M. (1995), 'Introduction: Verbs are words too', in M. Tomasello and W. E. Merriman (eds), *Beyond Names for Things: Young Children's Acquisition of Verbs*. Hove: Lawrence Erlbaum, pp. 1–18.

Nelson, K. (1995), 'The dual category problem in the acquisition of action words', in M. Tomasello and W. E. Merriman (eds), *Beyond Names for Things: Young Children's Acquisition of Verbs*. Hove: Lawrence Erlbaum, pp. 223–49.

Patterson, K., Lambon Ralph, M. A., Hodges, J. R., McClelland, J. L. (2001), 'Deficits in irregular past-tense verb morphology associated with degraded semantic knowledge'. *Neuropsychologia*, 39, 709–24.

Pinker, S. (1991), 'Rules of language'. *Science*, 253, 530–5.

Pinker, S. (1994), *The Language Instinct*. London: Penguin Books.

Pinker, S. (1999), *Words and Rules*. London: Phoenix.

Pinker, S. (2001), 'Four decades of rules and associations, or whatever happened to the past tense debate?' Online: www.ehess.fr/centres/iscp/persons/dupoux/ 2001j./papers/pinker.htm.

Pinker, S. and Ullman, M. T. (2002), 'The past and future of the past tense'. *Trends in Cognitive Sciences*, 6, 456–63.

Plunkett, K. and Juola, P. (1999), 'A connectionist model of English past tense and plural morphology'. *Cognitive Science*, 23, 463–90.

Plunkett, K. and Marchman, V. A. (1996), 'Learning from a connectionist model of the acquisition of the English past tense'. *Cognition*, 61, 299–308.

Plunkett, K. and Nakisa, R.C. (1997), 'A connectionist model of the Arabic plural system'. *Language and Cognitive Processes*, 12, 807–36.

Ramscar, M. (2002), 'The role of meaning in inflection: why the past tense does not require a rule'. *Cognitive Psychology*, 45, 45–94.

Rumelhart, D. E. and McClelland, J. L. (1986), 'On learning the past tenses of English verbs', in D. E. Rumelhart and J. L. McClelland, *Explorations in the Microstructure of Cognition, Volume 2*. Cambridge: MIT Press, pp. 216–71.

Taatgen, N. A. and Anderson, J. R. (2002), 'Why do children learn to say "Broke"? A model of learning the past tense without feedback'. *Cognition* 86, 123–55.

Tomasello, M. (1995), 'Pragmatic contexts for early verb learning', in M. Tomasello and W. E. Merriman (eds), *Beyond Names for Things: Young Children's Acquisition of Verbs*. Hove: Lawrence Erlbaum pp. 115–46.

Tomasello, M. and Bates, E. (2001), *Language Development. The Essential Readings*. Oxford: Blackwell Publishing.

Tyler, L. K., Randall, B. and Marslen-Wilson, W. D. (2002), 'Phonology and neuropsychology of the English past tense'. *Neuropsychologia*, 1373, 1–13.

Ullman, M. T. (1999), 'Acceptability ratings of regular and irregular past-tense forms: Evidence for a dual-system model of language from word frequency and phonological neighbourhood effects'. *Language and Cognitive Processes*, 14, 47–67.

Ullman, M. T., Corkin, S., Coppola, M., Hickok, G., Growdon, J. H., Koroshetz, W. J. and Pinker, S. (1997), 'A neural dissociation within language: Evidence that the mental dictionary is part of declarative memory, and that grammatical rules are processed by the procedural system'. *Journal of Cognitive Neuroscience*, 9, 266–76.

4 Seeing and saying for yourself: The roles of audio-visual mental aids in language learning and use

Brian Tomlinson and Javier Avila

1 Introduction

In first language learning and use the meaning of utterances listened to or read is typically represented multi-dimensionally in the mind (Tomlinson 2000b, 2001; Masuhara 2005), with visual imaging being one of the main means of achieving understanding, interpretation, representation, retention and recall of the language experience. Another of the means of doing this is by using the inner voice to repeat utterances in the mind and to talk about them. For example, when reading the line, 'I saw a tram' from the poem *Amsterdam* by John Hegley (Hegley 1997: 12) one of us saw a tram outside the main station in Amsterdam and then a tram on the promenade in Blackpool, whilst at the same time reciting the line mentally and having the following inner speech 'conversation': 'What a silly poem . . . anyone could write that . . . could use it though . . . get learners to write similar poems . . .'. Later, when recalling the poem, the tram outside the station image was dominant and words then came back to mind.

In addition, during the activities of speaking and writing native speakers typically see images representing partially what they want to say, they talk to themselves about what they are going to say, they sometimes try out various options in their minds and they frequently rehearse utterances mentally before producing them.

Audio-visual mental aids play a crucial part in native speaker understanding and use of language from a very early age and yet in the acquisition and development of another language from instruction they do not seem to be typically made use of effectively until advanced competence is achieved (Tomlinson 1998a; 2003a).

2 Visual imagery in L1 learning and use

Visual imagery is an aspect of mental imagery in which we see pictures in our mind, either as a recreation of something once perceived (e.g. a painting), as a representation of something communicated non-visually (e.g. a story) or as a creation of something new based on previous experience (e.g. a coach planning tactics for a game). The term 'visualization' is sometimes used in the literature as synonymous with 'visual imaging'. We differentiate it as the use of visual imagery with a deliberate, definite goal in mind (Arnold 1999: 260). Other aspects of mental imagery are motor imagery (through which we mentally experience physical activity) and the other sensory imageries (i.e. tactile imagery, olfactory imagery and auditory imagery).

Stevick (1986: 16) defines mental imagery as: 'a composite that we perceive (more or less vividly) as a result of the interaction between what we have in storage and what is going on at the moment'. This broad definition caters either for an experience through the sensory system, recalling stored information and interacting with new information to create a novel experience or for a similar vicarious experience in the absence of the sensory stimulus, where, for example, someone can see the Forest of Arden as a result of a speaker telling of their own experience in the forest. Mental imaging can be seen as a basic cognitive strategy in human cognition, discovering and problem-solving. Some researchers limit its scope to the cognitive realm, but that ignores an important feature of imagery, that of its relation with the affective component of learning, without which a complete picture of the learning process would be impossible. Other researchers (Tomlinson 2000b, 2001b; Masuhara 2005) stress the interaction of mental imaging, of affective engagement and of cognitive engagement to achieve the multi-dimensional mental representation vital for the deep processing (Craik and Lockhart 1972) required for effective and durable learning.

Recent discoveries of the neurological basis of the generation of mental imagery have shown that it is not located in any specific site in the brain but in different areas (Kosslyn *et al* 1995). Damasio (1994), for example, states that the basis of the mind is to be found in the inner responses of the body, especially those involving mental imaging; therefore, an essential condition of thought is the ability to generate and manipulate mental imagery. Petsche *et al* (1992) study and compare the mechanisms involved in perception and mental recreation of experience and conclude that there are significant similarities in the mental localization of both activities. They also find strong similarities between verbal thinking and thinking using images, with strong activity in the frontal areas in both tasks.

It seems that nearly all of us typically make use of visual imagery when using our L1 and that doing so facilitates understanding, retention, recall and production. For example, surveys of introspective reports of visual imaging among 80 L1 teachers of English at seminars in England, Japan and Spain (Tomlinson 1997) revealed that 95 per cent of them saw images in their minds (varying in detail and vividness) when reading a variety of texts. Stevick (1986: 3) also reports 95 per cent of visualizers in his experiments with L1 listeners and readers.

When using language both L1 learners and proficient L2 users seem to make frequent use of visual imaging to:

• Predict subsequent content of texts, for example seeing a piece of cheese in the mind whilst reading or listening to the utterance, 'First grate the . . . .'.

- Make inferences about what is not explicitly stated in utterances (Eysenk and Keane 1990), for example, seeing a mental image of a spade when reading, 'He dug a hole.'.
- Personalize utterances by representing what other people have said or written with familiar, meaningful images (Sadoski 1985; Tomlinson 1998a), for example, seeing an image of your own house when reading, 'At long last we reached home.'.
- Select between alternative representations whilst responding to ambiguous text (Tomlinson 1997, 1998a), for example seeing both a harbour and a bottle of fortified wine when hearing the question, 'Do you know where the port is?' and then selecting the harbour representation when subsequently hearing, 'I'm deciding whether to drive there or not.'.
- Represent linguistic utterances mentally by combining images from relevant prior experience with images generated by information in the texts (Paivio 1979), for example seeing images both of your own first day at school and those of the boy in the poem *First Day at School* by Roger McGough.
- Reinterpret utterances by changing images already seen as further information becomes available, for example, seeing an image of a car outside a theatre when told that somebody went to see a play in a friend's car then seeing the play performed in a car when told the play was performed by a company who specialized in putting on plays in cars.
- Achieve vague representation through a protypical image, before more detailed representation through a stereotypical image, before specific representation through a text-instantiated image (Tomlinson 1997), for example, changing an image from a vague brown bird to a big, black rook to a baby rook hopping on one leg when hearing more information.
- Achieve the 'experiencing' of the text and not just the comprehension of information (Esrock 1994).
- Follow instructions and directions by visualizing their intended outcomes before and whilst attempting to achieve them (Tomlinson 1997), for example, when following instructions from a driving instructor or following directions to get to the station.
- Retain representations of what has been read or listened to (Tomlinson 1998a), for example, retaining salient images of what happens in a story.
- Recall representations of what has been read or said (Tomlinson 1998a), for example, recalling images of a book read many years ago.
- Repeat and/or rephrase utterances retained and recalled as visual images (Tomlinson 1998a).
- Start the preparation for producing an utterance by imaging a visual representation of what you want to say or write (Tomlinson 1996, 1998a), for example, seeing the winning goal being scored again by Liverpool just before and whilst telling somebody about a game you had been to.

For a list of further uses of visual imaging in L1 language use see Tomlinson (1998a: 267–8)

All the uses of visual imaging listed above are important in first language acquisition and development as well as in language use. For example, imaging stories and descriptions can help to compensate for unfamiliar lexical items, retaining meaningful images can help you to remember newly experienced lexical items and having clear pictures of what you want to say can help to retrieve the language needed to say it. Visual imaging is also a powerful tool in the development of the ability to read and understand text (e.g. Sadoski, Goetz and Fritz 1993; Sadoski and Paivio 1994). Above all, visual imaging can provide the affective and cognitive power which drives the deep processing (Craik and Lockhart 1972; Sadoski and Quast 1990) which is required for effective and durable learning.

Imagine trying to learn or use a language without being able to make use of visual imaging.

3 Visual imaging in L2 learning and use

The literature above shows how valuable visual imaging is in L1 learning and use. It is a sound hunch therefore that its use in the learning of a second language is a determinant of effective learning.

Research has shown that visual imaging can be a powerful tool to understand and learn from L2 text (Tomlinson 1997; Avila 2005). Unfortunately there is also evidence that L2 learners typically do not make adequate or effective use of visual imaging until they reach an advanced level of L2 proficiency. In numerous experiments L2 learners have been found to make little use of visual imaging. For example, Knight *et al* (1985) found that imaging was significant for L2 readers but was not mentioned as a strategy at all by L2 learners, who, when reflecting on their reading process, focused primarily on low level decoding skills. Similar findings have been reported in Stevick (1986), Padron and Waxman (1988), and Barnett (1989) and Avila (2005) found that L2 students did not typically use visual imagery when reading in the foreign language (or were not conscious of it) and the ability to generate mental imagery seemed to be inhibited by the cognitive exhaustion of decoding each word in the text.

Tomlinson (1997, 1998a) reports results of numerous experiments with L2 learners at Kobe University and Nagoya Women's University in Japan and at the University of Luton, which revealed that less than 15 per cent of any cohort typically make use of visual imaging when reading in the L2. He did find though (as did Padron and Waxman 1988) that those who did report making use of visual imaging tended to achieve better comprehension and recall than those who did not. This, of course, could mean that the ability to make use of visual imaging is a consequence of language proficiency or it could mean that it is a contributor to language proficiency. Our experience of helping low level L2 learners to make use of visual imaging suggests that it is the latter and that more L2 learners could become proficient if they were helped and encouraged to make more use of visual imaging. It is also our experience though that L2 learners need to be trained to make effective use of visual imaging. Tomlinson (1998a: 270–1) reports experiments in which L2 learners were asked to visualize texts and only managed to do so with partial success. In addition to a failure to see what might be in the gaps in the text, Tomlinson also found that L2 learners attempting visualization typically suffered from 'premature commitment to a schema' (Rumelhart 1980). For example, a class of students who had been asked to draw a birthday party prior to reading an extract from Harold Pinter's *Birthday Party* continued to see the typical children's party they had drawn, even though the text made explicit reference to an adult 'booze-up'. Again though, Tomlinson found that those who achieved the most successful visualizations also achieved the best comprehension and recall.

Avila (2005) found significant evidence that helping learners to visualize through formal instruction and systematic use of mental imagery in the classroom resulted in greater visual imaging and improved reading ability. Those findings were also significantly correlated to higher interest and involvement in the reading activities.

4 The inner voice in L1 learning and use

4.1 What is the inner voice?

The inner voice is what we use to make sounds in our heads. We can use it to replay or create music, songs, utterances and sound effects in our heads, to read mentally what we see on a page, to comment on what we hear and read and to prepare for and rehearse what we intend to say. Its main role in relation to language use is to enable us to talk to ourselves in inner speech. We talk to ourselves all day long and would have great problems understanding, learning from and controlling our world without inner speech. As Steels (2003: 174) says, 'Every normal human being, including deaf people, reports hearing almost constantly a silent voice when they are not overtly speaking.' We also use private speech (inner speech spoken aloud) to comment to ourselves on what we are experiencing, frequently when we are children and sometimes as adults when we think nobody is listening. Inner speech and outer speech are very different both in their grammar and in their roles and we use our inner voice far more than we do our outer voice. Unlike our outer voice, which has to share many features with other voices in order for it to be understood, our inner voice is private, personal and unique.

The inner voice does not operate as an isolated phenomenon but rather plays a part in creating multi-dimensional representation and creation of meaning (Masuhara 1998). It does this by firing neural connections which trigger and interact with sensory, affective and, sometimes, even motor responses (Jacobs and Schumann 1992; Esrock 1994; Sadoski and Paivio 1994; Kosslyn *et al* 1995; Tomlinson 1996, 1997, 1998a). Thus, for example, I might read, 'At long last the food arrived' and respond by saying 'Great' with my inner voice, by seeing a visual image of my favourite food, by mentally tasting the food, by feeling pleased and, perhaps, even by moving my lips and swallowing in anticipation of the food.

4.2 What are the main characteristics of L1 inner speech?

Inner speech has been characterized as reduced and as lacking in organization by such researchers as Sokolov (1972) and Vygotsky (1986). In our view it follows the brain's basic principle of economy and it interacts with sensory imagery and affect to produce a representation of meaning far richer than can be communicated by the outer voice. In fact, inner speech is not reduced at all. It is the primary form of communication, which we need to expand in order to communicate with others. Sometimes, if we are communicating with intimates, the expansion required is minimal because we share referenced contexts with each other. At other times the expansion and elaboration required is extensive if, for example, we are attempting to communicate complex ideas or plans to people we have never met before.

In our view our inner voice uses a restricted linguistic code to interact with sensory images and affective electro-chemical impulses in order to achieve multi-dimensional self-communication. This linguistic code is similar to the Restricted Code claimed to be typical of the speech of the lower working classes in Bernstein (1971: 77–81) in that it is fundamentally elliptical, vague, implicit, concrete, descriptive and narrative. It also uses a narrow range of vocabulary and structures and it makes significant use of such non-verbal features as intonation and stress. Its grammar and lexis are similar to, but even simpler, than the grammar and lexis of spoken, unplanned discourse (Carter and McCarthy 1995) and its pronunciation and intonation are similar to those of intimate, colloquial conversation. It is an essentially cotext and context dependent code, which we understand by reference to previous utterances or to non-linguistic situations we have experienced. For example, 'Only an hour' is meaningful only to the speaker, who is the only one who knows its context and cotext. The inner voice is often very vague in reference but we have no problems in understanding such self-comments as, 'What! . . . That's terrible' because we know what we are referring to and we know in what way it is terrible. And, because our inner voice is private and rarely monitored by other people, we do not worry about false starts, repetitions, grammatical inconsistencies or even the occasional gibberish. We know what we mean.

We have listed below some of those characteristics of inner speech which we think are distinctive:

(1) It is very fast. Korba (1986, 1990) calculates it as being ten times as fast as outer speech and estimates that it would take the equivalent of 4,000 words to extrapersonally express one minute of inner speech. Wiley (forthcoming) points out how useful this is when responding to live situations and, in particular, to emergencies.

(2) It can be, according to Chautauga (1992) reflexive 'mindless' communication (e.g. 'Ouch') or intentional 'mindful' communication (e.g. 'How could I be so stupid?').

(3) It is usually elliptical. Because its reference is usually to our own experience our inner speech frequently consists of verbless phrases such as, 'Not yet', 'Same excuse' and 'After work'. We leave out words to save energy and time. We know what we are referring to and we only need to express our responses or intentions. If we used the outer voice for thinking (as many L2 learners do) we would never have time to think at all.

Other examples of elliptical use of the inner voice include: 'Oh, so short only, ah?'; 'Alright, nothing very unusual.'; 'So bleak.'. These examples (and those below) are just a few of many which were collected from an experiment with 16 L1 students at the National University of Singapore (NUS) (Tomlinson 2000a). They were asked to write down anything they noticed saying with their inner voice, first of all whilst reading a number of poems and then during the course of a day.

(4) It is exophoric. Our inner voice rarely refers directly to words or phrases in immediately previous or subsequent utterances but rather to the context which is in our mind or to a mental representation of a linguistic experience (e.g. 'Why did I do that ?'; 'Didn't he get the hint?'; 'Do something about it.').

(5) It is implicit and vague. Being explicit and specific to ourselves would be uneconomical as we are able to fill in linguistic gaps effectively with sensory and affective connections and with cotextual and contextual reference (e.g. 'Is money everything ?'; 'Just wait till I tell you what I have in mind.'; 'No, maids do it.').

(6) It is often partial. This is either because we have changed the focus of our attention (e.g. 'Must ring . . . Dam. It's ten already.'), because the completion is predictable (e.g. 'Tomorrow I'll read . . .') or because we complete the utterance with a visual image (e.g. 'I'll go by . . .').

(7) It is simple and narrow. Our inner speech uses a very narrow range of lexis and grammatical structures. We use core vocabulary and very basic structures to produce very short utterances which are semantically 'highly condensed' (de Guerrero 1994) and which often achieve 'semantic richness' (Centeno-Cortes and Jimenez 2004). In Tomlinson's (2000a) NUS inner speech corpus the average length of utterance is four words, all the utterances are in the active voice, nearly all of them have simple aspect, none of them have perfective aspect, none of them contain a subordinate clause, only three of them contain a conjunction (all coordinators) and most of them use only core vocabulary.

(8) What we say is novel. In inner speech we only say to ourselves what is new to us. So most of the time we focus on the comment rather than on the topic, on the predicate rather than the subject (e.g. 'Must be written by a kid.'; 'Still doing their work.'; 'Liked the picking of noses part though.'). 'In inner speech, it is never necessary for us to name that about which we are speaking, i.e., the subject. We always limit ourselves

only to what is being said about this subject, i.e., the predicate.' (Vygotsky 1956: 359).

(9) It is relevant. In inner speech we only say to ourselves what is directly relevant or necessary. 'Mental speech is structured according to the principle that statements be kept strictly to a minimum' in contrast to 'external speech (vocalized or written) which requires a great redundancy of communicated information' (Sokolov 1972: 260).

(10) It is egocentric and idiosyncratic (Vygotsky and Luria 1930). It is by and for us and it does not have to consider anybody else. 'Vocabulary frequently assumes a very individual, subjective significance and is complemented by graphic images' (Sokolov 1972: 3) and words are used according to their psychological meaning as experienced at a given moment rather than their logical meaning expressed as a formal definition.

(11) It is coherent. Lantolf and Pavlenko (1995: 111) say that, 'At the outset, private speech is structurally identical to social speech, but as it moves toward its mental function as inner speech, it becomes increasingly elliptical in appearance and less coherent to the ear of one listening to it'. It might be incoherent to an eavesdropper but it is coherent to ourselves. We know how an inner voice utterance is connected to what has gone before and we know our illocutionary intent. Salkie (1995) considers coherence to be achieved jointly by the producer of the text and the receiver of the text. In inner speech the producer is also the receiver and coherence is easily achieved.

In experiments which elicited private verbal thinking during problem solving Centeno-Cortes and Jimenez (2004) found most of the above characteristics plus others (e.g. fragmentation, breakdown and eureka expressions).

4.3 What are the main roles of inner speech in L1 use?

The main role of inner speech seems to be to define and guide the self by either expressing meaning or generating meaning (Johnson 1994). In doing this it links the individual and their environment, it aids the development and use of higher mental processes and it regulates behaviour (Dance and Larson 1976). It achieves this through performing many sub-roles, most of which were confirmed in the Tomlinson (2000a) experiment reported above. Responses to the question, 'On what occasions did you find you were talking to yourself in English?' included:

- Wondering what I'm going to do on Saturday.
- When under stress.
- Thinking about a problem.
- When alone and when talking to others (trying to get what they're saying).
- When I was happy and wanted to congratulate myself.
- When playing cards.

- When I didn't understand the textbook.
- Watching a movie.
- Reading.

Answers to the question, 'Why do you think you were talking to yourself on the occasions mentioned in 1 above ?' included:

- Preparing to speak to someone.
- Just thinking out my thoughts.
- Helps to relax when tense.
- Reasoning to myself.
- Clarifying doubts.
- Clarifying thoughts.
- Organizing thoughts.
- Advice to self.
- Reassurance – 'I tell myself things which will help me to feel better'.

Another group of L1 speakers of English at NUS (seven MA students) answered the same questionnaire orally as the 16 BA students had done in writing (Tomlinson 2000a). At first they were embarrassed to 'confess' that they talked to themselves all the time but when they realized that this was normal they independently revealed very similar uses of the inner voice to those listed by the 16 BA students and to those discovered by most researchers into inner speech. It seems that using the inner voice is crucial for our self-esteem, our self-control, the expression of our self and our interpretation and contribution to the world around us. Imagine being in an L2 classroom in which the activities you are involved in inhibit the use of your L1 inner voice and retard the development of an L2 inner voice.

Here are some of the sub-roles of inner speech:

To achieve reiteration of what has been heard or read

Teachers often warn learners of the bad habit of sub-vocalizing and yet all the research evidence suggests that we need to say other people's words in our head in order to understand them and to establish a mental representation of them.

This phenomenon has been demonstrated to be a normal and functional feature of the listening and reading processes by many researchers. Blonskii (1964) demonstrated that it is necessary to reproduce the speech of the speaker when listening. McGuigan (1964), Hardyck (1968), Cleland (1971), Sokolov (1972) and Klein (1981) conducted electromyographic studies of inner speech during silent reading (and in some cases, for example Sokolov, during listening activities) and came to similar conclusions. Sokolov, for example, demonstrated that, 'silent reading is always accompanied by motor speech tensions of varying intensity, depending on the complexity of texts and on reading habits' (p. 211) and Klein concluded that, 'Inner speech has been shown to be an important facilitative aid used by all normal readers, especially under difficult textual conditions' (p. 60). Gathercole and Baddeley (1993) regard this 'phonological loop' to be particularly important in the comprehension of long and syntactically complex sentences and Anderson (1995) considers it to be a way of achieving a 'back up store to be consulted during off-line linguistic analysis'. And yet the myth that inner speech during silent reading is detrimental is still perpetuated today (e.g. Nuttall 1996: 58; Willis 1996: 72).

To help us to achieve mental representation (Jenkin *et al* 1993)

We do not process a text (or any other experience) directly. We process our multi-dimensional mental representation of it. In an experiment conducted at the University of Luton in 1997, Tomlinson (1998b) asked 21 proficient readers to read an extract from *Brazil* (Updike 1994) and then to report on their reading process. All 21 said they visualized whilst reading and 18 said they talked to themselves in their heads. In a similar experiment at the National University of Singapore 12 of 16 proficient reader respondents reported using inner speech to help them to understand poems and 10 reported using visualization.

Sadoski and Paivio (1994) describe the interaction between the verbal and the non-verbal (i.e. sensory) codes during mental representation and Masuhara (1998) develops a theory of multi-dimensional representation in which inner speech, sensory images and affect all play a part in firing the neural connections which achieve mental representation for the reader.

Many of the inner speech utterances in Tomlinson's (2000a) experiment were helping the speaker to achieve mental representation of the poems they were reading: e.g. 'Sounds like a poem for kids.'; 'Must be quite old now.'; 'A person's reflection of his life.'.

To help us achieve connections

Connecting is a vital part of the process of understanding and representing experience, as it enables us to relate what we are reading, listening to, seeing or taking part in to our existing knowledge of the world and to our views about it. Many of these connections are made through sensory images but the inner voice also has an important part to play. In reading and listening, 'to establish connections and relationships of some kind between two sentences being comprehended separately, both of them must be kept in mind. Without a fixation of the preceding sentence it cannot be linked to the next' (Sokolov 1972: 117). In addition to this holding role, inner speech also helps us to remember similar phenomena and to use our understanding of them to help us to interpret and represent the phenomena we are currently experiencing. In other words, inner speech helps us to use the old to understand the new (e.g. 'Sounds like an archer or a shooter.'; 'Sounds like one of those Britons on social welfare.'; 'Sounds like that song . . .').

To help us to respond (i.e. express views on what we are reading, listening to or experiencing – e.g. 'So funny. Weird, doesn't make sense.'; 'Such a loser but yet quite a pitiable character.'; 'Willy thought, "Please don't come, Sarajini. Please don't come."' (Naipaul 2001, 116)).

Responding is governed by each person's prior experience and their views on life and is an extension of mental representation. The uniqueness of each response to the same text explains how, despite considerable convergence of decoding among a group of similar people, there can be considerable divergence of understanding too.

To help us remember

It is not normally the language we encounter which we commit to memory but our mental representation of it (Sadoski and Paivio 1994). Repetition of what we hear and read is necessary to achieve the short term memory which enables us to achieve mental representation of the utterance. The mental representations of those salient utterances which we rephrase, explain to ourselves and comment on are most likely to be remembered. In a number of experiments, Sokolov (1972: 113) showed that without speech movements when listening 'instantaneous amnesia' occurred but that even if words were repeated in an 'extremely abbreviated form, at times hardly perceptible hints at words' then their representations were likely to be remembered.

To help us recall

When trying to remember what we have heard, read or experienced, talking to ourselves can help to spark and supplement sensory images which can bring back our representations of what we are trying to recall (Sadoski and Paivio 1994; Tomlinson 1997; Avila 2001). These sensory images (mainly visual) can then be translated into inner speech in preparation for public recall.

The 16 first language respondents in Tomlinson (2000a) were asked to recall a poem without looking back at it or writing down their recall and then they were asked, 'What did you do in your mind whilst you were trying to recall the poem?'. Ten of them said that they talked to themselves about the poem (e.g. 'I asked myself . . .'; 'I imagined re-telling the story to somebody else.'; 'I tried to re-call the conversation.') and eleven of them said they visualized scenes from the poem. One of them said that she used words and pictures in her head at the same time to help her to recall the poem.

To help us to develop thought

As Johnson (1994: 180) says, it provides 'an extremely fast and efficient method of facilitating symbolic thought or making associations between or among concepts.' Huey (1968) accepts that thought starts as a sub-conscious, non-verbal phenomenon but says that, 'there can be little doubt that the main meaning comes to consciousness only with the beginning of the sentence-utterance' (he is referring to inner speech) 'and the reader does not feel that he has the complete sense until he has spoken it.' We think that most of our thoughts originate as sensory images but we would agree with Sokolov (1972: 121) that there is a 'presence within us of large thought complexes, expressed through slight verbal hints. In conveying our thoughts to others, we unfold them, using these semantic complexes as support . . .'.

To help us to plan and to decide

In planning future courses of action, we use visual imagery plus instructions to ourselves (e.g. when playing chess or cards, when working out an itinerary for a visit, when organizing a conference) (e.g. 'Now let me see, I can either do this or . . . . . .'; 'Oh dear. I'm going to be late. Should I run after the bus?'; 'I think I should go get some food.').

To help us to reassure ourselves

We often reassure ourselves when things are not going well by telling ourselves about our qualities, by talking of some potentially positive future event, by making excuses, by blaming other people, by giving ourselves advice or by just mumbling expressions of support ('All right, calm down now – there's nothing to be afraid of – he's just an ass-hole – there's no point getting this angry.'; 'Relax, don't panic.'; 'Everything will turn out fine.').

To help us to prepare for outer speech

Prior to and whilst speaking or writing to others we speak to ourselves. We do so as a preparation which involves developing thought and the expression of that thought prior to communicating it to others. According to Vocate (1994b: 25), 'Self-reflexive consciousness and intentionality are impossible without the mediation of inner speech between stimulus and response . . . ' and outer speech communication cannot occur 'without the coding process of inner speech'. Akhutina (2003) reports in some detail the views of Russian scholars such as Anan'ev, Luria, Sokolov and Vygotsky on how inner speech facilitates the development from a vague thought or motive to outer voice production. In particular Akhutina highlights Vygotsky's view that the transition from inner speech to outer speech involves restructuring and not just vocalization, and Luria's view that dynamic aphasics fail to produce coherent outer speech because they lack the facility to use inner speech to develop initial thought into expanded speech. It could be that many L2 learners, by not making use of their capability to use inner speech, are suffering the same effects and communicative consequences as dynamic aphasics. Kingsbourne (2000: 123) considers the effects of inner speech impairment of other types of aphasics and repeats Schuller's (1991) as yet unanswered question, 'What is inner life like without inner speech?'.

Ausubel *et al* (1980: 439–40) discuss the role of verbalization in facilitating the 'transformational processes involved in thought' and Sokolov asserts that, 'external speech is functionally dependent on inner speech' (1972: 65) and that prior to speaking or writing to others 'we fix our thoughts in our mind with the aid of inner speech . . .'.

The inner voice prepares for the outer voice by formulating vague phrases, expanding upon them, trying out alternatives, monitoring draft expressions for accuracy, appropriacy and potential effect and then monitoring and revising our actual public translations of our initial inner utterances. This is very difficult in spontaneous speech and often results in false starts, re-phrasings, repetitions, hesitations, pauses and incomplete utterances. L2 learners often do not use inner speech as a preparation for outer L2 speech and the result is often reticence, short, safe, shallow utterances or incoherence. It has been argued by Steels (2003) that this inner speech self-monitoring not only facilitates effective outer speech but plays a vital role in language acquisition. It does so by allowing us to listen to ourselves and to notice and repair comprehension failure by adding disambiguating features which we eventually acquire.

To help us to monitor and to self-evaluate

Whilst speaking or writing with the outer voice we are constantly monitoring our production for accuracy, appropriacy and effect. We are also constantly using inner speech to evaluate what we do and say, often with overt or implied second person subject (e.g. 'You silly sod.' 'Silly sod.'). Steels (2003: 181) refers to neurophysiological evidence that there is 'a re-entrant system in the human brain' which enables us to monitor language we have just produced. 'The same left inferior frontal region is activated both for listening to somebody else's speech and for listening to your own speech – even if this speech is not pronounced' and this same region is also used for 'self-awareness'.

Perhaps the most powerful statement about the centrality of inner speech in the processes of thought and communication is the assertion by Korba (1986: 33) that, 'All verbal interaction (and a great deal of non-verbal interaction) requires the use of inner speech, either in the preparation (encoding) of spoken language for others, or in the understanding (decoding) of the spoken language of others'. If this is true, not using inner speech would drastically inhibit the ability to think and communicate and it is not using inner speech that we are going to demonstrate below that is typical in L2 language learning and use.

If inner speech is impaired then many of the functions described above are inhibited and outer voice communication becomes unsuccessful (de Blesser and Marshall 2005). This is the situation for some types of L1 aphasics and for most L2 learners too.

For a recent review of literature on the use of L1 inner speech see Archer (2003).

5 The inner voice in L2 learning and use

It is very difficult to use an inner voice when learning an L2 from formal instruction, but not so difficult when learning an L2 naturally or in an immersion environment (Masuhara personal correspondence; experiments we report below). When we learn our L1 we do so in what is primarily a private and personal way. We talk to ourselves before we talk to others and even when we talk out loud we are often using a private voice which is self-directed (Vygotsky 1986). When we learn an L2 in the classroom we are usually required to use an outer voice from the very beginning. We are not normally given time to talk to ourselves but are required to participate in social interaction. Our L1 inner voice is inhibited by the need to produce L2 utterances which will be subjected to public scrutiny. So, instead of developing thoughts and ideas in our heads before speaking them aloud we put all our mental energy into finding the right L2 words in the right form and the right order. We use the L1 inner voice for translating from L1 to L2 and for monitoring the correctness of our utterances in the L2 (see Swain 1998 for an example of learners of French using their private English voices to monitor what they are producing in French). And in most cases we do not develop an L2 inner voice for a very long time because most of the activities we participate in as beginners demand instant responses and ask us to report our experience rather than to process it, because we are afraid to be 'ungrammatical' in our heads in case this interferes with what we say aloud, and because the de-contextualized triviality and blandness of much of the language we are required to process and produce does not encourage thought.

In experiments which Tomlinson conducted at Kobe University and the University of Luton, native speakers and L2 intermediate learners were asked to read short texts (poems and extracts from novels) and then to reflect on their reading process. In all the experiments the native speakers reported speaking to themselves and seeing mental images but very few of the L2 learners reported either of these processes (Tomlinson 1996, 1997, 1998b). A similar result was reported by Masuhara (1998) when she asked native speakers and L2 learners to think aloud as they were reading the beginning of a novel. The native speakers reported their inner speech and their sensory images whereas the L2 learners reported their attempts to decode and translate the words of the text (see also Jenkin et al 1993). And if we do develop an inner voice in the L2 and we let it out as a private voice during classroom activities we are monitored and corrected. For example, Frawley and Lantolf (1985), Frawley (1992) and McCafferty (1994) claim that what appears as erroneous L2 performance is often a reflection of the mental orientation of the speaker rather than a failure to use the L2 correctly. Confronted with this use of private speech when learners are compelled to interact in English whilst performing a task, teachers often monitor (and even correct) it as though it was public speech and thus discourage the learners from using inner speech in case they 'let it out'. But without an effective inner voice we cannot produce meaningful public speech and we cannot achieve self-regulation or self-monitoring. In addition, we cannot achieve the creativity which would make us intelligent and interesting individual human beings when using the L2, especially if we are also failing to use visual imaging prior to the creation of language. See Herrmann (1998) and von Oech (1998) for theories of the roles of visual imaging and inner speech in the creative process in the brain.

If the development of an L2 inner voice is retarded and the use of the L1 inner voice inhibited by tasks requiring the focusing of processing energy on low level linguistic decoding then very little interpretative, critical or creative thought or expression is possible and the learner feels diminished. And, of course, if thought is attempted in an imitation of the L2 outer voice, it is bound to be conventional, superficial and very slow ('The process of external speech needs. . . much more time than does inner speech to express thoughts.' (Sokolov, 1972)). One way of encouraging the use of L2 inner speech is to ask learners to keep inner voice diaries. When de Guerro (2004) did this she found that 45 per cent of the entries were in relation to concurrent processing of language being heard and read, 38 per cent to recall of language heard, read or used previously, 13 per cent to preparation before writing or speaking and just 4 per cent to silent verbalization of thoughts for private purposes.

It does seem though that advanced L2 learners make use of inner speech and private speech to help them to achieve mental representation. Appel and Lantolf (1994) report how advanced L2 English speakers trying to produce oral recalls of texts used private speech to try to understand as well as to recall the texts. de Guerrero (1994) conducted a large scale study of Puerto Rican college-aged learners and concludes that inner speech plays a central role in rehearsing short term memory features (phonological, lexical and grammatical) so as to transfer to long term memory and that it helps L2 learners to gain confidence and lose anxiety about speaking the language as a result of internal rehearsal. McCafferty (1998) gave narrative recall and picture relation tasks to Japanese and Venezuelan intermediate and advanced learners and found considerable use of private speech (often accompanied by gestures) in order to achieve object-, other- and self-regulation. He also found that the students used self-regulatory gestures after brief pauses and he suggests a possible connection with inner speech. Masuhara (1998) reports how advanced learners reported more inner speech and more visual images in their think aloud protocols of a reading activity than intermediate learners did.

In an experiment conducted at Leeds Metropolitan University and the University of Córdoba (Spain) we asked 23 proficient Spanish learners of English if they used their inner speech in their L1 and L2. They all reported using the inner voice and private speech in their L1. When asked about the use of inner speech in the L2, 22 students reported using L2 inner speech when they were abroad (in the target language country) for a time longer than an incidental trip. They also reported using inner speech while talking or writing in English and they mostly used inner speech when planning what to say in the target language if they were at home (Spain), but reported a higher frequency if they were in a linguistic immersion situation. Javier Avila (a proficient user of English as an L2) uses inner speech continuously in his everyday life, and has realized that when living in an English-speaking country for a couple of days, his inner speech turns into English; the effect even lasts a number of days when he is back at home and so it is for the majority of the people who took part in the experiment. Javier even remembers using inner speech when teaching English in the Czech Republic, his colleagues and friends were all Americans and English speaking Czechs and his inner speech was basically English during that academic year, with the only exception of counting, which is something he always does in Spanish regardless of where he lives.

Does the fact that L2 inner speech only seems to be typically used by advanced learners mean that advanced learners only make use of their inner voice once they have become advanced or does their ability to use the inner voice help them to become advanced? We are convinced that the inability to develop an effective L2 inner voice prevents many learners from achieving meaningful communication in the L2 and therefore prevents them from ever becoming advanced. As a failed learner of French Tomlinson (1997: 277–9) tried to reflect on the process of reading an advanced text in French and found that he was using all his processing energy in trying to decode the words that he did not know. As a result, he could not remember what the text was about when he had finished reading it. He then read another advanced text in French but this time he made himself read the text aloud in his head in French, he made himself visualize and at the end of each paragraph he did a mental summary using his L1 inner voice and the images he had created. The result was that he managed to stop himself from excessive decoding and translation, that he understood and enjoyed the text and that he maintained a durable mental representation of the text. How he wishes that he had been encouraged to use mental imagery in his French lessons.

We know from numerous experiments that 'input from the "outer ear" interferes with the use of the "inner ear"' and 'tying up the outer voice' interferes with use of the 'inner voice' (Smith *et al* 1992: 96). This is what happens in classroom conditions when teachers demand answers to questions during and immediately after a reading or listening task and when they ask learners to read aloud. If only L2 teachers would learn to leave their learners in silence more. Maybe then the L2 inner voice and inner ear would have a chance to develop.

For an overview of recent research into the use of inner speech in L2 language learning and use see de Guerro (2005).

6 Concurrent use of visual imaging and the inner voice

From much of the literature reviewed above the impression given is that visual imaging and the inner voice are used separately and independently.

This false impression comes from their separation as subjects of study. This separation has made it easier to focus research on the two phenomena but in most cases it has ignored the fact that they are often used together (either simultaneously or sequentially) to achieve mental representation.

Some researchers do relate inner speech and visual imaging. For example, Sadoski and Paivio (1994) focus in their dual-coding theory on the interaction between the linguistic and the visual codes and Leontiev and Ryabova (1981) discuss the roles of inner speech and visual imaging in the transition from vague thought to expanded utterance. Another researcher who does acknowledge that inner speech is used in interaction with mental imaging is Wiley (forthcoming: 4). He agrees with Collins (in press) that 'inner speech is usually accompanied by several other kinds of images and sensations' which are 'largely visual, though they can range far and wide in what they visualize, possibly well beyond the topic of the inner language.' Wiley (p. 18) illustrates his point by reporting how his wife selects her clothes for the next day by forming 'sentences' from a combination of visual images and a few inner voice words whilst lying in bed the night before. Interestingly Tomlinson (2003a: 183) gives a very similar example of his wife selecting what clothes to wear from the inner voice diary he had asked her to write. In this diary words often combine with images to represent quite complex thoughts. As Johnson (1994: 176) says, 'While using inner speech, we silently produce a few key words to help us to make associations with much larger ideas or concepts.'

Unfortunately there is evidence that whilst concurrent use of visual and auditory imaging is used in the L1 to achieve mental representation it is not so in L2 processing in which a 'word by word strategy' often occupies most of the available processing energy (Jenkin *et al* 1993).

We agree with Leontiev and Ryabova (1981: 65) that an L2 should be taught 'as a medium which will engage the thought, perception and imagination of the learner' and to facilitate this we advocate devising principled and systematic procedures for helping L2 learners to develop the ability to use visual and auditory imaging concurrently both in their responses to the L2 they are exposed to and in their production of it. See Chapter 5 for suggestions for how to do this.

References

Akhutina, T. V. (2003), 'The role of inner speech in the construction of an utterance'. *Journal of Russian and East European Psychology*, 41, (3/4), 49–74.

Anderson, J. R. (1995), *Learning and Memory–An Integrated Approach*. New York: John Wiley and Sons Inc.

Appel, G. and Lantolf, J. P. (1994), 'Speaking as mediation: A study of L1 and L2 text recall tasks'. *The Modern Language Journal*, 78, (4), 437–52.

Archer, M. S. (2003), *Structure, Agency and the Internal Conversation*. Cambridge: Cambridge University Press.

Arnold, J. (1999), 'Visualization: language learning with the mind's eye', in J. Arnold (ed.), *Affect in Language Learning*. Cambridge: Cambridge University Press, pp. 260–78.

Ausubel, D. P., Sullivan, E. V. and Ives, S.W. (1980), *Theory and Problems of Child Development* (3rd edn). New York: Grune and Stratton Inc.

Avila, F. J. (2001), 'La visualización y su relación con la memoria. Potencial didáctico en la clase de lengua extranjera', in D. Levey (ed.) *English Language Teaching: Changing Perspectives in Context*. Cádiz: University of Cádiz Press, pp. 71–77.

Avila, F. J. (2005), '*El Uso de la Imagen Mental en la Lectura en el Proceso de Adquisición de una Segunda Lengua*'. (Ph.D. Thesis (in press)).

Barnett, M. (1989), *More Than Meets the Eye: Foreign Language Reading*. Englewood Cliffs, NJ: Prentice Hall Regents.

Bernstein, B. (1971), *Class, Codes and Control. Vol. 1 Theoretical Studies Towards a Sociology of Language*. London: Routledge and Kegan Paul.

De Bleser, R. and Marshall, J. C. (2005), 'Egon Weigl and the concept of inner speech'. *Cortex*, 41, (2), 249–57.

Blonskii, P. P. (1964), 'Memory and thought', in *Selected Works on Psychology*. Moscow: Prosveshchenie Press.

Carter, R. and McCarthy, M. (1995), 'Grammar and the spoken language'. *Applied Linguistics*, 16, (2), 141–58.

Centeno-Cortes, B. and Jimenez, A. F. (2004), 'Problem solving tasks in a foreign language: the importance of the L1 in private verbal thinking'. *International Journal of Applied Linguistics*, 14, (1), 7–35.

Chautauga, (1992), 'Mindfulness, mindlessness and communication'. *Communication Monographs*, 59, (3), 299–327.

Cleland, D. L. (1971), 'Vocalism in silent reading'. *Visible Language*, 2, 145–57.

Collins, (in press) 'Internalised symbols and the social process of thinking'. *Interaction Ritual Chains*. Princeton: Princeton University Press.

Craik, F. I. M. and Lockhart, R. S. (1972), 'Levels of processing: A framework for memory research'. *Journal of Verbal Learning and Verbal Behaviour*, 11, 671–84.

Damasio, A. (1994), *Descartes' Error: Emotion, Reason and the Human Brain*. New York: Avon.

Dance, F. E. and Larson, C. E. (1976), *The Function of Human Communication: A Theoretical Approach*. New York: Holt, Rhinehart and Winston.

Esrock, E. (1994), *The Readers's Eye*. Baltimore: The Johns Hopkins University Press.

Eysenk, N. W. and Keane, M. T. (1990), *Cognitive Psychology. A Student's Handbook*. Hillsdale, NJ: Lawrence Erlbaum Associates.

Frawley, W. (1992), 'The Cross-language Study of Private Speech'. Paper Presented at the Conference for Socio-Cultural Research, Symposium on Private Speech and Self-Regulation. Madrid, August.

Frawley, W. and Lantolf, J. P. (1985), 'Second language discourse: A Vygotskian perspective'. *Applied Linguistics*, 6, 19–44.

Gathercole, S. E. and Baddeley, A. D. (1993), *Working Memory and Language*. Hove: Lawrence Erlbaum Associates.

de Guerro, M. C. M. (1994), 'Form and functions of inner speech in adult second language learning', in J. P. Lantolf and G. Appel (eds), *Vygotskian Approaches to Second Language Research*. Norwood, NJ: Ablex, pp. 83–116.

de Guerro, M. C. M. (2004), 'Early stages of L2 inner speech development: what verbal reports suggest'. *International Journal of Applied Linguistics*, 14, (1), 90–113.

de Guerro, M. C. M. (ed.) (2005), *Inner Speech – Thinking Words in a Second Language*. New York: Springer-Verlag.

Hardyck, C. D. (1968), *The Effect of Subvocal Speech on Reading*. Arlington, VA: (ERIC Document Reproduction Service No. ED 022 656).

Hegley, J. (1997), 'Amsterdam', in J. Hegley, *The Family Pack*. London: Methuen, p. 12.

Herrmann, N. (1988), *The Creative Brain*. New York: Brain Books.

Huey, E. B. (1968), *The Psychology and Pedagogy of Reading*. Cambridge, MA: M.I.T. Press.

Jenkin, H., Prior, S., Rinaldo, R., Wainwright-Sharp, A. and Bialystok, E. (1993), 'Understanding text in a second language: a psychological approach to an SLA problem'. *Second Language Research*, 9, (2), 118–39.

Johnson, J. R. (1994), 'Intrapersonal spoken language: an attribute of extrapersonal competency', in D. R. Vocate (ed.), *Intrapersonal Communication: Different Voices, Different Minds*. Hillsdale, NJ: Lawrence Erlbaum.

Kingsbourne, M. (2000), 'Inner speech and the inner life'. *Brain and Language*, 71, 120–3.

Klein, E. S. (1981), *Inner Speech Cue Preference in Reading Disabled and Normal Children*. Ann Arbor: University Microfilms International.

Knight, S. L., Padron, Y. N. and Waxman, H. C. (1985), 'The cognitive reading strategies of ESL students'. *TESOL Quarterly*, 19, 789–92.

Korba, R. J. (1986), '*The Rate of Inner Speech*'. (unpublished PhD thesis. University of Denver).

Korba, R. J. (1990), 'The rate of inner speech'. *Perceptual and Motor Skills*, 71, 1043–52.

Kosslyn, S. M., Behrmann, M. and Jeannerod, M. (1995), 'The cognitive neuroscience of mental imagery'. *Neuropsychologia*, 33, (11), 1335–44.

Lantolf, J. P. and Pavlenko, A. (1995), '*Sociocultural Theory and Second Language Acquisition*'. *Annual Review of Applied Linguistics*, 15, 108–124.

Leontiev, A. A. and Ryabova (1981), *Psychology and the Language Learning Process*. Oxford: Pergammon Press.

Leontiev, A. A. (2003), 'The phase structure of the speech act and the nature of plans'. *Journal of Russian and East European Psychology*, 41, (3/4), 33–8.

Masuhara, H. (1998), 'Factors Influencing the Reading Difficulties of Advanced Learners of English When Reading Authentic Texts' (unpublished PhD Thesis. University of Luton).

Masuhara, H. (2005), 'Helping learners to achieve multi-dimensional mental representation in L2 reading', *Folio*, 9, (2), 6–9.

McCafferty, S. G. (1994), 'Adult second language learners' use of private speech: a review of studies'. *The Modern Language Journal*, 78, (4), 421–36.

McCafferty, S. G. (1998), 'Nonverbal expression and L2 private speech'. *Applied Linguistics*, 19, 1, 73–96.

McGuigan, F. J. (1964), *Silent Speech During Silent Reading*. Arlington, VA: (ERIC Document Reproduction Service No. ED 003 312).

Naipaul, V. S. (2001), *Half a Life*. London: Picador.

Nuttall, C. (1996), *Teaching Reading Skills in a Foreign Language*. Oxford: Heinemann.

von Oech, R. (1998), *A Whack on the Side of the Head: How you can be more Creative*. Farmingdale, NY: Baywood.

Padron, Y. N. and Waxman, H. C. (1988), 'The effect of EFL students' perceptions of their cognitive strategies on reading achievement'. *TESOL Quarterly*, 22, 146–50.

Paivio, A. (1979), *Imagery and Verbal Processes*. Hillsdale N.J.: Lawrence Erlbaum.

Rumelhart, D. E. (1980), 'Schemata: the building blocks of cognition', in R. J. Spiro,

B. C. Bruce and W. F. Brewes (eds), *Theoretical Issues in Reading Comprehension*. Hillsdale, NJ: Lawrence Erlbaum Associates.

Sadoski, M. (1985), 'The natural use of imagery in story comprehension and recall: replication and extension', *Reading Research Quarterly*, 20, 658–67.

Sadoski, M., Goetz, E. T. and Fritz, J. B. (1993), 'Impact of concreteness on comprehensibility, interest, and memory for text: Implications for dual coding theory and text design'. *Journal of Educational Psychology*, 85, 291–304.

Sadoski, M. and Paivio, A. (1994), 'A dual coding view of imagery and verbal processes in reading comprehension', in R. B. Ruddell, M. R. Ruddell and H. Singer (eds), *Theoretical Models and Processes of Reading* (4th edn). Newark, Delaware: International Reading Association, pp. 582–601.

Sadoski, M. and Quast, Z. (1990), 'Reader response and long term recall for journalistic text: The roles of imagery, affect, and importance'. *Reading Research Quarterly*, 26, 463–84.

Salkie, R. (1995), *Text and Discourse Analysis*. London: Routledge.

Schuller, S. (1991), *A Man Without Words*. New York: Summit Press.

Smith, J. D., Reisberg, D. and Wilson, M. (1992), 'Subvocalisation and auditory imagery: Interactions between the inner ear and the inner voice', in D. Reisberg, *Auditory Imagery*. Hillsdale, NJ: Lawrence Erlbaum.

Sokolov, A. N. (1972), *Inner Speech and Thought*. New York: Plenum Press.

Steels, L. (2003), 'Language re-entrance and the "inner voice"'. *Journal of Consciousness Studies*, 10, (4/5), 173–85.

Stevick, E. (1986), *Images and Options in the Language Classroom*. Cambridge: Cambridge University Press.

Swain, M. (1998), *Integrating language and content teaching through collaborative tasks*. Singapore: RELC Annual Seminar.

Tomlinson, B. (1996), 'Helping L2 readers to see', in T. Hickey and J. Williams (eds), *Language, Education and Society in a Changing World*. Clevedon, Avon: Multilingual Matters.

Tomlinson, B. (1997), 'The Role of Visualisation in the Reading of Literature by Learners of a Foreign Language'. (unpublished PhD thesis. University of Nottingham).

Tomlinson, B. (1998a), 'Seeing what they mean: helping L2 readers to visualise', in B. Tomlinson, (ed.), *Materials Development in Language Teaching*. Cambridge: Cambridge University Press, pp. 265–78.

Tomlinson, B. (1998b). 'And now for something not completely different: an approach to language through literature'. *Reading in a Foreign Language*, 11/2, 177–89.

Tomlinson, B. (2000a), 'Talking to yourself: the role of the inner voice in language learning'. *Applied Language Learning*, 11, (1), 123–54.

Tomlinson, B. (2000b), 'A multi-dimensional approach'. *The Language Teacher*, 24, (7), 1–6.

Tomlinson, B. (2001), 'Connecting the mind: a multi-dimensional approach to teaching language through literature'. *The English Teacher*, 4/2, 104–15.

Tomlinson, B. (2003a), 'Helping learners to develop an effective L2 inner voice'. *RELC Journal*, 34, (2), 178–94.

Tomlinson, B. (2003b), 'Humanising the coursebook', in B. Tomlinson (ed.), *Developing Materials for Language Teaching*. London: Continuum, pp. 162–73.

Updike, J. (1994), *Brazil*. London: Hamish Hamilton.

Vocate, D. R. (1994b), 'Self-talk and inner speech: understanding the uniquely human aspects of intrapersonal communication', in D. R. Vocate (ed.), *Intrapersonal Communication*. Hillsdale, NJ: Lawrence Erlbaum.

Vygotsky, L. S. (1956), 'Thought and Language', in *Selected Psychological Investigations*. Academic Pedagogy of Science, Moscow: RSFSR Press.

Vygotsky, L. S. (1986), *Thought and Language*. Cambridge: MIT Press.

Vygotsky, L. S. and Luria, A. R. (1930), 'The function and fate of egocentric speech.' *Proceedings of the Ninth Internal Congress of Psychology: Proceedings and Papers – New Haven, September 1–7, 1929*. Princeton, NJ: The Psychological Review Company, 464–5.

Wiley, N. (forthcoming), 'The linguistics of inner speech: Saussure meets the social self'.

Willis, J. (1996), *A Framework for Task-Based Learning*. Harlow: Longman.

5 Applications of the research into the roles of audio-visual mental aids for language teaching pedagogy

Brian Tomlinson and Javier Avila

We have both found that imagery training can increase L2 learners' ability and inclination to make use of mental imagery in language learning and use. For example, Avila (2005) found a significant increase in the reported amount of student visualization after mental imagery instruction and treatment. In his study students reported using mental imagery far more frequently in a final questionnaire and interview than in an initial questionnaire administered prior to treatment. We have also found that increased use of imagery can lead to improved performance in the L2 (Tomlinson 1996, 1997, 1998a, 2001, 2003).

However, in a recent survey of the use of visual imaging and inner voice activities in Unit 3 of current EFL coursebooks we found only two visual imaging activities in *New Cutting Edge Pre-Intermediate* (Cunningham and Moore 2005a) and two visual imaging activities in *New Cutting Edge Intermediate* (Cunningham and Moore 2005b). We found no visual imaging activities at all in *Innovations* (Deller and Hocking 2000), *New Headway Beginner* (Soars and Soars 2002), *New Headway Intermediate* (Soars and Soars 1998), *Going for Gold* (Aklam and Crace 2003), *Wow* (Nolasco 1990), *Changing Skies* (Pulverness 2001) or *Wavelength Intermediate* (Burke and Brooks 2000), and we failed to find any inner voice activities at all in any of the nine books listed above. We did, however, find 12 visual imaging activities and one inner voice activity in Unit 3 of *Use Your English* (Tomlinson and Masuhara 1994) and five visual imaging activities and four inner voice activities in Unit 3 of *Openings* (Tomlinson 1994a), as well as numerous visual imaging activities and inner voice activities in materials written at Leeds Metropolitan University for projects in China, Ethiopia and Singapore led by Brian Tomlinson and involving Hitomi Masuhara.

The almost complete lack of activities in current global textbooks encouraging learners to use visual imaging and their inner voice suggests that the potential value of audio-visual mental aids is still not appreciated by most commercial publishers. This would in turn suggest that their potential value (whilst stressed by some specialist literature) is also not yet appreciated by mainstream books on methodology or on the teaching of the four skills, and that the use of these mental aids is not typically focused on by teacher training courses. We would strongly recommend that audio-visual mental activities should be included in language teaching coursebooks and that ways of facilitating their effective use should be taught on teacher training courses. We would, in particular, recommend the following activities, which can easily be included in textbook units or added to them to achieve multi-dimensional supplementation:

- Readiness activities which stimulate relevant mental activities prior to reading or listening to a text (e.g. 'See pictures in your mind of an interesting old lady you know and talk to yourself about why you find her interesting.').
- Initial response activities which facilitate multi-dimensional representation whilst reading or listening to a text (e.g. 'As you listen to the poem change your picture of an old lady into a picture of the old lady who is speaking in the poem.').
- Intake response activities which facilitate the development of personal responses to a text which has just been read or listened to (e.g. 'Do you like the old lady/ Give yourself reasons for your answer.').
- Development activities in which the learners visualize a localized version of the text they have just read prior to telling the new story to themselves mentally as a preparation for telling (or writing) the story to somebody else.
- Creating mental picture stories and descriptions prior to turning them into inner voice texts.
- Conducting inner speech dialogues.
- Writing down inner speech diaries (de Guerro 2004).
- Creating private speech diaries at the end of the day.
- Carrying out visual and inner speech summaries of sections of texts read or listened to.
- Extensive reading of stories which include samples of inner speech and/or encourage visual imaging and inner speech (Bivens and Hagstrom 1992; Tomlinson 2003).
- Mentally preparing and rehearsing for participation in conversation or to give an unscripted presentation (Hegelsen 2001).
- Writing the inner voice monologues of characters in texts in which their outer voice does not represent what their inner voice is saying (Tomlinson 2003).
- Drawing characters from texts whilst reading them (Tomlinson 1998a).
- Drawing interpretations of texts after reading or listening to them (Tomlinson 1998a).
- Completing or re-drawing illustrations to match the content of a text (Tomlinson 1998a).
- Miming a text whilst listening to it being read (Tomlinson 1998a).
- Problem solving by using private speech (McCafferty 1994a; Donato 1988; de Guerro 2004).
- Engagement in natural, colloquial discourse with teachers and other proficient users (Di Camilla and Anton 2004).

1 Other suggestions for helping L2 learners to make use of the audio-visual mental aids available to them

In L1 the inner voice develops naturally at the same time as (or possibly even before) the external voice and the two systems complement each other. The ability to make use of visual imaging both precedes and combines with the ability to use language. In L2 the external voice is given primacy from the very beginning. It inhibits the use of the inner voice and visual imaging, thus slowing down thought and retarding creativity. Instead of demanding public performance in the L2 from the very beginning we should encourage learners to talk to themselves in private, egocentric L2 speech and to make maximum use of their ability to use visual imaging to facilitate communication. But even before that we should allow them the privacy and silence to develop an inner voice by providing them with opportunities to listen to the L2 being used whilst being helped to respond in their minds. They can also respond physically (or even in the L1) but they must be given time to think and they must not be forced to perform in a public voice without having an inner voice available to help them to prepare.

One way of helping learners to develop L2 inner voices is to offer beginners an initial silent period of experiencing the language in contextualized use without having to focus on the correct features of the L1 outer voice or to produce any utterances publicly. Then they can be given problem solving tasks to do (in groups, in pairs, individually) and be encouraged to use inner speech, private speech, visual imaging, drawing and physical movement to help them to articulate and solve the problems. Any utterances they produce should not be monitored and must on no account be corrected. As McCafferty says (1994b: 199), private speech (provided it is not corrected) helps 'students learn how to control anxiety about a task'. Later in the course the learners can be asked to participate in tasks in which they use private and/or inner speech to help them to prepare for production in outer speech (according to de Guerro (1994), L2 learners gain confidence and lose anxiety about speaking the language as a result of internal rehearsal).

As Vygotsky (1956) says, inner speech is similar in many ways to colloquial speech. The L1 learner is exposed to colloquial speech most of the time but most L2 beginners are exposed only to planned and formal speech. It is important that L2 learners first experience the L2 in its colloquial, unplanned form so that they can acquire a variety of the language which can facilitate the development of inner speech. The teacher should chat to the learners naturally rather than delivering pre-planned sentences and stories, descriptions, instructions, etc. should be given informally and spontaneously rather than in the planned and often scripted form which characterizes many beginners' classrooms today.

Drills and controlled practice exercises can prevent the development of inner speech as they do not allow time for thought, do not offer any problems to think about and focus the learner's attention on correct forms of outer speech. Also damaging to the development of L2 inner speech and visual imaging are premature reading activities in which the learner is forced to focus processing energy on low level linguistic decoding of a short and empty text in order to answer discrete item comprehension questions focusing on the linguistic code of outer speech. Postponing reading until a substantial vocabulary has been acquired can facilitate the development of an L2 inner voice because the voice which has been developing during meaningful listening activities and problem solving tasks can then be used to help achieve multi-dimensional representation of reading texts in which a lot of the language can be automatically processed (Tomlinson 1998b). This is especially so if the reading is voluntary and extensive and does not require detailed comprehension of discrete items. However, there is not much point in encouraging learners to respond to reading texts with visual imaging and inner speech if there is nothing in the texts worth responding to. In a recent analysis of nine popular elementary level EFL coursebooks we found that all the texts were short, explicit, neutral, bland and non-provocative in a way that the texts we read in the real world rarely are and that low level linguistic decoding was all that was necessary to comprehend the texts. Wajnryb (1996) also analysed popular EFL coursebooks and concluded that they portrayed a world which was 'safe, clean harmonious, benevolent, undisturbed and PG-rated', which lacked 'jeopardy, face threat, negotiation implicature (or implied meaning)' and in which meaning was 'explicit and context-independent' (p. 291). As Tomlinson (1997) found from his numerous experiments, we tend to generate and retain visual images when we are affectively engaged by a text. More stimulating early texts could facilitate the use of inner speech and visual imaging.

Learner use of the L1 in the L2 classroom has been discouraged by most methodologists for a long time on the grounds that the more practice the learners get in using the L2 the better. This has led to lower level learners being restricted because they do not yet have the language to develop and express ideas and opinions nor to project themselves as intelligent, creative human beings. All they can do is to imitate models, to decode simplistic texts and to manipulate the decontextualized language of drills. Their representation of the L2 world is almost entirely linguistic and it lacks the multi-dimensional richness and variety of their L1 representation of the world. This narrow experience of the L2 world diminishes many learners, demotivates them and prevents them from ever achieving communicative competence in the L2. However many methodologists have begun to recognize the dangers of insisting on the exclusive use of the L2 and they are beginning to suggest greater tolerance of L1 use (e.g. Edge 1993; Willis 1996; Swain 1998). We would go much further and suggest that in some activities the use of the L1 should be positively encouraged so that the learners can respond intelligently to what they read and listen to and so that they can generate interesting content before they speak or write. If they are encouraged to use their L1 in response and preparation activities they are likely to use their L1 inner voices too and thus to fire the connections which will achieve the multi-dimensional representation necessary for meaningful processing and production of the L2 (Centeno-Cortes and Jimenez 2004). If they are forced to only use the L2 they will devote all their processing energy to producing correct L2 outer speech and they will be unlikely to achieve meaningful representation at all. Of course, ultimately the learners need to develop an inner voice in the L2 so, in addition to L1 thinking and discussion activities, they need activities in which they are first of all encouraged to think in an L2 inner voice and then to use an L2 private voice whilst taking part in problem solving activities. The aim is to make sure that the learners always use an inner voice and to help them to progress from exclusive use of an L1 inner voice, an L1 private voice and an L1 public voice to a stage in which they are able and willing to code switch between L1 and L2 in their inner, private and public voices and eventually, for some of them, to a stage in which they are proficient users of L2 inner, private and public voices.

In conclusion, here is a suggested programme for helping learners to develop the ability to use their inner voice and visual imaging in the early stages of L2 learning.

1.1 Stage 1

(1) Learners listen to dramatic readings of stories by the teacher (e.g. with gestures, sound effects and visuals) and then do imaging and L1 inner voice activities (e.g. 'See pictures in your mind of what the old man did and then talk to yourself about why he smiled.') before taking part in L1 discussions of the story.

(2) Learners take part in TPR activities (Asher 1977, 1994; Tomlinson 1990, 1994b) in which they are given time to image and to think in their inner voices before they follow simple L2 instructions that have been given to them by their teacher.

(3) Learners take part in TPR Plus activities (Tomlinson 1990, 1994b) in which they act out stories, events, processes, etc. narrated to them by their teacher and then try to recall what happened mentally before drawing it and/or re-telling it in the L1.

1.2 Stage 2

(1) Learners listen to dramatic readings of stories by the teacher, then do imaging and L1 inner voice activities before taking part in L1 discussions of the story. Then they try to continue the story in their heads in pictures and in the L2 before trying to tell each other their story endings in the L2.

(2) Learners take part in TPR activities in which they are given time to think before they follow the L2 instructions they have been given.

(3) Learners take part in TMR (Total Mental Response) activities in which the teacher instructs them in the L2 to form mental images and to discuss issues and problems with their inner voices. Then they discuss their mental experiences with each other. The inner voice and the group

discussions will be primarily in the L1 but the teacher can encourage the use of some L2 words.

(4) The learners are encouraged to read along in their heads and to visualize as the teacher reads emotive texts aloud. Then there are intake response activities in which the learners think about and then discuss their responses to what they have 'read'.

(5) The learners take part in problem solving activities in which they are encouraged to use their L2 private voices aloud individually, then in pairs and then in groups.

1.3 Stage 3

(1) Learners listen to dramatic readings of stories by the teacher, then do imaging and L2 inner voice activities before taking part in L2 discussions of the story. Then they try to continue the story in their heads in the L2 before taking part in a group story writing activity.

(2) Learners take part in TPR activities in which they are given time to think in their inner voices whilst following complex L2 instructions.

(3) Learners take part in TMR (Total Mental Response) activities in which the teacher instructs them in the L2 to form mental images and to discuss issues and problems with their inner voices. Then they discuss their mental experiences with each other in the L2 before using them as the basis for an L2 writing activity.

(4) The learners do extensive reading activities in which they read texts of their choice. There are no tasks but the learners are encouraged to talk to themselves as they read and to do visual and inner speech summaries and predictions at the end of sections of the text

(5) The learners do experiential reading activities in which pre-reading connection activities, whilst-reading think activities and post-reading intake response activities are used to stimulate the use of imaging and the inner voice.

(6) Learners in groups prepare to perform readings of extracts from texts they have already read silently and enjoyed.

(7) The learners take part in problem solving activities in which they are encouraged to use their private voices aloud individually, then in pairs and then in groups. They then report their solutions to other groups in outer speech.

By doing such activities the learners can gain the confidence, the self-esteem and the communicative competence which can come from effective use of imaging and the inner voice. Such activities are rarely advocated in TEFL methodology and are not generally used in coursebooks. However inner voice activities are used in Neuro Linguistic Programming (NLP) and in Suggestopedia and examples of mental response activities can be found in Sion (1995), Underhill (1996), Tuzi (1998) and Helgesen (2001).

It is now possible to use neuro-imaging scans to detect inner speech and visual imaging activity in the brains of normal subjects (Petsche *et al* 1992; Fujimaki *et al* 2004) and we intend to make use of this in a joint project between Nagoya University, Leeds Metropolitan University and Cordoba University in which we intend to measure inner speech and visual imaging activity and their effects prior to and after mental imaging training for groups of L2 learners (Tomlinson *et al* in progress).

References

Aklam, R. and Crace, A. (2003), *Going for Gold Intermediate*. Harlow: Longman.

Asher, J. F. (1977), *Learning Another Language Through Actions*. Los Gatos, CA: Sky Oaks Publications.

Asher, J. (1994), 'The total physical response: a stress-free, brain compatible approach to learning', *SEAL*, Autumn.

Avila, F. J. (2005), 'El Uso de la Imagen Mental en la Lectura en el Proceso de la Adquisición de una Segunda Lengua' (unpublished PhD Thesis, University of Seville).

Bivens, J. A. and Hagstrom, F. (1992), 'The representation of private speech in children's literature', in L. E. Berk and R. M. Diaz (eds), *Private Speech: From Social Interaction to Self-Regulation*. Hillsdale, NJ: Lawrence Erlbaum.

Burke, K. and Brooks, J. (2000), *Wavelength Pre-Intermediate*. Harlow: Longman.

Centeno-Cortes, B. and Jimenez, A. F. (2004), 'Problem solving tasks in a foreign language: the importance of the L1 in private verbal thinking', *International Journal of Applied Linguistics*, 14, (1), 7–35.

Cunningham, S. and Moore, P. (2005a), *Cutting Edge Pre-Intermediate*. Harlow: Longman.

Cunningham, S. and Moore, P. (2005b), *Cutting Edge Intermediate*. Harlow: Longman.

Dellar, H. and Hocking, D. (2000), *Innovations*. Hove: Language Teaching Productions.

Di Camilla, F. J. and Anton, M. (2004), 'Private speech: a study of language for thought in the collaborative interaction of language learners'. *International Journal of Applied Linguistics*, 14, (1), 36–69.

Donato, R. (1988), '*Beyond Groups: A Psycholinguistic Rationale for Collective Activity in Second Language Learning*' (unpublished PhD thesis. University of Delaware, Newark).

Edge, J. (1993), *Essentials of English Language Teaching*. London: Longman.

Fujimaki, N., Hatakawa, T., Matani, A. and Okabe, Y. (2004), 'Right-lateralized neural activity during inner speech repeated by cues', *NeuroReport*, 15, (15), 2341–5.

de Guerro, M. C. M. (1994), 'Form and functions of inner speech in adult second language learning', in J. P. Lantolf and G. Appel (eds), *Vygotskian Approaches to Second Language Research*. Norwood, NJ: Ablex, pp. 83–116.

de Guerro, M. C. M. (2004), 'Early stages of L2 inner speech development: what verbal reports suggest'. *International Journal of Applied Linguistics*, 14, (1), 90–113.

Helgesen, M. (2001), 'Innervoice, time, planning and practice', www.mgu.ac.jp/~ic/helgesen2/paper.htm.

McCafferty, S. G. (1994a), 'The Use of Private Speech by Adult ESL Learners at Different Levels of Proficiency', in J. P. Lantolf and G. Appel (eds), *Vygotskian Approaches to Second Language Research*. Norwood, NJ: Ablex, pp. 117–34.

McCafferty, S. G. (1994b), 'Adult second language learners' use of private speech: a review of studies'. *The Modern Language Journal*, 78, (4), 421–36.

Nolasco, R. (1990), *Wow!*. Oxford: Oxford University Press.

Petsche, H., Lacroix, D., Lindner, K., Rappelsberger, P. and Schmidt-Henrich, E. (1992), 'Thinking with images or thinking with language: A pilot EEG probability mapping study'. *International Journal of Psychophysiology*, 12, (1), 31–9.

Pulverness, A. (2001), *Changing Skies*. Swan Communication.

Sion, C. (1995), *Talking to Yourself in English–An Alternative Approach to Self-Study–Books 1 & 2*. Heerlen, Netherlands: Training Etcetera.

Soars, L. and Soars, J. (1998), *New Headway Upper-Intermediate*. Oxford: Oxford University Press.

Soars, L. and Soars, J. (2002), *New Headway Beginner*. Oxford: Oxford University Press.

Swain, M. (1998), *Integrating language and content teaching through collaborative tasks*. Singapore: RELC Annual Seminar.

Tomlinson, B. (1990), 'Managing change in Indonesian high schools'. *ELT Journal*, 44, (1), 25–37.

Tomlinson, B. (1994a), *Openings*. London: Penguin.

Tomlinson, B. (1994b), 'TPR materials'. *Folio*, 1, (2), 8–10.

Tomlinson, B. (1996), 'Helping L2 readers to see', in T. Hickey and J. Williams (eds), *Language, Education and Society in a Changing World*. Clevedon, Avon: Multilingual Matters, pp. 253–62.

Tomlinson, B. (1997), '*The Role of Visualisation in the Reading of Literature by Learners of a Foreign Language*' (unpublished PhD thesis. University of Nottingham).

Tomlinson, B. (1998a), 'Seeing what they mean: helping L2 readers to visualise', in B. Tomlinson (ed.), *Materials Development in Language Teaching*. Cambridge: Cambridge University Press, pp. 265–78.

Tomlinson, B. (1998b), 'And now for something not completely different: an approach to language through literature'. *Reading in a Foreign Language*, 11, 2, 177–89.

Tomlinson, B. (2001), 'The inner voice: a critical factor in language learning'. *Journal of the Imagination in L2 Learning*, VI, 26–33.

Tomlinson, B. (2003), 'Helping learners to develop an effective L2 inner voice'. *RELC Journal*, 3, (2), 178–94.

Tomlinson, B. and Masuhara, H. (1994), *Use Your English*. Tokyo: Asahi Press.

Tomlinson, B., Masuhara, H. and Avila, J. (in progress), 'The effects of mental imagery training on L2 learners' ability to read'.

Tuzi, F. (1998), 'The inner workbench in the EFL classroom'. *IATEFL Newsletter*, February–March.

Underhill, A. (1996), *Using the Inner Workbench to Enrich Learning*. Hiroshima, Japan: JALT Convention.

Vygotsky, L. S. (1956), 'Thought and Language', in *Selected Psychological Investigations*. Academic Pedagogy of Science, Moscow: RSFSR Press.

Wajnryb, R. (1996), *Death, taxes and jeopardy: Systematic omissions in EFL texts, or life was never meant to be an adjacency pair*. Sydney: ELICOS Association 9th Educational Conference.

Willis, J. (1996), *A Framework for Task-Based Learning*. Harlow: Longman.

6 Internalization and language acquisition

James Lantolf and Beatriz Centeno-Cortes

1 Introduction

This chapter addresses Vygotsky's concept of internalization as it relates to language acquisition in general and to L2 development in particular. Internalization is the process through which culture exerts its influence on human consciousness, and as such represents Vygotsky's attempt to overcome the long-standing and problematic mind-body dualism (see Vygotsky 1997). Wundt, the founder of modern psychology, resolved the problem by segregating human culture (the external) from the human mind (the internal) and in so doing ruptured, what in Vygotsky's view, was the organic interconnection between the two (Cole 1996). For Vygotsky the separation made it impossible for psychology to fully understand the nature of uniquely human forms of thinking and therefore set himself the task of developing a theory that would reunite culture and mind.

At the core of Vygotsky's proposal was the notion that human mental activity is mediated by culturally constructed artifacts, concepts and activities (Ratner 2002) that, once appropriated and internalized, imbue humans with the capacity to voluntarily control mental activity, including memory, attention, planning and execution, rational thought and learning. Vygotsky referred to these as 'higher mental functions,' not because they were superior to biological functions but because they were built upon the foundation of those mental capacities provided by human biology (Vygotsky 1987). Humans, unlike any other species, have the capacity to self-generate artificial stimuli and to use these to intentionally control, or mediate, our biologically endowed mental functions, as well as our relationship to the external (physical and social) world (*ibid.*). The artificial, or what he called, *auxiliary*, stimuli (Vygotsky 1978) have their origins in human cultural life.

2 Understanding internalization

The importance of internalization of cultural forms of mediation in Vygotsky's theory is captured in the following statement: '*I only want to say . . .* that without man [sic] (=operator) as a whole the activity of his apparatus (brain) cannot be explained, that *man controls his brain and not the brain the man*' (cited in Yaroshevsky 1989: 230). Recognizing that both biological and cultural factors were essential for human mental activity to develop, Vygotsky set himself the task of constructing a unified psychology – one that dialectically integrated our biological endowment with our social and cultural inheritance which included activities, artifacts and concepts. His proposal was that through the internalization of cultural factors, humans were able to develop the capacity to mediate (i.e. voluntarily control) the functioning of their biologically endowed mental activity.

Vygotsky understood artificial stimuli to be any artifact created by a culture to represent meaning. This could include something as simple as tying a string around one's finger as a memory aid to something as complex as linguistic signs. It is in fact the latter type of artifact that Vygotsky considered to be the most powerful form of representational system because language imbues humans with enormous social and mental flexibility. For one thing, it frees us from the constraints of the here-and-now and allows us to talk and think about virtually anything at any time and in any place. As a simple example, we can sit in our offices and think about what to buy for dinner. As a more complex example which Vygotsky borrowed from Marx, through symbolic mediation in the form of a blueprint (comprised of both linguistic signs and non-linguistic symbols) an architect is able to plan a virtual building prior to construction of the real thing.[1] Indeed, the capacity to plan (i.e. to carry out an activity in imagination before actualizing it in the material world) is an extremely powerful higher form of thinking. Among other things, it requires that we inhibit real activity so that the plan itself can be constructed. This is something that Luria (1982), in particular, showed develops in children over time as they gain increasing control of language.

The mechanism through which our inheritance occurs is, according to Vygotsky, *internalization*, a topic which he addresses in the often cited statement that every psychological function appears twice, first between people on the interpsychological plane and then within the individual on the intrapsychological plane. The problem is precisely how are we to interpret what Vygotsky meant by intrapsychological. Frawley (1997: 94–5), for example, notes that the original Russian term that Vygotsky used was *vrashchivanie*, which means something like 'ingrowing,' and is sometimes translated into English as 'interiorization'. This term implies the emergence of 'active, nurturing transformation of externals into personally meaningful experience' (Frawley 1997: 95). In the words of Luria (1979: 45), 'it is through this interiorization of historically determined and culturally organized ways of operating on information that the social nature of people comes to be their psychological nature as well'.

If we want to see how rearranging furniture in a room will look we can either physically move the pieces of furniture about or we can mentally carry out a parallel, though obviously not identical, activity on the ideal mental plane. We rely on the mental manipulation to plan out our eventual concrete activity in the material world. Equally, important, however, is that our mental manipulations are in most cases influenced by our knowledge of how the physical world operates; thus, normally we do not place sofas on the sides of walls and if we choose to do so, we recognize that some special devices will be required in the physical world to make such things happen. Moreover, we can mentally plan how to rearrange the room even if we are in some other place in the world. We do not have to be physically present in the room. Internalization thus enables humans to abstract from physical objects and material actions and thus, unlike in the case of appropriation in other animals, human thinking is freed from 'the realm of perception' (Arievitch and van der Veer 1995: 123). In this view, internalization does not imply that mental activity must be carried out solely on the ideal plane. We can, for instance, rearrange furniture by using a sketch pad or a computer display to help visualize the activity, the same way the architect plans a building in the form of a blueprint. The important point is that we do so free of the actual physical presence of the furniture. This crucial capacity, which sharply distinguishes humans from other species, is known as *displacement* (see Luria 1982). Language, in particular, imbues humans with an exceptionally flexible and powerful displacement ability.

Internalization (and its associated function of displacement) accounts for the sense of continuity across time and space experienced by individuals. Vygotsky argued for a genetic (i.e. historical) connection between inter- and intrapersonal speech. That is, in ontogenesis, children initially engage in social interaction with other more mature members of their culture. This interaction is mediated in large part by speech (and in literate cultures, writing). Eventually this interpersonal speech takes on a secondary (in the derivative sense), or intrapersonal, function in which the speech is directed not at others but at the individual. In intrapersonal communication, the 'I – You' of social interaction becomes an 'I – Me' dialogue in which 'I' makes choices on what to talk about and 'Me' interprets and critiques these choices (Vocate 1994: 12). Through intrapersonal speech, generally referred to as private speech, people are capable of regulating their memory, attention, thinking and learning. Clark (1998: 178) notes that our public language is ideally suited to be coopted for intrapersonal functions, because, as with social communication, the individual can employ it for inspection, critique, and the modification of ideas, concepts and problems. In intrapersonal communication we talk ourselves into development (Yingling 1994). Given our earlier discussion of the central role that imitation plays in internalization, we would expect imitation to be a pervasive feature of private speech aimed at internalizing the various affordances, linguistic and non-linguistic, available in the sociocultural environment. In the next section, we consider some of the studies on imitation in L2 private speech in both children and adults.

3 Imitation: The mechanism of internalization

According to Vygotsky, the process of internalization entails the uniquely human capacity to imitate the activity of conspecifics (1987: 210). For

Vygotsky, imitation does not carry any of the behaviourist baggage associated with the concept in psychology but instead is a complex and potentially transformative activity (Newman and Holzman 1993: 151). In fact, imitation has a long history in psychology that predates behaviourism. Baldwin (1895/1915), for example, made the concept a centre piece of his developmental theory. For Baldwin, imitation is not mere repetition of others' behaviour but is 'a method of absorbing what is present in others and of making it over in forms peculiar to one's own temper and valuable to one's own genius' (cited in Valsiner and van der Veer 2000: 153). According to Newman and Holzman (1993: 151) imitation is 'a critically important developmental activity because it is the chief means by which in early childhood human beings are related to as other than and in advance of who they are'. Members of the culture relate to children who imitate not as parrots, but as 'speakers, feelers and thinkers' (*ibid.*).

A central feature of imitation, distinguishing it from emulation and mimicking, is the perception of both the goal and means of an activity. In emulation, the goal is perceived but the means are not, while in mimicking, neither is perceived. Humans are capable of all three actions, while other primates, at least in the wild, emulate and mimic, but do not imitate the behaviour of conspecifics. The ability to distinguish goal from means in imitation is manifested in the (symbolic and concrete) play activity of children, because it is in play that the child decouples 'the intentional affordances from their associated objects and artifacts so that they may be interchanged and used with "inappropriate" objects playfully' (Tomasello 1999: 85). In playing with language, in particular, the child decouples language from its normal communicative function where attention is on purpose or goal and focuses instead on the means (i.e. the semiotic tools and performative gestures that make up communication) (Cazden 1976: 606).

4 Neuropsychology of imitation

Meltzoff (2002: 19) argues that 'imitation promises to be a hot research topic in the coming decade. Interest in imitation spread from a small band of aficionados to the broader community of cognitive scientists, evolutionary biologists, neuroscientists, philosophers, and development scientists.' Researchers have observed that neonates have the ability to imitate the movements of others from birth. An especially significant finding of this research is that infants can imitate the behaviour of caregivers following a delay, often of a day or more (Meltzoff 2002: 21). Thus, they are able to imitate on the basis of representations stored in memory and this in turn provides 'freedom from context specificity,' clearly a crucial capacity for language acquisition (p. 30).

Iacoboni *et al* (1999) have discovered that Broca's area is specialized for imitation of goal-directed activity, including both language and gesture. The mirror neurons located in this region of the brain fire whether the individual is performing or just observing someone else engaged in an action. When the action observed or carried out is not goal directed (e.g. random finger tapping), mirror neurons in a different region of the brain fire. According to Iacoboni's team, Broca's area is not specifically dedicated to an encapsulated language system; rather it incorporates an evolutionary continuity between action, recognition, imitation, and language supported by a shared set of neural mechanisms (Heiser *et al* 2003: 1128).

5 Imitation in Language Acquisition

Following Chomsky's critique of behaviourist accounts of acquisition, imitation was discarded as a mechanism supporting the process for several decades (Speidel and Nelson 1989). Somewhat ironically, however, even those such as Chomsky and Ervin, who argued against imitation, acknowledged that imitation indeed plays a role in language acquisition (Speidel and Nelson 1989: 14–15). Despite the aura of doubt surrounding imitation, psychologists, psycholinguists and neuroscientists are showing renewed interest in imitation as a central mechanism in acquisition, and indeed for some the interest never waned (Speidel and Nelson, *ibid.*). Arbib (2002) proposes an evolutionary model for language development based on the function of mirror neurons in Broca's area. According to Arbib (2002: 253), 'the human brain and body evolved in such a way that we have hand, larynx, and facial mobility suited for generating gestures that can be used in language, and the brain mechanisms needed to produce and perceive rapidly generated sequences of such gestures'. In Arbib's hypothesis, the key innovation that connects language learning with imitation and what separates humans from higher primates in this regard, is the brain's capacity to imitate complex rather than just simple actions (Arbib 2002: 257). In primates even simple imitation requires a lengthy and laborious process of instruction between parent and offspring (e.g. cracking a nut with a rock or stick), in humans even complex actions are imitated after a fairly brief time period. Crucially, in complex actions, humans are able to decompose the actions into the constituent components, including goals and means.

In a survey of research on imitation in child language acquisition Speidel and Nelson (1989) observe that it is a complex mechanism involving motoric and neurological processing. Imitation, as Tomasello pointed out, is not simple copying of what someone else says. It is intentional and self-selective on the part of the child and is not driven by frequency of exemplars in the input. Imitative processes in children change over time and vary across children. In the early stages of acquisition children are more likely to focus on words and later shift their attention to morphemes. Imitation can follow immediately after and entail rote repetition of the model, or it can reduce or expand the patterns provided in the model. It is in the reductive and expansive types of imitation where its transformative qualities can be observed. Beginning as early as 9 months of age, children can defer imitation of their models. This has important consequences as it permits children to analyse language 'off-line' (Meltzoff and Gopnik 1989: 38). Kuczaj (1983) and Weir

(1962) document off-line analysis in children's self-directed crib speech, produced when children are alone in their cribs. Moreover, deferred imitation points to a continuum between imitation and spontaneous language production, with deferred imitation serving as 'essential building blocks for spontaneous speech' (Speidel 1989: 163). Some argue that imitation comprises both observation and reproduction and these latter two processes are on a continuum 'with respect to the degree of activation and elaboration of the central representational networks involved in the reproduction of the response' (Speidel and Nelson 1989: 5). Thus, even acquisition through observation, in this view, 'entails covert or symbolic motor acts' (*ibid.*), a notion that challenges input processing models which assume that production is not a central mechanism in acquisition. Some children adhere more closely to the model in their imitations, while others may be more 'novel and adventurous' (*ibid.*: 17). Finally, not all imitative activity has acquisition as its goal. This is especially true during communicative interaction, where imitation can have pragmatic functions, such as sustaining the interaction and tightening the bonds between parents and children. Nevertheless, we cannot rule out the possibility that even this type of imitation may have an impact on acquisition. We present examples of various imitative processes later in the chapter.

6 A theory of acquisition

Tomasello (2003) proposes a psycholinguistic model of language acquisition which argues that 'children begin to acquire language when they do because the learning process depends crucially on the more fundamental skills of joint attention, intention-reading, and cultural learning – which emerge near the end of the first year of life' (p. 21). From this perspective, language is a special and complex type of 'joint attentional skill' that people employ 'to influence and manipulate one another's attention' (*ibid.*) Imitation is a central mechanism in Tomasello's model. However, in this case, it must take on a different perspective from other forms of imitative action (e.g. facial movements, gestures, etc.). If children merely put themselves in the place of adults when imitating communicative intentions, they would end up directing the communicative symbols at themselves rather than at other individuals. Children must 'engage in role reversal imitation' when learning to use symbols with adults in the same way adults use symbols with the child (Tomasello 2003: 27). The linguistic symbol that results from role reversal imitation is then 'understood intersubjectively from both sides of the interaction'; that is, the learning process guarantees that children acquire socially shared symbols through coming to realize that interlocutors can both comprehend and produce the same or similar symbols. Thus:

> using linguistic symbols in utterances is a social act, and when this act is internalized in Vygotskian fashion the product is a unique kind of cognitive representation that is not only intersubjective (involving both self and other), but also perspectival

in the sense that the child understands that the same referent could have been indicated in some other way – the speaker could have chosen another linguistic symbol to indicate a different aspect of this entity.

(Tomasello 2003: 28)

Role reversal imitation with linguistic symbols is complex and in early acquisition children frequently produce errors, especially with the pronoun *you* given that the second person pronoun is more frequent in speech directed at children than is the first person pronoun (Tomasello 2003: 203). Interestingly, young children often attempt to clarify the referent of pronouns through use of gesture, presumably indicating that an understanding that pronouns requires 'some supplemental indication of the intended referent (such as a gesture) in situations in which shared knowledge by speaker and listener cannot be assumed' (p. 207). Children are able to imitate not just language directed at them by adults, but are also quite good at imitating language they are exposed to by eavesdropping on third party conversations (p. 269). We will consider examples of this phenomenon from child and adult L2 learners below.

7 Interactive imitation in L1 child language

As we have mentioned, children imitate adult models in both social and private speech. Examples (1) and (2), borrowed from Lightbown and Spada (1993), illustrate imitation during adult–child social interaction.[2] In (1b) Cindy responds to Patsy's question and then in (1c) she imitates and expands upon her own utterance producing what on the surface is similar to a classroom pattern drill activity, a common occurrence in child imitation (see Kuczaj 1983).

(1) **Cindy** (24 months, 16 days) is playing with a stuffed rabbit
    a. **Patsy** (adult): What does this rabbit like to eat?
    b. **Cindy**:   (uninterpretable speech) eat the carrots.
                    (she then gets another stuffed rabbit.)
    c. **Cindy**:   He (uninterpretable speech) eat carrots. The other one eat carrots. They both eat carrots.

(Lightbown and Spada 1993: 4)

In (2) as David responds to his mother's command to get undressed, he appropriates and, rather creatively, plays with the final segment of her utterance, treating negative morpheme *un-* as a separable prefix:

(2) **David** (3 years, 11 months)
    a. **Mother**: Get undressed (after many repetitions)
    b. **David**: I'm getting undressed.
              I'm getting *on dressed.* (italics in original)
              I'm getting on dressed.
              I'm getting *off dressed.* (italics in original)

(Lightbown and Spada 1993: 5)

Finally, (3) is an example of deferred imitation involving an inappropriate but again quite creative lexical substitution:

(3) At a birthday party, adults propose several toasts with grape juice, as in the following utterance:
    Father: I'd like to propose a toast
                Following a period of time during which no toasting was going on, David (5 years, 1 month) utters:
    David: I'd like to propose a piece of bread.
                The adults not realizing that David was serious began to laugh, 'which sent David slinking from the table'
                                          (Lightbown and Spada 1993: 6)

8 Private speech and child L2 imitation

As we have noted, the function of imitation during communicative interaction is not always clear. Any given imitation may serve an interactional function, such as holding the floor, or acknowledging and possibly agreeing with an interlocutor's utterance. On the other hand, it may serve acquisition; or it may indeed serve both functions simultaneously. Disentangling the various functions of conversational imitation presents a substantial challenge for researchers (see Speidel and Nelson 1989). However, in the domain of private speech, that is, the intrapersonal communication that children engage in when alone, the function of imitation seems considerably less ambiguous (see Weir 1962; Kuczaj 1983; Meltzoff and Gopnik 1989). Private speech imitation clearly does not serve an immediate social function in that it is not intended as a contribution to an ongoing conversation. Thus, it seems less problematic to assume that in this case imitation promotes internalization of the linguistic features in its focus. On the other hand, it might be that even private imitation makes a contribution to a conversation, only in this case it is an imagined future conversation. Acquisition is not something that happens for its own sake; it serves linguistic interaction.

In this section we will discuss a study on child L2 private speech by Saville-Troike (1988) which provides abundant examples of imitation. However, unlike in the child L1 literature, where much of what has been documented in private speech is deferred imitation, Saville-Troike attests *immediate* private speech imitation. Several of the children disengaged from communicative interaction in English, while at the same time privately imitating the language patterns produced by their teacher and English-speaking classmates. The criteria the researcher used for classifying speech as private instead of social was reduced volume, lack of eye contact and no expectation of interlocutor responsiveness.

In (4A & B) the same three-year-old child produces immediate reductive imitation and, according to Saville-Troike (1988: 578) evidences Slobin's learning principle – pay attention to the ends of utterances. In (4B) the child seems to be practising English question intonation. Keep in mind that the child at this point is not engaged conversationally with either the peer or the teacher:

(4) Three-year-old child
    A. **Peer**:   I want you to ride the bike
       Child 1: Bike
    B. **Teacher**: I need you to walk?
       Child 1: Walk? Walk? Walk? Walk?

(Saville-Troike 1988: 578)

In (5) a four-year-old child immediately imitates the teacher's entire utterance.

(5) Four-year-old child
      Teacher: What's happened there. (sic)
      Child 2: What's happened there.

(Saville-Troike 1988: 578)

In (6) the same child produces a reductive imitation of the teacher's lengthy utterance and in so doing generates an inappropriate collocation, 'wipe your teeth' and deletes the plural marker from 'hands'.

(6) Four-year-old
      Teacher: You guys go brush your teeth. And wipe your hands on the towel.
      Child 2: Wipe your hand. Wipe your teeth.

(Saville-Troike 1988: 584)

An important aspect of Saville-Troike's study was that she was able to establish a connection between the L2 forms that appeared in the children's private speech and their use of these same forms when they eventually re-engaged in social speech, thus providing support for the argument that imitation, in this case, during private speech, promotes internalization (i.e. language acquisition).

9 Private speech and adult L2 imitation

Second language acquisition (SLA) research has generally not recognized imitation as a viable factor in acquisition, no doubt because of its behaviourist baggage. However, in the recast literature what is usually referred to as 'uptake' of a recast is indeed a form of imitation. In the L1 literature imitation no longer carries the negative connotations it did in the 1960s and 1970s. In fact, L1 researchers consider the recast itself to be a type of imitation that is often quite sensitive to the child's linguistic development (Speidel and Nelson 1989). L2 researchers have confronted the same difficulty as their L1 counterparts with regard to the function of imitation during communication. An advantage that accrues to L2 researchers is use stimulated recall to tease out the functions of imitative moves made by L2 learners.

Be that as it may, it turns out that as in the case of children, adults also imitate in their private speech linguistic patterns produced by their teachers and peers. Through use of individual recording devices, and using the same criteria developed by Saville-Troike, L2 researchers have begun to investigate the imitative behaviour of adult learners. To date, however, this research has not generated the same robust data as has L1 research. Several reasons have been advanced to account for the difference, including adult self-awareness which may make them more reticent to speak when under observation and the possibility that only individuals intentionally trying to learn a new language are likely to produce private speech. Not all students enrolled in language classes, especially university foreign language classes (i.e. non-English) where much of the adult L2 private speech data has been collected, make the effort to learn the language. Some are merely fulfilling a degree requirement (Gillette 1994; Lantolf 1997). Nevertheless, the findings are interesting and we hope that research on this important topic will continue. An important difference between the L1 and adult L2 private speech research is that so far, to our knowledge at least, all of the adult data has been collected in the social setting of the language classroom. No adult study has collected data that parallels Kuczaj's and Weir's work with children when they are alone. Some L2 studies have used interviews (e.g. Gillette 1994) or questionnaires (e.g. de Guerrero 1994; Lantolf 1997) to collect adult private speech data, but while first-person reports have documented that adults indeed engage in L2 focused private speech they do not provide the detail nor do that have the same validity as does direct observation.

In (7) a Korean L1 adult classroom an ESL learner focuses on the meaning of a new word 'argue':

(7)
     a. **Teacher:** Argue (loudly)
     b. **Learner:** Argue means . . . (with rising intonation and with sufficient volume to be social)
     c. **Teacher:** Disagree.
     d. **Learner:** Disagree (falling intonation, somewhat softly) Yeah. (very softly).
     e. **Teacher:** Thank you (addressing another student). And it means using words, you disagree using your words, not fight.
     f. **Learner:** Argue (very softly).

                                           (Lantolf and Thorne, forthcoming)

The teacher first provides a synonym, which the learner repeats softly telling herself that she understands, which is how we interpret her use of falling intonation accompanied by 'Yeah'. The teacher then offers a definition, after which the learner repeats, 'argue'. We interpret this as an attempt to keep the item within the focus of her attention while she mulls over its meaning.

In (8) we see an example that parallels some of the child L2 data presented by Saville-Troike in that the learner experiments with English collocations. The teacher asked one of the students a question, which the Korean learner then vicariously responded to (see Ohta 2001) but with focus on the formal rather than the communicative features of the question:

(8)
> **Teacher:** Were you taking a nap, a little sleep? [directed at another student]
> **Learner:** nap, I take nap . . . ing

The expression 'taking a nap' was apparently new for this learner. Her imitation of the pattern is reminiscent of a pattern drill behaviour documented in L1 children by Kuczaj (1983) and by Saville-Troike's L2 children. She first repeats the noun 'nap' and then substitutes the teacher's 'you' with 'I' in the full phrase, an example of Tomasello's 'role reversal' imitation. She also substitutes the simple present form of the verb 'take' for the teacher's progressive. The pause following the second instance of 'nap' is interesting. In trying to reproduce the original pattern, the learner seems to be about to produce a hybrid, '*I take napping,' a chunk of language that she might well try out later in communicative activity. Alternatively, she might have intended to attach the gerundive *–ing* to the verb 'take' as indeed occurred in the teacher's utterance but only after she realized that her imitation of the original model had omitted this segment. Thus, her externalization of the *–ing* could have been a reminder that the morpheme appeared in the model.

Centeno-Cortés (2003) carried out a longitudinal study of private speech produced by university L2 learners of Spanish. Among other things, this research further supports the findings of Lantolf and Yáñez-Prieto (2003) and Ohta (2001) that learners often focus on language features that diverge from the focus of a lesson, as is illustrated in (9):

(9)
> a. **Teacher:** Si estás comparando un nombre, entonces sí tiene género. Sarah tiene tanto (writing the sentence on the board).
> 'If you are comparing a noun, then yes it has gender. Sarah has as much'
> b. **Speaker outside the classroom:** Vale . . . vale, vale, vale. 'OK . . . OK, OK, OK';
> c. **Learner:** (laughs)
> d. **Teacher:** dinero 'money'
> e. **Learner:** vale vale vale (in a very soft voice and imitating the intonation of the person in the background)
> f. **Teacher:** como Kevin. 'as Kevin'
> g. **Learner:** ¿Por qué? 'Why'
> h. **Teacher:** Tanto dinero, porque dinero es un nombre masculino. 'As much money, because money is a masculine noun'
> i. **Learner:** Ah! (in very soft Private Speech)
>
> (Centeno-Cortés 2003)

By the time (9) occurred, the learner already knew that *vale* is the equivalent of *ok* in Spain. The teacher is explaining how the comparative word *tanto* may be masculine or feminine depending on the gender of the following noun, and the learner was paying attention to the explanation given by the teacher, as shown in the private comment uttered in the last turn of the example. However, she happened to hear someone outside the classroom saying *vale, vale, vale,* and she imitated privately the peculiar intonation that she had heard despite the fact that it was not related to the topic of the lesson. The example recalls Saville-Troike's study in which the children appropriated utterances from eavesdropping on peer interactions.

10 Private speech and spontaneous performance

The L2 research literature on adults has not paid much attention to the function of imitation per se in the acquisition process. However, it is interesting to note that one of the ways imitation has been framed in this literature is as uptake of recasts. In the child L1 literature, on the other hand, uptake of adult recasts of child utterances has been situated within the general framework of speech imitation (see Speidel and Nelson 1989).

An important feature of Centeno-Cortés's study is that to our knowledge it is the first study of adults to attempt to make a connection between L2 features that appear in private speech with the spontaneous use of those same features in interpersonal communicative performance. Both oral and written Spanish produced in or for the classroom was considered social speech.[3] In (10) the learner discovers that the English complex verb *to ask for* cannot be rendered in Spanish as **preguntar por*, but requires a single verb form, *pedir*. In (10b) the learner's 'Ah' means something like 'Now I understand'. Indeed, later in the course, the student responds correctly (10d) to the teacher's query on the Spanish equivalent of English 'to ask for'. Of course, this performance is not the same thing as spontaneous conversational production, and given the time lapse between the initial and the second teacher–learner interaction (45 days), it is possible that the leaner could have internalized the form in other venues. Nevertheless, we believe that the learner's private response played some role in the learning process. Furthermore, (10c) illustrates an additional feature of adult private speech that to our knowledge has not been documented in either child L1 or L2 private speech – use of metacomments. The learner's utterance does not contain an overt imitation per se (the learner could well have repeated the verb covertly before externalizing the metacomment). 'Ah' is frequently used in social speech as a marker of understanding of an interlocutor's utterance. Given that private speech is derived from social speech it is not surprising that speakers rely on the forms available to them in social speech to organize their inner order in private speech (Frawley 1997)[4]:

(10)
    a. **Teacher:** To ask for something. Ayer le pedí a Amy su número de teléfono. Pero *ask a question* es *preguntar*. Esto *preguntar POR* no existe.[5]
    b. **Learner:** ¿no? Ah! (softly to herself)

11 Conclusion

Carroll (2001: 16–17) argues that the process of language acquisition is 'not directly observable' and can only be inferred 'on the basis of other observable events such as the utterances that learners produce, the interpretation they assign to utterances they hear or read, the time it takes to interpret an utterance, their judgements of the acceptability of utterances, etc.'. We would like to suggest that private speech, including both imitation and metacomments, does indeed provide at least some direct access to the acquisition process. To borrow a phrase from Vygotsky (1987), private speech may well be acquisition 'in flight'. There are no doubt processes at work in language learning, or any kind of learning, that we may not ever be able to observe; nevertheless, what happens in private speech as documented in the type of data considered in this chapter might very well enable researchers to gain a glimpse of the learning process as it unfolds in real time. The presence of metacommentary in adult private speech seems to be a feature that distinguishes it from early childhood private speech. Frawley and Lantolf (1985), however, report that older children do produce metastatements in their private speech, but in this case the intent is not to internalize the language but to navigate themselves through difficult cognitive tasks.

The evidence from private speech also shows that learners apparently have their own learning agendas, which operate independently of their teacher's. This agenda may well be a manifestation of the learner's zone of proximal development (see Lantolf and Yáñez-Prieto 2003 and Ohta 2001 for further discussion). Finally, Nicholas *et al* (2001) in their review of the recast literature point out that despite the high frequency of recasts observed in teacher feedback, there is a fairly low level of apparent uptake by learners. Analysis of private speech suggests that learners may imitate teacher recasts with greater frequency than the research shows. Ohta (2001) documents that learners often vicariously respond to teacher queries and imitate their recasts even when they are directed at other students. While all of these are areas where a great deal of research remains to be carried out on private speech, imitation, and L2 development, we believe that the most important area is establishing the connection between private speech and social communication.

Notes

1   Other types of symbolic mediation include numeric systems, diagrams, art, music.
2   Lightbown and Spada do not share the perspective on imitation presented here. In their view, imitation is a copying process and while some of the speech produced by children mirrors adult patterns, much of it does not, and therefore for them, does not qualify as imitation (Lightbown and Spada 1993: 7).
3   The recordings were carried out only in the classroom; therefore, it may be possible that the learner targeted the same linguistic item outside of the classroom setting.
4   For further discussion of adult use of metacomments in private speech, see Lantolf and Yáñez-Prieto (2003).

5   *Preguntar por* is a possible collocation in Spanish but it does not have the meaning
    intended by the student in the context under consideration.

References

Arbib, M. A. (2002), 'The mirror system, imitation, and the evolution of language',
    in K. Dautenhahn and C. L. Nehaniv (eds), *Imitation in Animals and Artifacts*.
    Cambridge, MA: MIT.

Arievitch, I. and van der Veer, R. (1995), 'Furthering the internalization debate:
    Gal'perin's contribution'. *Human Development*, 38, 1113–26.

Baldwin, J. M. (1895/1915), *Mental Development in the Child and the Race*. New York:
    McMillan.

Carroll, S. E. (2001), *Input and Evidence. The Raw Material of Second Language Acquisition*. Amsterdam: John Benjamins.

Cazden, C. (1976), 'Play with language and meta-linguistic awareness: One dimensions of language experience', in J. Bruner, A. Jolly and K. Sylva (eds), *Play. Its Role in Development and Evolution*. New York: Basic Books, pp. 603–8.

Centeno-Cortés, B. (2003), '*Private Speech in the Second Language Classroom: Its Role in Internalization and Its Link to Social Production*' (unpublished PhD dissertation. The Pennsylvania State University. University Park, PA).

Clark, A. (1998), 'Magic words: how language augments human computation', in P. Carruthers and J. Boucher (eds), *Language and Thought: Interdisciplinary Themes*. Cambridge: Cambridge University Press, pp. 162–83.

Cole, M. (1996), *Cultural Psychology. A Once and Future Discipline*. Cambridge, MA: Belknap.

Frawley, W. (1997), *Vygotsky and Cognitive Science. Language and the Unification of the Social and Computational Mind*. Cambridge, MA: Harvard University Press.

Frawley, W. and Lantolf, J. P. (1985), 'Second language discourse: A Vygotskyan perspective'. *Applied Linguistics*, 6, 19–44.

Gillette, B. (1994), 'The role of learner goals in L2 success', in J. P. Lantolf and G. Appel (eds), *Vygotskian Approaches to Second Language Research*. Norwood, NJ: Ablex, pp. 195–213.

de Guerrero, M. C. M. (1994), 'Form and functions of inner speech in adult second language learning', in J. P. Lantolf and G. Appel (eds), *Vygotskian Approaches to Second Language Research*. Norwood, NJ: Ablex, pp. 83–116.

Heiser, M., Iacoboni, M., Maeda F., Marcus J. and Mazziotta, J. C. (2003), 'The role of Broca's area in imitation'. *European Journal of Neuroscience*, 17, 1123–8.

Iacoboni, M., Woods R. P., Brass M., Beekering, H., Mazziotta, J. C. and Rizzolatti, G. (1999), 'Cortical mechanisms of human imitation'. *Science*, 286, 2526–8.

Kuczaj, S. A. II. (1983), *Crib Speech and Language Play*. New York: Springer Verlag.

Lantolf, J. P. (1997), 'The function of language play in the acquisition of L2 Spanish', in W. R. Glass and A. T. Pérez-Leroux (eds), *Contemporary Perspectives on the Acquisition of Spanish. Volume 2: Production, Processing, and Comprehension*. Somerville, MA: Cascadilla Press.

Lantolf, J. P. and Yáñez-Prieto, C. (2003), 'Talking yourself into Spanish: Intrapersonal communication and second language learning'. *Hispania*, 86, 97–109.

Lantolf, J. P. and Thorne, S. L. (forthcoming), *Sociocultural Theory and the Genesis of Second Language Development*. Oxford: Oxford University Press.

Lightbrown, P. and Spada, N. (1993), *How Languages are Learned*. Oxford: Oxford University Press.

Luria, A. R. (1979), *The Making of Mind. A Personal History of Soviet Psychology*. Cambridge, MA: Harvard University Press.

Luria, A. R. (1982), *Language and Cognition*. New York: John Wiley & Sons.

Meltzoff, A. N. (2002), 'Elements of a developmental theory of imitation', in A. N. Meltzoff and W. Prinz (eds), *The Imitative Mind. Development, Evolution, and Brain Bases*. Cambridge: Cambridge University Press.

Meltzoff, A. N. and Gopnik, A. (1989), 'On linking nonverbal imitation, representation, and language learning in the first two years of life', in G. E. Speidel and K. E. Nelson (eds), *The Many Faces of Imitation in Language Learning*. New York: Springer-Verlag, pp. 23–51.

Newman, F. and Holzman, L. (1993), *Lev Vygotsky. Revolutionary Scientist*. London: Routledge.

Nicholas, H., Lightbown, P. M. and Spada, N. (2001), 'Recasts as feedback to language learners'. *Language Learning*, 51, 719–58.

Ohta, A. S. (2001), *Second Language Acquisition Processes in the Classroom: Learning Japanese*. Mahwah, NJ: Lawrence Erlbaum.

Ratner, C. (2002), *Cultural Psychology. Theory and Method*. New York: Kluwer/Plenum.

Saville-Troike, M. (1988), 'Private speech: Evidence for second language learning strategies during the "silent period"'. *Journal of Child Language*, 15, 567–90.

Speidel, G. E. (1989), 'Imitation: A bootstrap for language to speak?', in G. E. Speidel and K. E. Nelson, (eds), *The Many Faces of Imitation in Language Learning*. New York: Springer-Verlag, pp. 151–79.

Speidel, G. E. and Nelson, K. E. (1989), 'A fresh look at imitation in language learning', in G. E. Speidel and K. E. Nelson (eds), *The Many Faces of Imitation in Language Learning*. New York: Springer-Verlag, pp. 1–21.

Tomasello, M. (1999), *The Cultural Origins of Human Cognition*. Cambridge, MA: Harvard University Press.

Tomasello, M. (2003), *Constructing Language: A Usage-Based Theory of Language Acquisition*. Cambridge, MA: Harvard University Press.

Valsiner, J. and van der Veer, R. (2000), *The Social Mind. Construction of the Idea*. Cambridge: Cambridge University Press.

Vocate, D. R. (1994), 'Self-talk and inner speech: Understanding the uniquely human aspects of intrapersonal communication', in D. R. Vocate (ed.), *Intrapersonal Communication. Different Voices, Different Minds*. Hillsdale, NJ: Erlbaum, pp. 3–32.

Vygotsky, L. S. (1978), *Mind in Society. The Development of Higher Psychological Processes*. Cambridge, MA: Harvard University Press.

Vygotsky, L. S. (1987), *The Collected Works of L. S. Vygotsky. Volume 1. Problems of General Psychology. Including the Volume Thinking and Speech*. (ed. by R. W. Reiber and A. S. Carton). New York: Plenum Press.

Vygotsky, L. S. (1997), *The Collected Works of L. S. Vygotsky. Volume 4. The History of the Development of Higher Mental Functions* (ed. by R. W. Reiber). New York: Plenum Press.

Weir, R. (1962), *Language in the Crib*. The Hague: Mouton.

Yaroshevsky, M. (1989), *Lev Vygotsky*. Moscow: Progress Press.

Yingling, J. (1994), 'Childhood: Talking the mind into existence', in D. R. Vocate (ed.), *Intrapersonal Communication: Different Voices, Different Minds*. Hillsdale, NJ: Erlbaum, pp. 121–44.

7 Affect in teacher talk

Jane Arnold and Carmen Fonseca

> Your choice of words and your language selections are critical to the self-esteem, the academic success, and the healthy mental and emotional development of your students. There is an undeniable link between the words you speak and the attitudes and outcomes students create in their lives.
>
> (Moorman and Weber 1989)

1 Introduction

Introducing a concern for affect in the classroom is vital for learning. Even though learning is often associated with the cognitive, it cannot be disassociated from the affective. Jensen (1998: 71) points out that 'the affective side of learning is the critical interplay between how we feel, act, and think. There is no separation of mind and emotions; emotions, thinking and learning are all linked'. Likewise, in his work on the neurobiology of affect as related to language learning, Schumann (1994: 239) stresses that 'in the brain, emotion and cognition are distinguishable but inseparable. Therefore, from a neural perspective, affect is an integral part of cognition'. One of the reasons that this is so is that an affectively positive environment puts the brain in the optimal state for learning: minimal stress and maximum interest and engagement with the material to be learnt. In large part, this state is created by the teacher, with one of the ways of doing so being teacher discourse.

Affect covers a large area of concern in the field of language learning/ teaching as it includes not only individual factors such as self-esteem, anxiety, inhibition, willingness to take risks, tolerance of ambiguity, learning styles, introversion/extraversion, self-efficacy and motivation, but also relational aspects such as empathy, teacher–learner rapport or cross-cultural processes. According to Arnold and Brown, there are two main reasons for being concerned with affective factors in language learning. First, taking affect into account can further language learning where 'attention needs to be given both to how we can overcome problems created by negative emotions and to how we can create and use more positive, facilitative emotions'. The second reason they mention is that 'As we teach the language, we can also educate learners to live more satisfying lives and to be responsible members of society' (Arnold and Brown 1999: 2, 3). In other words, attention to affect connects to broader social goals.

Affect has also been shown to be a mediating force between the way interactions are organized and cognitive learning. For instance, first language learning is facilitated by parents and teachers through social interaction and cooperative activities. Similarities between L1 and L2 acquisition processes have been widely discussed in the literature, and the types of input in teacher talk and parental talk have much in common. From a linguistic point of view, both can be considered as simplified codes created to help the listener to learn and understand language (Chaudron 1993; Ellis 1994; Fonseca 2002). They share features such as the frequent use of repetition, formulaic expressions, expansions, preference for simplified vocabulary, change in voice volume and modification of intonational contours. From an affective point of view, the way parents interact with children undeniably has a central part in their development. Parents hold great expectations for their offspring to learn their mother tongue; therefore, they empower their children by using temporary supports, or scaffolds, to help them acquire the knowledge, skills and strategies they need to progress, to become autonomous. In a similar way, teachers' beliefs and expectations have been found to have greater influence than teachers' knowledge on the way they plan their lessons, on the kinds of decisions they make and on their general classroom practice (Pajares 1992). Among other things, the teachers' selection of words and their discourse organization play an important role in shaping learners' self-concept and their academic success.

2 A constructivist vision of learning

Language learning is a social event where significant adults, normally parents and teachers, provide the learners with mediated, meaningful experiences to help them to construct knowledge actively. This social event is of great importance as, according to Lantolf and Appel (1994: 26–7), this 'linguistic activity is not simply the means through which mental activity is reflected, but it is the means through which higher mental functions derive their sociocultural origins and through which a specifically human mind is organized and functions'.

Teaching is understood as an interaction between learner and expert to establish what learners need to learn to accomplish a task without assistance (Tharp and Gallimore 1994). Reading a story to a child is an example of how adults interact with children to empower them to acquire the reading strategies they need to become autonomous readers. At first, adults read aloud, generally making use of specific intonational contours to get and maintain the child's attention. Then, they point to pictures to facilitate meaning; they may also try to incorporate interaction and ask the child simple questions or to highlight something in the illustrations related to the story. Vygotsky (1978) defines these verbal and non-verbal behaviours as temporary supports (scaffolds) provided by adults that allow children to participate in this complex reading process before they are able to do so unassisted. The mediators or facilitators are working in the learners' zone of proximal development (ZPD) that Vygotsky (1978: 86) defined as 'the distance between the actual developmental level as determined by individual problem solving and the level of potential development as determined through problem solving under adult guidance or in collaboration with more capable peers'. Learners' autonomy evolves by offering them mediated experiences in which they can interact with the materials in various ways. The teacher's role in this sense has to do with 'helping learners to become autonomous, to take control of their own learning, . . . enabling them to become independent thinkers and problem-solvers' (Williams and Burden 1997: 68).

During the early stages of first language acquisition, parents play this empowering role. Parental talk or motherese has been classified as a simplified code used automatically to help the child to understand and learn language. Different studies have concluded that parents use shorter sentences, pause more, refer to here-and-now situations, make frequent use of nonverbal language and add information to their words by underlining them with expanded intonation contours. Parents interested in empowering their children do not hesitate to repeat words or sentences and they understand that learning is a process which needs time. Each performance of the child, verbal or not, is rewarded with a smile, a hug or an encouraging verbal comment. They do not consider their offspring as poor language learners; instead, they simply use a linguistic input slightly beyond the child's production level. They have high expectations for their children and believe that they will soon become good language producers. Intuitively, caring parents know that any bad learning experience can influence their children's opinion about their coping potential, that is to say, their beliefs about their capacity to carry out a task. In fact, it could affect their willingness to take risks in other learning situations or, as Chastain (1988: 167) states, 'experiences that have positive results tend to be repeated and those with negative outcomes avoided. Those that are associated with success are approached with confidence and those associated with failure or displeasure are approached with reluctance and distaste'.

In the context of the foreign language (FL) classroom, this constructivist vision of language learning is also applicable. In contrast to traditional teaching methods stressing individuality, rote-learning of vocabulary and a strong grammar-centred approach, the foundation of sociocultural theory approaches is that language is learned through emphasis on meaning and context negotiated in social interactions. Learners are considered active participants, whose language competence can be best developed if at the individual level they are assisted to learn metacognitive and metalinguistic skills and strategies and at the social level, they acquire the ability to communicate effectively in group situations which require cooperation and interaction. Sinclair and Brazil defined the teacher as a 'skilled verbal artist, able through little other than his conversation to control a large group of pupils, manage them and take them systematically through a curriculum, all at the same time' (1982: 4). A constructivist vision of language learning adds the reflection on how teachers through their 'conversations' can teach self-directed strategies and effective communication strategies that embrace linguistic and relational dimensions.

3 Teacher confirmation

One of the key reflections of humanistic educator Carl Rogers (1969) was on the necessity to facilitate real, significant learning in the classroom and that achieving this is, in large part, dependent not on things such as specific skills or scholarly knowledge of the teacher, or course planning or teaching aids, but rather on 'certain attitudinal qualities which exist in the personal relationship between the facilitator and the learner' (1969: 105–6). This type of learning will be accomplished most successfully in a classroom in which a climate of 'unconditional positive regard' has been established. The concept refers to the teacher's complete acceptance of his/her students, a respect for their worth and value as individuals. This is not the same as acceptance of all behaviour, but includes the ability to separate the doer from the deed; and thus when a student has turned in a messy assignment two days late, it means telling her 'your work is not neat enough and I asked for it two days ago' instead of 'you are really messy and lazy'.

Roger's work is closely connected to the development of Martin Buber's concept of confirmation, by which he means that one of our basic innate drives is to be confirmed by others, that is, to discover and reaffirm through interaction our identity as a human being. Through our contact with others, through interaction, we become what we are, and, indeed, confirmation may be the most important aspect of human interaction. 'Actual humanity exists only where this capacity unfolds' (Buber 1965: 102). In any educational setting confirmation is central; Watzlawick *et al* (1967: 84) refer to it as the 'greatest single factor ensuring mental development and stability'. A good deal of work on confirmation has been done in general communication studies where it is recognized that communication includes both content and relational dimensions. According to Duncan (1967: 249), 'We do not relate and then talk, but we relate in talk'.

In the case of a discipline such as second or foreign language learning, just as with learning our first language, interaction and communication are at the very centre of the learning process, especially in current contexts which stress being able to communicate effectively in the target language. In an activity such as classroom language learning, which is highly interaction-dependent and to no small extent influenced by teacher behaviour, teacher confirmation (Ellis 1998, 2004) is a factor to be taken into account, especially perceived teacher confirmation, which is a student's perception of receiving acknowledgement as a worthwhile individual from his/her teacher. As teachers, we send verbal and non-verbal messages, perhaps unintentionally, to students who receive them, perhaps unconsciously but nevertheless deeply, making them feel 'real or unreal, accepted or rejected, valued or scorned, understood or misunderstood, humanized or objectified' (Sieburg 1985: 188) – in other words, confirmed or disconfirmed.

In a study done to generate items of common confirmation and disconfirmation behaviours of teachers to include in the instrument TCS (Teacher Confirmation Scale), Ellis (1998) used a sample of 52 undergraduate university students from several subject areas in the United States to get a list of 406 examples, with a content analysis yielding 60 different teacher behaviours. From this data emerged the following four categories of behaviour patterns, all related directly to verbal and non-verbal affective aspects of teacher discourse. Some typical examples of each category are included:

- **Teacher questioning behaviour, especially teachers' response to students' questions/comments**. The confirming teacher indicates that students' responses are appreciated ('That's a good point'), listens to students, is available outside of class and is flexible about following the lesson plan.
- **Demonstrated interest in students and in their learning**. The confirming teacher gives constructive written or oral feedback on students' work (e.g. suggests ways to improve or states why the work is good), demonstrates that he/she knows students' names, communicates that he/she is interested in whether students are learning, makes an effort to get to know students, provides oral or written praise or encouragement on students' work, establishes eye contact during class lectures, communicates that he/she believes that students can do well in the class and smiles at the class.
- **Teaching style**. The confirming teacher checks on students' understanding ('Is that clear?', 'Are you ready to go on?'), uses an interactive teaching style, listens to students viewpoints regarding grading, is approachable, uses appropriate facial expressions and makes an effort to communicate the practical application of course material in students' lives.
- **Aberrant disconfirmation**. The disconfirming teacher belittles or makes 'put-down' statements to some students when they participate during class (e.g. the teacher makes comments like 'I've already discussed that'; 'If you'd been listening, you'd know the answer'), does not take students' input seriously, uses a rude tone of voice when responding to some students' comments or questions during class, talks down to students, embarrasses students in front of the class, focuses on only a few students during class while ignoring others, puts students on the spot during class, uses derogatory terms to describe the class (e.g. 'stupid'; 'lazy'), interrupts students when they are making a comment or asking a question, seems more concerned with getting through all of the lecture material for the day than with helping students to understand the material, talks above students' heads. (Adapted from Ellis 1998).

The concept of confirmation has been applied to the language teaching context by León (2005), who points out its vital importance for language learners since language learning is generally recognized as an especially anxiety-prone activity. Hence, there is a need to confirm learners and help to encourage their willingness to communicate (MacIntyre *et al* 1998).

4 Verbal teacher behaviour

Teacher talk has been described as a distinct linguistic code that is characterized by the modification of phonological, lexical and syntactic aspects of speech (Ellis 1985; Chaudron 1993) and by a specific organization of discourse (Nattinger and DeCarrico 1993) and it is generally considered that certain verbal and non-verbal modifications can enhance learners' comprehension and ability to process the target grammar and lexis. The nature of teacher discourse has a great influence on students' participation and on assimilation of instructional content.

Chaudron (1993: 50) revises studies done on 'the amount of teacher talk compared with students' speech in classrooms, the distribution of teacher talk in terms of pedagogical and functional moves or acts and the nature of teachers' explanations' and he finds that the most characteristic feature is the teacher's dominance in classroom discourse, approximately 70 per cent of the total. This verbal dominance can also be observed in a typical teacher behaviour called paraphrasing: teachers repeat what has already been said by the learners to ensure that what is being said is totally appropriate to the context and to show their personal approval:

> Teachers often *paraphrase* what children say, so as to present it back to them in a form which is considered by the teacher to be more compatible with the current stream of educational discourse. They also *reconstructively recap* what has been done by the children in class, so as to represent events in ways which fit their pedagogical framework. (Mercer 1994: 105)

Variability among teachers and among different classroom organizational models has also been reported. Instructional approaches based on the foundations of sociocultural theory imply that teacher verbal guidance would at certain moments of the course decrease to facilitate the learners to become truly self-directed. Within a constructivist vision of learning, Tharp and Gallimore (1994) report the following stages on the way towards learner autonomy:

(1) **modelling**;
(2) **scaffolding** vs. **shaping**. Shaping means simplifying a task by breaking it into a series of steps toward the goal, while scaffolding abridges the learner's role by means of graduated assistance from the expert;
(3) **encouraging, praising**;
(4) **instructing, questioning**;
(5) performance assisted by **the self** (at first, performance is not fully developed or automatized);
(6) **Feeding-back**.

Chaudron's (1993) review of the functional distribution of teacher talk reveals that teachers primarily tell things, get learners to do things, encourage them to say things and evaluate what learners do. In order to achieve their teaching goals, they model, repeat or expand teachers' and students' utterances, they clarify, request, check comprehension, confirm and repair in the language classroom when necessary what has been said or written. An affective view of the functions of teacher talk adds relevant information on how these functions can be better developed. Teachers may elicit responses in a way that produces negative affect; for example, their verbal expression ('Let's see if this time you can get it right') may be reinforced by their tone of voice, facial expression, etc. which imply that they do not expect a correct answer. On the contrary, they can smile and simply nominate a student to answer, facilitating the student's willingness to communicate. When eliciting responses, one technique that is useful both cognitively and affectively is the cooperative learning structure 'Think-pair-share' (Kagan 1994), where students are first given time to think of the answer ('How could we reduce violence in society?'), then they share with a partner and only after having had time to think and to practice what they want to say does the teacher finally ask them to 'go public'. Here, silence, also a part of teacher discourse, has the affective purpose of eliminating anxiety and inhibition by permitting the students to reflect and practise.

Many studies have been done on the importance of feedback for language learning (Corder 1981; Lightbown and Spada, 1990; Carroll *et al* 1992) but these generally refer to cognitive feedback. Stevick (1999) offers an interesting scheme in which we look at feedback along four main dimensions: cognitive, affective, external and internal. Each of these can be positive or negative. Thus, with external (teacher) feedback of a cognitive nature (what you said is correct/not correct) the student may receive both positive or negative feedback as helpful. However, if the feedback of an affective nature is negative (what you said is stupid, boring, doesn't interest me), the effect on the learner can be devastating. As Stevick (1999: 51) says, 'external affective feedback influences a learner's willingness to keep on trying to communicate in spite of occasional negative feedback of the external cognitive variety'. When determining their policy on error correction of spoken English, teachers need to consider not only what they want to correct but if the affective feedback they provide is negative. Constant praise or empty praise should also be avoided as students know perfectly well when they have accomplished something in an appropriate way. Instead, it is preferable to praise that part of an action that is correct and to signal what needs to be improved, for example, 'You were able to complete some of the exercises correctly, but you still need to work on your composition'. Knoll and Patti (2003: 42) note that '. . . teachers also know that true praise is specific rather than general. Instead of repeatedly saying, "Good job", they specify precisely what was good about the job, for example, "You identified some excellent resources for your group to use"'.

Ehrman and Dörnyei (1998) speak of the importance of empathy in the language classroom. Empathy can be expressed in teacher discourse in diverse ways. One is by learning and using students' names. As Dörnyei and Murphey (2003) note, a teacher knowing a student's name, and the student knowing that the teacher knows it, is extremely important for that student's constructed identity in that class. A student who even thinks the teacher does not know their name will often feel they are invisible in the group. Taylor (2005) adds the notion of perceptual position, referring to pronominal use, with first through fourth positions manifested respectively through I, you, they and we. She points to how the use in teacher discourse of the fourth position, *we* and related words such as everyone, can establish an empathic relationship with students. Gorham (1988: 50–1) suggests that the use of 'our' and 'we', addressing students by their name and asking their opinions is even more important in larger classes where it is harder to establish the atmosphere of psychological closeness that has been shown to have an influence on both motivation and cognitive learning.

5 Non-verbal teacher behaviour

Important though our words, or what Underhill (1999) calls our first voice, may be for teacher discourse, there are other non-linguistic aspects which greatly influence the affective impact of our discourse. As language teachers, we are often so focused on the 'essence' of our subject matter – verbal expression – that we may not be dedicating sufficient attention to the non-verbal aspects which relate to our discourse in the classroom and which are a vital source of support for the development of affect in teacher discourse. Some of the most significant of these are voice and vocal affect, eye contact, facial expression and proximity. It is essential that these be taken into account in the classroom because, as Ellis (1998) affirms, both the verbal and non-verbal channels are involved in students' assimilating content and relational information. In one study dealing with teacher immediacy (Richmond 1990) these behaviours, especially vocal variety, smiling and eye contact, were found to be responsible for a much greater variation in student motivation than factors related to use of power bases in the classroom in the study. They also found that immediacy, along with affinity-seeking variables (listening, disclosure of personal information, acting interested and involved in conversations, adapting messages to the student or situation, etc.) was more closely associated with cognitive learning than the power/behaviour alteration messages such as rewards, punishments, guilt or authority (Richmond 1990: 189, 191).

6 Voice and vocal affect

As language teachers our voice may well be our most important tool but unfortunately, teachers rarely receive any information regarding this. Not only is voice one of our main vehicles for providing language input, our voice is also a vehicle for presenting ourselves. If we are tired, enthused, angry,

never looks students in the eye seems to lack confidence and gives the students a sense of insecurity'. In addition to other benefits from making frequent and sensitive eye contact with students, such as monitoring comprehension and interest or determining aspects of classroom management, it can be an important part of Roger's 'unconditional positive regard' which helps students to feel accepted.

8 Facial expression

In any face-to-face communication our facial expression completes the meaning of our words. It helps the participants to understand each other's feelings, attitudes or other parts of the message we want to communicate. At times, it may be sufficient to carry the meaning of what we want to say; for example, when a student gives a correct answer, a smile may give more effective cognitive feedback than repeating mechanically 'Yes, that's right'. In conjunction with other body language, facial expression can be an effective, less-threatening form of error correction. Research (Chenoweth *et al* 1983) shows that learners want correction (and not only in grammar activities) but that insensitive policies of feedback on errors can lead to inhibition. Van Lier (1988) considers that correction by others is more likely to lead to negative affective reactions than self-correction; thus, facial expression could be an effective way to indicate to students that a mistake has been made which could be self-corrected.

Ellis (1998) has pointed out the importance of teachers communicating to their students that they are interested in them, and she points out that one way this is done is through facial expression. Similarly, teacher interest in the subject, a vital factor in developing learner interest, can be communicated through this channel.

9 Proximity

In the teacher-centred classroom, the teacher was generally found at the front of the class in a position of total control and authority, which conveyed the message, 'I have all the knowledge and you will pay full attention to what I say to get this knowledge.' In the social-constructivist view of learning all participants construct knowledge together and thus the teacher may also be found sometimes consulting with learners in groups or asking questions from other parts of the room so that she can relate to all students, not only those that sit in the first rows. In addition to what the teacher's words may be saying, her position in the classroom is telling students that she considers them part of the group.

10 Instructional conversations

In the EFL/ESL classroom teachers use the target language for many purposes: for classroom management and for pedagogical interventions, but also for establishing contexts of interaction in which students have the opportunity to use the language in authentic or semi-authentic ways to inter-act with others. This is an especially important function in EFL situations where the classroom may be the only option for interaction in the target language.

Describing how teachers through their 'conversations' can teach self-directed strategies and effective communication strategies that embrace lin-guistic and relational dimensions is not an easy task. Many language teachers rely on a non-conversational style of instruction that directly focuses on grammatical rules, vocabulary items and pattern drills (Tharp and Gallimore 1994). According to Donato (2000: 34) 'instructional conversations capture a wider range of communicative and cognitive functions of talk than current models of input, output, and interaction', that is to say, a conversational style capitalizes on strategies to facilitate language learning and on tactics to create significant discourse contexts where learners can freely express their thoughts. This conversational style is a main feature of humanistic approaches to language learning which claim that learners could optimize their learning process if they actively participate in class and develop their innate capacity for self-reflection on linguistic and vital issues. Stevick (1990: 60) explains one purpose of tasks in the humanistic methods:

> Some of the exercises employed by those methods encourage students to verbalize – to "share" with one another – their thoughts and feelings on a number of topics. At times, these topics are fairly personal, but proponents argue that their very immediacy and urgency allow the class to go beyond a mere quest for linguistic proficiency and to develop pride, self-confidence, and a sense of community.

In her research Johnson (1999: 37) presents the case of Sandra, a trainee teacher with a conflict between two goals: 'She feels compelled to be that teacher who "teaches the language" while at the same time is driven by an inner desire to recreate language learning experiences for her students that allow them to express who they are and what they know'. Sandra tells of establishing sufficient rapport through conversations with her students so they 'realized I was interested in hearing their ideas . . . At moments like these, they poke a few holes in the language barrier, and they can communi-cate as the people they are inside' (Johnson 1999: 36). Basically, what she is referring to is her ability to confirm learners.

11 Conclusion

Teacher discourse can facilitate the process of language learning, both as an immediate and a life-long activity, in different ways. Cognitively, teachers need to structure their discourse so that it is comprehensible and organized in ways that make the language easier to assimilate. This is important, but it is quite possibly even more important that affective aspects of discourse be taken into account and that teachers both verbally and non-verbally create a true learning environment where students believe in the value of learning a language, where they feel they can face that challenge and where they understand the benefit they can get from attaining it.

References

Arnold, J. and Brown, H. D. (1999), 'A map of the terrain', in J. Arnold (ed.), *Affect in Language Learning*. Cambridge: Cambridge University Press, pp. 1–24.

Busnel, M. C. (1979), 'Mesures intravaginales du niveau et des distorsions acoustiques de bruits maternels'. *Electrodiagnostique Therapie*, 16, 142.

Buber, M. (1965), *Between Man and Man*. New York: Macmillan.

Carroll, S., Swain, M. and Roberge, Y. (1992), 'The role of feedback in adult second language acquisition: error correction and morphological generalizations'. *Applied Psycho-Linguistics*, 13, 173–98.

Chastain, K. (1988), *Developing Second-Language Skills. Theory and Practice*. San Diego: Harcourt Brace Jovanovich Publishers.

Chaudron, C. (1993), *Second Language Classrooms. Research on Teaching and Learning*. Cambridge: Cambridge University Press.

Chenoweth, A., Day, R., Chum, R. A. and Lupescu, S. (1983), 'Attitudes and preferences of nonnative speakers to corrective feedback'. *Studies in Second Language Acquisition* 6, 79–87.

Corder, S. (1981), *Error Analysis and Interlanguage*. Oxford: Oxford University Press.

Donato, R. (2000), 'Sociocultural contributions to understanding the foreign and second language Classroom', in J. Lantolf (ed.), *Sociocultural Theory and Second Language Learning*. Oxford: Oxford University Press, pp. 27–50.

Dörnyei, Z. and Murphey, T. (2003), *Group Dynamics in the Language Classroom*. Cambridge: Cambridge University Press.

Duncan, H. D. (1967), 'The search for a social theory of communication in American sociology', in F. Dance (ed.), *Human Communication Theory*. New York: Holt, Rinehart and Winston, pp. 240–52.

Ehrman, M. and Dörnyei, Z. (1998), *Interpersonal Dynamics in the Language Classroom: The Visible and Invisible Classroom*. Thousand Oaks, CA: SAGE.

Ellis, R. (1985), *Understanding Second Language Acquisition*. Oxford: Oxford University Press.

Ellis, R. (1994), *The Study of Second Language Acquisition*. Oxford: Oxford University Press.

Ellis, K. (1998), 'The relationship among perceived teacher confirmation, cognitive learning and affective learning' (unpublished doctoral dissertation: University of Colorado, Denver).

Ellis, K. (2004), 'The importance of perceived teacher confirmation'. *Communication Education*, 53, 1–20.

Fernald, A. (1993), 'Approval and disapproval: Infant responsiveness to vocal affect in familiar and unfamiliar languages'. *Child Development*, 64, 657–74.

Feu Guijarro, Mª J. and Piñero Gil, E. (1996), 'El mundo sonoro infantil y la adquisición del lenguaje.' *Música, Arte y Proceso*, 2, 39–49.

Fonseca Mora, M. C. (2001), 'Los contornos melódicos como señalizadores de la fuerza ilocutiva del discurso del profesor de L2'. *Estudios de Lingüística Inglesa Aplicada, ELIA*, 2, 57–68.

Fonseca Mora, M. C. (2002), *The Role of the Musicality of Language in the Acquisition Process of English as a Second Language*. Ann Arbor, MI: UMI.

Gorham, J. (1988), 'The relationship between verbal teacher immediacy behaviors and student learning'. *Communication Education*, 37, 39–53.

Gower, R. and Walters, S. (1983), *Teaching Practice Handbook*. Oxford: Heinemann.

Jensen, E. (1998), *Teaching with the Brain in Mind*. Alexandria, VA: Association for Supervision and Curriculum Development.

Johnson, K. (1999), *Understanding Language Teaching*. Boston: Heinle and Heinle.

Kagan, S. (1994), *Cooperative Learning*. San Clemente, CA: Kagan Cooperative Learning.

Knoll, M. and Patti, J. (2003), 'Social-Emotional learning and academic achievement', in M. J. Elias, H. Arnold and C. Steiger Hussey (eds), *EQ + IQ = Best Leadership Practices for Caring and Successful Schools*. Thousand Oaks, CA: Corwin Press, pp. 36–49.

Lantolf. J. and Appel, G. (eds) (1994), *Vygotskian Approaches to Second Language Research*. Norwood, NJ: Ablex.

León, I. (2005), 'La confirmación del profesor de inglés percibida por el alumnado en educación secundaria' (unpublished MA thesis: University of Seville).

Lightbown, P. and Spada, N. (1990), 'Focus-on-form and corrective feedback in communicative language teaching: effects on second language learning'. *Studies in Second Language Acquisition*, 12, 429–48.

MacIntyre, P., Clément, R., Dörnyei, Z. and Noels, K. (1998), 'Conceptualizing willingness to communicate in a L2: A situational model of L2 confidence and affiliation'. *Modern Language Journal*, 82, 545–62.

Maley, A. (2000), *The Language Teacher's Voice*. Oxford: Macmillan Heinemann.

Mercer, N. (1994), 'Neo-Vygotskian theory and classroom education', in B. Stierer and J. Maybin (eds), *Language, Literacy and Learning in Educational Practice*. Clevedon, Avon: Multilingual Matters, pp. 92–110.

Moorman, C. and Weber, N. (1989), *Teacher Talk: What it Really Means*. Saginanaw, MI: Personal Power Press.

Nattinger, J. and DeCarrico, J. (1993), *Lexical Phrases and Language Teaching*. Oxford: Oxford University Press.

Pajares, M. F. (1992), 'Teachers' beliefs and educational research: Cleaning up a messy construct'. *Review of Educational Research*, 62, (3), 307–32.

Papousek, M. (1994), 'Melodies in caregivers' speech: A species-specific learning guidance towards language'. *Early Development and Parenting*. 3, 5–17.

Papousek, M. (1996), 'Intuitive parenting', in I. Deliège and J. Sloboda (eds), *Musical Beginnings: Origins and Development of Musical Competence*. Oxford: Oxford University Press, pp. 88–112.

Querleu, D., Renard, X., Versyp, F., Paris-Delrue, L. and Crépin, G. (1988), 'Fetal hearing'. *European Journal of Obstetrics and Reproductive Biology*, 29, 191–212.

Richmond, V. (1990), 'Communication in the classroom: Power and motivation'. *Communication Education*, 39, 181–95.

Rogers, C. (1969), *Freedom to Learn: A View of What Education May Become*. Columbus, OH: Merrill.

Schuman, J. (1994), 'Where is cognition?'. *Studies in Second Language Acquisition*, 16, 231–42.

Sieburg, E. (1985), *Family Communication: An Integrated Systems Approach*. New York: Gardner Press.

Sinclair, J. and Brazil, D. (1982), *Teacher Talk*. Oxford: Oxford University Press.

Snow, C. E. (1972), 'Mother's speech to children learning language'. *Child Development*, 43, 549–65.

Stern, D., Spieker, S. and MacKaine, K. (1982), 'Intonation contours as signals in maternal speech of prelinguistic infants'. *Development Psychology* 18, (5), 727–35.

Stevick, E. W. (1990), *Humanism in Language Teaching*. Oxford: Oxford University Press.

Stevick, E. W. (1999), 'Affect in learning and memory', in J. Arnold, (ed.), *Affect in Language Learning*. Cambridge: Cambridge University Press, pp. 43–57.

Taylor, L. (2005), 'Investigating affect through analysis of teacher generated language'. Presentation given at TESOL Spain, Seville, March 2005.

Tharp, R. G. and Gallimore, R. (1994), *Rousing Minds to Life: Teaching, Learning and Schooling in Social Context*. Cambridge: Cambridge University Press.

Tomatis, A. (1991), *The Conscious Ear*. New York: Station Hill Press.

Underhill, A. (1999), 'Facilitation in language teaching', in J. Arnold (ed.), *Affect in Language Learning*. Cambridge: Cambridge University Press, pp. 125–41.

Van Lier, L. (1988), *The Classroom and the Language Learner*. London: Longman.

Vygotsky, L. S. (1978), *Mind in Society: the Development of Higher Psychological Processes*. Cambridge: Harvard University Press.

Watzlawick, P., Bavelas, J. and Jackson, D. (1967), *Pragmatics of Human Communication*. New York: W.W. Norton.

Williams, M. and Burden, R. (1997), *Psychology for Language Teachers*. Cambridge, Cambridge University Press.

8 The attitudes of language learners towards target varieties of the language

Ivor Timmis

1 Introduction

We take it for granted that children acquire different varieties of their native language. It is likely, though not guaranteed, that a child growing up in Quebec will acquire a different variety of French than a child growing up in Paris; it is likely, though not guaranteed, that a child growing up in Manchester will acquire a different variety of English than a child growing up in New York. In most cases, this phenomenon is easy to account for: children will generally acquire the variety to which they are predominantly exposed, and a child growing up in Quebec is obviously more likely to have exposure to Quebec French than Parisian French. In some cases, however, it is more difficult to explain why children acquire different varieties of the first language. I would like to take an anecdotal example to illustrate the point. Two children are born in Stirling, Scotland to English parents who have moved there for work. The mother speaks RP British English and the father a Northern English variety of British English. At the time of writing, the older child (13) speaks with a noticeable Scottish accent and some other features of Scottish English such as 'wee' to mean small; the younger child (9) does not sound Scottish at all. In this case it seems unlikely that we can account for the difference in the variety in terms of exposure, especially as they have thus far attended the same schools. It seems likely that we will have to account for this difference in terms of the boys' attitudes, either conscious or subconscious, to the local variety. It is a well established notion in sociolinguistics (Wardhaugh 2005) that the variety of a language a speaker acquires, and even the variety a speaker chooses to use at a particular moment, can be influenced by the speakers' attitude to the peer group. A desire for inclusion will generally lead the speaker to adopt the variety of the peer group. One explanation for the speech differences of the two boys in this case, then, might be that they have different attitudes to the peer group.

Differences in exposure and peer group orientation will obviously still be relevant in the case of learners who are acquiring a second language in the second language environment (e.g. immigrant children), but they are less obviously relevant in the case of learners outside the second language environment who may not have extensive exposure to a particular variety and who do not have an immediate peer group of target language speakers. L2 learners' attitudes to the target variety of the language are likely to influence their motivation to learn the language which, in turn, is highly likely to influence their success in acquiring the language. In this chapter we will ask how and why L2 learners' attitudes to target varieties of the language are likely to affect motivation and we will address the following questions in relation to English Language Teaching (ELT):

(1) Why has the question of target varieties become so important in the context of ELT?
(2) What attitudes might learners have to different target varieties of English?
(3) Why are these attitudes important?
(4) What can teachers and other educators do to ensure that learners' acquisition is not negatively affected by their attitude to the target variety of English? Is there anything teachers and educators can do to help learners to have a positive attitude to the target variety?

2. Learner Attitudes and Motivation

Ellis (1994) argues that learners show different attitudes to:

(1) the target language;
(2) the target language speakers;
(3) the target language culture;
(4) the social value of learning the L2;
(5) particular uses of the L2;
(6) themselves as members of their own cultures.

This categorization is a good starting point for our discussion as it immediately raises a number of interesting questions. First, we need to question how far, or indeed, whether, it is possible to disentangle attitudes to the target language or, in our case, target variety of the language from attitudes to the speakers and the culture of that target variety. It would seem to be very difficult, perhaps impossible. There is a consensus among linguists that no language can be seen to be superior to another in purely linguistic terms – no functioning natural language is inherently more systematic, more complex or richer than any other, although these qualities are frequently attributed to particular languages. This consensus among linguists does not prevent, of course, lay people from making judgements about particular languages, sometimes quite strong ones: a Turkish student once told me in all seriousness that the Kurdish language 'has no grammar'. If such judgements are not based on linguistic grounds, it follows, then, that preferences for one language over another, for one variety over another, are likely to be motivated by social judgements. A second question which arises from Ellis' categorization is why learners' might differ in their attitude to the social value of learning the L2, particular uses of it and themselves as members of their own culture. I would like to use two quotations collected from Indian students in the course of my own research (Timmis 2003) to throw light on this question:

> [I am learning English because] English is becoming a common language in day to day communication, though not for our emotional feelings.

> I am learning English only as a mean of universal way to speak. And not as a impression upon our regional and national languages.

These students have clear and conscious views of the social value of learning English, purposes for which they want (and do not want) to use and learn English and of their responsibilities to their own culture. There is no reason to suppose, however, that all students in that context would share their views, or even their degree of awareness.

3 The nature of attitudes

Having established that learners might have attitudes towards different aspects of the target language variety, it will be useful to make some general observations about the nature of attitudes. Ellis (1994) considers attitudes to be one of a set of social variables with the potential to impact on acquisition. He goes on to note the following features of attitudes:

- They can change over time.
- They are a matter of degree rather than being absolutes.
- They are socially determined.
- They have the capacity to influence action, but do not necessarily determine it.

For our purposes, it is also important to observe that attitudes can be difficult to measure for two reasons:

(1) It is not clear how far the kinds of attitudes we are talking about are conscious.
(2) In terms of research, attitudes are probably most amenable to measurement by self-report questionnaire. Though much of my own research in this area is based on questionnaires, I would not argue that they are precision instruments. One can never exclude the possibility of bias and misunderstanding, and one can never be sure that respondents are giving a sincere rather than face-saving answer ('social desirability bias').

Nevertheless, I would argue strongly that the difficulty of measuring attitudes should not prevent us from trying. One of the problems with such debate as there has been about the issue of learners' attitudes to target language varieties is that much of it has been conducted by proxy, with expert commentators with little or no reference to the attested attitudes of learners (Widdowson 1994; Modiano 2001; Alptekin 2002). The actual attitudes of learners have, I would argue, an important role to play in the argument.

4 Language learning and identity

Why should the kinds of attitudes we have discussed above matter? A learner in Japan, for example, might have the choice of American English, British English, Australian English or, more speculatively, some yet-to-be defined World Standard English. The matter is even more complicated when there is one or more local varieties as well, as for example in Singapore, Nigeria, or India, though in these cases the extent of exposure to a particular variety may make the notion of choice rather hypothetical. Why should the learner have a preference, and why should it matter? Again, our initial answer can be simple, one word in fact: identity. But as before, the simple answer raises another question: why is identity involved in the learning process?

Norton (1997: 410) defines identity as '. . . how people understand their relationship to the world, how that relationship is constructed across time and space and how people understand their possibilities for the future'. She then goes on to argue that it is through language that learners negotiate their social identity and that their degree of 'investment' in a language is crucial. For others (Prodromou 1997a, 1997b; Modiano 2001; Alptekin 2002), it is the learner's cultural identity which is at stake with the target language variety acting as a kind of Trojan horse for the cultural values of its native speaker community. We will return to this question of social and cultural identity when we discuss learners' attitudes in the context of ELT.

For a critical overview of the literature on identity in L2 learning see Ricento (2005).

5 Attitudes to the target variety and the effect on motivation

If we accept the argument that learners' social and cultural identities are necessarily involved in the language learning process, we can clearly see that learners' attitudes to target language varieties have strong potential to affect motivation. What kind of effect should we expect? Ellis (1994: 200) expresses the commonsense argument that 'In general, positive attitudes towards the L2 and its speakers, and its culture can be expected to enhance learning'. Motivation in terms of positive attitudes to the L2 and its speakers can be regarded as an affective factor in language acquisition. Arnold and Brown (1999) define affect as 'aspects of emotion, feeling, mood or attitude which condition behaviour'. An interest in the role of affect in language acquisition is not new – Krashen and Terrell (1983) posited the notion of the affective filter – but there has been a recent emphasis in language teaching research on the importance of affect in language acquisition (see Arnold 1999). Schumann (1999) argues that there is a neurobiological basis for relating positive affect to language acquisition. In terms of our argument, evidence from affect research would suggest that there is a much stronger link between positive attitudes and successful acquisition: positive attitudes will not just 'enhance learning' (Ellis 1994: 200); positive attitudes are central to effective acquisition.

It is important to note, however, that this need not be the case. Ellis refers to the phenomenon of 'Machiavellian motivation', where negative attitudes to the target language community actually lead to a stronger motivation to learn the language because of a desire to exert control over that community. I think the following quotation from a teacher collected in the course of my research (Timmis 2003) sheds interesting light on this kind of motivation: '[Ultimately, I would like my students to be able to] switch between a socio-politically dominant variety of English and "accent of their country" and use this ability both for advancement and resistance'.

5 Varieties and the changing face of the English-speaking world

We have acknowledged that the question of learners' attitudes to target language varieties is not unique to ELT. In this respect, it is interesting that, in the context of French teaching, Salien (1998) mounts 'a defense of Quebecois as an acceptable and teachable form of the French language' and speaks of 'international French'. We also argued, however, that there are reasons why the question is of particular current relevance in ELT. It is to these reasons that we now turn.

The rapid growth in the international use of English is much discussed and something we are all aware of, even if the pace of this growth is understandably difficult to capture in figures. For the purposes of this chapter, however, I am going to argue that the following estimate about English language use is particularly significant: 'So, if current population and learning trends continue. . . Within 10 years there will certainly be more L2 speakers than L1 speakers. Within 50 years there could be up to 50 per cent more' (Crystal 1997a: 11). Indeed, there have already been estimates that up to 80 per cent of communication in English is between non-native speakers. We may or may not agree with Crystal (1997a: 10) that 'world English exists as a political and cultural reality', but it is clear that the face of the English-speaking world is changing significantly. If we want to talk about the different varieties of English available for learners, we will need to make sense of the wide, varied and growing use of English. The division of the English-speaking world into 'three circles', proposed by Kachru (1982), is a well known and influential attempt to provide a descriptive model of the English-speaking world.

The three circles are characterized thus by White (1997: 1) and Crystal (1997b: 53–4):

(1) The inner circle refers to the traditional bases of English, where it is the primary language. Included in this circle are the USA, the UK, Ireland, Canada, Australia and New Zealand. The varieties used here are

'norm-providing'. In other words, they set the standards for other varieties to follow.

(2) The extended circle includes countries and territories where English has long been established and plays an important institutional role and an important 'lingua franca' role in a multilingual setting. India, Pakistan, Singapore, Nigeria and over 50 other territories are included in this circle. The varieties in this circle are not 'norm-providing', but 'norm-developing'.

(3) The expanding circle includes countries which recognize the current importance of English as an international language. However, these countries were not colonized by inner circle countries and English has no special status within the country itself. These varieties are 'norm-dependent'.

It is important to acknowledge that this model has come under attack for two main reasons:

(1) It is an oversimplification which blurs important distinctions within the circles, particularly within the outer circle.

(2) By placing native speaker communities in the centre and describing them as 'norm-providing', it seems to present native speaker dominance of the English-speaking world as a permanent feature.

In spite of these weaknesses, I am going to argue that it is a serviceable model for an initial exploration of the English-speaking world as it does capture something of the historical development of English and the socio-political contexts in which it is used.

This rapid and continuing growth of the international use of English has led to some commentators (Widdowson 1994; Graddol 1998) raising questions about the 'ownership' of English. The question is clearly an important one for us in considering learners' attitudes to different varieties of English. It is argued that native speakers will soon be a minority constituency in the English-speaking world: 'English speakers of North America, the British Isles and the Antipodes will become minority stakeholders in the language' (Graddol 1998: 24). Widdowson (1994) asks if standard British English has any genuine claim to be 'the real thing' among the different Englishes which have emerged. He points out that advocates of standard British English argue that the maintenance of this standard will facilitate international communication. He argues, however, that grammatical conformity to standard British English is not crucial to communication and that the language has grown beyond the legitimate control of the native speaker community. In similar vein, Alptekin (2002) argues that if preferred language patterns are socially determined, it is not appropriate to impose these on any other community. We are faced with a situation where non-native use of English is rapidly gaining ground and where we can no longer assume that learners will have the need or desire to interact with native speakers. Ellis (1994) notes that learners tend to favour the prestige variety of a language and that much second language acquisition research has been based on this assumption. We have shown in this section, however, that it is no longer axiomatic that learners will see native speaker varieties as the prestige varieties to learn.

6 Questioning native speaker target varieties

A number of commentators have indeed challenged the validity of native speaker varieties as a target. Alptekin (2002: 63) challenges the validity of the native speaker model on a broad level, arguing that, given the increasing international use of English, we should be aiming for 'intercultural communicative competence' rather than a version of communicative competence based on the native speaker: 'With its standardised norms, the [native speaker] model is found to be utopian, unrealistic, and constraining in relation to English as an International language (EIL)' (Alptekin 2002: 57). It is utopian, he argues, as it perpetuates the 'linguistic myth' of the native speaker and tends to a 'monolithic portrayal' of native speaker culture. It is unrealistic in that it does not take proper account of the lingua franca status of English, and constraining in that it 'circumscribes both teacher and learner autonomy by associating the concept of authenticity with the social milieu of the native speaker' (Alptekin 2002: 57).

Jenkins (1998: 119) is concerned with the implications of the international use of English for pronunciation teaching: 'The recent growth in the use of English as an International Language has led to changes in learners' pronunciation needs and goals'. Jenkins (1998) suggests that the majority of learners no longer aspire to a native-like accent and that their main motivation is not to communicate with native speakers. Although Jenkins (1998) refers exclusively to pronunciation concerns, her arguments, as they are concerned with questions of sociocultural appropriateness and international intelligibility, are central to the wider debate about which model of English we should offer our learners.

Jenkins (1998) observes that there has not been much research into the English used among non-native speakers and that as far as pronunciation is concerned the emphasis has been on intelligibility for the native speaker receiver. Her focus, however, is on intelligibility in an international context and her recommendations are clear and specific: 'We should concentrate the productive focus of pronunciation teaching on the three areas that appear to have the greatest influence on intelligibility in EIL i.e. certain segmentals, nuclear stress (the main stress in the word group) and the effective use of articulatory setting to the extent that it underpins the first two areas' (Jenkins 1998: 121). In terms of pronunciation, Jenkins (1998: 124) advocates: 'A universal, realistically learnable and teachable core, based on the native speaker model ("model" being singular in the sense that the designated areas are common to all native varieties) which are then fleshed out according to a wide range of acceptable, local non-native norms'. More recently, Jenkins (2006) has emphasized the need to teach accommodation strategies so that intelligibility will depend less on the technical production of particular sounds and more on the willingness and capacity to adjust to other varieties.

Willis (1999), as he acknowledges, takes up Jenkins' arguments about the need to adapt goals and models in the context of English as an International Language and applies these argument to grammar. Willis (1999) introduces another dimension to the traditional accuracy/fluency distinction with the notion of conformity. 'Conformity' is the attainment of native speaker norms, whereas 'accuracy' is consistent and intelligible production so that the speaker communicates what he or she wants to say.

Willis (1999) questions the validity of aspiring to native speaker norms on the grounds of both principles and pragmatism, posing the following questions for teachers:

(1) Are you aiming at conformity to a native speaker standard? If so, which native speaker standard are you aiming at and can you define it?
(2) How many of your students need to achieve this native speaker standard and how many are likely ever to achieve it?

According to Willis (1999), rather than aiming at native speaker conformity, then, 'What we should be doing is helping them to develop a negotiable dialect of English. . . . Provided they have this ability their deviations from the standard form are no more important than the deviations displayed by native speakers'. It is interesting in this respect that Graddol (1998: 24) considers that these skills of negotiation may, in themselves, form an important part of the learning process: 'Learners will need to examine some of the strategies required for negotiating understanding with others who use either different varieties of English or who speak very little of the language. Such skills will be a basic requirement of world citizens'.

Carter (1998: 43) focuses on the cultural aspect of taking native speaker varieties as a target: 'Do we want the native speaker as our model, particularly if it means we have to take the native speaker culture too?'. As we noted earlier, it can be argued that a native speaker target variety of the language will act as a Trojan horse for the native speaker culture. It seems particularly unnecessary to risk this kind of 'enculturation' if the learners are unlikely ever to come into contact with the native speaker culture. Modiano (2001: 343) notes that global communication and cultural diversity are competing forces:

While on the one hand there is a call for a language of wider communication, for a common space, we have on the other hand a sincere desire to preserve cultural diversity. These two movements, which are contradictory, are bound to result in conflict and irresolution.

Prodromou (1997a: 13) is concerned about English as a vehicle for American domination:

but to put it even more directly, the teaching and learning of English today, though not completely identified with the pursuit of the American dream, are inseparable from United States hegemony worldwide – English is both an instrument for furthering American interests and in turn it is furthered by the successful promotion of those interests.

It seems, then, that the native speaker model carries with it the threat of cultural and linguistic imperialism. Modiano (2001: 339) summarizes this threat: 'Those who view the spread of English as linguistic imperialism question the English language teaching and learning enterprise because, from their point of view, it compromises the cultural integrity of the non-native speaker'. Modiano (2001: 340) goes on to link this threat to cultural integrity specifically with conformity to native speaker target varieties:

> For learners who primarily want to acquire the language because it is a cross-cultural communicative tool, pressure to attain near-native proficiency may result in establishing them as auxiliary members of the culture which is represented by the prescriptive educational standard, something not in harmony with their own self-image.

Alptekin (2002: 58) speaks of the dangers of 'enculturation' if learners are forced to 'convey appropriate, coherent and strategically effective meanings for the native speaker'. Enculturation, for Alptekin (2002: 58) involves acquiring 'new cultural frames of reference and a new world view, reflecting those of the target language culture and its speakers'.

7 In defence of native speaker target varieties

We have examined above some of the questions raised about using a native speaker model to teach English for use in an international context. We need to recognize, however, that there may be dangers in moving away from a native speaker model. Cook (2002) notes that any fully-fledged language, whether it is widely spoken or spoken only by a small community, must be rich enough to fulfil all the varying communicative needs of its speakers. Davies (1991) has argued that, for example, speakers of Singaporean English, as they do not use that language for all their communicative purposes, may simply not get enough exposure to Singaporean English to achieve full competence in it. Similarly, to use evidence from my own research (Timmis 2003), when my Nigerian interviewee tells me that she uses English formally, at work, but a local language for all other purposes, is it not likely that her variety of English will lack an affective dimension simply through lack of exposure? While Jenkins (1998) argues that we should focus on those aspects of phonology that are teachable and learnable, there is a danger of confusing 'what is teachable and learnable' with what can be conveniently systematized for teaching purposes. We should note, however, Jenkins' (1998) insistence that she is not arguing for some kind of minimalist lingua franca, but for a mutually intelligible core to be the focus of teaching with non-core elements supplied by local varieties. It is not clear, however, where, for example, a Hungarian student would look for non-core elements, unless we are going to class European English as a variety – but this itself could be classed as a lingua franca short on non-core elements.

'We need to be careful that in paring down the syllabus, we do not force the learner to "accept" a role which is less desirable than he would ordinarily achieve' (Harder 1980: 268). To illustrate what may be lost by a precipitate paring down of the syllabus, I would like to take an example from my own experience which shows the affective function of ellipsis. While writing to a professional colleague from another institution, I was uncertain whether to end the letter:

> *'Look forward to seeing you shortly.'*
> or
> *'I look forward to seeing you shortly.'*

I felt they struck quite different tones and I was not sure which to use as I had friendly relations with this colleague, but he was in a formal relationship to the university (external examiner). Such grammatical choices are not a matter of life and death, but they can make a difference to how relationships are established and maintained

There is nothing wrong, of course, with trying to focus on those structures which will be maximally useful to our students in EIL, but we need to be careful that we do not focus exclusively on the transactional to the detriment of the interactional. We do not want our students to be reduced, in Harder's (1980: 268) words, to the status of 'a coarse and primitive character from an interactional point of view'.

8 Learner attitudes to varieties of English

As we argued earlier, one of the problems with the debate about target varieties is that it is not a debate in which the voices of learners have been heard (Timmis 2002). We have already made the case that a positive attitude to the target variety is likely, though not certain, to enhance acquisition, so the actual attitudes of learners will be of real importance to us. Jenkins (1998: 125) sounds an interesting warning note: '. . . it is important that we should all guard against political correctness in the sense of telling our learners what their goals should be: in particular that they should not want to sound like native speakers if they clearly wish to do so'. It is quite possible that our learners will actually want a native speaker model. We may well be persuaded ourselves by the arguments of Jenkins (1998), Willis (1999), Modiano (2001) and Alptekin (2002), but what if our learners do not hold such views? If we insisted on moving away from target varieties against their wishes, would we not, to use Alptekin's phrase 'constrain the autonomy' of the learners?

Timmis (2002; 2003) carried out a survey designed to investigate learners' (and teachers') attitudes to conforming to native speaker norms. The survey involved over 400 students in 15 countries and Timmis (2002) reached the following tentative conclusions:

(1) There remains a significant attachment to native speaker norms, and it seems to be greater among learners than teachers. Learners who aspire to native speaker norms often do so even when they know they are unlikely to attain them or to need them.
(2) There is less attachment to native speaker norms in outer circle countries (in this case, South Africa, India and Pakistan).

Timmis (2002) concedes that it would be ludicrous to suggest that such a survey can give an accurate picture of learners' attitudes in general, but it does show that, just as we cannot assume that learners will prefer a native speaker target variety, we cannot assume that we will not. We also need to be aware that learners' views may differ from those of teachers or expert commentators and question whether we have the right to foist our views on learners. To illustrate a number of issues relating to learners' attitudes to native speaker target varieties, I would like to refer in some detail to an interview carried out for my own research (Timmis 2003).

The interviewee, "R", lives in Nigeria where she is a women's group leader. Her work involves giving seminars and workshops in different parts of the country. She conducts the seminars and workshops in English, so she is effectively using English as a lingua franca for professional purposes. Her stated motivation for coming to England, however, was to 'improve her pronunciation', 'to learn how words are said'. It emerged that the people in her workshop groups had no problems understanding her, but she felt the need to improve her pronunciation because the workshops were sometimes attended by Nigerian doctors and lawyers. It is interesting that though she came to England to improve her pronunciation, she had no particular desire to 'sound like these people'. On the other hand, she admitted to being quite gratified when a neighbour remarked that she was making progress and beginning to sound like 'one of us'. When I put it to her that adopting a native speaker accent might compromise her cultural identity, she was quite emphatic: 'I know I'm black, I know I'm African, I just want to speak English like you'. 'R' also mentioned on a number of occasions that she would not use all she had learned in England when she returned to Nigeria: if she used colloquial language, for example, she would not be understood, and would be regarded as showing off.

This interview then highlighted a number of themes from my research into learners' attitudes to native speaker norms:

- The weak link between stated motivation and actual aspiration as a language learner: learners may aspire to native speaker performance even when they clearly do not need it.
- The idea that there is, somewhere, one correct way to speak English (the

use of the passive in 'to learn how words are said' is interesting in this respect).

- The notion that native speaker English confers prestige.
- The notion that acquiring native speaker proficiency is a benchmark of achievement.
- The fact that it is difficult to disentangle the prestige notion from the benchmark notion.
- The fact that students seem to be less worried about and less sensitive to issues of cultural identity than teachers and expert commentators are on their behalf.
- The idea that students can be flexible communicators who can adapt their language to the communicative context.

9 Implications for classroom practice

How can we deal with the question of target varieties in a principled way? The tenor of my argument above is clearly that we should consult learners, but this alone is not enough. Learners may be too young to have formed a view, learners in the same context may have conflicting views, learners may differ in how consciously they hold their views, and learners' views may change over time. Willis (1999) gives a set of options which provide an interesting framework for discussion. We will discuss each of the six options in turn.

9.1 Option 1: Teach standard British English

Willis (1999) considers this to be both 'undesirable and impractical'. It is certainly undesirable to force British English on our students and probably impractical to expect many of our students to approximate to native speaker standard. It would certainly seem to be perverse to carry on without making any adjustments at all, oblivious to the changing face of the English-speaking world. British English does seem, however, still to be an attraction for many students. There are extensive, but not, of course, complete grammatical descriptions of British English, so it represents a definable target for students and one which, rightly or wrongly, they recognize as 'authentic'. The same arguments would, of course, apply to American English or other native speaker varieties.

9.2 Option 2: Define a form of 'International English' and teach that

There is, as Willis (1999) acknowledges, a formidable problem of description to be overcome before this becomes a viable option. Willis (1999) is also concerned that even if we could satisfactorily describe International English, to teach it would be simply to 'substitute one form of tyranny for another'. Crystal (1997a) is far more positive about this option: 'Eventually, I imagine, we will all be teaching World Standard English, once it exists, rather than British, American, or any other regional English, unless there are grounds for not doing so'. The international English option is also supported by Modiano (2001: 344):

> The teaching and learning of a geographically, politically and culturally 'neutral' form of English, which is perceived as a language of wider communication and not as the possession of the native speaker, is one of the few options we have at hand if we want to continue to promote English language learning while at the same time attempting to 'neutralize' the impact which the spread of English has on the cultural integrity of the learner.

Widdowson (1994: 385) suggests that given the desire to be mutually intelligible and the global communication network, International English will tend to 'stabilize'. Timmis (2003) showed that, while most teachers would be willing to teach this hypothetical form of English, there was no great enthusiasm for it, one common objection being that its cultural neutrality would make it a bland variety to learn and teach. It is certainly questionable whether an international variety of English could ever be codified, and it may be more fruitful as Roberts (personal communication) suggests, to speak of English for International Purposes rather than International English. This might well involve considerable re-prioritizing of the language forms we teach, and may well involve a greater role for teaching communication strategies such as accommodation, but it would not involve teaching a new variety of English.

9.3 Option 3: Offer a range of Englishes in the classroom

The problem here, as Willis (1999) points out, is that there is real potential for confusion, even frustration in the classroom. If I returned to my French studies, for example, I would not want to face an indiscriminate mix of Parisian French, Tunisian French, Senegalese French, Quebecois and Martinique French. That is not to say, however, that I would not enjoy the occasional song or story presented in one of these varieties or the occasional text discussing the development and nature of the variety. The notion that you can prepare learners in any practical way for the range of varieties they are likely to meet outside the classroom seems to me to be fanciful. Occasional exposure to Indian English, for example, is unlikely to help learners with decoding problems when they meet Indian English outside the classroom. It may well be, however, that in engendering a more positive attitude to varieties we can help our learners with communication. As Kramsch (2002) remarked, goodwill is a very important factor in communication. Goodwill itself is not teachable, but a respect for other varieties, a willingness to accommodate, and some idea of how to accommodate may be areas where we can help our learners. There are obvious implications for teacher education here. In this respect, it is interesting that Crandall (2003) refers to a

World Englishes and Their Speakers programme at the University of Maryland whose aims are to:

- foster increased understanding of the cultures and communities of World English speakers;
- help create an awareness of the varieties of English spoken by these students;
- identify ways of validating these students' English varieties and assisting them in acquiring the standard American English expected in their classrooms; and
- provide strategies to assist these students in developing academic literacy and skills.

Crandall (2003) also has a number of practical and specific suggestions for fostering a positive attitude to variety. Although these are designed for learners who speak other varieties of English and are studying in the USA, many of the ideas seem transferable to other contexts:

- Introduce literature (folk tales, stories, proverbs, etc.) in which different English varieties are used.
- Engage students in written dialogues with teachers where they can use their variety of English but also see the standard American English forms in the teacher's responses.
- Allow the use of different varieties in prewriting and drafting of papers and in language experience stories.
- Base early writing assignments on personal, family or traditional stories.
- Include students' writings in the collection of texts that students read.
- Engage students in investigating language differences, language attitudes, and dialect diversity.

9.4 Option 4: Offer successful L2 speakers as models

What Willis (1999) has in mind here is that a group of French learners of English could be offered successful French learners of English as models. Alptekin (2002: 63) also argues that 'successful bilinguals' would make good models, especially because of their 'intercultural insights and knowledge'. Willis (1999) concedes that this may be a hard option to sell, and we can also ask how this applies to the multilingual classroom. It is legitimate to ask, too, why the native speaker should be left completely out of the picture if it turns out that students want exposure to native speakers. It is possible, however, that, as with the previous option, we could fashion a judicious compromise. Cook (2003) makes a strong case for a more positive portrayal of learners or, to use his term, L2 users, in course materials. We can extend this argument from L2 users to L1 culture. Alptekin (2002) argues for materials which are based in the local culture, but there is no evidence that this is what learners want and we would risk negative attitudes, and negative affect, by going against what they want. A positive portrayal of L1 cultures, however, along-side a more critical portrayal of the target variety culture seems to be a more principled option.

9.5 Option 5: Give learners exposure to native speaker English but adopt a C-R [consciousness-raising] methodology which places a very low premium on conformity

As this is clearly Willis' (1999) favoured option I will quote him in full on this one:

> See language as a meaning system and encourage learners to develop their own systems. Carry out C-R [consciousness-raising] work which encourages learners to focus on form, but place a very low premium on testing for conformity. Cut out the focus on forms which have little communicative value (e.g. question tags). Look for productive generalisations (e.g. V+N+Infin) and pay much less attention to exceptions like *suggest.*

The potential problem here is that it may appear that the teacher is imposing a low premium on conformity and to be running the risk of imposing an impoverished syllabus.

We are always faced with problems of selection when teaching, but as Carter (1998: 51) remarks:

> Learners should not be patronised by being told that they do not need to bother with all this real English. They should not be disempowered and syllabuses should not be deliberately impoverished. Also, learning a language should, in part at least, involve developing something of a feel for that language.

It would seem to respect learners' attitudes more if we offered exposure to one main native speaker variety with a negotiable premium on conformity.

9.6 Option 6: Include the study of language and dialects in a language teaching programme

We have already argued in relation to option 4 that there is a strong case for developing an awareness of and a positive attitude to variety. I would prefer to see this as a leitmotif in the programme using the kinds of activities which Crandall (2003) suggests rather than as a formal sociolinguistic component.

10 Conclusion

In this chapter we have argued that learners' attitudes to the target language variety are one important social factor which can impact on acquisition and we have reached the following conclusions:

(1) It is better for one variety of English to be used consistently in the class-room, but not to the total exclusion of others.
(2) As native speaker varieties cover the full range of communicative

functions, it is probably better that the variety which is consistently used should be a native speaker variety.

(3) The emphasis placed on conformity to this variety should be negotiable.
(4) Classroom materials should portray L2 users and L1 cultures more prominently and in a more positive light.
(5) Learners should be encouraged to show curiosity about and a respect for other varieties of the target language.

References

Alptekin, C. (2002), 'Towards intercultural competence in ELT'. *ELTJ*, 56, 1, 57–64.

Arnold, J. (ed) (1999), *Affect in Language Learning*. Cambridge: Cambridge University Press.

Arnold, J. and Brown, D. (1999), 'A map of the terrain', in J. Arnold (ed.), *Affect in Language Learning*. Cambridge: Cambridge University Press.

Carter, R. (1998), 'Orders of reality: CANCODE, communication and culture'. *ELTJ*, 52, 1, 43–56.

Cook, G. (2002), 'The E of TESOL'. Unpublished Colloquium Paper with J. Jenkins, C. Kramsch, D. Larsen-Freeman, B. Seidlhofer and H. Widdowson, *36ʰ TESOL Conference*, Salt Lake City.

Cook, V. (2003), 'Materials for adult beginners from an L2 User Perspective', in B. Tomlinson (ed.), *Developing Materials for Language Teaching*. London: Continuum.

Crandall, J. (2003), 'They DO speak English: World Englishes in US Schools'. ERI26/3. Available at: www.cal.org/ericcll/news/2003summer/englishes.html. Accessed 15 February 2006.

Crystal, D. (1997a), 'Watching world English grow'. *IATEFL Newsletter*, 135, 10–11.

Crystal D. (1997b), *English as a Global Language*. Cambridge: Cambridge University Press.

Davies, A. (1991), *The Native Speaker in Applied Linguistics*. Edinburgh: Edinburgh University Press.

Ellis, R. (1994), *The Study of Second Language Acquisition*. Oxford: Oxford University Press.

Graddol, D. (1998), 'Will English be enough?', in A. Moys (ed.), *Where Are We Going With Languages? Consultative Report of the Nuffield Languages Inquiry*. London: Nuffield Foundation, 24–33.

Harder, P. (1980), 'Discourse as self-expression: on the reduced personality of the second language learner'. *Applied Linguistics*, 1, 3, 262–70.

Jenkins, J. (1998), 'Which pronunciation norms and models for English as an International Language?'. *ELTJ*, 52, 2, 119–26.

Jenkins, J. (2006), 'The spread of EIL: a testing time for testers'. *ELTJ*, 60, 1, 42–50.

Kachru, B. (1982), *The Other Tongue. English Across Cultures*. Urbana, IL: University of Illinois Press.

Kramsch, C. (2002), 'The E of TESOL'. Unpublished colloquium paper with G. Cook, D. Larsen-Freeman, B, Seidlhofer and H. Widdowson, *36ʰ TESOL Conference*, Salt Lake City.

Krashen, S. and Terrell, T. (1983), *The Natural Approach: Language Acquisition in the Classroom*. Oxford: Pergamon Press.

Modiano, M. (2001), 'Linguistic imperialism, cultural integrity and EI'. *ELTJ*, 55, 4, 339–46.

Norton, B. (1997), 'Language, identity and the ownership of English'. *TESOL Quarterly*, 31, 3, 409–29.

Prodromou, L. (1997a), 'Global English and the octopus'. *IATEFL Newsletter*, 135, 12–15.

Prodromou, L. (1997b), 'From corpus to octopus'. *IATEFL Newsletter*, 137, 18–22.

Ricento, T. (2005), 'Considerations of identity in L2 learning', in E. Henkel (ed.), *Handbook of Research in Second Language Teaching and Learning*. Mahwah, NJ: Lawrence Erlbaum, pp. 895–910.

Salien, J-M. (1998), 'Quebec French: Attitudes and pedagogical perspective'. *Modern Language Journal*, 82, 1, 95–102.

Schumann, J. (1999), 'A neurobiological perspective on affect and methodology in second language learning', in J. Arnold (ed.), *Affect in Language Learning*. Cambridge: Cambridge University Press.

Timmis, I. (2002), 'Native speaker norms and international English: a classroom view'. *ELTJ*, 56, 3, 240–9.

Timmis, I. (2003), 'Corpus, Classroom and Context: The Place of Spoken Grammar in ELT.' (unpublished PhD thesis. University of Nottingham).

Wardhaugh (2005), *An Introduction to Sociolinguistics* (5th edn). Cambridge: Blackwell Publishing.

White, R. (1997), 'Going round in circles: English as an International Language, and cross-cultural capability'. *Cross-cultural capability conference*, Leeds Metropolitan University. Available at: www.rdg.ac.uk/app_ling/circles.htm.

Widdowson, H. (1994), 'The ownership of English'. *TESOL Quarterly*, 28, 2, 377–89.

Willis, D. (1999), 'An international grammar of English?', Unpublished paper, *33rd IATEFL Conference*, Edinburgh.

Part 2

RESEARCH REPORTS

9 The value of recasts during meaning focused communication – 1

Brian Tomlinson

1 Introduction

A common phenomenon in communicative interaction between parent and very young child is recasting of some of the child's utterances by the parent(s). The parent interprets the child's intended meaning and then echoes it by using a different way of communicating the same meaning. The difference could entail, for example, using different words, changing the word order, changing word endings, adding function words, pronouncing a word differently or using a different intonation pattern. So, for example the mother might echo the child's, 'Daddy go work.' by saying, 'Yes, daddy's gone to work.' or the child's, 'Cow' with, 'Yes, there's a cow.' The phenomenon is very common and seems to be considered by the parents to be useful in:

- providing correct models;
- providing more effective models;
- enriching the child's vocabulary;
- enriching the child's repertoire of structures;
- confirming the validity of the child's observation;
- seeking confirmation of the child's meaning;
- seeking clarification of the child's meaning;
- restating the child's position prior to an elaboration or modification of it by the parent.

Very often the parent recasts affirmatively and supportively and provides negative evidence in a positive way. The corrective function of parental recasts has been frequently examined and is reported in the literature in, for example, Bohannon and Stanowicz 1988; Farrar 1990, 1992; Marcus 1993; Morgan *et al* 1995.

The main question raised in this chapter is, 'Does supportive recasting during L2 classroom communicative interaction have the same positive value as parental recasting of children's L1 utterances seems to have?'.

2 What the literature tells us

Long (1996: 434) defines recasts as, 'utterances that rephrase a child's utterance by changing one or more sentence components . . . while still referring to its central meanings'. He considers it to play an important role in negotiation of meaning, which he defines as, 'denser than usual frequencies of semantically contingent speech' which 'serve to make target forms salient independent of increased frequency' (p. 452). In a similar way Morris (2002) defines recasting as providing the learner with 'a target language sample of what the interlocutor perceives to be the learner's intended message. The central meaning of the learner's original utterance is retained while morphological, syntactic, or lexical elements are changed' (p. 396). Morris identifies four properties of recasts: '(1) they reformulate an ill-formed utterance; (2) they expand the utterance in some way; (3) the central meaning of the utterance is kept, and (4) recasts immediately follow the ill-formed utterance. . . .' (pp. 396–7). Morris also states that recasts can provide three things: '(1) implicit negative feedback, (2) positive evidence because the target language form is provided, and (3) enhanced salience through the juxtaposition of the original ill-formed utterance and the target language recast form. . . .' (p. 397). Like most researchers of recasting, the primary concern of Long and of Morris is with its value as an instrument of correction. This is true of those L1 development researchers referred to above and also of most researchers of teacher–student interaction in L2 classrooms. For example, Oliver (1995) coded as recasts those responses which 'maintained the central meaning while reformulating the syntactic structure of the NNS error' (p. 468), Izumi (1998) says, 'a turn was deemed to be a recast when the NS response maintained the central meaning of the NNS utterance while reformulating its incorrect part' (p. 10) and Byrd (2005) says that recasts involve error correction which 'provides implicit negative feedback along with implicit positive feedback' (p. 553). Other similar definitions of recasts by teachers of L2 learner utterances are given by, for example, Ayoun 2001; Doughty 1994; Doughty and Varella 1998; Ellis *et al* 2001; Leeman 2000; Lyster 1998; Lyster and Ranta 1997; Long *et al* 1998; Mackey 2000; Mackey and Philp 1998; Morris 2002; Ohta 2001; Oliver 2000; Roberts 1995; Saxton 1997, 1998; Thornbury 1997. Most L2 researchers have focused on oral interaction but Hedge (1988) and Johnson (1988), for example, have proposed recasting activities in which the teacher reformulates the learner's written text. Nearly all L2 researchers have found that teacher recasting of form in meaning focused activities is a very common teacher intervention, especially in immersion approaches, in which the learners focus primarily on meaning (e.g. Doughty 1994; Faneslow 1977; Lyster and Ranta 1997; Roberts 1995).

Many L2 researchers have concluded that teacher recasting of learner utterances in meaning focused activities may play a useful role in L2 acquisition and development. Morris (2002), for example, lists studies which have reported a positive impact of 'Implicit Negative Feedback (INF), such as recasts and negotiation moves' (p. 397) and Williams (2005) provides a list of researchers who report that recasts 'have been found effective . . . both in experimental . . . and classroom studies' (p. 685). Many researchers also agree with Long and Robinson (1998) that learners benefit most in terms of acquisition from paying attention both to form and to meaning, especially when there is a brief shift of attention from meaningful content to linguistic form. This is what can happen as a result of teacher recasting of learner utterances. However Lyster (1998) refers to studies of teacher recasting of learner utterances in 'communicatively oriented L2 classrooms where there is a primary focus on content' (p. 52) and comes to the conclusion that 'the majority of recasts used naturalistically by teachers in such contexts are unlikely to be either negotiated or noticed by young L2 learners as evidence' (p. 52). This is a point made also by Byrd (2005: 558), who says that:

> Recasts are difficult to do well in typical classrooms for at least two reasons: (a) the teacher's attention is both focused and scattered as he or she works with the individual but it also involves awareness of the whole group and (b) students are likely to misunderstand the recast if they are focused on communication.

Lyster (1998) also reports a study by Lyster and Ranta (1997) in which they investigated the use of corrective feedback by teachers in four primary French immersion classrooms and found that 'recasts were by far the most widely used form of feedback' (p. 52). They also found that recasts 'did not lead to any student generated forms of repair because recasts already provide correct forms to learners' (p. 53). They maintained that 'negotiation of form' activities might be more useful to learners than teacher recasts because they lead to student-generated repair. But they also conceded that 'it is impossible to claim that learner uptake is in itself an instance of L2 learning or that no uptake implies the absence of L2 learning' (p. 53). This is a point taken up by Morris (2002) who argues that, even if learners fail to repair or even notice that recasts are providing feedback, recasts might promote L2 development by 'making the target language form salient and providing positive evidence' (a position supported by Leeman (2000) and Saxton (1997)). Mackey and Philp (1998) found that recasts may be beneficial for short-term L2 acquisition even when not immediately made use of by learners and Mackey (2000) found that some learners who had not noticed the forms that were corrected actually developed those forms. The challenge is to find a way of ascertaining the immediate, short-term and long-term value of meaning focused recasts and to discover the characteristics of a potentially beneficial recast.

A number of researchers have investigated the value of learner recasting of learner utterances. For example, Morris (2002) 'assessed the provision and use of Implicit Negative Feedback in the interactional context of adult beginning learners of Spanish working in dyads (NNS-NNS)' (p. 395) and found that the 42 learners provided recasts and negotiation moves to each other, with lexical errors favouring the negotiation of form and syntactic

errors inviting recasts (a generalization also made by Lyster (1998) in relation to his study of teacher–learner interaction in French immersion classrooms). Morris found that getting learners to work together in pairs on a
communicative task did sometimes lead to modified output and that negotiation moves 'proved more effective in immediately repairing errors than did
recasts' (p. 395). He warns though that feedback and immediate repair do
not necessarily lead to L2 acquisition. Morris and Tarone (2003) also investigated the value of learner recasting of learner utterances. They investigated
the interactions of three dyads of young adult learners of Spanish as a
Foreign Language and found that:

> although learners corrected each other's errors using recasts, in several cases the
> learners continued to produce the erroneous form in posttests. Stimulated recall
> revealed that negative feelings about their conversation partners seemed to have
> caused some learners to interpret recasts not as helpful corrective feedback, but as
> criticism and even mockery.
>
> (Morris and Tarone 2003: 325)

It seemed that recasts were ineffective 'on those occasions in which feedback
was provided but included overt negative attributions or was immediately
followed by interpersonal conflict' (p. 342). This reinforces Byrd's (2005)
contention that 'activities in and of themselves are neutral to communication
and learning' and that it is how they are used that matters. Certainly it seems
that in order for recasts to be useful to learners they need to be perceived by
them as positive and communicatively useful interventions.

Some L2 researchers have doubted the corrective value of teacher recasts
on the grounds that they do not provide negative evidence if the learners do
not notice they are being corrected. For example, Lyster (1998: 52) says that
'the majority of recasts as used naturalistically by teachers . . . are unlikely to
be either negotiated or noticed by young learners as negative evidence'. This
is a point made by Thornbury when he quotes Chaudron (1988: 152) that
'the greatest error teachers make may be the assumption that what occurs as
"correction" in classroom interaction automatically leads to learning on the
part of the student' and when he refers to the point made by Schmidt and
Frota (1986) that learners need to know when they are being corrected and
to match their current level with the target level. Lyster and Ranta (1997)
found in their analysis of interaction in four primary immersion classrooms
that recasts did not lead to any student-generated forms of repair, Allwright
and Bailey (1991: 104) say that recasting 'may be useless if learners cannot
perceive the difference between the model and the erroneous forms they
produce' and Calve (1992) dismissed recasts as remnants of audiolingualism
which minimize the value of student utterances.

Whilst most L2 researchers have focused on the corrective value of recasts
some have been more interested in their communicative value. Lyster
(1998), for example, reports that three quarters of the teachers' recasts in his
reported study of four immersion teachers 'were used in . . . ways that kept

learners' attention focused on content by primarily providing confirmation or additional information related to the student's message and, to a lesser degree, by seeking confirmation or additional information related to the student's message' (p. 74). He argues that the corrective value of recasts could be reduced by such discourse functions and by the signs of approval that teachers use to value content whilst recasting form. This is a position taken by Vigil and Oller (1976), who argue that the positive affective feedback provided by recasts negates their potentially corrective value and suggest that positive affective feedback should be combined with negative cognitive feedback which indicates that changes in the learners's output are desirable. Lyster, however, appreciates the value of recasts in 'advancing the lesson by keeping students' attention focused on content in spite of gaps in L2 proficiency' (p. 75), in providing positive feedback, in encouraging diversity of use, in signalling topic continuation and in allowing the teacher to keep the floor.

3 What experience tells me

I have taught English in Indonesia, Japan, Nigeria, Singapore, the UK, Vanuatu and Zambia. And I think I have frequently used recasting in the classroom.

It seems that when I am teaching I do use recasting during meaning focused activities, both deliberately as a teaching strategy and naturalistically as an instinctive contribution to communicative interaction. When I use it instinctively it tends to be in order to contribute to the coherence of the interaction by, for example, seeking clarification, confirming validity, supporting the speaker or reassuring the speaker. When I use it deliberately it tends to be as part of an attempt to get learners to acquire or develop a particular linguistic feature. In both types of use though my recasting does not always constitute a response to an 'ill-formed utterance' (Morris 2002: 396). Quite often my recasts are in response to a well-formed and appropriate utterance and when I respond to such utterances deliberately it tends to be for enrichment rather than correction. Or I do it in order to help learners to communicate effectively as well as accurately and appropriately.

I can certainly remember responding to learners' grammatically inaccurate but communicatively effective utterances during informal conversation by recasting them as both an affirmation and a provision of negative evidence. For example, I remember such exchanges as:

T: Heh, I like your new shirt. Where did you get it?
L: Get it from Next. Only costed £15 in sale.
T: It only cost £15? It's better than mine. I got it from John West's and it cost me £50.

I think I used to do this quite instinctively to aid cohesion but when I noticed myself doing it, it became more deliberate and I probably started to script my utterances in a slightly unnatural way to enrich the input and ensure redundancy. Of course, strictly speaking this does not conform to the definition of recasting as reformulating the learner's own words but is instead a way of the teacher using the learners' words more accurately as part of a contribution to the interaction. Many teacher trainers (e.g. Timmis: personal communication) argue that this form of recasting has no effect on learner repair or revision as the learners do not notice the difference between their utterances and the equivalent utterances of the teachers. My view on this is that the varied repetition provided by the teachers' recasting (especially if it is frequent and meaningful) provides important input information in a situation which is positively relevant for the learner and therefore likely to facilitate acquisition (Maley 1994).

I vividly remember as Head of a Language School doing a cover lesson and developing a lesson plan in my head as I went up the stairs to the top floor classroom. The lesson I developed eventually involved groups of learners competing to remember the most differences between a scene from a film they had acted out from my directions and the equivalent real life event they had been given a very short time to read about. They scored points if they were able to report a difference when it was their turn or if they were able to find fault with a group's report of a difference. What I found was that nobody was using 'but' to contrast events or descriptions and I soon found myself recasting statements to model the contrastive function of 'but', as in the example below:

L: In the film the old lady called Mrs King. The old lady real name Mrs Barlow.
T: So what you're saying is that in the film the old lady was called Mrs King but in real life she was called Mrs Barlow.

What I noticed was that after a few such recasts the learners started to use 'but' in their reports of differences. Even so I continued to recast the utterances as this had the communicative function of clarification for the other groups who were trying to spot factual inaccuracies in the reports:

L: In the film she went to bank by taxi but she went by bus.
T: You're saying that in the film the old lady went to the bank by taxi but in real life she went by bus.

It seemed that the frequent but varied repetition of 'but' as a mid-sentence marker of contrast in meaningful contexts had an impact (despite nobody seeming to notice it consciously) and by the end of the competition most groups were reporting differences using mid-sentence 'but'. When teaching other classes I used this lesson again and found that my by now deliberate recasting had a similarly successful effect on uptake. I also found that the learners used 'but' in this way quite frequently in a contrastive written task I set them over a week later. My hypothesis was that frequent similar recasting in meaningful and slightly varied contexts could facilitate both repair and acquisition and I decided to try to find experimental confirmation of this hunch. The resultant experiment is detailed in 'The Mrs King Experiment' below.

Interestingly when I proudly demonstrated my lesson on teacher training courses I found that native speakers were using 'and' instead of 'but' to mark contrast. For example, they were saying, 'In the film the old lady was called Mrs King and in the film she was called Mrs Barlow'. This led me to a hunch that native speakers typically use 'but' to mark contrast in writing and planned speech but often use 'and' to mark contrast in unplanned speech. I checked this against the spoken corpus of English assembled by Carter and McCarthy at the University of Nottingham and my hunch was confirmed (Carter: personal communication). This made me question whether helping learners to do something which native speakers typically do not do is in fact useful. My decision was that if the activity facilitated the use of contrastive 'but' in writing then it was useful and if the learners also used it in unplanned speech they might be using it untypically but not incorrectly and they would be easily understood.

4 'The Mrs King Experiment'

Following my discovery that recasting contrastive utterances using mid-sentence 'but' during a group competition seemed to encourage learner use of 'but' both immediately and subsequently, I developed a classroom activity into an action research experiment and I prepared a script for teachers.

In the script I gave instructions for the following activities:

Activity 1

The students are told:

1 'I'd like you to think about your typical Wednesday in your own country. Try to see pictures in your mind of where you are and what you are doing.'

They are then given three minutes to think about their typical Wednesday.

2 'Form pairs. Tell your partner about one thing you do on a typical Wednesday in your own country.'

They are then given five minutes to talk about their typical Wednesday.

3 'I'd like you to think about a typical Wednesday in your life in England. Try to see pictures in your mind of where you are and what you are doing.'

They are then given three minutes to think about their typical Wednesday in England.

4 'Write a comparison for a newspaper in Leeds in which you highlight the differences between your typical Wednesday in your own country and your typical Wednesday in England. You have 30 minutes to write your article.'

After 30 minutes the teacher collects in the articles and tells the students that she wants to find out about their countries and about how well they write, and that she will give them feedback on their articles later.

Activity 2 (to be done in the next lesson from Activity 1)

The students are told:

'I'm going to show you a film today, a new British film. First though I'd like you to think about the beginning of a film you've seen recently. It could be on tv or in the cinema; it could be in your country or in England. Try to see pictures in your mind of what happened at the beginning of the film. Now think about your film for three minutes.'

The students form pairs and are given five minutes to describe to their partner the beginning of their film.

The teacher then leads a class discussion about the films and asks for examples of different types of films (e.g. comedy; drama; science fiction)

The teacher then follows this script:

'The film I'm going to show you is a comedy, a drama and a crime film. It's called "Mrs King Strikes Back". What do you think it's about? Just think about the title for a few minutes.'

(Write Mrs King Strikes Back on the board or the OHP.)

'Well, what do you think? Any guesses?'

(Encourage as many students as possible to have a guess.)

'Mrs King is an elderly widow. Her husband died recently. She lives alone in a large apartment in West Kensington, a wealthy part of London, where apartments are very expensive. What do you think the film is about now?'

(Encourage as many students as possible to have a guess.)

'Unfortunately I've left the video at home. So, instead of watching the film we're going to act it instead. You're going to act the first scene from the film and I'm going to direct you. You're all going to play Mrs King, you're all going to play a letter, you're all going to play a taxi, you're all going to play a taxi driver, you're all going to play a queue in a bank, you're all going to play a beautiful young girl, you're all going to play a bank clerk and you're all going to play a British policeman.

Right. I'll describe the actions and you all act them together.

Mrs King was in her apartment. She was getting ready to go to her friend's apartment to play cards. You're Mrs King. Get ready.

Suddenly a letter came through the letter box. You're the letter.'

(Pause to let the students play the letter coming through the letter box. Pause, also, after each subsequent sentence to let the students perform the action(s).)

'Mrs King got up and went to the door to pick up the letter. She opened the envelope, took out the letter and began to read it. At first she was surprised and then very angry. She screwed up the letter and threw it across the room. Then she went to her wardrobe and took out her coat and hat. She put them on and then took her stick from the wardrobe.'

(If none of the students understand an instruction, act it out for them first. Don't worry if some students don't take part. Leave them to join in when they're ready.)

'She went quickly downstairs and into the street. Then she started to walk very slowly like a very old lady with a stick.

She saw a taxi coming down the road and hailed it with her stick.

The taxi screeched to a halt. (Encourage the learners to make the sound of a taxi screeching.)

Mrs King got into the taxi and said, "Barclays Bank please. Kensington High St."

"Yes, maam," said the taxi driver and the taxi roared off down the road.

When the taxi got to Barclays Bank the taxi screeched to a halt again.

Mrs King got out of the taxi and walked slowly into the bank.

In the bank, Mrs King joined a very long queue.

Standing in front of Mrs King was a beautiful young woman. The woman turned round to Mrs King and said, "Could I borrow a pen please?"

Mrs King opened her handbag and took out a gun.

She put the gun in the back of the beautiful young woman and said, "Go to the counter, quick!"

The young woman went to the counter and Mrs King said to the bank clerk, "Give me all your money."

The bank clerk started to give Mrs King money with her right hand and with her left hand she pushed an alarm button.

The alarm went off. (Encourage the learners to make the sound of an alarm going off.)

Mrs King panicked. She said, "Just give me £50,000!"

The bank clerk gave Mrs King £50,000.

Mrs King put the money in her handbag and then ran out of the bank.

As Mrs King was leaving the bank a policeman was just coming in.

Mrs King knocked the policeman over and then ran out into the street.

In the street Mrs King started to walk very slowly like a very old lady.'

Activity 3 (to be done in the same lesson as Activity 2)

Tell the students:

'This is actually a true story; the old lady did rob a bank. But the film changed many of the facts.

I'm going to give you a report on the trial of the old lady. I want you to read it to spot the differences between what happened in real life and what happens in the film.

I'd like you to get into groups as we're going to have a group competition. I'll give each person a copy of the report but I'm going to put it face down. Don't turn it over until I clap my hands. When I clap my hands turn it over and look for all the differences. You've only got two minutes to find all the differences so you won't have time to read the whole passage carefully. You can help each other in your group.'

(Give out the passage face down. When everybody has a copy, clap your hands so that the students can start to look for differences. After exactly two minutes stop the students and tell them to turn the paper face down again.)

Activity 4

Tell the students:

'You're going to play a game now. We're going to start with Group 1 and they must tell me one difference between what happened in real life and what happened in the film. Listen carefully to what they say and if you think they are wrong, shout out, "Challenge!" Then try to correct their statement. If nobody challenges then Group 1 gets two points. If a group challenges correctly they get two points and Group 1 lose two points. If a group challenges incorrectly they lose two points and Group 1 get two points. Then we go on to Group 2 and then Group 3, etc. When it is your group's turn you only have ten seconds to speak. If you don't speak within ten seconds you lose your turn. When your group get another go, a different person must speak from the previous time. You cannot speak again until everybody in the group has given a difference. All the members of the group can help each other though. Any questions?'

Start to play the game. After each person has given a difference or made a challenge rephrase their utterance so that it uses 'but' to highlight the differences. Don't draw attention to this though and don't tell the students to use 'but'.

e.g.

Student: Her name is Mrs Barlow in real life. In the film she's called Mrs King.

Teacher: You're saying that, 'In real life she is called Mrs Barlow but in the film she's called Mrs King.' Any challenge?

If possible, record the game and later count the number of times that the students use 'but' to give a difference and the number of times they don't use 'but' to give a difference. If it's not possible to record the game try to note down these numbers. Try also to note the number of re-phrasings you make before somebody uses 'but' correctly on their own initiative.

Play the game until most of the differences have been mentioned and each group has had an equal number of turns. Work out the difference between the top group score and the bottom group score (let's say it's 10). Then say:

'I'm going to give every group a chance to win. When I clap my hands the first person to put their hand up can have the chance to give one more difference. If there is no challenge or an unsuccessful challenge that person's group get 12 points (if the difference between the top group and the bottom group is 10). A successful challenge will also get 12 points.'

Play the final turn and then announce the winning group.

Activity 5 (to be done as homework as soon as possible after Activity 4)

The students are told:

'Mrs Barlow was walking home after playing bridge with her friends. As she was passing a cinema in West Kensington, she noticed an interesting looking film called 'Mrs King strikes Back'. She looked at the poster for the film and at photos of scenes from the film. As the film was just about to start she decided to go and watch it.

As she was watching the film she soon realized that the film was about her. She was furious because there were so many differences between the film and what happened in real life.

When she got home Mrs Barlow decided to write a letter to *The Times* newspaper complaining about the film.

For homework tonight write the letter from Mrs King to *The Times*. In your letter complain that the film is not true and mention the differences between what happens in the film and what happened in real life.'

Activity 6 (to be done one week after Activity 4)

The students are told:

1 'I'd like you to think about a typical Saturday in your life in your own country. Try to see pictures in your mind of where you are and what you are doing.'

2 'Form pairs. Tell your partner about one thing you do on a typical Saturday in your own country.'

3 'I'd like you to think about a typical Saturday in your life in England. Try to see pictures in your mind of where you are and what you are doing.'

4 'Write a comparison for a newspaper in Leeds in which you highlight the differences between your typical Saturday in your own country and your typical Saturday in England. You have 30 minutes to write your article.'

After 30 minutes the articles are collected in.

The written work from Activities 1, 5 and 6 is analysed by the researcher and then given back to the teacher so that she can give feedback to the students.

The experiment outlined above makes use of teacher meaning-focused recasting of form not so much as a means of facilitating learner repair but as a means of confirming content with the speaker, clarifying content for other listeners and offering an implicit model for future learner output. It differs from most other recasting experiments reported in the literature both in the intended communicative functions of the recasting and in the fact that the recastings are predetermined in an attempt to implicitly influence the learners' acquisition and development of a specified form (what Williams (2005) refers to as 'intensive recasting' and considers to be the main reason for the apparent success of the recasting experiments of Doughty and Varela (1998)). The recastings in the experiment are, however, similar to those reported by Hauser (2005) when developing an argument that the criteria for coding interactional turns sometimes lead to misinterpretations because the 'maintenance of meaning' is not achieved by one turn because it is 'inseparable from the local context of interaction' (p. 310). Hauser gives an example of a teacher turn which could be coded as a corrective recast but 'is not designed to maintain or restore intersubjective understanding between T and Y, but rather to put Y's answer into a form that T finds acceptable for forwarding to the rest of the class' (p. 300). In the same way the teacher's recasting of the differences expressed by learners in the competition in Activity 4 of the Mrs King Experiment could be misinterpreted as corrective recasts but are actually utterances intended for 'forwarding to the rest of the class'. They could be seen as reformulations, a teacher intervention recommended by Thornbury (1997) and defined as a rephrasing of student utterances 'using the content the student has provided, but recasting it so that' it 'approximates as closely as possible to a putative target language model' (p. 327).

5 The Mrs King Experiment in action

I conducted the experiment with a class of 20 primary school teachers of English and a class of 20 middle school teachers of English. Both groups are from Guangzhou, China and both groups speak Cantonese as their mother tongue and English as a foreign language and all the students gave permission for their work to be analysed as part of an experiment on some aspect of methodology. Their average level of English was estimated as Upper Intermediate.

I would have preferred a lower level class to try the experiment with but my being timetabled in Week 1 of both the Guangzhou teachers' classes gave me an opportunity to gain a sample of 40. I also thought it was a good opportunity to demonstrate an unusual methodological approach and to engage the teachers in an activity which they could later read about and discuss in relation to the second language acquisition (SLA) component of their course. Given the timetabling constraints I had to modify my template for the experiment, as is inevitable in any action research in which the researcher is not in complete control of the environment of the research. So, for example, I had to ask the teachers to do Writing Activity 1 and Writing Activity 3 without any readiness activities and in their own time rather than in class.

At the beginning of their 12 week intensive methodology and language improvement courses at Leeds Metropolitan University both classes were asked to write in their own time a one page response to the following task:

Writing Task 1

Please write below a comparison between a typical Tuesday in Guangzhou and your first Tuesday in England.

They were told that their responses would be used as part of an experiment, that they would get feedback on their writing and that it was not compulsory to respond.

Towards the end of their first week's course both classes were given a five hour session on SLA. As part of these sessions I conducted the Mrs King meaning-focused recasting experiment. I told them it was a demonstration of a pedagogic approach but I did not discuss the objectives, principles or procedures at all. At the end of the 'demonstration' both groups wrote a one page response in class to the following task:

Writing Task 2

You are Mrs Barlow. Write a letter to *The Times* newspaper complaining about the differences between what happened in the film Mrs King Strikes Back and what happened to you in real life.

They were also asked to wait until after the weekend and then to write a one page response to the following task:

Writing Task 3

Please write below a comparison between a typical weekend in your life in Guangzhou and your first weekend in England.

5.1 Results

Differences competition

In both classes the 20 participants formed four groups. They were given two minutes to read the newspaper account of Mrs Barlow's bank robbery and each group was then given two attempts at specifying the differences between the scene from the film which they had acted out and the real life event it was based on. In both classes there was also one final chance for a group to be the first to put their hands up in order to try to specify another difference. After each attempt at specifying a difference I repeated the difference using the structure 'In real life . . . but in the film . . .'. See Activity 4 in the Mrs King Experiment above for more details of the competition.

The number of respondents who used 'but' when specifying a difference between the film and real life in the group competition were:

Table 9.1 Response of Class A/Class B

Response	Class A	Class B
1	Yes	No
2	No	Yes
3	Yes	Yes
4	Yes	Yes
5	No	No
6	Yes	No
7	Yes	Yes
8	Yes	Yes
9	Yes	Yes
10	Yes	Yes
11	Yes	Yes
Total	**9/11**	**8/11**

Implications

My recasting in both classes of the early groups' attempts to contrast what happened in the film and what happened in real life seemed to influence subsequent groups' expression of the contrasts. A typical example would be a member of a group saying, 'The lady is Mrs Barlow. In the film Mrs King', with me recasting this as, 'So you're saying that in real life the lady is called Mrs Barlow but in the film she's called Mrs King'. As far as the participants were concerned the main objectives of my recasts were to check what the group were saying and to make it clear to the other groups in case they wanted to make a challenge. I did not draw attention to my use of 'but' in my recasts, yet from the sixth response onwards in both classes all the groups phrased their contrasts using the structure 'In the film . . . but in real life . . .' or 'In real life . . . but in the film . . .'. I would suggest that it was the varied repetition of the use of 'but' and its obvious value in making contrasts clear that influenced its subsequent use by the participants.

It would seem that the teacher can influence the immediate production of others by implicitly modelling a communicatively useful structure which can help to achieve the intended outcome of an activity.

Writing Activities

(1) The teacher's implicit oral modelling of a communicatively useful activity during the group difference competition seemed to influence the participants' written expression in the subsequent letter writing activity. There was a very frequent use of 'but' (every 3.5 sentences in Class B) and many participants used a very similar sentence medial 'but' structure to the one they had used in the group difference competition, e.g.:

'I was pinned to the wall but in the film nobody pinned me to the wall.' (39)

Table 9.2 Number of 'but's per sentence in writing tasks 1–3

	Writing Task 1		Writing Task 2		Writing Task 3	
	Sentences	Buts	Sentences	Buts	Sentences	Buts
Class A						
1	15	0	9	2	14	1
2	30	1	12	0	X	X
3	7	1	10	5	11	0
4	9	1	11	1	32	0
5	25	0	11	2	X	X
6	12	1	9	3	22	2
7	8	0	15	1	17	0
8	14	1	12	2	20	3
9	14	0	15	2	20	1
10	6	2	11	0	7	0
11	12	1	12	0	16	1
12	12	2	6	2	11	1
13	18	0	8	1	12	1
14	8	0	10	5	19	1
15	19	0	9	1	11	0
16	13	1	7	4	14	0
17	11	1	7	1	21	0
18	14	1	X	X	X	X
19	24	0	9	3	16	0
20	17	2	9	0	20	1
Total	286	15	192	34	283	12
Class B						
21	14	4	6	3	5	1
22	13	1	8	4	16	0
23	12	2	8	3	8	1
24	24	1	11	2	19	2
25	X	X	13	1	18	1
26	11	1	6	4	13	1
27	22	2	17	4	29	1
28	27	1	13	2	10	0
29	18	0	13	4	17	1
30	25	0	9	0	18	0
31	18	1	15	8	24	2
32	35	0	7	0	X	X
33	12	1	12	0	12	0
34	25	1	16	0	20	1
35	46	1	8	1	X	X
36	17	1	16	1	18	0
37	X	X	16	4	X	X
38	48	5	11	8	30	0
39	16	0	10	7	20	0
40	8	2	15	9	15	0
Total	**391**	**24**	**229**	**65**	**293**	**11**
A + B	**677**	**39**	**421**	**99**	**576**	**23**

Table 9.3 Proportion of sentences using 'but'

	Task 1	Task 2	Task 3
Class A	Every 19.0 sentences	Every 5.6 sentences	Every 23.5 sentences
Class B	Every 16.3 sentences	Every 3.5 sentences	Every 26.6 sentences
A + B	Every 17.4 sentences	Every 4.2 sentences	Every 25.0 sentences

'I just asked £50,000 but £85,000 in your film.' (27)

'I went to a London bank, but not a Kensington bank.' (31)

'the second difference is Mrs King took a gun but in real life, I just had a perfume spray . . .' (3)

'What's more, I'm 70 years old this year, but the film said I pretended to be an old lady.' (19)

Other participants used sentence initial 'But' to mark a contrast with the content of the previous sentence, e.g.:

'But in the film I was arrested by three policemen.' (28)

'But in the real life, I was seventy years olds.' (5)

(2) The use of 'but' was much more frequent in the letter writing activity (Task 2) than in the written activity comparing Tuesdays (Task 1). This could be because Task 1 was done before the teacher's implicit modelling of 'but' for contrast and because the participants' were still strongly influenced by this implicit modelling when they did Task 2. If this was the case it could be that the teacher's implicit modelling made salient an already acquired structure which was then frequently retrieved and made use of during the participants' inner speech formulation of output in Task 2 (Tomlinson 2000). The point about salience is also made by Leeman (2003), whose study suggests that recasts can facilitate learning because they enhance salience rather than because they provide negative evidence. It could also be that in the Mrs King Experiment the implicit modelling developed the participants' acquisition of 'but' in a new way. Also it could be that the kinaesthetic nature of the acting out of the film scene led to powerful visual images being associated with the teacher's use of 'but' during the differences competition and that the recall of these images during the writing of Task 2 triggered the recall of the associated structure (Tomlinson 1998). However it could also be that comparing a typical Tuesday in Guangzhou with the first Tuesday in England is much less likely to lead to the frequent use of 'but' than contrasting the differences between a real life event and a film version of it. The first task seems to lend itself more to the writing of two implicitly contrastive paragraphs whereas the second one seems to lend itself more to an itemizing of the differences. I would need to replicate the experiment with the same number of native speakers to find out whether this is so. What many of the

participants did in Task 1 was to write about half a page on a typical Tuesday in Guangzhou and then half a page on their first Tuesday in Leeds. Others did make contrasts within sentences but some used 'while' rather than 'but' to mark the contrasts, e.g.:

'Firstly I am a teacher in Guangzhou while I am a student in England.' (17)

'Last Tuesday, I was a teacher while this Tuesday I am a student.' (4)

'While in England I have a quite different Tuesday.' (19)

'I felt exhausted in the college while I was interested in the study in Leeds Metropolitan University on Tuesday.' (27)

(3) The use of 'but' was much less frequent in Task 3 than in Task 2. This could be because Task 2 was done immediately after the teacher's implicit modelling of a 'but' structure whereas Task 3 was done three or four days later. This could mean that implicit modelling of form during meaning-focused activities can lead to immediate rehearsal of that form in a related activity but as a one-off activity it does not necessarily play a significant role in the actual acquisition and development of the form. It could also be though that comparing a typical weekend in Guangzhou with the first weekend in England is much less likely to lead to the frequent use of 'but' than contrasting differences between a real life event and a film version of it. Again I would need to replicate this experiment with an equivalent number of native speakers to find out.

Although 'but' was used infrequently in Task 3 it was used more often than in Task 1 to connect a first part on Guangzhou with a second part on England, e.g.:

'But here in England, we are new comers.' (23)

'But the first weekend that I spent in England was so different.' (29)

'But things changed quite a lot at this weekend because we are now in England.' (25)

'But yesterday, it was my first weekend in England.' (21)

Even so most participants just wrote about half a page on Guangzhou (usually starting 'In Guangzhou . . .') and then about half a page on their first weekend in England (usually starting 'In England . . .' or 'My first weekend in England . . .') without marking the contrast explicitly at all. Maybe that is the way most native speakers would write such a comparison too.

One participant though, after writing two implicitly contrastive paragraphs used 'but' in the conclusion:

'In brief, the typical weekend in Guangzhou is busy, bustling and a little bit boring. But my first weekend in London was peaceful, comfortable and exciting.' (31)

It was also noted that 'while' instead of 'but' was used only once ('While in

England, I'm only a student and I needn't do any of the work.' (19)) whereas in Task 1 it was used more often.

While this experiment does not prove anything conclusively about the value of re-casting it does suggest that repeated but varied meaning-focused recasting of the same form within a meaning focused activity can:

- influence learner output in the same activity;
- influence learner output in immediately subsequent and related activities;
- have some influence on learner output in related activities performed up to four days after the intervention.

6 Conclusions

The apparent value of the recasts in the Mrs King Experiment could be attributed to the fact that:

- the teacher focused the recasts exclusively on one linguistic feature and ignored other problematic forms;
- the learners were provided with frequent and varied repetition of the 'same' recasts;
- the recasts were made salient by the teacher's emphasis;
- the recasts were of communicative value to the learners;
- the recasts were provided during an activity in which most of the learners were positively engaged;
- the recasts were addressed to all the learners not just the producers of the utterances which were recast;
- the recasts invited learner responses rather than signalling that the teacher was keeping the floor;
- the recasts were not provided as negative evidence but as positive evidence of an effective way of expressing contrasts.

It could be that one of the above characteristics or a combination of a few or all of these characteristics was responsible for facilitating effective production (see Lyster (1998) on the value of combining teacher strategies).

I have by no means proved the value of form-focused recasts in meaning-focused activities but I think I have at least indicated the potential of such interventions. What I am most convinced of though, from my reading of the literature, my own experience and my experiment is not that recasting is better than not recasting but that it is the quality of the learning experience in which recasts are made or not made that really matters. Just as there are good and bad approaches to grammar teaching and good and bad approaches to using TPR, there are good and bad approaches to recasting too. Some positively beneficial ways of making use of recasts in meaning focused activities could include:

- Setting a linguistically demanding task and then recasting predetermined utterances during monitoring (e.g. a task requiring the learners to use reported speech whilst solving a crime in which a number of witnesses change their statements).

- Recasting learner utterances during the retelling stage of a TPR Plus narrative activity (Tomlinson 1994).
- Recasting learner utterances during the story dictation phase of a TPR Plus narrative activity (Tomlinson 1994).
- Recasting parts of a story during the reading phase of a TPR Plus sequence (Tomlinson 1994).
- Recasting in a communication task in which the teacher plays a role (e.g. as a bank clerk, waiter, shop assistant, train information provider, etc.).
- Recasting in a Community Language Learning Task in which the teacher gives the learners the utterances they need in order to make the points they want to.
- Recasting during the post-mortem phase of a Scenario activity (di Pietro 1987).
- Recasting during a complicated game in which the teacher as umpire has to keep repeating the rules (e.g. cricket).
- Recasting for dramatic effect whilst reading a story.

My conclusion then is that supportive recasting during L2 communicative interaction can have value in providing positive feedback, in facilitating communication and in providing salient input. I suspect that recasting is most valuable when it is intensive, when it helps learners to achieve intended task outcomes, when it is repeated over a substantial period of time and when the learners have other meaningful opportunities to meet the form in comprehensible input.

Acknowledgements

I would like to thank Javier Avila for finding me much of the literature referred to above during his stay at Leeds Metropolitan University as a Visiting Scholar in 2005.

I would also like to thank the 40 teachers from Guangzhou who took part in the Mrs King Experiment whilst doing Methodology and Language Improvement courses at Leeds Metropolitan University in September 2005.

References

Allwright, D. and Bailey, K. M. (1991), *Focus on the Language Classroom: An Introduction to Classroom Research for Language Teachers*. Cambridge: Cambridge University Press.

Ayoun, D. (2001), 'The role of negative and positive feedback in the second language acquisition of the Passe Compose and the Imparfait'. *Modern Language Journal*, 85, 226–43.

Bohannon, J.N. III and Stanowicz, L. (1988), 'The issue of negative evidence: Adult responses to children's language errors'. *Developmental Psychology*, 24, 684–9.

Byrd, P. (2005), 'Instructed grammar', in E. Hinkel (ed.), *Handbook of Research in Second Language Teaching and Learning*. Mahwah, NJ: Lawrence Erlbaum, pp. 545–62.

Calve, P. (1992), 'Corriger ou ne pas corriger, la n'est pas la question'. *The Canadian Modern Language Review*, 48, 458–71.

Chaudron, C. (1988), *Second Language Classrooms: Research on Teaching and Learning*. Cambridge: Cambridge University Press.

Doughty, C. (1994), 'Finetuning of feedback by competent speakers to language learners', in J. Alatis (ed.), *Georgetown University Roundtable (GURT) 1993*. Washington, DC: Georgetown University Press, pp. 96–108.

Doughty, C. and Varela, E. (1998), 'Communicative focus on form', in C. Doughty and J. Williams (eds), *Focus on Form in Classroom Second Language Acquisition*. Cambridge: Cambridge University Press.

Ellis, R., Basturkman, H. and Lowen, S. (2001), 'Learner uptake in communicative ESL lessons'. *Language Learning*, 51, 281–318.

Faneslow, J. (1977), 'The treatment of error in oral work'. *Foreign Language Annals*, 10, 583–93.

Farrar, M. J. (1990), 'Discourse and the acquisition of grammatical morphemes'. *Journal of Child Language*, 17, 607–24.

Farrar, M. J. (1992), 'Negative evidence and grammatical morpheme acquisition'. *Developmental Psychology*, 28, 90–8.

Hauser, E. (2005), 'Coding corrective recasts: the maintenance of meaning and more fundamental problems'. *Applied Linguistics*, 26, 3, 293–316.

Hedge, T. (1988), *Writing*. Oxford: Oxford University Press.

Izumi, S. (1998), 'Negative feedback in adult NS-NNS task-based conversation'. Paper given at AAAL Seattle.

Johnson, K. (1988), 'Mistake correction'. *ELT Journal*, 42, 2, 89–96.

Leeman, J. (2000), 'Towards a New classification of Input: An Empirical Study of the Effect of Recasts, Negative Evidence and Enhanced Salience on L2 Development' (unpublished PhD dissertation, Georgetown University, Washington DC).

Leeman, J. (2003), 'Recasts and second language development'. *Studies in Second Language Acquisition*, 25, 37–63.

Long, M. (1996), 'The role of the linguistic environment in second language acquisition', in W. C. Ritchie and T. K. Bhatia (eds), *Handbook of Language Acquisition: Vol. 2 Second Language Acquisition*. New York: Academic Press, pp. 413–68.

Long, M., Inagaki, S. and Ortega, L. (1998), 'The role of implicit negative feedback in SLA: Models and recasts in Japanese and Spanish'. *Modern Language Journal*, 82, 357–71.

Long, M. and Robinson, P. (1998), 'Focus on form: Theory, research and practice', in C. Doughty and J. Williams (eds), *Focus on Form in Second Language Classrooms*. New York: Cambridge University Press, pp. 15–41.

Lyster, R. (1998), 'Recasts, repetition and ambiguity in L2 classroom discourse'. *Studies in Second Language Acquisition*, 20, 51–81.

Lyster, R. and Ranta, L. (1997), 'Corrective feedback and learner uptake: negotiation of form in communicative classrooms'. *Studies in Second Language Acquisition*, 19, 37–66.

Mackey, A. (2000), *Interactional Feedback in the L2 Classroom: Learner's Perceptions and Developmental Outcomes*. Plenary Address, PennTESOL East Conference.

Mackey, A. and Philp, J. (1998), 'Conversation interaction and second language development: Recasts, response and red herrings?', *Modern Language Journal*, 82, 338–56.

Maley, A. (1994), ' "Play it again Sam": A role for repetition'. *Folio*, 1, 2, 4–5.

Marcus, G. (1993), 'Negative evidence in language acquisition'. *Cognition*, 46, 53–85.

Morgan, J., Bonamo, K. and Travis, L. (1995), 'Negative evidence on negative evidence'. *Developmental Psychology*, 31, 180–97.

Morris, F. A. (2002), 'Negotiation moves and recasts in relation to error types and learner repair in the foreign language classroom'. *Foreign Language Annals*, 35, (4), 395.

Morris, F. A. and Tarone, E. E. (2003), 'Impact of classroom dynamics on the effectiveness of recasts in second language acquisition'. *Language Learning*, 53, (2), 325–68.

Ohta, A. (2001), *Second Language Acquisition Processes in the Classroom: Learning Japanese*. Mahwah, NJ: Lawrence Erlbaum Associates.

Oliver, R. (1995), 'Negative feedback in child NS-NNS interaction'. *Studies in Second Language Acquisition*, 17, 459–81.

Oliver, R. (2000), 'Age differences in negotiation and feedback in classroom and pair work'. *Language Learning*, 50, 119–51.

di Pietro, R. J. (1987), *Strategic Interaction*. Cambridge: Cambridge University Press.

Roberts, M. (1995), 'Awareness and the efficacy of error correction', in R. Schmidt (ed.), *Attention and Awareness in Foreign Language Learning*. Honolulu: University of Hawaii, Second Language Teaching and Curriculum Center, pp. 162–82.

Saxton, M. (1997), 'The contrast theory of negative input'. *Journal of Child Language*, 24, 139–61.

Saxton, M. (1998), 'The long term effects of corrective input: An experimental approach'. *Journal of Child Language*, 25, 7, 1–21.

Schmidt, R. and Frota, S. (1986), 'Developing basic conversational ability in a foreign language: A case study of an adult learner of Portugese', in R. Day (ed.), *Talking to Learn*. Rowley, MA: Newbury House.

Thornbury, S. (1997), 'Reformulation and reconstruction: tasks that promote "noticing" '. *ELT Journal*, 51, 4, 326–35.

Tomlinson, B. (1994), 'Materials for TPR'. *Folio* 1,2, 8–10.

Tomlinson, B. (1998), 'Seeing what they mean: helping L2 readers to visualise', in B. Tomlinson (ed.) *Materials Development in Language Teaching*. Cambridge: Cambridge University Press.

Tomlinson, B. (2000), 'Talking to yourself: the role of the inner voice in language learning'. *Applied Language Learning*, 11, 1, 123–54.

Vigil, N. and Oller, J. (1976), 'Rule fossilization: A tentative model'. *Language Learning*, 26, 281–95.

Williams, J. (2005), 'Form-focused instruction', in E. Hinkel (ed.), *Handbook of Research in Second Language Teaching and Learning*. Mahwah, NJ: Lawrence Erlbaum, pp. 671–91.

10 The value of recasts during meaning focused communication – 2

Javier Avila

1 Introduction

I was aware of Brian Tomlinson's research on recasting at Leeds Metropolitan University (see Chapter 9 in this volume) and decided to replicate his Mrs King Experiment with learners of Spanish as a Foreign Language. I produced a version of the scripts in Spanish and then conducted equivalent experiments with classes of learners. Before I report on my findings I would like to do what Brian Tomlinson did in his chapter and reflect on my experience of the intuitive and the deliberate use of recasts in the classroom.

2 Javier's experience of recasting

I have taught English as a Foreign Language (EFL) in Spain (secondary education, University) and in the Czech Republic, where I also taught Spanish as a Foreign Language (SFL) at a University. When attempting to recreate my own experience with recasting in a second language I realized that I have been using it unconsciously as a technique to foster communication with my students and to overcome entropy. The use of the technique falls into two interconnected processes that might work together or autonomously in the pursuit of optimal communication and learning. I may recast an utterance just to solve a mismatch in the content, but also to try to redirect a grammatical problem or just to contribute with a supporting move to make the student feel at ease with his own contribution and therefore foster interaction.

I remember realizing the common errors of my Czech students and trying to overcome them by means of recasting their utterances in an indirect way. The same has happened with my Spanish students, experience has told me what kind of typical mistakes get into errant deviations and which ones are no more than occasional instances out of the unstable nature of interlanguage that will get into the right track just through exposure to the target language.

The kind of activities and materials that I normally use in my class do not normally focus on the form of the language, but try to maximize the benefits of systematic exposure to the target language through listening and reading activities that work as a springboard for productive skills. We do not normally have typical closed-ended questions on the content of the texts we use, but open-ended questions or tasks where the student do not have to find 'the answer' but their answer from interaction with the text. Therefore, I normally recast the students' utterances to make sure I understood what they meant and to make their points clear to the rest of the group, regardless of the grammar being right or wrong, just recasting the utterance in the right way when there is a mistake. The extremely complex nature of our raw material when teaching will ask us to recast in a variety of forms according to each learner, some of them you may realize that they are nodding after a slight recast and therefore realizing its aim, some others might need a more direct recast with a stronger intonation focus on the specific element and even different body language.

In my experience as a teacher trainer in Spain, I have realized that the majority of our fellow teachers will recast as their initial strategy to correct student mistakes and errors, thus trying to provide a supporting recast rather than negative evidence.

3 The 'Mrs King Experiment' conducted with learners of Spanish and learners of English in Spain

During my stay as a visiting scholar at the School of Languages, Leeds Metropolitan University, Brian Tomlinson suggested replicating his study on recasting with Spanish students. Since my experience with recasting supported his hunches and research I agreed to conduct the experiment in Spanish. I initially translated and adapted the lesson plan to the Spanish situation and we decided to use it in two institutions, one where I might teach the lesson plan and the other one where I was going to conduct it having a different teacher for the lesson plan. During the editing process of this chapter I also decided to conduct the experiment with Spanish learners of English at the University of Cordoba.

3.1 The conduct of the experiment

I conducted the experiment in a rather small class of English learners of Spanish at the School of Language, Leeds Metropolitan University[1] (four senior students, low intermediate level of Spanish – B1 in the European Reference Framework) and at the Instituto Cervantes (Leeds) where Mr José Ruiz, an experienced and up-to-date teacher of Spanish taught the lesson plan (seven senior students, low intermediate – B1 as well). At both institutions the Mrs King Experiment was inserted in the normal classroom dynamics, not implying a significant alteration of the course programme. As for the Spanish students of English at the University of Cordoba (Spain), the sample was also rather small (just four students), but the enthusiastic nature of the students pushed me to undertake the experiment again.

3.2 School of Languages, Leeds Metropolitan University

Four students attended the first session where they were asked to do the pre-writing activities of the study. I then got them to write Task 1 of the Mrs King Experiment (see Chapter 9 in this volume for details). They wrote about the differences between a typical Wednesday in England and a typical Wednesday in Spain for '*El País*', a nationwide newspaper in Spain.

They were told it was a study to measure the appropriateness of a lesson plan and they would receive feedback on it later, no information on the objectives or contents of the study was provided.

A week later, in the next lesson, we did Activity 2. The acting was a great success, all the students were involved in the acting procedure and they seemed to enjoy it a lot. Then we did Activity 3 (reading the report of the trial of the old lady) and Activity 4, the group competition. It must be noted here that since we only had four students, they were doing this individually. The experience was amazing; they were really involved in it and tried to beat their colleagues. At this point it occurred to me that the fact that they might acquire the use of 'but' or not was not so important from the pedagogic point of view as how the students were using the target language, and how important in quality as much as in quantity was the effort they were making to express what they wanted. It is difficult to see from the teacher's point of view how they could not be learning something from the experience, not only at this stage of the experiment, which was superb, but also at the initial acting stage, which had all of the components of Gardner's (1983: 223) equation on motivation:

MOTIVATION = EFFORT + DESIRE TO ACHIEVE A GOAL + ATTITUDES.

As it is generally agreed in the profession, given motivation, almost every student can learn a language, as Scarcella and Oxford (1992: 51) assert: 'Unquestionably motivation and attitude are very important in language learning success'.

The students did Activity 5 (writing the complaint letter) as homework. In the next lesson they did Activity 6, commented with their partners on a typical day in England and finally wrote about the differences between a typical Saturday in Spain and England for a Spanish newspaper.

The students were really enthusiastic about the acting and the game; they asked me to do another similar activity next time. I personally value the students' perception of the activity as one of the key elements in the communicative process of teaching (see Bandura 1986), and my personal experience tells me that when rapport is achieved in the classroom the flow experience of learning may move from utopia to praxis (Csikszentmihalyi 1990).

3.3 Instituto Cervantes, Leeds

Mr Ruiz taught the Mrs King Experiment lesson plan. The students were told it was a study but as in the other institution they were not informed about the objectives or contents of the study. They wrote about the differences between a typical day in England and a typical day in Spain.

On the information sheet, Mr Ruiz wrote a number of comments that will be useful to realize the real progress of the teaching-learning experience. Initially he wrote that the attitude of the students towards the activities was rather curious: 'They were rather willing to know about the objectives of the study'. Mr Ruiz was really interested in the study; he likes trying new experiences and stated, 'the activities incidentally fitted perfectly into the contents of the teaching programme'.

The first activity was performed on the 28 May 2005, it took 45 minutes and there were four students. 'Initially they were rather surprised and didn't know what to write, then they got into it and wrote extensively. There were different points of view, from the personal "I" to the impersonal "an engineer, a student in Spain . . .".'

The second activity was done on the 4 June and it lasted 25 minutes. There were six students this time. Mr Ruiz wrote that the students talked a lot about films, but for the dramatization activity he had to illustrate it initially, but then all but one of them took part. 'We all had great fun,' wrote Mr Ruiz.

As for Activity 3 (4 June), six students took part in it. 'Students complained about the scarce time for reading; more than complaining they were sort of joking on that because they sort of predicted there was a competition later'. Then in Activity 4 (same day, more or less half an hour later) 'the six students were really involved (but for the one that stood aside before – he is really shy and rather a slower learner). They were really competitive. Sometimes they might just invent the differences and I had to reread the story to check them and give the points'.

Activity 5 was done at home (4–11 June) and unfortunately some of the students did not do it.

Activity 6 was done on 11 June for 40 minutes and there were six students in class. The teacher states: 'It was easier for them since they knew the kind of activity and it seemed to be easier on Saturday – the day they were attending the session'.

3.4 Faculty of Philosophy, University of Cordoba

I had a mixed ability class, with two students just coming from high school and two other students in their last year at university, having left English aside for a while – i.e. two high intermediate and two low intermediate students. Since they were used to the kind of activities they were about to do in the Mrs King Experiment, I did not inform them of the nature of the experiment in order to encourage natural behaviour in the classroom.

All the students attended the different sessions of the study; we started with the pre-writing activities, following the original script of the experiment (see Chapter 9 in this volume). A week later we did Activity 2; three students were very active in the acting procedure, but one student who is really shy was reluctant to take part. I invited her to do what she pleased and she sat down providing indications and working as the prompter of the acting. Then we did Activity 3 and the group competition (Activity 4), during which I formed two pairs to facilitate intergroup communication in the target language. The competition was a great success, the students getting very involved in the game and seeming to enjoy it a lot. Finally, they did Activity 5 and 6 as in the previous cases.

My personal assessment of the activity in the English class is absolutely positive, as in the Spanish experiments, the students interacted, used their English and were eager to undertake the different steps. As commented above, that is definitely a crucial part of the learning process.

3.4 The results

Differences competition

Table 10.1 Differences competition

	School of Languages	Instituto Cervantes	University of Cordoba
Times they said '*pero*' (*but*)	0	8	5
Times '*pero*' was not used	5	8	4
Times the teacher paraphrases before '*pero*' is uttered	5	3	3

Implications

In the School of Languages the students were initially just using juxtaposition to contrast what happened in real life and in the film. My reiterative use of 'but' didn't seem to lead the students to change their use of 'pero' (but), it rather got them to use 'y' (and), an informal way to express contrast colloquially in Spanish (see Chapter 9 for a report of a similar use of 'and' to mark contrast by native speakers of English).

At the Instituto Cervantes it took Mr Ruiz three rephrasings before 'pero' or 'y' was said, but in the end the students uttered the adversative conjunction as many times as not, this suggesting that the recasting was having an effect on the students.

Table 10.2 Number of 'but's per sentence in writing tasks 1–3

	Writing Task 1		Writing Task 2		Writing Task 3	
	Sentences	Buts	Sentences	Buts	Sentences	Buts
School of Languages						
1	8	0	3	2	13	0
2	6	2	7	0	12	1
Total	**15**	**2**	**10**	**2**	**25**	**1**
Instituto Cervantes						
1	29	0	29	2	25	0
2	19	3	22	1	16	1
Total	**48**	**3**	**51**	**3**	**41**	**1**
University of Cordoba						
1	17	0	15	4	9	2
2	26	1	22	3	19	2
3	18	0	9	1	15	2
4	15	2	18	5	10	3
Total	**76**	**3**	**64**	**13**	**53**	**9**
A + B + C	**139**	**8**	**125**	**18**	**119**	**11**

Table 10.3 Proportion of sentences using 'but'

	Task 1	Task 2	Task 3
School of Languages	7,5	5	25
Instituto Cervantes	16	17	41
University of Cordoba	25.33	4.92	5.88
A + B + C	**17.375**	**6.94**	**10.81**

Implications

The teachers' recasting of the oral utterances of the students during the group difference competition seems to have influenced the use of the recast linguistic item in the ulterior written performance. At the school of languages we find the use of *but* every 7.5 sentences in Task 1, and every 18.75 sentences at the Instituto Cervantes, whereas in Task 2 we find it every 5 sentences at the School of Languages and every 11 sentences at the Instituto Cervantes. If we consider both groups together we find *but* used every 15 sentences in Task 1 and every 9.5 sentences in Task 2.

The students used 'pero' (but) in medial and initial position to express contrast, e.g.:

'In the film I took a taxi to the bank but in fact I used the bus.'
'In the film I got a letter that made me angry, but in fact I didn't get any letter.'
'[. . .] But it was sort of a gangster film and I was astonished.'
'It is true, I got a customer, but I didn't talk to her while in the cue.'
'In the film I got a taxi, but in fact I got the bus.'
'In the bank I got a flask of perfume that worked as a fake gun but in the film they showed me with a real gun.'
'I didn't ask for money at the counter but to the bank manager.'
'I know she is not seventy years old but I don't know exactly how old is she.'

As in the competition above, many students used 'y' (and) instead of 'pero' (but) to express contrast, e.g.:

'In the film she didn't take a customer and she didn't take her to the bank manager office.'
'The hostage was not called Julia Exposito and she didn't push Mrs. Martin against the wall.'
'Her name was Mrs. Martin not Martínez, and she is not 70 years old.'

The average use of the structure in Activity 2 was more frequent than in Activity 1, and, though the number of students in the sample does not allow us to make strong inferences about the effectiveness of the treatment, it does provide an indication of the potential of meaning-focused recasting in the foreign language classroom. I do agree with Tomlinson (Chapter 9 this volume) and Leeman (2003) that recasts can increase salience and that may foster the learning of the structure which is recast. I also agree that the combination of the kinaesthetic activities together with the recasting and the atmosphere of the competition may have fostered the connection between the structure being recast and the juxtaposed information; that connection may be verbal, in the form of adversative sentences, and non-verbal, in the images stimulated by the dramatic representation and the reading of the report of the story (Sadoski 1983; Sadoski *et al* 1988; Sadoski *et al* 1990).

As in Tomlinson's study, the average use of 'but' was more frequent in Activity 2 than in Activity 3. The reason for this outcome may be due to the fact that Activity 2 was performed right after the recasting activity, therefore affecting short-term production. Another possibility may be that Activity 2 drew on the modelled activity itself, being therefore contextually related to the competition and thematically related, whereas Activity 3 asked the students to extrapolate their input to another thematic activity where the connection was basically formal rather than based on content.

As in the competition reported above, many English speakers tend to use 'and' instead of 'but' to express contrast and they transfer that use to their second language. It should be noted that in Activity 1, the students were mostly enumerating their activities in one country and another, whereas in

Activity 2 and 3, the comparison of the activities in the different countries by means of juxtaposition and copulative and adversative coordination was far more frequent.

4 Conclusions about recasting

Though conclusions can only be impressionistic from such a small sample, the indications of the study are that the recasts in the Mrs King Experiment lesson plan may have exerted some influence on the use of the specific structure by the students. The reasons for that might be due to the nature of the activities that were connected with the recasting procedure itself and to the very recasting procedure, its communicative value and the salience it provided to the structure, providing positive evidence of contrast being achieved. It may also be inferred from the study that learners need far more exposure to the recasting procedure, in order to be able to transfer the effect of the recasting to their competence in Spanish once the thematic connection has been removed.

These inferences are by no means conclusive but a more ambitious study (in terms of the size of the sample, different levels and different learning environments) might help to extrapolate the implications to the population of Spanish learning students, therefore achieving a higher external value. Tomlinson's opening question in Chapter 9 in this volume might be best answered by means of such further research, the evaluation of the amount of intensive recasting needed to find significant improvement and the length of the exposure to the recasting process are key questions still to be determined. However, both teachers involved in the study (Mr Ruiz and myself) agreed on the potential of supportive recasting embedded in communicative interaction in the foreign language classroom and we have found from the literature and the teaching experience itself a justification for what we have intuitively been doing in our teaching.

Acknowledgements

Special thanks to the Spanish Department at the School of Languages (Leeds Met.) and the Instituto Cervantes (Leeds) for their cooperation and to all the students who took part in the different experiments.

References

Bandura, A. (1986), *Social Foundation of Thought and Action; a Social Cognitive Theory.* Englewood Cliffs, NJ: Prentice Hall.
Csikszentmihalyi, M. (1990), *Flow, The Psychology of Optimal Experience.* New York: Harper and Row.
Gardner, H. (1983), *Frames of Mind.* New York: Basic Books.
Leeman, J. (2003), 'Recasts and second language development'. *Studies in Second Language Acquisition,* 25, 37–63.

Sadoski, M. (1983), 'An exploratory study of the relationships between reported imagery and the comprehension and recall of a story'. *Reading Research Quarterly*, 20, 658–67.

Sadoski, M., Goetz, E. T. and Kangiser, S. (1988), 'Imagination in story response: Relationships between imagery, affect and structural importance'. *Reading Research Quarterly*, 26, 463–84.

Sadoski, M., Goetz, E. T., Olivarez, A., Lee, S. and Roberts, N. M. (1990), 'Imagination in story reading: The role of imagery in reading and a dual coding alternative'. *Reading Research Quarterly*, 26, 463–84.

Scarcella, R. C. and Oxford, R. (1992), *The Tapestry of Language Learning*. Boston: Heinle & Heinle.

11 Output like input: Influence of children's literature on young L2 learners' written expression[1]

Irma-Kaarina Ghosn

1 Introduction

This paper reports on the results of an experimental research study, which investigated the influence of story-book reading on young English language learners' written expression. More specifically, it aimed at determining whether story-reading and follow-up activities can enhance the vocabulary base and coherence in children's writing. Young Arabic-speaking children (*n* 140) in grades 4–6 (ages 9.5–12) in Lebanon participated in the project. At the beginning of the school year, students were randomly assigned to experimental and control classes. The experimental classes received 15 weeks of story-based instruction (SBI) once per week while the controls continued with their regular English language programme. The findings indicate that SBI had a positive influence on children's L2 writing, resulting in longer and more expressive writing with clearer organization and supporting detail.

2 Writing in a second language

In beginning level English language courses for young learners writing is not usually emphasized, and here I use the definition of writing that Hudelson (1989: 5) adopts from Berthoff (1981):

> Writing is the creating of original text using the individual's intellectual and linguistic resources rather than copying someone else's text, using prepared lists of words to create sentences or stories.

Writing tasks in primary ELT courses rarely call for creation of original texts, but consist mainly of filling in the blanks, compiling lists and constructing short messages and letters. Explicit focus on organization and idea development is rare, if it exists at all. In 1988, Samway found that writing tasks in primary school English as a Second Language (ESL) texts served an exercise function and that even at 'the most advanced levels most ESOL texts for elementary grade children present writing in an artificial way' (p. 3). A look at more recent texts confirms this to be true even today. This is rather surprising in the light of what is known about the role of writing in children's L2 development.

The work of Graves (1983) and Kress (1994; 1997), in particular, has been fundamental in shaping our thinking about how children develop as writers in their native language, and we now know that even very young children can construct original and interesting texts when given appropriate supportive environment. One of the most delightful accounts of a young child's L1 writing development is Bissex's (1980) in-depth study of her son, Paul. In her *Gnys at wrk*, Bissex shows how Paul's writing, which began as notes 'written' in a system he had invented himself and which gradually merged with the conventional writing system, was closely intertwined with his reading development. Paul was of the opinion that 'once you can write a word you can read it'. It appears that Paul was right. Research over the past 20 years shows that young second language learners can also produce stories early in their L2 development (Edelsky 1982; Hudelson 1984). Neither sophisticated oral language nor the ability to read seem to be prerequisites (Rigg 1981; Edelsky 1982; Hudelson 1984; Zamel 1992).

In fact, writing is argued to contribute to young L2 learners' reading development, since:

> writing requires these beginning readers/writers to make decisions about purpose, sequence, and language, because it helps them to understand how and why texts are written, gives these learners insight into the goals, constraints, and concerns of authors, insight which they apply to their reading.
>
> (Zamel 1992: 469)

When composing and revising their writing, students become aware of how the meaning of the text is created by the writer, who is in a kind of dialogue with the text, constantly trying to understand how to make the text say what they intend it to say. As Zamel (1992: 471) puts it, 'Writing, because it gives rise to our own ways of probing and working with texts, is thus a way out to construct, to compose the reading'. The same argument has been voiced also by Smith (1982) and Freeman and Freeman (1992), who have argued for a holistic approach to teaching reading and writing. Halliday (1975) and Kamii (1991), on the other hand, have stressed the social nature of language development, arguing that children construct language by interacting and manipulating language, and by engaging in meaningful use of language within a community of language learners. Maquire and Graves (2001: 561) quote Heddie, a 9-year-old second language learner who brings her experience to bear upon the L2 writing theory in this poignant statement: 'The more you write, the more you learn how to write. It's like speaking, the more you speak, the more you learn how to speak'.

Moreover, Hudelson (1984) suggests that, for some L2 children, writing may also facilitate other schoolwork. Writing, therefore, deserves special attention in contexts that Ghosn (2001: 19) has referred to as 'foreign language for academic purposes in the primary school' (FLAPPS). In FLAPPS settings, such as Ghana, Nigeria, Botswana and Zambia, for instance, a foreign language serves as a mandatory vehicular language in the general curriculum. In the case of Lebanon, the context of this study, English or French is used in the general curriculum at the latest from year 7. Therefore, children, whose native language is Arabic, must develop, early on, sufficient L2 writing skills to demonstrate their learning in written tests and examinations administered in the L2. (An added confounder in their case is the distinctive difference between the colloquial Arabic, spoken in Lebanese homes, and the literary, classical Arabic, *fusha.*)

Take, for instance, the following objectives from the Lebanese National Curriculum for Mathematics and Science, respectively, of the basic cycle, which is taught in English, a foreign language to the children:

> Express understanding correctly, both verbally and/ or in writing; Argue by analogy, giving examples and counter arguments (Ministry of National Education 1995: 296–301), and

> Give descriptions of [nature's cycles] and state [their] importance; Identify and define; explain with examples; Explain results of experiments; state expectations of what will happen (*ibid*: 460–78).

Clearly, in order to be able to demonstrate the above abilities in written examinations, students must have some practice with this kind of writing, which is very different from the writing tasks in typical English language coursebooks.

3 Story-book influence on language development

The positive influence of stories on first language development is well documented in the literature. Gunderson and Shapiro (1988: 433), for example, found that children in one US first grade class, where story books were regularly used, developed vocabularies 18 times larger than what would be expected in a skills-based programme. The findings are not surprising in light of Cohen's (1968) much earlier study, in which 285 grade 2 children increased their vocabulary base and word knowledge significantly in comparison to the control group after listening to stories daily and completing follow-up activities. Research also shows that exposure to stories of high literary quality significantly improves children's quality of writing, regardless of their reading ability (Dressel 1990), with children's L1 writing reflecting the linguistic structures, format, and style of their reading materials (DeFord 1981; Mikkelsen 1984; Dressel 1990). When investigating the quality of primary school children's talk during story discussions, Strickland *et al* (1989) found that children also developed competence in organizing their explanations, learned to modify their speech according to the purpose and audience, and developed analytical ability. It is not unreasonable to assume that these skills could transfer also to their writing, including L2 writing.

4 Story-based programmes and L2 writing

Several studies show story reading to have a positive influence on children's L2 vocabulary development and writing. For example, Carger (1993) found that just after three readings of a picture storybook, three 5–6-year-old Spanish-speaking kindergartners, with little or no knowledge of English, increased their total word count, two-syllable words, meaning units and target vocabulary. Tudor and Hafiz (1989) and Hafiz and Tudor (1990) report on the influence of extensive reading of graded readers on written expression of 16 Pakistani children, aged 10–11, in the UK and on 50 adolescents (aged 15–16) in Pakistan. They report statistically significant gains from the first study in the story groups' syntactic, semantic and spelling accuracy while children's writing became simpler and more basic. Their second study reports statistically significant gains of the experimental group's writing readiness, vocabulary base and accuracy of expression, but not on syntactic accuracy. While students wrote more, their vocabulary ratio declined. This is not surprising, bearing in mind the findings of DeFord (1981), Mikkelsen (1984), and Dressel (1990) of children's L1 writing. The researchers, who do not present any writing samples, argue that the gains were due to the input provided by the graded readers. However, the gains could have been simply due to the significantly more exposure the experimental groups had to the target language – a total of 92 hours in the second study!

By far the most compelling evidence in favour of 'real' (as opposed to graded or simplified) stories as medium of second and foreign language instruction comes from the 'book flood' studies conducted by Elley and his colleagues in Niue (Elley 1991), Fiji (Mangubhai and Elley 1982; Elley and Mangubhai 1983), Sri Lanka and Singapore (Elley *et al* 1996), and South Africa (Elley 2000). In these studies, children have been exposed to large quantities of high-interest story books in an effort to provide extensive exposure to L2 in the challenging FLAPPS contexts. These studies, involving literally hundreds of primary school children, have documented gains in all four language skills, including writing.

However, the above-cited studies have not reported on qualitative aspects such as organization, support and voice in children's writing. When Huie and Yahya (2003) compared writing samples of 168 native English-speaking children and 228 limited English proficient (the term used by their school district) children in Florida, they found striking differences between the two groups in these three areas. Native English-speaking children's writing had a clearer organizational structure and they used more adjectives and two-syllable words that their non-native-English-speaking counterparts, which produced not only more detailed and lively texts but also texts with more personal style. The authors note that the L2 learners' writing indicated the kind of writing instruction they had received: 'children had been given prepared sentences in which they were asked simply to fill in the blanks' (p. 27), in other words, writing tasks typical in the English language teaching texts.

MacGowan-Gilhooly (1996) notes that L2 writers lack the adequate control over the language that would enable them to write fluently and with clarity. Fluency implies 'the ability to generate one's ideas in writing intelligibly and with relative ease' (p. 52) while clarity refers to 'the ability to write expository pieces with a clear focus, sufficient support for that focus, logical development of ideas, and effective introductions and conclusions' (p. 53). These are areas believed by many to be the most difficult to teach. Second language learners' writing fluency is also hindered by lack of adequate vocabulary (Arndt 1987; Raimes 1987), with young ELLs having to depend on the few limited structures they know (Clay 1998).

The present study attempted to find out whether story-based instruction can enhance second language writing skills, particularly vocabulary, organization and use of supporting detail.

4.1 Context and participants

In one private K-12 school in Beirut, Lebanon, 140 children, aged 9.5–12, participated in the study. The school is located in a disadvantaged suburb of the city, serving primarily children from lower middle class families. Reflecting the common practice in Lebanon, children in the school begin formal English language instruction in the kindergarten and receive some subject matter instruction – primarily science and mathematics – in English. (According to the requirements of the National Curriculum, students must begin English-medium learning of all general curriculum subjects at the latest in the 7th year of schooling, at age 12–13, with the exception of Arabic language and civics education.) The children in the study were all native speakers of Arabic and had received 5–6 hours of English language instruction per week since kindergarten.

Of the total of 140 children, 68 were assigned into the experimental and 72 into the control group. Teacher A taught two experimental and two equivalent control groups and teacher B taught one experimental and one equivalent control group. Both teachers had a university degree and had taught full-time in the school for four years.

4.2 Data collection and procedures

Picture stimuli from the story construction component of the TOWL-3 (Hammill and Larsen 1996) were used to collect data on children's writing. In one form of the test, children are asked to construct a story to go with a picture depicting a pre-historic group of people battling a herd of mammoths, while the other form presents a futuristic picture set in space. The story compositions were used to collect data on children's vocabulary base as well as organization, support and voice.

At the beginning of the school year, children were randomly assigned to experimental and control groups. A random of half of each class was further assigned into pre-test–post-test condition (n 82). Form A of the story construction was used as pre-test and Form B as post-test. While the random grouping and post-test-only condition (n 58) increased the internal validity of the study and reduced any possible testing effect, the pre-test–post-test condition enabled measurement of gains in individual children's writing. (However, the main reason for the post-test-only condition was that reading comprehension data were also collected from the same group of children; in order to minimize the time taken from teaching, half the children took the reading test while the other half took the writing test. The post-tests were administered during the mid-year examination period when no classes were scheduled.)

4.3 Data analysis

Quantitative and qualitative data were collected from a total of 221 TOWL-3 compositions from pre- (n 82) and post-tests (n 140). The compositions were first scored for vocabulary base (number of total words, discrete items, 2-syllable and polysyllable words) and the results applied to analysis of variance and covariance. While word count does not necessarily distinguish quality writing from poor writing, it has been used to determine L2 learners' fluency. A broad vocabulary base undoubtedly enhances writers' ability to express their meaning more accurately. A repertoire of one-syllable words, on the other hand, even when considerable, is likely to result in much less accurate expression of complex ideas than what is possible with polysyllable words. The procedure described by Huie and Yahya (2003: 26) was then used to collect qualitative data from the papers. The researcher and two student teachers specializing in TESL first read the stories independently and, using a scoring rubric adapted from the national primary cycle English language coursebook (Ghosn *et al* 2000: 193), scored them as low, average-low, average-high, or high. The three readers reached an agreement of 91 per cent on the low and high papers and 78.5 per cent on the low and high average papers. From the total sample, anchor papers were selected that each scorer had scored the same, two papers per rubric level for experimental and control Groups 1 and 2 (32 papers), and one paper per rubric level in Group 3 (8 papers). These anchor papers were then analyzed for organization, support and voice. The anchor papers were then matched with the pre-test papers and analyzed for any qualitative improvements. The discussion of the qualitative aspects of the children's writing is based on these 80 papers.

4.4 Intervention

For 15 weeks, the experimental groups received story-based instruction once a week instead of their regular language programme while the control groups continued with their regular English language programme. The three groups were exposed to a different intervention each. Group E1 children selected picture story books for silent reading and completed simple 'Book Review' checklists, which required no writing, yet enabled the researcher and the teacher to determine how many stories each child read (see Appendix

A). Group E2 children selected picture story books to read and then chose written reader response tasks from a set designated for each story. These included literary journals, letters and news reports (Johnson and Louis 1987), extensions and changes, as well as personal reactions and reflections (see Appendix B). The teacher of Group E3 was instructed on how to conduct literature circle discussions, and the researcher visited the class twice to model the procedure. At the beginning of each week, the children were each given the same story to read. These stories were then discussed in a literature circle towards the end of the week. Children were divided into groups of four and given discussion starters that encouraged both efferent and aesthetic responses (see Appendix C for samples). The teacher circulated from group to group to listen in, making occasional comments and asking clarifying questions. The group discussions were given approximately 15 minutes, after which the teacher brought the groups together for a whole class session, during which she invited children first to summarize the main events of the story and then their most important thoughts and questions. The researcher observed three of these sessions, once at the onset of the study, once in the middle and once at the conclusion of the study. All groups' selections included a number of award-winning titles as well as classic fairytale-type stories. During the study, the experimental group children read an average of 10 titles each.

4.5 *Quantitative results*

Table 11.1 shows the means and standard deviations of the groups. In the post-test, all three experimental groups scored a higher mean than the controls in total word count, discrete item count and, subsequently, in the composite as well. However, the differences failed to reach statistical significance at alpha level 0.05, with the exception of E2, whose discrete item mean was significantly higher than the mean of their counterparts (t 2.21, df 24, $p<0.03$). Since all three control groups had begun with higher means in the pre-test in all but TW, analyses of covariance (ANCOVA) were carried out. These revealed that when the pre-test scores were partialled out, the story-based interventions had a significant influence on children's writing in all three experimental groups. In Group 1, differences in favour of the experimental, silent reading group were found in total words (TW) (F 9.69, df 2, $p<0.001$), discrete items (DI) (F 6.86, $p<0.003$), and in 2-syllable words (2S) (F 13.45, $p<0.001$). In Group 2, statistically significant differences were found between the experimental (written response) and control groups in TW (F 5.13, $p<0.1$), DI (F 18.87, $p<0.001$), 2S (F 12.14, $p<0.001$) and the composite score (CS) (F 6.48, $p<0.07$). In Group 3, the experimental, literature circle group scored higher means in 2S (F 5.35, $p<0.02$), with differences in total word count and composite score failing to reach statistical significance at alpha level 0.05 (F 3.34, $p<0.07$ and F 3.44, $p<0.07$, respectively).

Analysis of variance (ANOVA) revealed also a statistically significant difference between the experimental and control groups in post-test rank scores in

Table 11.1 Means and standard deviations – pre-test–post-test Groups

	Group	N	Pre-test		Post-test	
TW	E1	21	94.04	45.49	142.95	51.11
	E2	10	85.2	25.64	157.1	43.57
	E3	6	87.5	30.7	130.33	51.67
	C1	25	74.2	42.94	110.76	50.16
	C2	13	89	39.85	134.69	35.80
	C3	7	114	27.07	148.14	24.25
	Total	82				
DI	E1	21	44.47	19.15	64.8	22.69
	E2	10	46	11.41	72.7	16.79
	E3	6	51.66	15.87	89.33	43.27
	C1	25	52	33.24	77.32	37.23
	C2	13	59.8	31.2	101.23	27.47
	C3	7	64.71	19.98	80.85	12.96
	Total	82				
2S	E1	21	4.38	3.82	3.23	2.23
	E2	10	8.7	3.77	16.6	4.08
	E3	6	11.66	5.5	14.5	7.71
	C1	25	7.76	4.45	8.92	6.28
	C2	13	7.3	3.0	12.3	4.15
	C3	7	11.28	2.69	15.85	3.62
	Total	82				
3S	E1	21	0.55	0.6	1.04	1.28
	E2	10	2.7	1.76	3.06	4
	E3	6	2.66	2.25	5.33	3.26
	C1	25	1.4	0.91	2.16	2.71
	C2	13	1.46	0.77	2.69	1.84
	C3	7	3	0.57	5.71	3
	Total	82				
CS	E1	21	143.42	58.93	212.04	61.64
	E2	10	142.6	36.39	250	65.36
	E3	6	153.5	51.39	239.5	94
	C1	25	135.28	80.4	208.84	100.76
	C2	13	154.15	73.94	251	65.86
	C3	7	193	47.46	250.57	38.36
	Total	82				

Key: E1 = silent reading group; E2 = written response group; E3 = literature circle group; C1, C2, C3 = respective control groups.
TW = total word count; DI = discrete items; 2S = 2-syllable words; 3S = polysyllable words.
CR = composite score.

favour of the experimental group ($F 5.03$, $df 1$, $p < 0.02$) while the groups had begun with similar means ($F 0.54$). Figure 11.1 shows the percentage of pre- and post-test papers according to their rank scores. The experimental groups' 'High' scores increased 15 percentage points (7 to 22 per cent) whereas no increase was noted in the control group. Similarly, the experimental groups' 'Average low' scores decreased by 14 percentage points (41 to 27 per cent) while the control groups showed no change. The control group's 'Average-high' papers increased by 25 percentage points (from 17 to 42.5 per cent) while the experimental groups' gains were 18 percentage points (26 to 44 per cent). However, the experimental groups' 'Low' papers decreased by nearly 25 percentage points (from 25.5 to 0.7 per cent) compared to the control group's decrease of 22 percentage points (36 to 14 per cent).

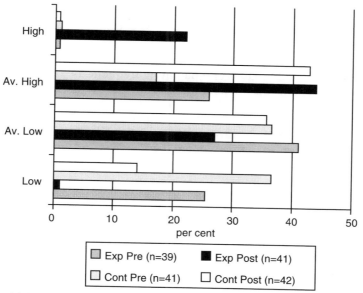

Figure 11.1 Percentage of Rank scores in the pre- and post-test in the two groups

4.6 Qualitative results

Qualitative analysis of the anchor papers revealed that, as anticipated, the word count was not necessarily associated with quality of writing in terms of organization and support. In all groups, there were long rambling papers that lacked coherence as well as short papers that read better. However, the experimental groups' anchor papers reflected overall clearer organization, more detail to support the main ideas, and, in many cases also more creative expression, as compared to the control groups in all three groups. Children in the experimental groups often used more effective opening sentences, such as the following (all student compositions have been typed exactly as written, with all spelling and punctuation left as in the originals):

> Long ago we had many astronauts went to the moon to discover. . . (S.H., 11)
>
> Hundred years ago, there were a lot of American scientists who wanted to discover (M.S., 11).
>
> In 3095, the columbian astronauts dicided to make a station on the moon. They prepared themselves to make what they dream for (L.B., 10).

In contrast, the control groups either began with 'once upon a time' or were similar to these three:

> In this picture there is a planet and there are some people dig the . . . (D.K., 11)
>
> I love the astronaut from the first time I see this picture. . . (S. M., 11)
>
> In the night there is a man his name Sally. . . (M.F., 9.5).

The experimental groups used more transitions such as 'One day', 'after two days', 'suddenly' and 'finally', and had more frequent use of words showing cause-effect relationships (mainly 'because'), and time sequence ('first', 'second', 'then', 'after that'). The experimental groups' writing also featured more colourful adjectives and adverbs, such as 'scary', 'astonishing', 'by chance', 'underground', 'source', and 'immediately', which provided better support for the ideas than the frequent 'bad', 'nice', and 'good' frequenting the control groups' papers. The story groups also used clear closings:

> At the end, they came back and were very happy of discovering gold. (M.S., 11)
>
> Finally, when he arrived on earth he took many gifts and presents, *not only to him, his friends also* . . . (emphasis mine) (S.S., 11)
>
> And at the end they found the petrole and they gave it to Lebanon, because Lebanon don't have petrole, and he took 'Nobel' prize. As one can see it was an 'Extra Adventure'. (W.S., 12)

Note the attempt at 'not only . . . but also' construct by an eleven-year-old S.S. The following closing is particularly reflective of the writer's ability to engage the reader and his budding ability to form hypotheses:

> . . . He went to the tomb and diged more immidiatly. He found a whole cimetry of people and took it back to earth. . .Now there are two questions: "*Are these earth people or not? And if they are, how did they die?*" (emphasis mine) (A.R., 12)

Overall, the control group children's stories about the picture often sounded like a series of sentences from an exercise book, not unlike the writing of LEP children in Huie and Yahya's above cited study:

> There is in the space peapol they are doing something
>
> And there is one in the back and there is one poting something in the rock
>
> And there is a something in the sky and there is a big tree in the tree there
>
> Is inside it airplane and there is many peapole. (Grade 5)

In contrast, the experimental groups' compositions featured more connected discourse as in the following example, ranked by the raters as 'High'. Despite the spelling errors, the writing has a clear organizational structure with a setting of the context, logical sequence of events and a clear conclusion. The repetition of the word 'groups' in different ways, the use of transitions and the reference to the passing of the three months, all contribute to coherence, as Michael Hoey (personal communication, 7 December 2003) also concurred (emphases mine):

> There was many people wants to go to space. They go in groups and every group wants to take things with them. The first group take clothes, second group brings shevel, third brings a map to tell them the way. The next Saturday they went. They go up by airplanes and fly. *Only they have 3 months.* When they arrive they saw many people diging and the airplanes, and a very big people, the aliens also, and trains. Every group put his thing on the ground. And they started to work. They want to find how many stars, and moon, and if they have more spaces. One of the group find a very big train. They go a far away with it. The other group dig in the ground. *The 3 months go on* and they have to go. The next Monday they went in the airport and all the people go to see them. They take all of the story to them and what they did and they were very happy. (J. K., 10)

Here is a beginning of another example from the experimental group. Note the two subordinate clauses in the third sentence (emphasis mine):

> One day there were an athrunate who want to go to space. The ground was very mudy. *They were shouting for them leader, but he didn't care because there was something in the ground.* They were working with there shovls to pick up the mudy sand, and driving the trucks to pick up the big rocks . . . (M. K., 10)

The following pre- and post-test sample from a 12-year-old student, whom the teacher identified as one of the weakest students in her class, is a striking illustration of the potential influence of stories on L2 children's written expression.

> I am see in the pickesher the people hit the elephant because the elephant atacked to the people there are eight people is hit the elephant and the elephant is very big the people is hold a big roll to hit him and the threes is put new [end of writing] (19 December 2002)

The pre-test was given just before the winter vacation, and the intervention started at the beginning of January. This is what the same student wrote in the post-test, after 15 weeks of the story-reading and literature circles (emphases mine):

> Discovery the moon
> Long ago we have many astronauts went to the moon to discovery, they went to bring the petrol, they went with him three Garph to dug the rock to discovery the patrol, then they arived in the rocked to the moon, then they bring all the tools to

dug the rock, they bring to the moon ten astaudents to discovery, then they start there warek very well, they have Garph to dug, they have astronauts to dug the rock with shovel, when they warek one astaudent when they warek they see under he rock a petrol then they showet ‾I found the petrol I found the petrol‾ then the friends tell ‾yes, yes, yes,‾ alvehim very happy then they went to the America strat, and they have the petrol. (15 April 2003)

Although the story is one long run-on, there is a clear sequence of events and attempts at transitions, with 'long ago', 'then' and 'when' contributing to coherence. The story has a clear beginning and an end. The word 'Garph' had the readers first puzzled, until it became clear that, in Arabic, a bulldozer is referred to as a *jarraf*, suggesting that the writer is drawing on her knowledge of letter names to invent the transliteration of the L1 word. Note also the dialogue bit, albeit without quotation marks. (Needless to say, other variables, beyond the knowledge and control of the researcher or the teacher may well have contributed to the change.)

Curiously, the words 'astronaut' and 'space' appeared in almost every composition, being particularly prominent in the compositions of the grade 5 children. Further investigation revealed that, while none of the stories used in the study involved space, the language book of Group 2 and 3 featured a lesson unit about space and space travel. The space lesson was, in fact, covered in Group 2 shortly before the post-test, explaining this group's particular facility with relevant vocabulary and concepts.

5 Discussion and conclusions

The purpose of this study was to examine the influence of story-based intervention on young L2 learners' written expression. The results corroborate the findings from the book flood studies and further suggest that story-reading and appropriate follow-up tasks not only contribute to the development of L2 children's vocabulary base but also to the coherence in their writing. This is evidenced by the story-based groups' use of more and clearer opening and closing sentences, transition signals, and supporting detail than their counterparts.

The qualitative differences between the experimental and control groups' writing further reflect the differences that Huie and Yahya (2003) found between native English-speaking children and their non-native English-speaking counterparts in terms of organization, support and voice. This suggests that story-reading and related follow-up activities, particularly written tasks, can bridge the gap between native and non-native English-speaking learners when it comes to learning language needed in tackling academic subject matter.

Despite the relatively short intervention period, some significant gains were noted. The findings are in line with Lazar's (1994: 116) claim that stories enable learners to move beyond word- and sentence-level awareness of language to a more overall awareness that includes differences in discourse sequence and the way words link, an awareness evident in many of the experimental group's anchor papers. The findings also resonate with Gregory's (1998: 118) 'knowledge centre' theory, which suggests that story books provide scaffolding for young second language learners' lexical, syntactic and ortho/graphophonic knowledge of the L2. The contextualized language of stories may also assist learners in the effort to communicate their ideas in writing.

In conclusion, this study supports the research findings from L1 classrooms that have found positive links between story-based instruction and children's written expression and shows that stories have a positive influence also on young L2 learners' written expression. Further research is needed to validate the findings in different cultural contexts.

Notes

1   The study reported here was supported by a grant from the Lebanese American University Research Council.

References

Arndt, V. (1987), 'Six writers in search of text: A protocol-based study of L1 and L2 writing'. *ELT Journal*, 41, 257–67.

Berthoff, A. E. (1981), *The Making of Meaning: Metaphors, Models, and Maxims for Writing Teachers*. Portsmouth, NH: Heinemann.

Bissex, G. (1980), *Gnys at Work. A Child Learns to Write and Read*. Cambridge, MA: Harvard University Press.

Carger, C. (1993), 'Louie comes to life: Pretend reading with second language emergent readers'. *Language Arts*, 70, 542–7.

Clay, M. M. (1998), *By Different Paths to Common Outcomes*. York: Stenhouse Publishers.

Cohen, D. (1968), 'The effect of literature on vocabulary and reading achievement'. *Elementary English*, 45, 209–17.

DeFord, D. (1981), 'Literacy: Reading, writing and other essentials'. *Language Arts*, 58, 652–8.

Dressel, J. H. (1990), 'The effects of listening to and discussing different qualities of children's literature on the narrative writing of fifth graders'. *Research in Teaching of English*, 24, 397–414.

Edelsky C. (1982), 'Writing in a bilingual program: the relation of L1 and L2 texts'. *TESOL Quarterly*, 16, 211–28.

Elley, W. (1991), 'Acquiring literacy in second language: The effects of book-based Programs'. *Language Learning*, 41, 3, 375–411.

Elley, W. (2000), 'The Potential of book floods for raising literacy levels'. *International Review of Education* 46, 3/4, 233–55.

Elley, W. and Mangubhai, F. (1983), 'The impact of reading on second language learning'. *Reading Research Quarterly*, 14, 1, 53–67.

Elley, W., Cutting, B., Mangubhai, F. and Hugo, C. (1996), 'Lifting Literacy levels with story books: Evidence from the South Pacific, Singapore, Sri Lanka and South Africa'. Paper presented at the World Conference on Literacy, Philadelphia, March 12–15 (ERIC Document Reproduction Service No. ED416441).

Freeman, Y. S. and Freeman, D. E. (1992), *Whole Language for Second Language Learners*. Portsmouth, NH: Heinemann.

Ghosn, I.-K. (2001), 'Teachers and Children Interacting Around the Textbook: An Exploratory Study of Children Developing Academic Second Language Literacy in Primary School English Language Classes in Lebanon' (unpublished Ph.D. thesis, University of Leicester). DAI 3049590.

Ghosn, I.-K., Hadba, C., Kanafani, J. and Richani, A. (2000), *English in Progress, National Textbook, Basic Education, Grade 6*. Sin-El-Fil, Lebanon: Educational Center for Research and Development.

Graves, D. (1983), *Writing: Teachers and Children at Work*. Portsmouth, NH: Heinemann Educational Books.

Gregory, E. (1998), *Making Sense of a New World*. London; Paul Chapman Publishing.

Gunderson, L. and Shapiro, J. (1988), 'Whole language instruction: Writing in 1st Grade'. *The Reading Teacher*, 41, 430–7.

Hafiz, F. and Tudor, I. (1990), 'Graded readers as an input medium in L2 learning'. *System*, 18, 1, 31–42.

Halliday, M. (1975), *Learning How to mean: Explorations in the Functions of Language*. London: Edward Arnold.

Hammill, D. D. and Larsen, S. C. (1996), *TOWL-3 Test of Written Language*, (3rd edn) Austin, TX: pro-ed.

Hudelson, S. (1984), 'Kan yu ret and rayt en Ingles: children become literate in English as a Second Language'. *TESOL Quarterly*, 18, 221–38.

Hudelson, S. (1989), *Write On. Children Writing in ESL*. ERIC Document Reproduction Service ED309653.

Huie, K. and Yahya, N. (2003), 'Learning to write in the primary grades: Experience of English language learners and mainstream students'. *TESOL Journal*, 12, 1, 25–31.

Johnson, T. and Louis, D. (1987), *Literacy Through Language*. Portsmouth, NH: Heinemann.

Kamii, C. (1991), 'What is constructivism?', in C. Camii, M. Manning and G. Manning (eds), *Early Literacy: A Constructivist Foundation for Whole Language*. Washington, DC: National Education Association.

Kress, G. (1994), *Learning to Write* (2nd edn). London: Routledge.

Kress, G. (1997), *Before Writing. Rethinking the Paths to Literacy*. London: Routledge.

Lazar, G. (1994), 'Using literature at lower levels'. *ELT Journal* 48, 2, 115–24.

MacGowan-Gilhooly, A. (1996), 'Fluency first: Reversing the traditional ESL sequence', in B. Leeds, (ed.), *Writing in a Second Language*. London: Longman, pp. 48–59.

Mangubhai, F. and Elley, W. (1982), 'The role of reading in promoting ESL'. *Language Learning and Communication*, 1, 2, 121–232.

Maquire, M. and Graves, B. (2001), 'Speaking personalities in primary school children's L2 writing'. *TESOL Quarterly*, 35, 561–93.

Mikkelsen, N. (1984), 'Literature and the storymaking powers of children'. *Children's Literature Association Quarterly*, 9, 9–14.

Ministry of National Education, Youth and Sports (1995), *The New Framework for Education in Lebanon*. Sin-El-Fil: Center for Educational Research and Development.

Raimes, A. (1987), 'Language proficiency, writing ability, and composition strategies'. *Language Learning*, 37, 439–68.

Rigg, P. (1981), 'Beginning to read in English the LEA way', in C. W. Twyford, W. Diehl and K. Feathers (eds), *Reading English as a Second Language: Moving from*

Theory. Monographs in Teaching and Learning 4. Bloomington, IN: Indiana University, pp. 81–90.

Samway, K. (1988), 'The writing processes of non-native English speaking children in the elementary grades'. *Dissertation Abstracts.* (UMI No. 8803327).

Smith, F. (1982), *Writing and the Writer.* New York: Holt, Rinehart and Winston.

Strickland, D. with Dillon, R., Funkhouser, L., Glick, M. and Rogers, C. (1989), 'Research currents: Classroom dialogue during literature response groups'. *Language Arts*, 66, 192–200.

Tudor, I. and Hafiz, F. (1989), 'Extensive reading as a means of input to L2 learning'. *Journal of Research in Reading*, 12, 2, 164–78.

Zamel, V. (1992), 'Writing one's way into reading'. *TESOL Quarterly* 26, 463–85.

Appendix A

Book Review

I Hate English! (Ellen Levine)

Name of reviewer . . . .

Put a tick in the box that best tells what you think.

	☹	☺	☺
This was an interesting book.			
I enjoyed reading this book.			
I would recommend this book to my friends.			
I think that boys and girls will like this book.			
I think that mainly girls will like this book.			
I think that mainly boys will like this book.			
This book is good for children of my age.			
This book is good for children younger than I.			
This book is good for children older than I.			

Appendix B

Reader Response

The Dragonfly Surprise (Irma Ghosn)

After reading the story, choose ONE of the following activities to complete:

1. *Add or change something.* Here are some suggestions:
   - Write what Mallika tells her mother about the contest and what happened.
   - Write a different ending to the story. Begin from the point where Heba enters the dragonfly in the contest, or from the point when the winner is announced.
   - Continue the story. What happens next?
2. *Write a diary entry.* Imagine that you are one of the characters in the story. Write a diary entry where you describe something that happened to you in the story. Use the first person pronoun 'I' (for example, Today my best friend Heba did something I will never forget . . .)
3. *Write a letter to one of the characters.* Here are some suggestions:
   - A letter from Mallika to her sister in Sri Lanka.
   - A letter from you to Mallika, telling how you feel about what happened.
   - A letter from you to Heba, telling what you think about what she did.
   - A letter from Miss Randa to her friend, telling about what happened.

Appendix C

Literature Circle Reflections

Sarah, Plain and Tall (Patricia McLachlan)

After reading the story, think about the story and talk about it with your literature circle partners. If you don't know how to start the discussion, here are some questions for you to think about.

What went on in your mind when you read about Anna's and Caleb's father putting an ad in a paper to get a wife?

Did you think Sarah would stay? When did you begin to think that she would?

What about Anna and Caleb? Is it easy to accept someone to replace one's mother?

What kind of a person makes a good mother? What qualities did Sarah have that made the relationship work?

12 The value of comprehension in the early stages of the acquisition and development of Bahasa Indonesian by non-native speakers

Erlin Susanti Barnard

1 Introduction

This study investigates the effect of applying the 'comprehension approach' in classroom instruction of Indonesian as a foreign language. The comprehension approach, also known as the 'input-based approach', claims that for acquisition to take place there must be a period of time allowed to process input without any pressure to produce output. In other words, instruction will be more effective if it is based on input rather than output practice.

The input presented to the learners is specially contrived and manipulated in order to induce comprehension of the target structure. It is achieved by gradually introducing new target items using gestures, visual aids, contextual clues or cognates to assist understanding. Learners are required to indicate their comprehension of the input stimuli in non-verbal or minimally verbal responses, e.g. by acting, drawing, or selecting one of the available answers. This could be considered an outcome-based approach whereby rather than being required to produce language output, learners produce an outcome of learning in the form of those non-verbal activities that indicate their comprehension. The term 'outcome' refers to the effect of a communication, as opposed to the term 'output', which is the language produced. The outcome could be getting a job, influencing somebody, solving a problem, producing a drawing, performing an appropriate action, etc. At the early stages of language learning, learners (especially in a comprehension approach) often do not produce an output but they can produce an outcome. Doing so can be much more motivating than simply receiving input or attempting premature output (Brian Tomlinson, personal communication). Most Indonesian language training, especially during the beginning stage of acquisition, has ignored this input-based approach, emphasizing the output or production approach.

2 The literature on comprehension-based approaches

Research into input-based instruction has been inspired by several theories of L2 acquisition, such as input hypothesis, input-processing theories, and/or skill-learning theories. The proponents of input-processing theories argue that human beings' processing capacities are limited. VanPatten (1996), for instance, suggests that elementary learners in particular may have difficulty in simultaneously attending to form and meaning in the input. Thus, it could be disadvantageous to require students to produce form while processing input for meaning. Skill learning theorists such as Anderson (1993) and McLaughlin *et al* (1983) suggest that learning takes place as a result of practice, and that a large amount of input is needed in order to provide sufficient practice that will lead from declarative to procedural knowledge, and from control to automatization of knowledge. This procedural knowledge is highly specific, and practice in comprehension will build comprehension skill, while practice in production will invoke production skill. Krashen (1985) puts forward a theory that mere exposure to input is not enough; rather, it is comprehensible input that promotes acquisition in motivated learners. The learner acquires more language when exposed to language that contains structures that are slightly beyond his/her current level of competence, yet are comprehensible through context and other extra-linguistic cues directed to the learner.

On the other hand, Swain's (1985) 'output hypothesis' argues that comprehensible output facilitates acquisition. It is only during the output or production stage that learners attend to the syntactic analysis of the input, whereas during the input processing stage, learners mainly focus on the semantic interpretation of the data. By pushing learners to produce coherent and appropriate output, learners are encouraged to move from semantic/top-down processing to syntactic/bottom-up processing, thus promoting interlanguage development.

Studies that look into the effects of instruction under different conditions on learners' performance can be used to examine these different theoretical views. The results of several experiments carried out by Reeds *et al* (1977), as well as Postovsky (1974, 1981), endorse the effectiveness of input-based instruction. So do results of various experiments conducted by VanPatten and Cadierno (1993a, 1993b), Cadierno (1995), VanPatten and Sanz, (1995) and VanPatten and Oikkenon (1996).

Despite the fact that most of the studies by VanPatten and co-workers (1993a and b, 1995, 1996) seem to support the effectiveness of input-based instruction, there remain a few problems concerning the design of the studies. A major problem lies in the fact that the groups not only received different types of practice, they also received different types of explicit instruction. For example, in the input group, the explicit instruction included an explanation of the contrast between the subject and object of a verb, followed by a presentation of subject and object pronouns. Next, the explanation emphasized the importance of keeping in mind the position of object pronouns in Spanish in contrast to those in English. In the output group, explicit instruction involved an explanation of objects and object pronouns, followed by a paradigmatic presentation of the form and position of object pronouns within the sentence.

With differences in explanation as well as in practice it is difficult to

determine the main variable affecting results. Is the difference in performance caused by the different explanations, or is it caused by the different
types of practice that the experimental groups received? Although VanPatten
and Oikkenon (1996) sought to address this issue in a subsequent study by
narrowing down the variables, i.e. explicit instruction versus input practice,
the study did not include any comparison with the output group. Thus, the
study only managed to partially resolve the issue by showing that the input
practice, as compared to explicit instruction, held greater significance in
enhancing the acquisition process. Thus, the superiority of input practice
versus output practice in its contribution to the acquisition process needs to
be further established by conducting a study which compares input and
output practice groups who both receive either the same type of explicit
instruction, or no instruction.

With regard to production skills, the existing studies report conflicting
evidence as to the effectiveness of comprehension or input-based training. In
relation to the question of whether input-based instruction may result in a
transfer to production skill, several of the above studies have provided some
evidence that indeed transfer is possible. For example, these studies indicated that transfer did occur in the input group, who, although not receiving
production practice, performed as well as the output group in production
tasks. However, another major problem with the studies that endorsed input-
based instruction concerned the design and measure of production tasks,
which were focused, controlled, and limited to discrete items. Besides the
objection that this type of task induced explicit knowledge, it is also possible
that the production task actually resembled the practice that the input group
received, thus enabling them to perform well in a controlled production test.
As a result, it may appear that training in comprehension skills brought
about transfer into production skills. In their attempt to address this issue,
VanPatten and Sanz (1995) used various production tests that also included
open-ended, online production tasks. While this study seemed to confirm
that without production training the effect of input-based instruction can be
applied to the written narration test, unfortunately no comparison was made
with an output-based instruction group. Thus, the question of the superiority
of input practice remains unconfirmed: had the performance been compared to those who were trained in output-based instruction, would they
have fared better or not? Consequently, the necessity of conducting a study
which employs open-ended tasks, and one which compares the results and
performance of input- and output-based training in such tasks cannot be
overlooked.

Although another study by Allen (2000) attempted to measure production
in a more open-ended format, the nature of the task may still have been
restrictive in the sense that students were required to focus on certain structural elements. Moreover, the test format and topic very much resemble the
practice the output group received, which may have augmented their
performance in the test.

With the exception of Postovsky's study (1974), most if not all the studies have focused on a few linguistic structures as their teaching target and assessed the acquisition of those particular forms. In their study, VanPatten and Sanz (1995: 172–3) stated that, 'the input is not free-flowing and spontaneous, like the input one might receive in a communicative interaction. Instead, the input is purposefully prepared and manipulated to highlight particular grammatical features'. The problem confronting studies that focus on specific grammatical forms is their failure to take into account the natural order of acquisition. Salaberry pointed out the lack of a comprehensive and reliable theoretical model of L2 development to guide the choice of linguistic structures to be taught, and argued that, 'the identification of developmental stages in L2 acquisition is not an accurate process. Hence, the identification of linguistic structures to be taught (and how they are taught) represents a problem . . . Furthermore, not all language learners may be at the same level of development of their L2 at any given time' (1997: 427).

No longitudinal study has yet been conducted that measures students' global language proficiency as a result of input versus output training where training lasts for an extended period of time. Most, if not all, of the studies were carried out over relatively brief intervals of time. One study with a relatively longer period of treatment is Postovsky's (1974) four week experiment. DeKeyser and Sokalski rightly admit that, 'Given the limited amount of practice received by participants in both our study and VanPatten and Cadierno's (1993a, 1993b), the results shed no light on automatization processes at all; we can speak only of declarative and nonautomatized procedural knowledge' (1996: 636). Hence, it is essential to conduct a longitudinal study with broader focus than a few linguistic target structures, which assesses the effect of long-term systematic comprehension and production practice on automatization processes, as well as on development of implicit knowledge.

3 The study

The aim of the present study was to further investigate the effects of comprehension versus production training conducted over the course of two semesters of college study on beginning students' achievement.

Unlike other studies, where the new treatments were introduced for a short period of time in the midst of the students' regular course of learning (in relation to the restricted grammatical structures as the target form), in the current study students received either comprehension training or production training throughout the course of their study in order to increase the strength of the treatment.

3.1 Research questions

The research questions that guided the design of this study are formulated as follows:

(1) How do comprehension and production training differently affect stu-

dents' overall achievement in comprehension tasks and production tasks by the end of their first semester?

(2) Will the effects of training be the same in the second semester?

3.2 Hypotheses

With respect to the research questions, the following hypotheses were formulated:

(1) After receiving comprehension training for one semester, students will perform better on comprehension tasks than those who receive production training.

(2) After receiving comprehension training for one semester, students will perform at least as well on production tasks as those who receive production training.

(3) After receiving comprehension training for two semesters, students will perform better on comprehension tasks than those who receive production training.

(4) After receiving comprehension training for two semesters, students will perform at least as well on production tasks as those who receive production training.

3.3 Participants

The participants for this study were tertiary undergraduate students from various faculties in a major university in Singapore who took beginning Indonesian language module 1 as a voluntary option. In order to ensure equality of the subject pools in terms of language proficiency, background and education, students were required to take a pre-survey questionnaire and a pre-test. Those who were included in the experiment had the following characteristics: between 20–23 years of age, with no background in the Indonesian language, bilingual speakers of English and another language, either Chinese or Tamil, which was studied as a subject matter in their primary and secondary schools. Hence, the subjects were reasonably homogeneous in terms of age, English proficiency and learning background. A total of 200 students in semester one and 58 in semester two were divided into input and output groups, both of which were taught using equal amounts of time and materials by the same team of teachers.

3.4 Design

The quasi-experimental design was chosen for the study, which was conducted in a real-life situation over two semesters. Cohen *et al* maintain that, 'Often in educational research, it is simply not possible for investigators to undertake true experiments. At best, they may be able to employ something approaching a true experimental design' due to the lack of control factors in the complexities of real-life (2000: 214). Nonetheless, undertaking an experimental study under real life conditions (as opposed to in a laboratory setting) may seem to be more favourable for the current study's purposes. Hatch and Farhady rightly stipulate that:

> Our goal should be to approximate as closely as possible the standards of true experimental design. The more care we take, the more confident we can be that we have valid results that we can share with others. However, if we reduce our experiments to highly artificial laboratory-type experiments, we must also worry about whether the results can be directly transferred and shared as valid for the classroom.
>
> (1982: 23–4)

One significant goal of conducting this study was to bring about improvements in teaching practice based on what can be learned from the outcome of the study. For this reason, it was also considered more beneficial to conduct a study that accurately reproduced a real life situation that teachers and practitioners could easily relate to.

The subjects of the current study were divided more or less equally into two treatment groups according to availability (105 in the comprehension/input group, and 95 in the production/output group). They were given the choice to register for either the morning classes or afternoon classes on a first come first served basis until the quota for each division was filled. The morning and afternoon division represents the division of the input and output groups and was decided arbitrarily. Although the treatment groups were intact classes, the groups represented some characteristics of random sampling because the assignment to each respective group was for the most part determined automatically according to students' time availability.

In the second semester, the grouping could no longer be determined on availability but by the number of students in each respective group who decided to continue with module 2. As it turned out, there were 26 in the output group and 32 in the input group.

3.5 Independent variables

The independent variables are the types of training. The comprehension/input group was taught with an emphasis on input-practice training, and the production/output group received instruction with an emphasis on output-practice training.

In the output-practice training, students were required to produce oral and/or written responses to the input presentation, for example by performing dialogues, role plays, interviews; whereas in the input-practice training, students were to respond in non- or minimal verbal activities such as pointing, miming, acting out, drawing, selecting or matching the pictures to the correct responses, etc.

Both groups followed a functional–notional syllabus, instead of a structural syllabus. In an effort to establish equality in terms of types of explicit instruction received, in the first semester of their study (in module 1) neither group received explicit instruction, whereas in the second semester (in module 2), where complexity of the language is greater, both groups received some explicit instruction of the same amount and type. Hence, in accord with Ellis (1993), the structural syllabus was incorporated into the course to 'serve as a facilitator' rather than as a primary syllabus.

To control the teacher variable, both types of group were taught by the same teachers. Each teacher equally taught input and output groups for the same number of hours each week.

3.6 Dependent variables

In order to assess the effects of comprehension versus production training on students' proficiency, students took both comprehension and production types of tests. In this respect, open-ended and online production tests were employed to better gauge students' acquisition. Such tests are necessary to avoid reliance upon explicit knowledge. Accordingly, rather than focusing on specific linguistic forms, the tests measured the development of students' global language achievement at different stages of their study, including their ability to use the target language in communication, a skill which procedural implicit knowledge underlies (Ellis 1993).

Post- and delayed post-tests were administered to evaluate students' performance at the beginning, middle and end of each semester. In addition, an oral interview was administered at the end of each term. Table 12.1 presents the template for the evaluation design and outline. In sum, both the post-tests and delayed post-tests comprised comprehension and production types of test to measure students' performance in these respective areas, bringing the number of tests administered in this study to a total of 18 tests, nine for the first module and nine for the second module.

Table 12.1 Evaluation outline

			Input group	Output group
4th week	Post test 1	1. Comprehension test		
		2. Production test		
8th week	Post test 2	3. Comprehension test		
		4. Production test		
11th week	Post test 3	5. Cloze test		
		6. Production test		
13th week	Delayed post test 1	7. Oral production test		
15th – 16th week	Delayed post test 2	8. Production test		
		9. Comprehension test		

The format of the oral test included performing a role-play with a partner based on a given situation, and giving a picture narration individually, followed by a question–answer session with a partner and/or teacher. The written production test incorporated various formats including dialogue elicitation, in which students were presented with a situation of two people conversing. One person's utterances were provided, and the other's were left blank. Students taking the role of B had to write utterances that connected to A's utterances. The other tasks were question formation (students had to write questions that elicited given answers, describing objects and their locations based on a picture, writing a minimum of 100 words (for module 1, but 150 words for module 2) of dialog or composition based on a given topic/situation).

The various tasks and formats of the comprehension test incorporated reading or listening to a narration followed by a true/false, and/or multiple choice task, listening to a passage and then drawing features of it, reading or listening to a text, followed by a labelling task and filling in blanks in a cloze passage.

3.7 Results

The results of the data analysis presented in Table 12.2 demonstrate that with the exception of the cloze test, the input group outperformed the output

Table 12.2 Tests results from Semester 1

Tests	Groups	N	Mean	S.D.	T	Sig.
1. comprehension test	Output	94	61.92	12.53		
	Input	103	66.54	11.87	2.65	0.0087
2. production test	Output	95	73.13	11.64		
	Input	102	67.31	13.24	3.28	0.0012
3. comprehension test	Output	92	30.44	9.91		
	Input	105	33.19	9.50	1.98	0.0490
4. production test	Output	92	38.81	5.36		
	Input	105	38.61	5.67	0.25	0.7995
5. cloze test	Output	92	23.06	7.18		
	Input	104	22.04	7.26	0.99	0.3247
6. production test	Output	92	21.30	3.06		
	Input	104	20.04	3.49	2.69	0.0077
7. oral production test	Output	93	66.94	6.21		
	Input	105	66.17	6.74	0.87	0.4039
8. production test	Output	93	56.70	9.26		
	Input	102	57.45	8.99	0.57	0.5673
9. comprehension test	Output	93	10.95	2.94		
	Input	102	11.89	3.28	2.11	0.0361

group in all the comprehension tests that were conducted throughout the semester as immediate post-tests. Furthermore, at the end of the first semester of study, the input group outperformed the output group in the delayed comprehension test. The T-test results reveal that the differences between the groups' performance were statistically significant at $p < 0.05$.

However, there were mixed results in the production tests conducted throughout the semester as immediate post-tests, two of which favoured the output group, whereas one production test showed that there was no significant difference between the two groups. Interestingly, by the end of the first semester, no significant difference was found between the input group and the output group, both in oral as well as written production tests.

The second research question was formulated to explore whether the effects of training would be the same in the second semester of study. In this present study, the treatment, i.e. the pattern of training from the first semester was, in general, extended into the second semester. The only difference in treatment from the first semester was that explicit grammar lessons were added to both the input and output groups in the second semester, in the same manner and quantity by the same teacher in each group.

It can be seen from the results presented in Table 12.3 that the effects of training in the second semester did not seem to be the same as in the first semester. In all tests, except in the oral production test, there was no significant difference found between the output and input groups' performance. Although the descriptive statistics indicate that the output group's mean

Table 12.3 Tests results from Semester 2

Tests	Groups	N	Mean	S.D.	T	Sig.
1. comprehension test	Output	26	69.99	16.40		
	Input	32	68.21	14.23	0.44	0.6647
2. production test	Output	26	75.45	10.23		
	Input	32	71.49	10.76	1.43	0.1578
3. comprehension test	Output	25	53.28	10.79		
	Input	32	49.34	10.23	1.40	0.1678
4. production test	Output	25	72.32	13.43		
	Input	32	73.23	10.84	0.28	0.7839
5. cloze test	Output	26	73.87	12.99		
	Input	32	70.52	13.06	0.97	0.3342
6. production test	Output	26	63.90	9.03		
	Input	32	62.42	8.81	0.63	0.5330
7. oral production test	Output	26	73.11	5.12		
	Input	32	69.78	5.82	*2.32*	*0.0243*
8. production test	Output	26	66.21	11.65		
	Input	32	61.41	13.00	1.48	0.1421
9. comprehension test	Output	26	73.42	13.60		
	Input	32	67.47	16.17	1.52	0.1337

scores were higher than the input group's in some of the tests – both comprehension and production – and the input group's mean score was higher than the output group's in one of the production tests, these differences were not statistically established according to the T-test analysis. The only result that strongly demonstrates the output group's superiority over the input group was found in the oral production test conducted at the end of the semester. By the end of the second semester, the production training resulted in greater oral production skills for the output group than the comprehension training.

3.8 Discussion

First semester of Indonesian study

The results from the first semester indicate that the input group had a clear advantage in terms of comprehension skill. In this course, instruction that focused on providing ample input processing activities allowed students to gain better comprehension skill compared to those who were taught under the production-focused type of instruction. This result is in line with the Input and Input Processing Hypotheses' claims, as indicated in Hypothesis 1.

There was one deviation in the cloze passage format in post-test 3, where there was no difference found between the performances of the input and output groups. In this case, it can be argued that the cloze passage format does not solely measure comprehension skills, as the test also requires students to produce language items in written form. Hence, in addition to comprehension skill, production skill is also required to accomplish the cloze passage task. This finding will be further discussed in the section below. At the same time, this result also implies that at this stage, the output group may have demonstrated comprehension skill equivalent to that of the input group. However, this comprehension skill was not durable as shown by the delayed post-tests results, in which the output group's comprehension skill was not on a par with that of the input group's. These findings confirm the first hypothesis that the input-based training, on balance, seems to produce more stable and durable results in developing comprehension skill.

The results of this study also seem to uphold the second hypothesis, namely that after receiving comprehension training for one semester, students will perform at least as well as those who receive production training on production tasks. Indeed, students from the input and output groups performed equally in both the oral and written delayed post-tests. However, an examination of the individual post-tests conducted early on during the semester shows that the output group actually performed better than the input group in several production post-tests.

It may appear that these results are explicable from the skill-building point of view (Anderson 1993), with its claim that students' learning is the result of the training they receive and that if they are trained in comprehension activities they will do well in that skill and, likewise, if they are trained in production activities they will perform well in production skill. Nonetheless, this does not explain the fact that although the input group did not receive much training in the area of production, they performed as well as the output group in some of the production tests, i.e. the written post-test 2, the cloze passage in post-test 3, and the delayed written test, as well as the oral post-tests. The skill-building theory is not able to account for the fact that without much training in production activities, students in the input group were still able to perform as well as those who were exclusively trained in that mode. More importantly, it should be noted that the output group, which performed better in most of the production post-tests, did not perform better than the input group in the delayed post tests. This indicates that the output-based training appeared to result in superior skill for immediate production (as shown in the output group's better performance in some of the post tests), but this superior performance does not appear to be durable.

The results also suggest that the training received by the input group was likely to enable the students to develop the knowledge not only to comprehend, but also to eventually produce, albeit more slowly than those trained using the production approach. Furthermore, the results support the current claim that training learners to comprehend meaning results in intake which, in turn, facilitates their interlanguage development (Ellis 1993, 1995; VanPatten and Cadierno 1993a). It is possible that at the early stage of learning, the input group was not ready to produce consistent or reliable output immediately as they were still processing the new input they had just received, working on accommodating the input into intake, and incorporating the intake into their interlanguage system, and hence, they had not reached direct readiness to produce. In other words, when compared to output-based training, in terms of production skill, input-based training may not produce an effect that is immediately and strongly perceptible, but rather produces a delayed and more enduring effect. In light of the information processing theory (McLaughlin *et al* 1983), it is possible that at the early stage, attentional resources were still employed for processing meaning, which resulted in production skills being held back. However, once understanding has been automatized, attentional resources would eventually be allocated to process forms, which signify the production process. The delayed written and oral post-tests were of integrative tests rather than tests on newly taught items which involved online production; hence, the gain measured is likely to be more indicative of procedural knowledge that, in turn, is a better measure of acquisition. In this regard, confirming the second hypothesis, the input group performed as well as the output group on production tasks by the end of the first semester.

In summary, similar to the previous findings by VanPatten and Cadierno (1993a, 1993b), Cadierno (1995), and Tanaka (1996), the results from the first semester of Indonesian study suggest that in the early elementary level of language learning, input-based training may have an advantage over output-based training, in that input-based training results in comprehension as well as production skill, whereas output-based training results in production but not comprehension skill.

Second semester of Indonesian study

While, in general, the treatment and procedure in the second semester of Indonesian study were similar to that of the first semester, the present study yielded different result patterns between the first and second semester classes. Overall, in the second semester class, the input group seemed to be consistent in their performance in comprehension as well as in written production tasks. These results lend support to the input-processing theory that continued treatment with input-based instruction will most likely be effective in increasing proficiency, both in terms of comprehension and production skills.

The findings, however, do not seem to verify the third hypothesis, namely that after receiving comprehension training for two semesters, students will perform better on comprehension tasks than those who receive production training. On the contrary, at this stage, the production group seemed to have managed to catch up with the input group in terms of comprehension skill.

The results partly confirm the fourth hypothesis, namely that after receiving comprehension training for two semesters, students will perform at least as well as those who receive production training on production tasks, particularly in terms of written production tasks. In the area of oral production skill, however, the output group seemed to have an advantage over the input group.

Thus, the output group showed improved comprehension skill compared to the first semester, as in the second semester they performed as well as the input group on comprehension tasks. In addition, the output group outperformed the input group on oral production tasks.

Now the onus of explanation is on how the output-based training generates improved comprehension skill in the second semester – but not in the first semester – and how the output training produces better results on developing oral skill. It seems quite logical to conclude that the advantage in oral skill can be attributed to the large amount of oral practice provided in the production-based instruction, in line with the claim proposed by the skill-building theory. However, output practice per se may not be the only or main reason for the good performance of the output group, either on comprehension or oral production tasks. It could be argued that the role of input is still of critical importance in understanding this observable fact. While the predominant emphasis of the output-based instruction was on output production, the production activity was mostly implemented in an interactive mode. Thus, unlike the traditional mechanical production practice, the production tasks in this study were focused on meaning. Meaning being negotiated during a two-way communication constitutes one type of input. This view was expressed by Long in his 'interaction hypothesis' (1983b) that states, 'It is not input only that is important to second language acquisition but input that occurs in interaction where meaning is negotiated'. Hence, it is not input per se that is significant in the process of acquisition, but interaction input that promotes comprehension. During this process of interaction that aims at getting one's message across, linguistic input is adjusted to the participants' comprehension level by way of paraphrasing, repetition, clarification and/or expansion. In this process, one of the key conditions for acquisition, i.e. comprehension input, is met. It is important to note, however, that the primary contributing factor towards acquisition may not be the output produced, but rather the input generated through the interaction. Krashen *et al* (1982) has said that, rather than playing a direct role in the acquisition process, output has an indirect role, namely, as a means to obtain further comprehension input. By the second semester, it is possible that the interaction (comprehensible) input generated over time through numerous interactions largely contributed to the improvement of the output group's comprehension skill. The question that follows is why, then, did interaction input not seem to produce the same results in the first semester.

In relation to the interaction hypothesis, Krashen (2003) posed an interesting question: 'Is interaction necessary or just helpful?'. Implied in this question is: without interaction, would acquisition be jeopardized? The findings of the current study indicate that this is not the case. In the first semester of Indonesian study, without necessitating interaction, the input training seems to be the likely victor in procuring comprehension skill and production skills. Conversely, output training that incorporates the interaction input does not seem to have an advantage over input training in terms of production skills, written as well as oral. As a matter of fact, output training seems to disadvantage the output group in terms of comprehension skill. In this study, interaction input only reveals its positive effect in the second semester. It could be argued that the different types and amount of input received by the input and output groups is still likely to be the determining factor in the outcome of this study.

During the first semester, the quantity and/or quality of input, i.e. 'interaction input' received by the output group may not be equal to the 'comprehension input' received by the input group that was processed in the silent mode. Recall that the input training was presented in the form of audio or written texts to which students responded in non-verbal or minimally verbal mode. This type of 'comprehension input' could well be more beneficial for the early beginners. Learners were allowed sufficient time and freedom to process the input without any pressure to produce. The 'interaction input' may not work as well during this early stage of learning for the reason that students may need to have a silent period as they process input into intake and incorporate intake into their interlanguage. From the view point of the human being as 'limited capacity processor', it is unlikely that learners could process optimally both form and meaning at the same time. In order to produce utterances, learners have to pay attention to form in the formulation of sounds into words, words into phrases, and phrases into sentences, etc. during such a process, and their attention to meaning may thus not be as optimal. Hence, at a stage where learners are still in the controlled processing stage, a focus on production activity may impede comprehension.

In addition, the production activity – although it is interactive in nature and focuses on negotiation of meaning – may not constitute much in the way of interaction input yet, since at this initial stage of learning the students lack a substantial amount of linguistic repertoire to use and manipulate. In this case, the interaction may well be restrictive, contrived and, thus, pseudo-communicative. Furthermore, the quality of the input generated through interaction may not be optimal, as learners are likely to hear language production by their peers that is imperfect or includes errors.

To sum up, in comparing the nature of input in the input and output groups in the first semester of learning, it could be inferred that:

(1) The input received by the output group was not as extensive as that of the input group. In the practice activities that follow input presentation, the input group listened to or read texts, dialogues, narration, etc. whereas the output group performed dialogues, narration, etc. Long (1983a), as quoted in Ellis (1990: 99), maintains that 'greater quantities of comprehensible input result in better (or at least faster) acquisition'.

(2) The quality of input received by the input and output groups was different: the source of input for the input group was mainly the teacher's or native speaker's speech presented through the audio and written texts, whereas the source of input for the output group was the teacher's and, to a large extent, peer's speech that could have been restrictive, contrived and contained errors.

(3) The processing of input by the output group could have been held back by the fact that learners had to attend to meaning and form simultaneously.

For the above mentioned reasons, the input training (processing comprehensible input in the silent mode) produced a better effect than the output training (processing interactive input in the verbal mode) in the first semester of learning. The question to be addressed next is what was occurring differently during the second semester of learning? How did the interaction input function differently in the second semester, such that it appeared to cause the improved performance of the output group?

One function of output, as claimed by Swain (1985), is to provide opportunity for meaningful use of one's linguistics resources. However, it can be argued that it is not until learners' linguistic repertoires have gradually developed, that learners are able to freely manipulate them for output production which, in turn, would generate more comprehension input to be processed into intake. As indicated earlier, this may explain why, in the second semester, students who were trained in output-based activity were able to perform well in comprehension tasks compared to their comprehension performance in the first semester. By this time, students' comprehension skill was greater because they had experienced substantial comprehension input, generated over time through numerous meaningful interactions during their output activity. Hence, it is reasonable to say that the effectiveness of pushed output was not that apparent during the early stage of learning, whereas over time, with an increasing amount of comprehensible input, the effect of pushed output was more perceptible. Particularly in oral production skill, its effect was superior compared to the effect of input processing.

The improvement of the output group learners' comprehension skill suggests that by this stage, input has become more automatically comprehended. As a result, learners can afford to release more attentional resources to form, as their attention is not absorbed so fully on processing meaning. As indicated earlier, the process of producing language causes learners to be more aware of language form, during which they are more conscious about the mechanism of combining linguistic elements to formulate utterances. Consequently, the quality of learners' production also improves.

In connection with the superiority of oral production skill, Swain (1985) strongly argues the merit of comprehension output. Language output is not merely seen as a means to generate more comprehension input – as implied in the Input Hypothesis – but it is perceived to have its own role in the process of acquisition. It is true that during two-way interaction, meaning negotiation is crucial and thus brings about comprehension input as well. Nonetheless, beyond the issue of comprehension input, a successful interaction also calls for learners to devote effort to fine-tuning their output in order to send across meaning satisfactorily. They may need to repeat, revise, and/or rephrase their utterances to convey their intention accurately in order to get appropriate responses during interactions. Especially in overcoming a communication breakdown, learners will be challenged and pushed to use alternate means to express themselves clearly. During this process of making use of the language, rather than comprehending the language, learners will be given opportunities to experiment with language, try out means of expression and see if they work. At the same time, they will be forced to move from semantic processing to syntactic processing of the language.

It is possible that the input group's oral production skill in the second semester is not on par with the output group's skill because they were not pushed in their output production in the same way as the output group. The Output Hypothesis maintains that 'acquisition takes place when there is a communication breakdown, and learners are pushed to use alternative means to get across . . . the message . . . precisely, coherently, and appropriately' (Swain 1985: 248–9). The input group may have equal written production skill with the output group because writing is a private activity and they can do so independently and, as demonstrated by this result, they do not exhibit problems in this area. However, what is lacking from the input training is the amount of interactive tasks in which learners are likely to encounter communication breakdown and which, in turn, could provide them with opportunities to put their language into use in a real/online communication mode. Although students were allowed more opportunities to use verbal responses during the input training in the second semester, the bulk of the activity still required predominantly non-verbal or minimally verbal responses. As the Output Hypothesis claims, opportunities to speak may not in themselves be sufficient; it is only when a learner is pushed that output contributes to acquisition. Hence, the input group may not have experienced the push to fine-tune their language production online as much as the output group did. Furthermore, with most of the activity being focused on comprehension, this focus on meaning may in fact prevent learners from paying attention to linguistic form in the input. As a result, during the speaking test in which there was more pressure for students to manipulate forms in online production mode, they may not be able to make use of their skills as smoothly as the output group.

4 Conclusion

It is not viable to conclude from the present study that the input training worked best, because the differences between the input and output group in comprehension and written production tasks in the second semester were not significant. The input-based instruction and the output-based instruction had almost the same effect on developing comprehension and written production skills in the long run. Furthermore, by the end of the second semester of learning, the output training produced better results on oral production tasks.

The implication is that while comprehension input may well be paramount in contributing to the process of language acquisition, it may also be necessary to implement output practice once the learners have developed sufficient linguistic repertoires, which in this study appeared to be in the second semester of learning. The results of this study suggest that a focus on comprehension input activities works very well in the early stage of Indonesian acquisition in developing comprehension and production skills. However, a prolonged focus on comprehension activities exclusively may not be as beneficial in developing optimal oral production skills. Learners fail to benefit from the opportunity to experience pushed output that the output group has. On the other hand, production training may develop comprehension as well as written-cum-oral production skills in the long run, although a focus on production activities at the early stage of acquisition does not seem to work well in developing comprehension skills.

One practical implication based on the results of this study could be introducing a new instructional approach whereby students begin their course with a focus on comprehension and then move towards a greater focus on production. For example, the input-based instruction could be implemented in the first semester of learning, in order for the learners to concentrate on input processing without being distracted by the requirement to produce. Subsequently, in the second semester, once learners have attained a foundational level of proficiency, output-based instruction can be added. In this way, learners can manipulate the language resources they have to further generate more input, and be pushed to practice the comprehension output by which they continue developing and refining their interlanguage systems.

References

Allen, L. (2000), 'Form-meaning connections and the French causative. An experiment in processing instruction'. *Studies in Second Language Acquisition*, 22, 69–84.

Anderson, J. (1993), *Rules of the Mind*. Hillsdale, NJ: Lawrence Erlbaum.

Cadierno, T. (1995), 'Formal instruction from a processing perspective: An investigation into the Spanish past tense'. *The Modern Language Journal*, 79 179–93.

Cohen, L., Manion, L. and Morrison, K. (2000), *Research Methods in Education*. London: Routledge Falmer.

DeKeyser, R. and Sokalski, K. (1996), 'The differential role of comprehension and production Practice'. *Language Learning*, 46, 613–42.

Ellis, R. (1990), *Instructed Second Language Acquisition*. Oxford: Basil Blackwell Ltd.

Ellis, R. (1993), 'The structural syllabus and second language acquisition'. *TESOL Quarterly*, 27, 91–113.

Ellis, R. (1995), 'Interpretation tasks for grammar teaching'. *TESOL Quarterly*, 29, 87–105.

Hatch, E. and Farhady, H. (1982), *Research Design and Statistics for Applied Linguistics*. Rowley, MA: Newbury House Publishers, Inc.

Krashen, S. (1985), *The Input Hypothesis: Issues and Implications*. London: Longman.

Krashen, S.(2003), *Explorations in Language Acquisition and Use*. Portsmouth, NH: Heinemann.

Krashen, S., Scarcella, R. and Long, M. (eds) (1982), *Child-Adult Differences in Second Language Acquisition*. Rowley, MA: Newbury House.

Long, M. (1983a), 'Native speaker/non-native speaker conversation in the second language classroom', in M. Clarke and J. Handscombe (eds), *On TESOL '82: Pacific Perspectives on Language Learning and Teaching*. Washington, DC: TESOL.

Long, M. (1983b), 'Native speaker/non-native speaker conversation and the negotiation of comprehensible input'. *Applied Linguistics*, 4 (2), 126–41.

McLaughlin B., Rossman, T. and McLeod, B. (1983), 'Second language learning: An information-processing perspective'. *Language Learning*, 33, 135–58.

Postovsky, V.A. (1974), 'Effects of delay in oral practice at the beginning of second language Learning'. *The Modern Language Journal*, 58, 229–39.

Postovsky, V.A. (1981), 'The priority of aural comprehension in the language acquisition process', in H. Winitz (ed.), *The Comprehension Approach to Foreign Language Instruction*. Rowley, MA: Newbury House.

Reeds, J. A., Winitz, H. and Garcia, P. A. (1977), 'A test of reading following comprehension training'. *International Review of Applied Linguistics*, 15, 307–19.

Salaberry, M. (1997), 'The role of input and output practice in second language acquisition'. *Canadian Modern Language Review*, 53, 422–51.

Swain, M. (1985), 'Communicative competence: some roles of comprehensible input and comprehensible output in its development', in S. Gass and C. Madden (eds), *Input in Second Language Acquisition*. Rowley, MA: Newbury House Publishers, Inc.

Tanaka, Y. (1996), 'The Comprehension and Acquisition of Relative Clauses by Japanese High School Students through Formal Instruction' (unpublished EdD dissertation, Temple University, Japan).

VanPatten, B. (1996), *Input Processing and Grammar Instruction in Second Language Acquisition.* Norwood, NJ: Ablex.

VanPatten, B. and Cadierno, T. (1993a), Explicit instruction and input processing. *Studies in Second Language Acquisition* 15, 225–43.

VanPatten, B. and Cadierno, T. (1993b), 'Input processing and second language acquisition: a role for instruction'. *Modern Language Journal,* 77, 45–57.

VanPatten, B. and Oikennon, S. (1996), 'Explanation versus structured input in processing instruction'. *Studies in Second Language Acquisition,* 18, 495–510.

VanPatten, B. and Sanz, C. (1995), 'From input to output: processing instruction and communicative tasks', in F. Eckman, D. Highland, P. Lee and R. Weber (eds), *Second Language Acquisition Theory and Pedagogy.* Mahwah, NJ: Lawrence Erlbaum.

13 Enhancing the language learning process for reticent learners of Vietnamese and of English in Vietnam

Bao Dat

1 Background: The construct of reticence

Although it is estimated that 20 per cent of the population suffers from communication reticence (Richmond and McCroskey 1992), classroom reticence ranks among the least discussed phenomena in language acquisition studies. While reticent behaviour in general has received serious attention among social psychologists for over a century (Daly and McCroskey 1984), in applied linguistics research on learner reticence has lagged behind research on other affective issues, such as classroom anxiety and language learning motivation. Yet in the five countries I have worked in, teachers have agreed that learner withdrawal from verbal discussion in the classroom is common and poses an obstacle to communicative instruction.

The phenomenon of reticence has been a major topic of discussion in social psychology and an issue of occasional mention in applied linguistics. Reticence (Phillips 1965) often comes under a wide variety of related constructs such as shyness (Zimbardo 1977; Buss 1984; Crozier 2001), stage fright (Clevenger 1959), social avoidance (Bruch and Cheek 1995), avoidance personality (Widiger 2001), novelty anxiety (MacIntyre 1999), communication anxiety (Hilleson 1996), communication apprehension (McCroskey 1984), foreign language speaking anxiety (Young 1990), classroom anxiety (Bailey 1983), speech apprehensiveness (Bannai 1980), reluctance (Burns and Joyce 1997), slow motivation (Wu 1991), communication avoidance (Daly and McCrosky 1984) Miller (1984), passive speech role (Littlewood *et al* 1996), lack of social skills (Friedman 1980), quietness (Richmond 1984) and withdrawal (Fu 1995). In general, language learners who suffer from reticence tend to withdraw from verbal interaction in the classroom despite the teacher's efforts at soliciting voluntary communication. The functional passiveness associated with reticence can be mild or extreme, ranging from waiting to be called upon for participation to insisting upon complete silence despite the teacher's attempt to elicit speech. To understand more specifically what reticence means, it may be useful to set this concept against a term that is closely related to it: the notion of silence. Although they take the same linguistic form, being both manifested by a state of muteness, there are fundamental similarities and dissimilarities between the two notions.

The first difference lies in the question of motives. Silence is viewed as an aspect of language and a form of conversational dominance (Brown and Attardo 2000). It parallels speech in achieving certain communicative tasks and so these two dimensions are complementary to each other. Silence, therefore, represents an indispensable layer of interpersonal discourse and is a natural part of conversational skill, accompanying speech to express a variety of meanings and perform a range of language functions – including to comfort, to support, to accept, to attract attention, to negotiate power, to scold, to interrupt, to challenge, and so forth (Wardhaugh 1992). Reticence, on the contrary, tends to suggest subordination or a potential handicap in activating such communicative skills. In much of the research, it indicates some level of reserve in speech that might fall in line with undesirable affective features such as shyness and communication apprehension (Evans 1996).

A second difference has to do with their significance in an educational setting. Silence can be an active factor in communication with facilitative uses that serve successful communication and that represent a set of skills to be learned and acquired (Wardhaugh 1992). For example, silence is employed by the teacher as a positive strategy to leave wait time so that students will participate more effectively (Evans 1996; Tomlinson 2000). A reasonable amount of silence provided by the teacher can convey a sense of patience – that is, in adapting the rate of teaching to the learning pace of learners, based on the understanding that the quickest way of learning is the students' own way (Knibbeler 1989). Reticence, on the contrary, does not demonstrate such a level of positive control and is never viewed as a teacher strategy towards any particular communicative effect. Instead it is often identified as showing learners' inadequate ability in self-expression (Chen 1985; Burns and Joyce 1997), a problem in verbal response to the learning situation (Tsui 1996), or a lack of initiative in negotiation of meanings (Wu 1991).

A third distinction concerns their ongoing impact on language development. Silence may characterize a mentally active period during which learners go through the process of building up language proficiency – so that once this is acquired enough learners will begin to talk (Krashen 1982; Burt and Dulay 1983; Stevick 1989). Reticence, on the other hand, does not embrace a preparedness that works towards linguistic facility. Instead it is often recognized as an impediment to communication capabilities (Foss and Reitzel 1988) and a source of disadvantage in second language improvement (Allwright 1984; Tsui 1996).

Both silence and reticence, in many cases, also demonstrate communication breakdown (Yoneyama 1999), a lack of ability to communicate, or failure of language (Tannen 1985) stemming from shyness, anxiety or a lack of knowledge (Buss 1984; Foss and Reitzel 1988; Hilleson 1996; Tsui 1996; Phillips 1999). Despite what we know, silence and reticence remain complex aspects of educational settings that are not always easy to identify. To this end, Malamah-Thomas (1996) suggest silence as a worthwhile object of linguistic investigation in the second language classroom as it sometimes causes confusion in which communication fails to be understood. Tsui (1996) also believes that reticence is worth examining further and suggests finding ways to help students cope with and overcome it to improve second language development.

2 The need to deal with reticence in L1 and L2 classrooms in Vietnam

In the traditional Vietnamese classroom, it is the teacher who decides who talks, when they talk, what they say, how they say it and when they stop talking. This model makes students believe that the teacher is the centre of knowledge and ideas. To shift such a centre of ideas from the teacher to the learner in the Vietnamese educational setting could be considered a revolt within the culture.

In Vietnam, classroom events are often organized in the lecturing mode, as was the case of five English classrooms that I recently observed in Ho Chi Minh City. Due to teacher control, interaction hardly occurs among peers but predominantly between the teacher and students. Such exchanges usually occupy from 15 per cent to 30 per cent of the lesson, in which teacher talk often takes up from 90 to 95 per cent of classroom talk.

Vietnamese students often seem to lack negotiation skills and seem very cautious during the lesson: they choose to speak as little as possible to avoid the risk of making mistakes. This behaviour severely restricts learning opportunities and results in a lack of genuine interaction between teachers and learners. It is often hard to find reciprocation of each other's attitudes and intentions. Without effective negotiation skills, learners lack not only a strong desire to communicate but also the willingness to explore the language and take risks, which as Seliger (1988: 32) believes, is an important factor that increases chances of encountering the target language and thereby favourably affecting second language learning. As many generations of Vietnamese teachers follow and consolidate this unproductive pattern, learners are actually trained to adopt it as an appropriate behaviour that keeps them comfortable in the classroom. Clearly, this routine poses a major hindrance for any teacher who wishes to employ an interactive mode of teaching.

Compared to reticent students in English language classrooms, reticent students in mother tongue classes seem to participate with less difficulty when they are guided and encouraged through class discussion. It is observed that L1 teachers are not only more fluent but also seem to know the subject matter better and are more pedagogically confident compared to L2 teachers. In a series of classroom observations, Anh (2004) collected and reported six strategies that many Vietnamese teachers often employ when teaching L1 to students, which he then recommends as ways to keep students from being reticent:

- When a student contributes an idea, repeat that idea to demonstrate interest before interacting with it.
- When a student provides an answer, ask more questions to the student to stretch that answer to the maximum.
- When a student expresses her view, invite the rest of the class to raise their hands if they support that view.
- When all the students keep silent when the teacher asks a question, give them one trial answer and ask them to judge it.
- When a student's contribution sounds good, compliment it and challenge it with follow-up questions.
- When a student's answer is not satisfactory or sufficient, provide assistance by giving clues in the form of questioning.

It seems clear that many Vietnamese teachers' favourite technique of helping students to speak is asking questions. In the meantime, getting learners to voluntarily voice their thoughts or raise questions proves to be much more difficult. Some Vietnamese linguists believe that focusing on questioning methods to increase verbal responses is helpful but not sufficient. They highlight the need for increasing learners' emotional involvement as the next solution. Phuong Nga (2002) maintains that teacher use of voice plays an affective role in leading out learner desire to open up. She suggests that the articulation should be clear, animated and pleasant. Besides, the teacher's suitable choice of words in relation to learner proficiency will facilitate comprehensibility while long-windedness in talk can be irritating and may put students off. Thai (1997) argues that setting a learning goal for students to follow is not as important as helping them develop the love for learning. Once taken by inspiration students will form objectives of their own and might broaden them beyond expectation. Tinh and Huong (2001) believe that one method of involving students actively in their mother tongue study is to assign extensive reading followed by sharing stories in class through oral presentation and story-telling competitions.

In recent years the Vietnamese Ministry of Education in its Direction No 24 GD has appealed for educators in the country to help students promote an active learning style, which includes verbal contribution during the lesson, self-learning and application of knowledge in practice (Chinh 2000). The Ministry has also conducted a number of workshops aiming at making Vietnamese language classrooms more interactive through role-play, group-work, problem-based tasks and self-regulated learning (Tinh and Huong 2001). Anh (2004) maintains that the burning question in Vietnamese education today is how to create more profound conditions for students to be actively and verbally involved in classroom interaction.

3 How reticence affects language-learning ability

Learners' reticent behaviour seems to interfere with second language classroom norms because it restrains a number of communicative activities that require learners' active verbal involvement. Many important arguments offered by the literature indicate that learners who are shy about using the spoken language will tend to receive less exposure to the target language; and that those who refrain from initiating interaction may well receive input but lack opportunities to turn it into intake (Seliger 1983; Allwright and Bailey 1991). Besides, reticence also restricts linguistic assistance from the teacher and peers (Scarcella and Oxford 1992) and limits the development of the lesson in ways that fail to pertain to learners' needs (Harker 1988; Green *et al* 1988). Reticence, in a word, might result in three deficiencies in the learning process: limitation of input, lack of practice opportunities to turn such input into intake, and 'the effects of all that happens on the receptivity of the learners' (Allwright and Bailey 1991: 149).

4 The causes of reticence in the literature

4.1 Rejection experiences

'Rejection experiences' is a term used by Bruch and Cheek (1995: 174) to indicate students' negative relations with peers and teachers, which cause individual learners to internalize a sense of ridicule during verbal participation. In this situation, learner silence acts as a safety measure to reduce the threat of rejection by the teacher.

4.2 Viewing oneself from other people's perspectives

People who are bothered by the thought that others may not think highly of them often behave reticently and withdraw from verbal performance so as to avoid being judged in negative ways. Widiger (2001) highlights this condition as avoidance personality, which develops into fear of criticism and makes one unwilling to communicate with other people or engage in new activities unless they feel certain of being liked.

4.3 Communication anxiety

One of the key explanations of communication avoidance has always been anxiety, also known as apprehensiveness (Foss and Reitzel 1988; Hilleson 1996; Tsui 1996; Phillips 1999). This may vary from stage fright in front of large audiences to nervousness in small group situations.

Second language learners have to deal with difficulties in understanding others, a problem that is not common among native speakers (Foss and Reitzel 1988; Hilleson 1996; Vogely 1999). Furthermore, foreign language anxiety involves fear that they cannot perform adequately in the new language, feeling incompetent not only in grasping the language in the first place but also in their ability to present themselves in a way compatible with their self-image.

4.4 Culture of learning

It is commonly recognized that the problem of getting students to respond in the classroom is particularly acute with Asian students, who are generally considered to be more reserved and reticent than their Western counterparts (Fu 1995; Tsui 1996; O'Sullivan 1997; Cortazzi and Jin 1999). In seeking an explanation, Cortazzi and Jin (1996, 1999), and Johnson (1995) stress the need to consider the culture of learning because what the students bring to the language-learning situation makes classroom interaction no longer just a matter of methods but a product of culture.

4.5 Teacher intolerance of silence

One method of supporting learners' speech is to add more waiting time until they are able to perform. Yet in reality, many teachers prove to be impatient towards learner silence by putting a great deal of pressure on students to speak, holding the misconception that an effective teacher should be able to invite immediate participation from them (Tsui 1996). By demanding that learners instantly report their experience, the teacher denies them the right to process and develop their response through an inner voice (Tomlinson 1998). Another explanation why students suffer the lack of opportunities to speak English in class could be that too much class time is taken up by teacher talk (Littlewood *et al* 1996), which rests on the assumption that a responsible teacher should be talking all the time (Tsui 1996).

4.6 Uneven allocation of turns

It is sometimes suggested that the teacher's uneven allocation of turns can account for classroom reticence (Tsui 1996). My classroom observation has led me to believe that the group that tends to receive more teacher attention normally comprises brighter or more enthusiastic students, while those who receive the least attention are often less active members. Receiving less support from the teacher, reticent students continue to be deprived of opportunities for classroom participation.

4.7 Incomprehensible input

Incomprehensible input is recognized by Tsui (1996) as another inhibiting factor in that learners will refuse to speak once they fail to understand the teacher's language. Psycholinguistic theories also suggest that comprehensible input is a key factor in second language acquisition (Dulay *et al* 1982).

4.8 Linguistic incompetence

It is believed that communication reluctance may stem from linguistic factors (Burns and Joyce 1997). It often results from concern about making mistakes and appearing foolish in front of peers (Phillips 1999). Wu (1991) believes that poor pronunciation is also the reason why students do not like to talk. When students cannot find ways or are not taught how to improve their accent, they will continue to be discouraged from participation for fear that the teacher may not be able to understand them or that their classmates will not respect them because of defective articulation.

5 Remediation of learner reticence in the literature

Kelly *et al* (1995) discuss a number of interesting strategies to remedy reticence. These include:

- Building an empathic relationship by showing that the teacher understands students' problems and concerns. One way to find out their concerns is by having a conversation with students before the class begins.
- Making sure the language used by the teacher is familiar to students so that the language serves to communicate ideas rather than claiming status.
- Providing structure to make answers more manageable. For example, the question 'What do you think?' should be replaced with 'Which position do you support?'. Alternatively, instead of asking reticent students to discuss 'happiness and goals in life' they can be given this structure to complete: 'A lot of people want . . . in life,' or 'Most people I know look forward to . . .'.
- Developing a signal system to tell the teacher what learners are ready to do. For example, students may use a multicoloured block so that they can face the green side forward when they have an answer to the teacher's question and the red side when they don't.
- Using visualization as a strategy to reduce communication apprehension by guiding reticents through a narrative that invites them to visualize the moment they give a speech in public and become successful. Researchers such as Ayers and Hopf (1990, cited in Kelly *et al*) found that the effect of visualization in the communication classroom is long lasting and more rewarding than a public speaking class without a visualizing component.
- Using positive feedback by an authority (Rosenthal and Jacobson 1968; Cialdini 1984, cited in Kelly *et al*). If an authority figure tells a student that he or she is making progress, such a compliment can build trust and may influence the behaviour of that individual.

6 Action research on reticence in Vietnam

This section reports my longitudinal action research project on reticence, which managed to perform two significant tasks that are not often carried out: to gather knowledge about appropriate methodology from students themselves; and to discover the changeability of an established learning behaviour that, for a long time, has been thought by many local Vietnamese teachers to be virtually impossible to modify.

One of the dangers in explaining classroom reticence is the overwhelming reliance on the issue of national culture. As Guest (2002: 157) points out, culture should be perceived as an interplay between social and personal schemes in the awareness of specific group dynamics rather than 'national cultures en masse.' This understanding gave me the urge to investigate the contemporary cultural framework of the local teacher in Vietnam and how it may contribute to learner reticence. In other words, I was hoping to investigate the relationship between the local culture of teaching and learner reticence. To take this intention one step further, I also wanted to test how far local teachers, who are accustomed to their traditional roles, are capable of stretching their roles and adapting their cultural framework in a way that could influence learners' conventional behaviour towards a more active verbal role. So I decided to conduct an action research study to test how much verbal reluctance can be repaired, not through a separate training programme but in the real, everyday classroom.

7 Research method and procedure

To conduct the project, I worked with 300 students and 15 teachers at the Centre for Foreign Languages (CFL) at the National University of Vietnam in Ho Chi Minh City. The students come from 15 lower and upper-immediate classes and the teachers are those who work with these classes. I gathered data by four different methods: classroom observation, survey questionnaires, in-depth interviews and a work journal. The study took place in eight stages:

Stage 1: I conducted a survey on the students to find out their perception of roles, their reflection on verbal reluctance, and their learning preferences.

Stage 2: Through interviews, I consulted the teachers on whether and why they think their students are verbally passive, and compared the teacher's view with their students' view learned from stage 1.

Stage 3: I observed classes to investigate visible factors that caused learner reticence and to measure the levels and types of learner participation. What the students and teachers said during the survey and the interview above set me in a focused direction for what I needed to observe.

Stage 4: I performed in-depth interviews with a number of selected students and teachers to gather in-depth information and pursue interesting data collected from the survey, interview, and observation in stages 1, 2 and 3.

Stage 5: Based on all observation, survey, and interview data put together, I worked out a set of pedagogical principles to help students reduce their reticent behaviour and participate more actively.

Stage 6: I invited the 15 teachers to come for a two day workshop in which I disseminated my findings and presented them together with my suggested pedagogical principles for an open discussion. We came up with a set of teaching strategies to remedy reticence and agreed to incorporate them in a set of experimental lessons in the actual classrooms. Each of the teachers then agreed to teach at least one such lesson to their students in their real class.

Stage 7: I made appointments with each of the teachers to discuss a new lesson plan in which we incorporated the new teaching strategies. We then decided on an actual class time to launch the experiment, with the teacher doing the experiment and me observing the class. Eventually the eight teachers conducted ten experiments in their own classrooms (some of them did the experiments more than once while others gave up due to their busy schedules). I then sat in and observed each of the experiments to compare the levels and types of learner participation with the behaviour I already observed in stage 3.

Stage 8: I collected teacher and student thoughts about the experiment through a survey of the students and personal interviews with the teachers.

During fieldwork, I regularly kept my work journal to record my personal reflections on various events and anecdotes from the research location that concentrate on critical incidents with a particular significance. The entire project took place over four years and great care was taken so that each time we proceeded to a new stage, we proceeded by making our decision based on the knowledge gained from the previous stage. This new idea then laid the foundation for the subsequent stage.

8 The causes of reticence learned from the study

To discover the causes of reticence I obtained data from interviews with local teachers and students, which were then combined with my classroom observation. Several of the resultant explanations overlap to some extent with the literature, but some of them stretch beyond it because they not only highlight the phenomenon of reticence from a new angle of a local context but also reveal the students' perspective of their teachers' performance in the light of how that performance may account for their lack of desire for participation.

8.1 Respect for and apprehension of the teacher

Of the students under study, 65.6 per cent are conscious that reticence sometimes serves as a means of showing respect for the teacher and a sense of modesty on their part. On the basis of this, loud or talkative class members are often viewed as not showing sufficient courtesy to others and hence will not gain much appreciation in return. In addition, 35 per cent of the students also admit a feeling of intimidation vis-à-vis the teacher for unexplainable reasons and such fear often holds them back from participating. For many others, the boundary between respect and fear seems indefinable as they admit keeping quiet from a mixture of both sentiments. Besides, reticence also denotes politeness, which becomes the ethical basis for maintaining a low profile. Many students feel that unauthorized speech or speaking without being invited by the teacher is a rude act because it means interrupting the teacher's words or, as stated by 8 per cent of respondents, a waste of class time.

8.2 Heavy dependence on the teacher

Many students view the teacher as the only source of knowledge. They feel that class time is best used when the teacher is lecturing and knowledge is best transferred when it is written down on the blackboard. A large number of students feel that it is the teacher who has the most power to make communication happen. As they indicate, the teacher should encourage everyone to speak out by trying different eliciting methods and by providing more vocabulary and sentence patterns. Some even take it for granted that moving towards a more interactive classroom atmosphere is solely the teacher's responsibility.

8.3 Dissatisfaction with teachers' personal styles

Of the students, 95.6 per cent experience various levels of dissatisfaction with their learning environment as a result of less inspiring teacher personality and a lack of stimulus in the teaching approach. Interestingly, many students connect classroom atmosphere with how their teacher behaves. Furthermore, 35 per cent of the student respondents feel that their teacher often walks into the classroom with an unsmiling, serious face. In line with this appearance, a formal lecture is then delivered in a calm, unvarying tone serving a strictly pedagogical aim rather than a social purpose where the teacher and students establish a rapport or a sense of community.

8.4 The communal mentality and fear of breaking norms

Of the respondents, 17.6 per cent feel that they are bound by an implicit responsibility to share a common behaviour with the group. In other words, everyone's reluctance results from the fact that everyone else does not talk, as one student reveals: 'If the rest of my class participate more, I'll be more willing to speak . . .'. Another student says, 'It is ridiculous to volunteer, especially when I'm in a large class. I just don't find this a normal thing to do. . . .'. If one wishes to act differently, it might suggest that the person is trying to step out and betray the group.

8.5 Consciousness of poor performance

Of the students, 23.3 per cent feel ashamed of their English, which they view as imperfect and clumsy and this feeling poses a psychological impediment to any desire to practice speaking. Another 5 per cent are seriously sensitive about the quality of their pronunciation and even their own voice.

8.6 Low self-esteem

Much of the learning shyness in the classroom also stems from a sense of inferiority, as experienced by 37.3 per cent of the students who are constantly aware of being surrounded by more proficient class members. Instead of trying to compete, these low-esteem students feel disconcerted by better performance and become even more withdrawn, believing that they would verbalize more in a class with equally or less competent classmates.

8.7 Negative attitudes toward verbal interaction

Some students admit not wanting to participate in classroom events even when feeling capable of doing so simply because the questions asked by the teachers often seem too easy. This is reflected by 46.6 per cent of the respondents believing that speaking a little but correctly is more valuable than speaking a lot but incorrectly and suggest that accuracy is the ultimate target of their speech. This prevents them from participating unless they feel confident that their contribution is perfectly flawless. Such extreme desire for correctness also causes this group to develop negative attitudes towards mistakes, which they view as useless and harmful. Of the students, 33.6 per cent state that the inquiry they form in their minds is often not an urgent need, and thus is not worth the embarrassment of voicing it publicly.

8.8 Lack of verbal practice in previous English courses

Although 70.3 per cent of the students express a willingness to participate during the lesson, they often feel restricted by a lack of conditions to perform. Over many courses, explicit knowledge of the language has been carefully taught while the skills to use such knowledge have not, and 89.3 per cent of the students mentioned that they did not receive much conversational practice in their previous courses. Besides the lack of skills development, much of the instruction in many EFL classrooms has been in the mother tongue, which is employed whenever convenient to smooth out comprehension in a monolingual context. Arguably, such indulgence in the use of native tongue poses another obstacle to the process of generating target language input.

Although most students in the survey do not volunteer to participate during lessons, 97.6 per cent admit that they constantly process ideas in their mind throughout most of the lesson, especially when a question is raised by the teacher. Of these students, 95 per cent express the wish that they could be encouraged to speak out their answer.

9 Suggestions for remedying reticence

The following strategies are processed from student responses to two main questions in a survey: 'What makes you reticent?' and 'What conditions do you wish to have so that you can participate more?'. Student responses were also combined with teacher suggestions during in-depth interviews as well as with my judgement based on class observation. The recommendations aim to help Vietnamese students under study and were introduced into a series of innovative lessons in their own classrooms, the results of which will be reported later in this chapter.

9.1 Ensure learner preparation

Student preparation prior to the lesson is a factor facilitating the best use of class time and the lack of learner preparation poses an obstacle to classroom interaction. It is also important to distribute more equal attention among all students, by keeping in mind that frequent performance from better students might intimidate the weaker ones.

9.2 Make lesson content more practical

There is a realistic need for the existing syllabus to link to the students' personal needs, by adapting every lesson toward more relevant contexts of Vietnamese life. Of the respondents, 23.5 per cent feel that to inspire better participation, classroom discussion should be directly related to their thoughts and personal experiences. Many students express interest in topics that involve various aspects of their everyday life, present society and job opportunities, methods and experiences in learning English, economics and the environment, among others. The fact that teacher and learner partici-pants come from the same socio-cultural background suggests that it is not difficult for teachers to evaluate teaching content and decide whether it makes use of learners' shared knowledge and experiences and whether it is likely to catch the learners' attention and touch their emotions.

9.3 Use a multi-layered approach to eliciting speech

Allow shy students to speak while keeping a low profile, such as speaking to a classmate. If a question requires a public answer, look for signs of willingness before inviting any speaker; or encourage a quick exchange of ideas between peers. When the answer is ready, it can be provided either by individuals or in choral response. Choral response is a favourite classroom behaviour among students from many Asian cultures, where decisions are frequently made in groups. For students who are strongly oriented to the printed word and do not enjoy interacting with others, be aware that their oral skills may be considerably weaker than their visual skills, so tell them to use a visual prompt when necessary.

9.4 Discuss student willingness to make changes

Convince learners of the rationale for interaction. Invite students to take part in constructing a new classroom environment with new rules of participation and make clear statements about what the teacher expects in terms of academic performance, such as informing the whole class that everyone is welcome to interrupt the teacher at any time. Although many learners may feel uncomfortable when diverging from certain norms that are culturally approved, strategy instruction can help them see the value in new methods that are not necessarily within their norms.

9.5 Warmly accept and value students' contributions

Make sure in every lesson there are positive moments, such as a chance to laugh, and acknowledge and develop student contributions. Provide positive experiences which students can associate with instances of participation every time they are inclined to participate.

9.6 Respect students' potential and do your best to increase their self-esteem

This can be done by smiling, nodding, acknowledging their attempt to communicate, listening attentively, interacting appropriately, providing positive feedback, encouraging students to talk more about themselves, using students' ideas for further discussion and making positive comments to develop the students' awareness of their personal worth. Bearing in mind that many reticent learners tend to have lower self-esteem than their more successful peers, make students feel good about themselves on a regular basis and make them believe that they are becoming better every day. Set classroom goals in the light of student ability and, to help increase a sense of achievement, allow one activity to include different tasks at different levels of challenge, in which reluctant students can play a more achievable role. When students begin to show some sign of progress, no matter how little, it should be noticed and acknowledged to motivate students towards engaging in further communication.

9.7 Increase class sociability

This can be done by creating conditions for more student–student communication and friendly relationships. Understand that unwillingness to communicate can be a result of social influences. If breaking the silent norms of the whole class proves too difficult, attempt to do so in small groups first by making reluctant learners feel well received at least by group members.

9.8 Patiently utilize what students know rather than forcing them to perform what they don't know

Invite students to write down topics for which they know some relevant vocabulary and structures to talk about and have content knowledge of. Use those topics in brief discussions with classmates and to supply them with more new language. When linguistic support comes in, make sure that it is always provided in the context of immediate need and interest rather than in isolation, being incorporated in practical tasks that lead to verbal facility.

9.9 Create a caring climate by responding positively to student talk

The teacher is the 'atmosphere' of the classroom. His or her personality is a major factor in students' learning. If the teacher is sulky, students become anxious; if he or she only lectures, students keep silent; if he or she criticizes harshly, students withdraw from contact to avoid risk and vulnerability. Teacher talk, besides what is previously planned for the lesson, should also develop from instances of student talk so as to actively involve them in sustained interaction related to their personal thinking, and to expose them to purposeful input.

10 Outcomes of the innovation

Following the remedial strategies suggested above, I then organized for the teachers to conduct a series of ten classroom experiments to test out the strategies. The outcomes were:

10.1 Findings about learner behaviours

The innovation has provided inspiring conditions for oral communication. Of the students, 73.75 per cent are aware that their oral communication during the experiment has become greater than before, as they could speak out at ease without much fear of making mistakes. Some feel that the experiment has provided the kinds of activities that stimulated more active thinking; others appreciate interacting more personally with the teacher and peers. In addition, 26.5 per cent of the respondents view the teaching methods as stimulating to their thinking and creativity as it got them more actively involved in classroom discussions both within and beyond the coursebook. Furthermore, 28.5 per cent recognize that the classroom atmosphere was more enjoyable with a better sense of cooperation among classmates as well as a warmer teacher–student relationship.

Class observation also shows that learners developed more extended speech rather than short utterances and the content of their talk came from their own ideas rather than being simply based on the coursebook as before. The range of language functions was broadened. Thanks to well-prepared lesson scripts with more localized content, many teachers were able to provide learners with more realistic conditions to communicate their individual feelings and thoughts.

By and large, the innovation manages to reconstruct the role relationship between the teacher and the learner. It provides students with a broader range of speaking opportunities that might not have existed before, surrounding them with a more pleasant and secure environment to open up at ease. Besides, the project also provides evidence that it is not impossible to reform a traditional classroom, especially when teachers and learners are willing to modify their styles. As it turns out, Vietnamese students do not obstinately avoid oral communication to the extent that one might have assumed, but much of their behaviour tends to be conditioned by the culture of teaching at the institute under study. Even so, classroom culture is not something permanent but, as Holliday (1994) and Fu (1995) believe, is temporary and can be changed.

Despite all this, a number of complexities have also emerged. Learner feedback after the experiment reveals that spontaneous interaction might not benefit all learners in the same way. Some students who appreciate some level of freedom and spontaneity may accept a classroom rule where they are given conditions to volunteer to speak out. Others find the idea of self-initiation somewhat threatening. Instead, they feel the need to rely on some form of support, such as their own written notes or being called on by the teacher, in order to feel more secure.

Observation shows a cultural behaviour which demonstrates the ideal of social harmony built into the participating act. When the teacher directs an activity that happens to challenge or undermine this ideal, such as by getting some learners to debate with their good friends, they are not likely to respond. This type of behaviour among many Vietnamese learners is characterized by Kramsch and Sullivan (1996: 199) with the term 'classroom-as-family', a setting deeply influenced by Vietnamese national culture. Another aspect of such an harmonious ideal is manifested in choral response.

Reynolds (2005: 13) remarks: 'If an experiment works, something has gone wrong'. This teasing statement consoles my disappointment when part of the innovation in fact has failed to work. The classroom atmosphere was not enjoyed by 18 per cent of the students and 17 per cent felt that speaking opportunities did not reach them. These groups comprise both weaker students, who admit having problems understanding spoken English, and stronger students, who comment that some teachers still used too much mother tongue during the lesson and that discussion topics were not inspiring enough for participation. In addition, 11.25 per cent of the learner participants who seem to be addicted to conventional classrooms react negatively to the experiment by commenting that the lesson did not provide a sufficient amount of knowledge that a lesson should give, that it failed to provide correction of pronunciation errors and was limited in teaching grammar rules. Arguably, each student participated in the project with a different kind of awareness, and this made it difficult for the teacher to cater to all the various needs.

10.2 Findings about teacher behaviours

Compared to my class observation before the experiment, teacher performance was markedly enhanced. The teachers were seen at many instants during the experiment to extend beyond their traditional role as a knowledge transmitter and to successfully establish a connection between the syllabus lesson and students' life experience, which produced visible effects on learner behaviour. Notwithstanding this, teacher resistance to change is revealed through the experiment. There were moments when some teachers became less concerned with making classroom interaction fresh and exciting than with tightly controlling learner performance, and less concerned with instilling in the learner a desire to communicate than practicing what the teacher was accustomed to doing. Other teachers feel they did not have the power over the class if they failed to decide who should speak and when. Even when leaving students alone with pair or group activities, these teachers were afraid of not fulfilling their responsibility unless they eventually check the outcome by inviting group representatives to perform in front of an audience. In many cases the norms exhibited were not necessarily what the teachers strongly believed in, but were established habits that they simply could not resist following. It has been reported from many studies since the 1970s that innovation conductors often find their theory incompatible with the project's philosophy (Karavas-Doukas 1998). Many teachers feel 'reluctant to abandon tried and tested methods for new ones, which they may be afraid will fail' (Sikes 1992: 47) and thus tend to 'translate innovatory ideas to conform to their existing practices' (Karavas-Doukas 1998: 26–32).

The study reveals the impact of the teacher culture on the experiment. Arguably, teacher proficiency affected every moment of the innovation. Those with good proficiency in spoken English had more advantage in handling the remedial method. They could be easily trained to welcome, facilitate and inspire verbal communication among their students. Their less proficient counterparts, instead of constantly teaching what students needed and in the way that students preferred to learn, subconsciously reverted back to what they were most comfortable with, whether it was explaining a reading text, reciting a list of grammatical rules or lecturing on vocabulary. These teachers tended to adhere to the textbook and were rarely engaged in spontaneous interaction, causing their students to respond with the same behaviour. In many lessons, while fluent teachers pursued what students said by responding to meaning to build further interaction, less fluent counterparts often responded to student contributions with a pedagogical remark, such as highlighting grammatical errors and drawing attention to linguistic form. They also had a tendency to read out questions from a written text, causing learners to follow the textbook and participate by reading out words from the printed text rather than communicating their candid thoughts.

Teachers' view of appropriate socio-cultural behaviour also plays a part in the teaching. Many revealing moments during the innovation stemmed from the teacher's belief in appropriate classroom conduct, which influenced classroom management and transferred to learner response. Some teachers did not allow their students to act silly. Instead of focusing on how actively and comfortably learners were involved in their discussion, they guided learners towards their sense of appropriate conduct. This guidance sometimes severely interfered with learner enthusiasm and interest that was not always easy to build up.

In many cases, much of students' level of responsiveness is influenced by teacher personality and perception of self-image. Having observed the same class being taught by different teachers, I could see how students respond to them with different hospitalities. It was uncommon to see a class getting bored and uncooperative when working with a cheerful, approachable and dedicated teacher. When a teacher seemed approachable and popular among students, they responded with more active involvement. Conversely, a teacher who cared about maintaining hierarchy tended to prevent language tasks from developing into dynamic interaction.

11 Concluding remarks

It must be acknowledged that given differences inherent in participants' learning and teaching styles, the remedial methods introduced in the project have worked with some learners and have 'turned off' others. Moreover, how well a strategy works also depends on many other factors, including the nature of the language task as well as individual learners' and teachers' personalities and competences. Although the recommended remedial strategies may not suit everyone, by trying them out we have offered more options for language learning and seen that any of them can contain the potential to facilitate more dynamic oral communication.

References

Allwright, R. L. (1984), 'The importance of interaction in classroom language learning'. *Applied Linguistics*, 5, 2, 156–71.

Allwright, D. and Bailey, K. M. (1991), *Focus on the Language Classroom.* Cambridge: Cambridge University Press.

Anh, B. N. (2004), 'Mot so chien luoc su dung ngon ngu cua giao vien trong viec nang cao tinh tich cuc hoc tap cua hoc sinh'. [Strategies in teacher talk to boost learner activeness]. *Linguistic Issues 2004*, Hanoi: Social Sciences Publisher, 241–51.

Bailey, K. (1983), 'Competitiveness and anxiety in adult second language learning', in H. W. Seliger and M. H. Long (eds), *Classroom Oriented Research in Second Language Acquisition.* New York: Newbury House, pp. 67–102.

Bannai, H. (1980), 'Socio-cultural influences on the communication development of Asian ESL students', in J. C. Fisher, M. A., Clarke and J. Schachter (eds), *On TESOL '80. Building Bridges: Research and Practice in Teaching English as a Second Language.* Washington, DC: Teaching English to Speakers of Other Languages, pp. 147–58.

Brown, S. and Attardo, S. (2000), *Understanding Language Structures, Interaction, and*

Variation–An Introduction to Applied Linguistics and Sociolinguistics for Nonspecialists. Michigan: The University of Michigan Press.

Bruch, M. A. and Cheek, J. M. (1995), 'Developmental factors in childhood and adolescent shyness', in R. G. Heimberg, M. R. Liebowitz, D. A. Hope and F. R. Schneier (eds), *Social Phobia – Diagnosis, Assessment, and Treatment.* New York and London: The Guilford Press, pp. 163–82.

Burns, A. and Joyce, H. (1997), *Focus on Speaking.* Sydney: National Centre for English Language Teaching & Research (NCELTR).

Burt, M. K. and Dulay, H. C. (1983), 'Optimal language earning environment', in L.W. Oller Jr. and P.A. Richard-Amato (eds), *Methods that Work – A Smorgasbord of Ideas for Language Teachers.* Rowley, MA: Newbury House Publishers, Inc., pp. 38–48.

Buss, A. H. (1984), 'A conception of shyness', in J. A. Daly and J. McCroskey (eds), *Avoiding Communication – Shyness, Reticence, and Communication Apprehension.* California: Sage Publications, pp. 39–49.

Chen, I. M. (1985), 'Elimination of student's fear towards English learning', in C. Chen, H. Huang, L. Hsiao, J. Kuo, M. Chen and G. Wang (eds), *Papers from The Second Conference on English Teaching and Learning in the Republic of China.* Taipei: The Grane Publishing Co, pp. 87–96.

Chinh, H. C. (2000), 'Cai tien quan ly qua trinh day hoc nham thuc hien viec doi moi Phuong phap day hoc', [Improving pedagogy management towards methodological reform]. *Educational Studies No 2/2000,* Ha Noi: Nguyen Thi Minh Khai Press, 145–72.

Clevenger, Jr., T. (1959), 'A synthesis of experimental research in stage fright'. *Quarterly Journal of Speech,* 2, 134–45.

Cortazzi, M. and Jin, L. (1996), 'Culture of learning: Language classrooms in China', in H. Coleman (ed.), *Society and the Language Classroom.* Cambridge: Cambridge University Press, pp. 169–208.

Cortazzi, M. and Jin, L. (1999), 'Cultural mirrors – Materials and methods in the EFL classroom', in E. Hinkel (ed.), *Culture in Second Language Teaching and Learning.* Cambridge: Cambridge University Press, pp. 196–219.

Crozier, W. R. (2001), *Understanding Shyness – Psychological Perspective.* London: Palgrave.

Daly, J. A. and McCroskey, J. (1984), *Avoiding Communication – Shyness, Reticence, and Communication Apprehension.* California: Sage Publications.

Dulay, H., Burt, M. and Krashen, S. (1982), *Language Two.* New York & Oxford: Oxford University Press.

Evans, M. A. (1996), 'Reticent primary grade children and their more talkative peers: Verbal, nonverbal, and self-concept characteristics'. *Journal of Education Psychology,* 88, 4, 739–49.

Foss, K. A. and Reitzel, A. C. (1988), 'A relational model for managing second language anxiety'. *TESOL Quarterly,* 22, 3, 437–54.

Fu, D. (1995), *My Trouble is My English'–Asian Students and the American Dream.* Portsmouth, NH: Boynton/Cook Publishers Heinemann.

Green, J. L., Weade, R. and Graham, K. (1988), 'Lesson constriction and student participation', in J. L. Green and J. O. Karker (eds), *Multiple Perspective Analysis of Classroom Discourse.* New Jersey: Ablex, pp. 11–47.

Guest, M. (2002), 'A critical 'checkbook' for culture of teaching and learning'. *ELT Journal,* 56, 2, 154–61.

Harker, J. O. (1988), 'Individual and team approaches: An introduction', in J. L.

Green and J. O. Karker (eds), *Multiple Perspective Analysis of Classroom Discourse.* New Jersey: Ablex, pp. 215–30.

Hilleson, M. (1996), '"I want to talk with them, but I don't want them to hear": an introspective study of second language anxiety in an English-Medium School', in K. M. Bailey and D. Nunan (eds), *Voices From the Language Classroom.* Cambridge: Cambridge University Press, pp. 248–75.

Holliday, A. (1994), *Appropriate Methodology and Social Context.* Cambridge: Cambridge University Press.

Johnson, K. E. (1995), *Understanding Communication in Second Language Classrooms.* Cambridge: Cambridge University Press.

Karavas-Doukas, K. (1998), 'Evaluating the implementation of educational innovations: Lesson from the past', in P. Rea-Dickins and K. P. Germaine (eds), *Managing Evaluation and Innovation in Language Teaching: Building Bridges.* London: Longman, pp. 25–50.

Kelly, L., Phillips, G. M. and Keaten, J. A. (1995), *Teaching People to Speak Well. Training and Remediation of Communication Reticence.* Cresskill, NJ: Hampton Press Inc.

Knibbeler, K. (1989), *The Explorative-Creative Way – Implementation of a Humanistic Language Teaching Model.* Tubingen: Gunter Narr Verlag Tubingen.

Kramsch, C. and Sullivan, P. (1996), 'Appropriate methodology'. *ELT Journal*, 50, 3, 199–212.

Krashen, S. D. (1982), *Principles and Practice in Second Language Acquisition.* New York: Pergamon Press.

Littlewood, W., Liu, N. and Yu, C. (1996), 'Hong Kong tertiary students' attitude and proficiency in spoken English'. *RELC Journal*, 27, 1, 70–88.

MacIntyre, P. D. (1999), 'Language anxiety: A review of the research for language teachers', in D. J. Young (ed.), *Affect in Foreign Language and Second Language Learning – A Practical Guide to Creating a Low-Anxiety Classroom Atmosphere.* Boston: McGraw-Hill College, pp. 24–45.

Malamah-Thomas, A. (1996), *Classroom Interaction.* Oxford: Oxford University Press.

McCroskey, J. C. (1984), 'The communication apprehension perspective', in J. A. Daly and J. C. McCroskey (eds), *Shyness, Reticence and Communication Apprehension.* Beverly Hills, CA: Sage, pp. 13–38.

O'Sullivan, N. (1997), *Teaching English in Southeast Asia.* Chicago, Ill.: Passport Books.

Phillips, G. M. (1965), 'The problem of reticence'. *The Pennsylvania Speech Annual V,* 22, 22–38.

Phillips, E. M. (1999), 'Decreasing language anxiety: Practical techniques for oral activities', in D. J. Young (ed.), *Affect in Foreign Language and Second Language Learning – A Practical Guide to Creating a Low-Anxiety Classroom Atmosphere.* Boston: McGraw-Hill College, pp. 124–43.

Phuong Nga, L. (2002), *Day Hoc Tap Doc o Tieu Hoc [Teaching Reading Skills in Vietnamese Primary Classrooms].* Hanoi: The Education Publisher.

Reynolds, T. (2005), *Wit and Wisdom. Inspirational Thoughts on Life.* London: Exis Publishing Limited.

Richmond, V. P. (1984), 'Implication of quietness – Some facts and speculations', in J. A. Daly and J. McCroskey (eds), *Avoiding Communication – Shyness, Reticence, and Communication Apprehension.* California: Sage Publications, pp. 145–55.

Richmond, V. P. and McCroskey, J. C. (1992), *Communication: Apprehension, Avoidance, and Effectiveness – Third Edition.* Scottdales, AZ: Gorsuch Scarisbrick.

Scarcella, R. C. and Oxford, R. L. (1992), *The Tapestry of Language Learning – The Individual in the Communicative Classroom.* Boston, MA: Heinle & Heinle Publishers.

Seliger, H. W. (1983) 'Learner interaction in the classroom and its effect on language acquisition', in H. W. Seliger and M. H. Long (eds), *Classroom Oriented Research in Second Language Acquisition.* Rowley, MA.: Newbury House, pp. 246–67.

Seliger, H. W. (1988), *Psycholinguistic Issues in Second Language Acquisition.* New York: Newbury House Publishers.

Sikes, P. J. (1992), 'Imposed change and the experienced teacher', in M. Fullan and A. Hargreaves (eds), *Teacher Development and Educational Change.* London: Falmer Press, pp. 36–55.

Stevick, W. E. (1989), *Success with Foreign Languages. Seven Who Achieved It and What Worked for Them.* Hertfordshire: Prentice Hall International English Language Teaching.

Tannen, D. (1985), 'Silence: Anything but', in D. Tannen and M. Saville-Troike (eds), *Perspectives on Silence.* Noerwood, NJ: Ablex, pp. 93–111.

Thai, L. X. (1997), *Boi Duong Hung Thu Cua Hoc Sinh Doi Voi Bo Mon Tieng Viet [Increasing Learner Interest in the Vietnamese Language Classroom].* Hanoi: Social Sciences Press.

Tinh, H. L. and Huong, T. M. (2001), *Giai Dap 88 Cau Hoi ve Giang Day Tieng Viet o Tieu Hoc [Responses to 88 Inquiries about Vietnamese Language Instructions in Primary Schools].* Hanoi: The Education Publisher.

Tomlinson, B. (ed.) (1998), *Materials Development in Language Teaching.* Cambridge: Cambridge University Press.

Tomlinson, B. (2000), 'Talking to yourself: the role of the inner voice in language learning'. *Applied Language Learning,* 11, 1, 123–54.

Tsui, A. B. M. (1996), 'Reticence and anxiety in second language learning', in K. M. Bailey and D. Nunan (eds), *Voices from the Language Classroom.* Cambridge: Cambridge University Press, pp. 145–67.

Vogely, A. (1999), 'Addressing listening comprehension anxiety', in D. J. Young (ed.), *Affect in Foreign Language and Second Language Learning – A Practical Guide to Creating a Low-Anxiety Classroom Atmosphere.* Boston: McGraw-Hill College, pp. 106–23.

Wardhaugh, R. (1992), *An Introduction to Sociolinguistics* (2nd edn). Oxford: Blackwell.

Widiger, T. A. (2001), 'Social anxiety, social phobia, and avoidance personality', in W. R. Crozier and L. E. Alden (eds), *International Handbook of Social Anxiety. Concepts, Research and Interventions Relating to the Self and Shyness.* John Chichester: Wiley and Sons, Ltd.

Wu, Y. H. (1991), 'Why don't they speak up? A study of factors that affect classroom participation in English language learning', in L. Yaofu, H. Huang, H. Jeng, S. Liao, S. Chou, S. Lin and A. Hadzima (eds), *Papers from The Seventh Conference on English Teaching and Learning in the Republic of China.* Taipei: The Grane Publishing Co, pp. 159–87.

Yoneyama, S. (1999), *The Japanese High School – Silence and Resistance.* London and New York: Routledge Japanese Studies Series.

Young, D. J. (1990), 'An investigation of students' perspectives on anxiety and speaking'. *Foreign Language Annals,* 23, 6, 539–53.

Zimbardo, P. G. (1977), *Shyness: What It Is, What to Do About It.* Reading, MA: Addison-Wesley.

14 A sort of puzzle for English as a lingua franca

Luke Prodromou

1 Introduction

This study was sparked off by a plenary presentation in March 1995 given by a British corpus linguist at a TESOL Conference in Athens, Greece. The speaker referred to the interesting insights that corpus linguistics had uncovered about 'spoken grammar' and how different this grammar was from traditional grammars (Carter and McCarthy 1995, 1997, 2001). The speaker ended his talk by suggesting that the teaching of English as a foreign language should reflect more of the 'real' English that corpora had uncovered. After the applause, one member of the audience asked what the relevance of these insights from 'native speaker' corpora was to the 'non-native speaker' teacher and learner of English as an international language. My research, on which this chapter is based is, in part, a response to that question.

My research grew out of the conviction that a corpus-based investigation of idiomaticity in L1 and L2 use of English was necessary if we were to understand how appropriate corpus-based discoveries were to the development of English as a Lingua Franca (ELF). I will use the term 'ELF' to refer to the use of English in an international context as a lingua franca between people with a different L1, including L1 speakers of English when they are using English with L2 speakers. This definition differs significantly from those who define ELF as involving only users of English for whom the language is not an L1 (Firth 1996; Haegeman 2002; Seidlhofer 2002; Lesznyák 2004; Jenkins 2005). While one agrees with Widdowson that 'native speakers' have no right to dictate rules to 'non-native speakers' of English (Widdowson 1994: 385), 'native speakers' are, nevertheless, a part of the rich tapestry that is English as an international lingua franca, both as potential interlocutors of 'non-native speakers' and as speakers of the most codified and widely accepted variety of English we have. To ignore the diversity of this tapestry 'would simply mean ignoring reality' (Knapp 2002: 221).

2 Defining idiomaticity

The focus of this chapter is idiomaticity in ELF. A useful definition of the phenomenon is provided by Wray:

A sequence, continuous or discontinuous, of words or other meaning elements, which is, or appears to be, prefabricated; that is stored and retrieved whole from the memory at the time of use, rather than being subject to generation or analysis by the language grammar.

(Wray 2000: 465)

Figure 14.1 sums up the range of formulae and fixed phrases which are frequently brought together in the literature under the umbrella of 'idiomaticity'.

This paper takes as its main hypothesis that it is in the area of idiomaticity (and phonology (Jenkins 2000)) that English as a Native Language (ENL) and ELF necessarily differ and not in the relatively unproblematic area of grammar. Broadly speaking, the pattern uncovered in my L2 user corpus is that ELF users tend to deploy the type of idiomaticity classified under A in Figure 14.1; they tend to use B and C to a lesser degree and the least frequent variety of idiomaticity of all in ELF is Type D, 'cultural idioms'.

3. The idiomatic paradox

As long ago as 1904, Jespersen described phraseology as an 'indispensable' though 'irrational' dimension of language competence (Jespersen 1904: 16–17). Time has vindicated Jespersen's prioritizing of formulaic language. In recent years, the area of phraseology has evolved from its peripheral status in Chomskyan linguistics (Chomsky 1965) to having a fundamental role in language description and acquisition (e.g. Bolinger 1961; Sinclair 1991; Gibbs 1995; Weinert 1995; McCarthy 1998; Skehan 1998; Stubbs 2001). Nattinger and DeCarrico (1992: xv) go so far as to describe 'lexical phrases' as 'the very centre of language acquisition' while, for Hopper (1998: 168), formulaic language is so integral a feature of language that it is 'difficult or impossible to draw a line between a formulaic and a non-formulaic expression'. In short, the experts agree that idiomaticity is important to L1 fluency. This much is uncontroversial. It is the unquestioned transition from L1 to L2 fluency via idiomaticity that I am querying in this paper.

The importance of phraseology in L1 language use has been highlighted by recent work in corpus linguistics; indeed, one of the major insights of the corpus analysis of English has been the profoundly phraseological nature of much of what we say and write. Erman and Warren (2000), in their empirical study of the idiom principle, found that as much as 50 per cent of the language may be explicable in idiomatic terms. However, Sinclair's (1987) suggestion that idiomaticity would allow learners, like 'native speakers', to produce English more confidently and 'with less effort' (Sinclair 1987: 159) did not always seem to be borne out by experience and the available research data.

It is these claims about idiomaticity that I was curious to explore in embarking on my research (Prodromou 2005): the reasons for the difficulty that even very advanced learners and users of English have with idiomaticity is the main puzzle this paper attempts to address.

Type A	Formulae	Examples
1	Clusters and pragmatic formulae	a bit of a; If you look at; you know; I mean; sort of; you see
2	Connectors	First of all, what's more, on the one hand
3	Conversational gambits	Pleased to meet you; How do you do; how's it going
4	Prepositional phrases	At the end; in the long term; in sight; at home
5	Transparent Binomials	Bed and breakfast; knife and fork, salt and pepper
6	Transparent trinomials	Tall, dark and handsome
7	Lexical sentence stems	It is interesting/likely/true that…
8	Compounds	Dry cleaner; phonecard; card phone
9	One-offs	Arms akimbo; by dint of; kith and kin
10	Grammatical frameworks	e.g. NP X of NP Y: A distribution of labour
11	Repeats	Again and again; try, try and try again
12	Colligation	Set about + ing
Type B	**Collocations**	
1	Restricted Collocations	jog+ someone's memory
2	Open collocations	River+rise; make+application
Type C	**Phrasal verbs**	
1	Verb + particle	Pop music turns them on
2	Verb + preposition	The machine turns on a pivot
3	Complex phrasal verbs	Lose track of; turn one's back on
Type D	**Cultural Idioms**	
1	Colourful Binomials	Spick and span; footloose and fancy free
2	Colourful Trinomials	Hook, line and sinker; lock, stock and barrel
3	Tournures	Kick the bucket; pull your socks up
4	Metaphors, figurative	Sail close to the wind
5	Similes	As cool as a cucumber
6	Proverbs and sayings	Kill two birds with one stone
7	Quotations	To be or not to be; the best laid schemes
8	Cultural allusions	Marks and Sparks; Basil Fawlty
9	Catchphrases, slogans	Drinka Pinta Milka Day; Arsenal rules OK
10	Slang phrases	Ghetto blaster; a whiz-kid; trouble and strife
11	Taboo expressions	Get pissed, fuck off
12	Mottoes	Aim high; he who dares, wins
13	Understatement	That was a showstopper, wasn't it; a bit of a twit
14	Hyperbole	There's millions of them
15	Lexicalised clauses	A don't-call-us-we'll call-you-situation
16	Nursery rhymes	Little Jack Horner; Mary had a little lamb
17	Limericks	There was a young lady named Bright…
18	Pop-song lyrics	She loves you, yeah, yea, yeah
19	Dyadic Discourse routines	See you later alligator; not if I see you first
20	Creative idiomaticity, puns	Last tangle in Westminster. It's raining kittens'n'puppies

Figure 14.1 Varieties of idiomaticity

4 Danger: Idiomaticity

The territory of idiomaticity is described through metaphors such as 'capricious', 'tyrannical' (Jespersen 1894: 22), 'a jungle' (Bolinger 1976: 9; Sinclair 1985: 254), 'dangerous minefield' (McCarthy and Carter 1994: 109) and 'treacherous' (Altenberg and Granger 2001: 174). The conceptualization of idiomaticity as a difficult, even dangerous, area reflects the widespread view of this central feature of English as a particular challenge in L2 acquisition; the metaphors we use to describe idiomaticity in the learning context reflect the frequently observed phenomenon of learners and L2 users attempting to deploy idiomaticity in spoken language and ending up sounding dysfluent and un-natural. As Irujo (1986: 299) says, 'colorful idioms, even when correctly produced, often sound strange and unnatural when spoken by "non-native speakers" of English'. Irujo is here referring to the traditional 'big words' of idiomaticity (Ellis 1996: 111), for example, *kick the bucket, spill the beans* but the strangeness of idiomaticity in 'non-native speech' also applies to the more frequent collocations and formulaic phrases (Fox 1998).

Idiomaticity, then, 'sounds' different and comes with great effort in 'non-native' speech and it is where even highly competent users of English as an L2 'are bound to make mistakes, even if (they have) mastered the grammar' (Coulmas 1981: 150). Why should this be so? Sinclair describes the relationship of idiomaticity to word meaning as 'mysterious' (Sinclair 2004: 27) and, likewise, Wray (2002: ix) describes this apparent conflict in the behaviour of idiomaticity in 'native' and 'non-native' speech as a 'mystery'. This mystery is the starting point for my own exploration of the 'puzzle' of idiomaticity in 'non-native-like' fluency.

5 The idiomatic deficit: Research evidence

The difficulty of idiomaticity for the L2 learner has been uncovered by repeated empirical investigations. Bahns *et al* (1986) set out to identify the *uses* of idiomaticity in learner speech but failed to find any instances of 'commonplaces, proverbs and idioms' in their data (Bahns *et al* 1986: 696). In a later paper, Bahns and Eldaw (1993) found that collocations were a persistent problem even with advanced students and accounted for a larger proportion of errors than single lexical items (Bahns and Eldaw 1993: 101). Dechert and Lennon's (1989) investigation of advanced learners' use of collocational blends led them to wonder:

> why, in spite of their many years of learning, plus, in some cases, months of exposure to native speakers in England, had their apprehension of collocational affinities between lexical items not reached a state of proceduralized automaticity?
>
> (Dechert and Lennon 1989: 165)

Similarly, Yorio (1989) investigated idiomaticity as an indicator of second language proficiency and discovered that 'studies do not appear to find extensive use of pre-fabricated language in untutored adult learners' (Yorio 1989: 57). Biskup's (1992) research into 'lexical collocations' (e.g. *reach a verdict, lift a blockade*) confirms their difficulty for learners, but only in production, not recognition (Biskup 1992: 86). Biskup concludes that 'only the experience of a "native-speaker" of a language allows him or her to produce collocations characteristic of that language' (Biskup 1992: 87). Granger (1998) found an 'underuse' of collocations in advanced learners' writing and concludes that 'learners use far fewer prefabs than "native-speaker" counterparts' (Granger 1998: 151). Like Granger, Arnaud and Savignon (1997), investigated advanced French learners' knowledge of 'rare words' and 'complex lexical units' as they call them, such as *a red herring* and *kick the bucket*, and concluded by questioning the degree to which advanced EFL learners could ever acquire idiomaticity:

> Can non-natives reach native-like proficiency with respect to rare words and complex lexical units? The answer would seem to be yes in the first case and no in the second.
>
> (Arnaud and Savignon 1997: 167)

The mystery of phraseology concerns not only idioms and collocations but multi-word discourse markers; De Cock (1998, 2000) found that learners of English used a smaller range of lexical phrases such as *you know, sort of* and *I mean* and, in particular, used far fewer expressions of vagueness (*sort of thing, like that, and everything*).

There is thus ample empirical evidence for the unique difficulty idiomaticity in its various manifestations poses for the learner and seems to reinforce the view that idiomaticity is the 'last and most challenging hurdle in attaining near-native like fluency' (Spöttl and McCarthy 2004: 191) and 'may floor even the proficient non-native' (Wray 2000: 463). Moreover, these findings raise important questions for the claims made on behalf of corpus linguistics and the application of its insights to language teaching.

6 ENL v ELF

The phraseological and corpus developments described above have taken place against the background of increasing resistance to native-centric views of English in the modern world. The last two decades have seen a growing debate about the 'break-up' of English or the emergence of 'world Englishes' (Quirk 1990; Kachru 1991; Mair 2003). For Quirk, standard English is 'the best candidate' for an international language, while for Kachru, Quirk is subscribing to a 'deficit' view of the new Englishes (Kachru 1991: 5–6). The centrifugal forces at work in world Englishes have in turn lead to a questioning of the role of 'native speaker' teachers and 'native speaker' models of English in the classroom. Alptekin (2002) challenges 'native-speaker' norms in the description of English as an international language and, by extension, methodologies that are dominated by an Anglo-American cultural perspective (Alptekin 2002 : 63).

Thus, one area of possible controversy surrounding corpus linguistics is the degree to which its findings can or should be applied to ELF. Is the full canon of modern English as revealed in spoken corpora (grammar, vocabulary, idiomaticity, phonology) an appropriate model for ELF? Seidlhofer (2001a and 2001b), for example, wonders whether there shouldn't be a grammatical common core for ELF, similar to Jenkins' phonological core (Jenkins 2000).

Where is this 'common core' to be found? Beyond the differences, what do ENL and ELF 'varieties' or uses of English share? Two areas in which the new Englishes and ENL diverge quite palpably is phonology and idiomaticity. Jenkins has developed a Lingua Franca Common Core for phonology (Jenkins 2000, 2005) but little attention has been paid to the role of idiomaticity in ELF. Seidlhofer (2001a) identifies idiomaticity as one of the areas in which English as a 'native' language and English as a lingua franca part ways:

> (ENL) is full of conventions and markers of in-group membership such as characteristic pronunciations, specialized vocabulary and idiomatic phraseology.
>
> (Seidlhofer 2001a: 136)

Seidlhofer coins the term 'unilateral idiomaticity' for those situations in ELF when one of the interlocutors uses an idiomatic expression which the other participant does not understand. Unilateral idiomaticity occurs when L1 speakers are involved in ELF and may lead to 'pragmatic failure' (Thomas 1983); ELF encounters consisting of L2–L2 users tend to avoid opaque uses of idiomaticity (Haegeman 2002; Meierkord 2005) and achieve understanding through accommodation and mutual construction of discourse (Meierkord 1998) and the application of a 'let-it-pass' principle (Firth 1996).

7 The empirical gap in research

Before the emergence of corpus linguistics, there had been few analyses of 'non-native' use of idiomatic language in speech and those that have been conducted were based on different kinds of elicited data such as interviews, thinking aloud, blank-filling, memory tests, written composition, questionnaire, translation, picture story narrations and multiple choice tests (see, for example, Bahns and Eldaw 1993; Kövecses and Szabo 1996; de Cock 2000; Adolphs and Durrow 2004). Useful though all of these studies have been, they provide insights into learning rather than acquisition (Nattinger 1980; Krashen 1981). They are studies of what the learner *knows about* formulaic language and not the use of formulaic language in spontaneous performance. Schmitt *et al* (2004), who conducted research into the acquisition of formulaic phrases by foreign students in the UK, acknowledge that 'the ability to complete a cloze test successfully does not demonstrate the ability to use the formulaic sequence at will in discourse' (Schmitt *et al* 2004: 67). Spöttl and McCarthy (2004) found 'a pattern of perceived receptive knowledge that is not matched with productive performance' (p. 216). It is important to bear in mind that here what Spöttl and McCarthy mean by 'productive performance' is no more than the ability to translate from L2 to L1 and complete multiple choice tests.

The artificial nature of data on which the research above is based has tended to generate an inadequate picture of the L2 user of English who is invariably found to be wanting when compared to 'native speakers', the description of whose discourse is based on huge corpora and naturally-occurring data. Nattinger (1980) warns against the danger of conflating the ability to 'learn' about idiomaticity and the ability to use it in pragmatically appropriate ways (Nattinger 1980: 342).

8 L2 user corpora

Apart from the L2 learner, then, little research is available into what adult users actually do with the language in ELF contexts. Cook's (2002) edited collection of articles *Portraits of the L2-user* does not include any analyses of naturally-occurring samples of L2 user speech. Early research into authentic L2 user conversation has focused mainly on discourse in institutionalized settings, such as business negotiations (Firth 1990; Erlich and Wagner 1995; Firth 1996) and academic advising sessions (Bardovi-Harlig and Hartford 1996). Cheng and Warren (1999) draw on a 50–hour corpus of 'native' and 'non-native speaker' everyday conversation in Hong Kong' while Pölzl (2003) bases her analysis on a corpus of 20 hours of naturally-occurring conversations among ELF users of 'rather fluent' but 'diverse proficiency' levels in the Middle East.

Meierkord (1998, 2005) refers to a small corpus of ELF speakers collected in a student hall of residence for overseas students in Great Britain and comprises 40,474 words or a total of 24 hours of informal interactions; the speakers participating in the conversations include both less competent and more competent speakers drawn from the 'outer circle' (ESL) and 'expanding circle' (EFL) of L2 users (Kachru 1985). Lesznyák (2004) bases her research into ELF on a 40–minute, quasi-natural discussion between 'NNS of English recorded at an international conference in the Netherlands' (Lesznyák 2004: 94).

A corpus of spoken ELF in academic settings (0.5 million words) is currently being collected at Tempere University (Mauranen 2003) and a corpus of general ELF (1 million words) is being built at the University of Vienna (Seidlhofer 2004).

9 The present corpus

My corpus differs from previous work on 'non-native' speech in focusing on natural, spontaneous speech produced by *proficient* L2 users of English as a foreign language from a number of different L1 backgrounds. Figure 14.2 summarizes the basic design of my L2-user corpus.

Date of recordings: 2000–2003
Type: Spoken, spontaneous, unscripted.
Length of complete corpus (including 'native speaker' interlocutors): 200,000 words
Length of L2 sub-corpus: 160,000 words
Number of participants/successful users: 42
Gender: 50% male, 50% female
Nationality: European (18 countries) and Latin American (6 countries).
Age: Adult: 25–50.
Education: University graduates and postgraduates.
Profession: EFL teachers, trainers, lecturers, applied linguists but also politicians, journalists, business people, publishers and administrators.
Level of English: Advanced/Proficient.
Register: Informal or non-formal conversation and some informal interviews between friends.
Roles: Family (married couples), friends, colleagues, acquaintances.
Setting: Home, office, car, train, restaurant, cafe, hotel.
Topics: Social chat, gossip, conversation about work, friends, politics, some discussion.

Figure 14.2 Summary of the Successful User of English (SUE) corpus

My 'successful' users are based on the concepts of 'expertise' (Rampton 1990) and 'accomplishment' (Edge 1988; Firth 1996; Wagner 1996) in ELF contexts rather than on extrinsic native-centric criteria such as examination passes or a high degree of idiomaticity. Expertise and accomplishment involve the speaker's orientation towards the interlocutor and the achievement of understanding through the use of all available linguistic means at their disposal; this understanding may be achieved in ways which are 'unidiomatic' by L1 standards (Firth 1996). My use of the concept of 'expertise' differs, however, from previous definitions in attempting to satisfy the criterion of classroom acceptability. I was attempting to respond to the requirement referred to by Alptekin (2002) that teachers in ELF contexts should be 'successful bilinguals with intercultural insights'; I have thus included accuracy in core grammar as part of my definition not because I see it as essential in all ELF encounters but as a pedagogic necessity given the current balance of forces in the teaching of English today.

The participants in my corpus are not 'learners': they have all completed their formal study of the language and gone out into the world to use English in a variety of social, personal and professional contexts. The subjects in my study exemplify a high degree of success in the use of English both in local and in a variety of international, cultural contexts; they are people who have occasion to use English with interlocutors from ethnic backgrounds other than their own and to code-switch effectively depending on their interlocutor. This, in practice, may mean a good command of 'core grammar' and, ironically, the ability to avoid rather than select opaque, culturally-laden idiomatic language. There follows a brief summary of the selection process:

(1) On visits to Europe and Latin America I frequently interacted, in social and professional contexts, with L2 users who sounded fluent in English, grammatically accurate and pragmatically successful. I arranged to record some of these individuals in informal, spontaneous contexts.

(2) On several occasions, a third party who knew what my research was about would recommend I record someone who they considered an outstanding user of English, again as a result of interaction with the individual in question.

(3) For many of the participants, I was able to contact people, L1 and L2 users, who knew them and ask these 'objective observers' to express an opinion on the subject's English.

(4) A fair proportion of my L2 users are widely recognized experts in the teaching or description of English or are recognized by ELT professionals who know them as successful users of English.

(5) I asked each participant to complete a questionnaire designed to elicit relevant bio-data; from this data, it emerged that all of the subjects had spent most of their life in an EFL rather than an ESL context.

(6) All of the informants use English regularly in personal, social or professional contexts with 'native' and 'non-native speakers', from ethnic backgrounds other than their own; they thus need to code-switch effectively depending on their interlocutor, an important aspect of ELF competence or 'expertise'.

(7) I circulated anonymous samples of the transcriptions to 100 professional ELT people (both L1 and L2 users) and asked them to give each sample a score to indicate the level of English suggested by the sample. The assessment was invariably very positive.

Thus, the process by which SUEs were selected involved my own knowledge and experience as a professional 'insider' and bilingual user of ELF but it also involved the knowledge and experience of members of the peer group, both L1 and L2 users (Edge and Richards 1998: 352).

10 A corpus and discourse-based approach

Having built my corpus, I began to explore the data inductively, in the form of frequency lists and concordance lines. Similarities and differences in frequency between the SUE and L1 corpora, such as the BNC and CANCODE, were noted. The differences were investigated using concordance lines to identify patterns of lexical and grammatical co-occurrence. The two kinds of software used at this stage were frequency lists of two-word phrases (TWPs) using the 'cluster' function of Wordsmith Tools and concordancers for the generation of Key Words In Context (KWIC; Scott 1996).

The identification of patterns involved looking at the way words and, in my case, TWPs, combine with other words (collocation) and with grammatical structures (colligation).

The more one uncovered of the co-text of a search phrase the more one detected patterns which made the concept of an 'extended unit of meaning' (Sinclair 1996) a natural and appropriate choice, emerging from the data itself. 'Extended units of meaning' are often made up of semantic and pragmatic prosodies. This means the dictionary definition of a word acts as a background or system of norms against which particular use is perceived; but the meaning of a word is also the effect of the words with which it habitually collocates; these collocates, in turn, may form typical patterns of meaning. Sinclair (1996, 2004) refers to these patterns as the word or phrase's 'semantic preference' (on a conceptual level) or 'semantic prosody' (on a pragmatic level). These patterns will give the word particular connotations, positive or negative.

11　Two word lexical phrases: Frequency

Given the vast and fuzzy nature of idiomaticity (see Figure 14.1) it was difficult to know where to begin investigating the phenomenon in 'L1 user' and 'L2 user' discourse. I therefore took the simplest definitions of 'idiom' I could find as my starting point: 'an idiom is a combination of two or more words which function as a unit of meaning' (Cowie and Mackin 1975: viii–ix).

The procedure I adopted was to begin with this minimal unit of idiomaticity, and work outwards from form to meaning, from meaning to context and from context to pragmatics. To identify examples of these units of meaning without pre-judging what counts as 'idiomatic', I created a list of frequent two-word 'clusters' based on the CANCODE corpus, using the Wordsmith Tools cluster function (Scott 1996). Scott (1996: 41) describes clusters as 'words which are found repeatedly in each other's company'; thus they are a kind of collocation but they 'represent a tighter relationship than collocates, more like groups or phrases' (Scott 1996: 35): *a lot of; a bit of a; I don't know if; If you look at; you know; I mean; sort of; you see.*

These clusters, in contrast to the low frequency of opaque idiomatic expressions, are frequent occurrences in spoken and written English and, unlike idioms and fixed expressions, are very common in L2 user discourse, too (Moon 1994; Biber *et al* 2004). McCarthy and Carter (2002) see a social significance in the frequency of these clusters and underline their importance in the shaping of interaction: they are not random fragments but pragmatic devices made 'visible'.

12　Quantitative analysis

If we compare the SUE corpus to the L1 corpus, we notice a considerable similarity in the most frequent two-word clusters in the two corpora (Table 14.1):

Table 14.1 TWPs in SUE corpus (200,000 words) and CANCODE, an L1 user corpus (5m words; normalized to occurrence per million words)

	Phrase	L1 pm	L1 per cent	L2 pm	L2 per cent
1	You know	5,602	0.58	4,113	0.41
2	I mean	3,431	0.36	3,060	0.31
3	I think	2,817	0.29	3,093	0.31
4	Sort of	1,917	0.18	546	0.05
5	And then	1,547	0.16	1,613	0.16
6	Don't know	1,323	0.14	1,426	0.15
7	Have to	1,182	0.12	1,766	0.18
8	You can	1,165	0.12	1,520	0.15
9	Going to	1,106	0.11	1,093	0.11
10	A bit	1,068	0.11	446	0.04
11	I know	994	0.10	660	0.07
12	As well	980	0.10	553	0.05
13	A lot	971	0.10	1,146	0.12
14	Like that	851	0.09	546	0.05
15	All right	842	0.09	226	0.02
16	Used to	728	0.08	987	0.11
17	You see	727	0.08	387	0.04
18	I thought	688	0.07	353	0.04
19	Kind of	663	0.07	1,113	0.11
20	I said	654	0.07	680	0.06

The degree of similarity in the two lists is striking. Generally, there is a remarkable overlap in the two corpora of most frequent TWPs, though the level of frequency of individual items, as we shall see, shows interesting differences to which I will return later in this paper.

12.1 Pragmatic markers

The first pattern that strikes one is that the majority of the TWPs, in both corpora, are items that have a pragmatic rather than a referential function. They are what are variously referred to in the literature as discourse particles (Schourup 1985; Aijmer 2002), pragmatic markers (Brinton 1996) or pragmatic particles (Holmes 1988).

These small items, though elusive and thin on semantic content, are among the most frequent items in the lexicon and are by no means insignificant; they have a wide range of context-embedded functions which 'emerge from the immediate speech context' (Cook 2001: 177).

The most frequent two-word pragmatic markers (*you know, I mean, I think sort of*) contain a non-literal, holistic element which has led some scholars to include them in the general category of idiomaticity, fixed expressions or formulaic language (Fromkin 1973: 42; Alexander 1978: 15; Gramley and

Pätzold 1992: 54; Powell 1992: 28; Carter 1998: 66; McCarthy 1998: 121; Moon 1998: 94).

Thus, pragmatic phrases, as I will refer to them in order to foreground their idiomatic dimension, are made up of a string of words with a single meaning which is usually at variance with the literal meaning of the individual words. I will, therefore, consider pragmatic phrases as examples of minimal idiomatic units, in contrast to the more extended idiomatic units of the 'colourful' variety (proverbs, sayings, nursery rhymes and so on).

12.2 Divergence

Turning to those items where the SUE corpus and L1 user corpus seem to diverge most, we notice that the following pragmatic phrases occur twice as frequently in L1 user conversation than they do in L2 user conversation: *sort of, a bit, as well, you see.*

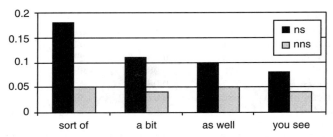

Figure 14.3 Two-word lexical phrases: deviations between L1 user and SUE corpora (%)

Interestingly, three out of the four most divergent pragmatic phrases in L1-user and SUE corpus (*sort of, a bit* and *you see*) have been described as pragmatic phrases of 'shared knowledge' that regulate interpersonal relations and modify attitudes towards propositional content on the part of the speaker (Erman 1987; Schiffrin 1987). These semantic and pragmatic features may be clues to why these three items display a different pattern of occurrence in the two corpora. I will explore this hypothesis by focusing on one of these items, *sort of.*

12.3 A sort of puzzle

Sort of is the fourth most common two-word lexical phrase in the CANCODE corpus and BNC. *Sort of* is, moreover, the 120th most frequent lexical item of any length in the informal spoken English captured in the CANCODE corpus. It is as frequent as *want* in L1 user conversation and almost as frequent as *okay. Sort of* is more frequent in CANCODE than *thing* and *come* and phrases such as *going to* and *I know.*

Why should *sort of* be less frequent in the discourse of even ELF users? To begin to answer this question, it is important to look at *sort of* and indeed all pragmatic phrases, not in isolation, but as part of wider combinations of form, meaning and use. Holmes (1984) warns against the danger of describing linguistic devices in isolation from other items with which they co-occur (Holmes 1984: 363). Figure 14.4 shows the most common collocates of *sort of* in L1 spoken discourse, occurring within five words to the left or right of the node phrase:

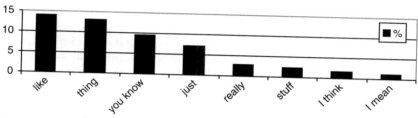

Figure 14.4 Most frequent collocates of *sort of* in L1-user corpus (out of a total of 250 random hits)

The first thing about the collocates of *sort of* that strikes the researcher is that they are all (apart from *really*) potential realizations of hedges and mitigating devices, often expressing vagueness. Bearing in mind that *sort of* itself is a kind of hedge, what we seem to have on, a semantic level, is the tendency for vagueness to attract vagueness or, pragmatically-speaking, that hedges attract hedges. In other words, *sort of* collocates frequently with individual words or phrases which foreground and reinforce its role as a pragmatic device through which the speaker expresses an appeal to shared knowledge.

12.4 Discourse rhapsody: The function of collocate repetition

A second observation we should make is that *sort of* occurs so frequently with one or more of its collocates that the resulting combination may be said to constitute an extended fixed phrase or what I call collocational complexes:

(1) It was **sort of** well **sort of like really** weird
(2) **you know** and kissing his feet and **sort of you know** bathing him in oil
(3) And **you know** she **just sort of** eats. . .
(4) and it's very short **like** cos it's **sort of** quite **sort of** it's **just like** in panels

In the full flow of conversational interaction, whether during monologues or dialogues, the discourse marker collocates of *sort of* are woven in and out of the discourse. On reading, in the cold light of print, the way these collocates of *sort of* combine to form larger units in spoken discourse, one can almost feel the speaker tacking on item after item, semantic chunk after semantic chunk, under the pressure of the ongoing evolution of the utterance in real-time. Yet, in actual discourse, these complexes pass almost unnoticed and contribute to the sense of flow in informal conversation. What we hear are small phrases which, in combination, have an integrative effect on the utterances and help construct what Bakhtin refers to as a 'chain of communication' (Bakhtin 1986: 93).The repeated collocates are not merely mechanical – they have a cumulative impact on their context of situation and the pragmatic outcomes. It seems likely, in other words, that such pervasive repetition is motivated in terms of the pressures of the sequential development of discourse and serves a range of constructive or co-constructive purposes in the discourse: turn-taking conventions, holding the floor, repair-strategies and generally establishing and maintaining the desired interpersonal relationship between the interlocutors.

On another level, one can interpret this collocational repetition as a way of intensifying the speaker's appeal to the real – or manipulated – shared background knowledge of the addressee. The closer we look at the data the more we realize that these patterns of co-occurrence are part of a wider lexical and semantic configuration which serve to promote speaker–hearer convergence. In the following examples we can sense the operation of this 'you-know-what-I-mean' factor shared by members of the same speech community:

(5) I try to **just sort of just** hope my life isn't affected
(6) It's like quite **sort of like** a pet

Fluency, then, is not to be found on the level of formulaic expressions in isolation but in the construction of 'extended units of meaning' or the 'idiom principle' broadly defined in textual, contextual and pragmatic terms.

12.5 Semantic and pragmatic prosodies of sort of

The general semantic and pragmatic patterns formed by the collocations we find with *sort of* are summed up in Figure 14.5.

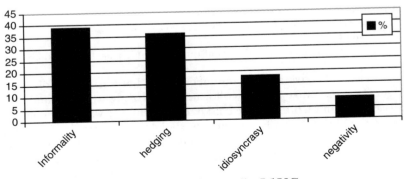

Figure 14.5 General prosodies of *sort of* in L1UC

(1) Informality: this includes individual items of vocabulary such as *pad, guy,* many idiomatic expressions, taboo words and most hedges.
(2) Hedging: this includes 'hedges' such as *you know, like, just etc,* vagueness, numbers and times.
(3) Idiosyncrasy: this includes negative meanings, taboo words, formal and technical items and literary-metaphorical expressions.
(4) Negativity: this includes words expressing negative feelings, complaints, anger, taboo and swear words.

These broad areas of meaning are activated in discourse to express a wide range of interpersonal functions and particularly in achieving the convergence and co-construction of discourse which is so characteristic of informal conversation. It is not surprising that, given the casual nature of the spoken data in the L1 speaker corpus (CANCODE), the most prominent general pragmatic prosody of *sort of* is 'informality'. This informality is realized in a number of ways, drawing on the various semantic resources available in the system of which *sort of* is a pivotal part: idiomaticity, taboo words and other individual lexical items that carry traces of informality. Informality is thus a strategic means of achieving convergence between speakers.

A deviation from the tone of informality by, for example, selecting a formal, technical or literary lexical item, will activate the need to use some kind of hedge to bring the discourse back into line or within the limits of comfortable, common ground. Hedging and vagueness are thus a major function in maintaining equilibrium in conversation and this is reflected in the predominance of the 'hedging' pragmatic prosody of *sort of* in L1 user discourse.

Idiosyncrasy is, par excellence, an occasion when *sort of* needs to be mobilized to re-establish the common ground when the speaker slips into some violation of the linguistic or social norm. This includes a multitude of sins, from unusual or rare words, words which mean 'strange' 'funny', and so on; words which are borrowed from other genres, such as literary genres, technical genres, etc. and of course, curses, oaths, taboo words. In all such cases, *sort of* can *re*-present the speaker's self in the light of shared background knowledge and the safe familiarity of the speech community to which the interlocutor belongs or which is salient in a particular encounter. It is a process of making the subliminally dialogic nature of discourse more conscious.

Finally, 'negativity' also occurs frequently in the company of *sort of* in various guises, and this is predictable given the function of *sort of* in promoting cooperation and convergence. Talk of problems, death, failure, dislike, enmity, disappointment are all occasions when speakers deviate from the agreeable, often phatic, default position of so much casual conversation and from which interlocutors, notoriously, desire to slip away from and return to more pleasant matters.

12.6 The 'difficulty' of sort of

Sort of, then, is not difficult in itself, in its dictionary sense. But it has a range of semantic and pragmatic prosodic functions that can only be acquired in situated interaction. Its main semantic prosody – idiomaticity – makes of *sort of* a kind of extended lexical or idiomatic unit. But its frequency in L1 discourse is inseparable from its full range of accompanying prosodies; the 'difficulty' or 'avoidance' by L2 users can only be explained in terms of the whole complex of relationships with which it co-occurs (informality, idiosyncrasy, hedging, negativity).

The socio-pragmatic rootedness of *sort of* may be one reason why the L2 user might find it a difficult item to acquire: its 'meanings' are not pre-packaged, ready-made but emergent (Hopper 1979, 1998), actively constructed in real-time in response to the pressures of face-to-face interaction; one cannot understand *sort of* by looking it up in a dictionary or by artificial classroom activities.

One can appreciate why *sort of*, in its extended sense, prosodies and co-occurrences included, is such a handy device in the informal spoken interaction of L1 users but the question is whether L2 users express the kinds of meanings that *sort of* has evolved to serve, and whether L2 users bring to the complex of shifting meanings to which *sort of* belongs the depth of commonality that would make this pragmatic phrase, and others like it, a frequent and natural choice. One will not choose *sort of* if one doesn't also choose idiomatic, idiosyncratic and informal modes of interaction. These modes of interaction may in turn be inextricably embedded in the cultural constraints of the L1 user speech community.

Taking due account of the relatively small number of instances of *sort of* contained in our L2 corpus we can surmise that *sort of*:

(1) Has a range of semantic meanings which expand on the core meaning of imprecision.
(2) Has relational and discoursal uses which are inseparable from its collocations; these uses are not random but driven by pragmatic need, especially the need speakers feel to hedge and mitigate the force of the utterance.
(3) Collocates with 'idiomaticity' and is associated with informality and idiosyncrasy or deviation from a norm. It helps to regulate the speaker's relationship with the listener, projecting and manipulating feelings and attitudes in order to present an image of self which is appropriate to the context and the interpersonal aims of the discourse.
(4) Forms wider networks of meaning or semantic prosodies (including idiomaticity) which, on a discourse level, serve to hold the text together as a unified whole. In this sense it is an 'extended lexical unit' or 'extended idiomatic unit'.
(5) Forms links, frames and chains that facilitate the online, real-time improvisation of fluent, informal spoken discourse. *Sort of* and its constellation of associated meanings is an integral feature of L1 fluency.

(6) Forms a closed system of pragmatic markers that serve convergent relational needs: *you know, I mean, I think, sort of* and other items in the same class all involve the listener in establishing commonality; in L1 discourse, these pragmatic phrases build rapport and define common space.

A possible explanation for the relative rarity of *sort of* in L2 spoken discourse might be that when most SUEs were acquiring the language they were not exposed to the kind of interactions in which *sort of* is frequent. Moreover, teachers and textbooks typically avoid the informality, vagueness and hedging which would promote the use of *sort of.*

12.7 Implications and future research

We have seen that the frequency of *sort of* is echoed in the richness of its pragmatic uses and this frequency and flexibility makes TWPs like *sort of* and *you know* a good place to begin to describe the way spoken English works across speech varieties. The rich layers of meaning underlying the 'little words' of English, when uncovered, may give us an insight into the nature of the differences between L1 and L2 as a whole. We can compare two-word pragmatic phrases to a pebble in a pool generating multiple circles of meaning; they are microcosm of the linguistic world of L1 and L2 users.

In the pedagogic domain, where time is short and acquisition long, we need to draw up a common core of idiomatic expressions which can form the basis for constructing syllabi in different contexts where English is being taught as a lingua franca. The scale of idiomaticity I drew up in Figure 14.1 may be helpful in deciding on what basis to include items in the common core, always in response to *emergent* local needs and any *emerging* common patterns in global ELF.

With firsthand knowledge gained from impromptu speech, we may hope to develop further hypotheses about the significance both of minimal idiomatic units and 'extended idiomatic units', which can be tested against further empirical data of a cross-cultural nature and incorporated into a theory of socio-cultural networks and sociolinguistic variation. Specifically, we need to explore the behaviour of more two-word pragmatic phrases which differ in frequency in the two kinds of corpora and attempt to identify common features across different pragmatic phrases. In my corpus, for example, *you see* and *a bit*, were less frequent than they are in L1 corpora: are *you see* and *a bit*, like *sort of* small but powerful bits of language?

A major area for future research is the link between phonology and idiomatic competence in spoken English. Are minimal idiomatic units 'primed' as Hoey says 'to occur with certain pitches or tones?' (2005: 188). If the answer is yes, as I suspect it is, then the acquisition of idiomatic competence after a certain age is a daunting task.

13 Conclusion

When I embarked on my research I thought I would be exploring the manifold nature of idiomaticity and thus when I found myself analysing small expressions like *sort of* I initially felt disappointed. I now realize I was not, in fact, looking at single lexico-grammatical items but at multiple extended units, composed of a whole range of related linguistic items, be they full lexical categories or pragmatic markers. I also realize that 'minor' grammatical categories do not necessarily express minor meanings. We have been looking at 'small words with big meanings' (McCarthy 2003: 60).

On another level, this paper has been a prolonged response to the arrival of corpus linguistics on the ELT scene. It is the continuation of a dialogue which began with the question raised by a classroom teacher at a TESOL Conference, querying the relevance of corpus linguistics to ELF. English has gone forth and multiplied – it has proliferated into Englishes, both 'nativized' Englishes and international lingua franca Englishes, and this heteroglossia reigns supreme, with all the potential for innovation that this entails. Any 'models' of English we decide to work with must be capable of accommodating this diversity and the creativity that all language users, be they L1 or ELF users, are heir to.

I feel it is too early to draw firm conclusions about the performance features of successful users of English as an international language from such a small corpus of language. My SUE corpus, however, has given me, and I hope the reader, some tantalizing glimpses as to why certain apparently simple features of English such as pragmatic phrases may be elusive for the L2 user. The search and re-search continues.

References

Adolphs, S. and Durrow, V. (2004), 'Social-cultural integration and the development of formulaic sequences', in N. Schmitt (ed.), *Formulaic Sequences: Acquisition, Processing and Use*. Amsterdam: John Benjamin, pp. 107–26.

Aijmer, K. (2002), *English Discourse Particles*. Amsterdam: John Benjamin's Publishing Company.

Alexander, R. (1978), 'Fixed expressions in English: a linguistic, psycholinguistic, sociolinguistic and didactic study, (Part 1)'. *Anglistik & Englischunterricht*, (6), 1978, 171–88.

Alptekin, C. (2002), 'Towards intercultural communicative competence in ELT'. *ELT Journal*, 56, 1, 57–64.

Altenberg, B. and Granger, S. (2001), 'Grammatical and lexical patterning of *make* in student writing'. *Applied Linguistics*, 22, (2), 173–94.

Arnaud, P. and Savigon, P. (1997), 'Rare words, complex lexical units and the advanced learner', in J. Coady and T. Huckin (eds), *Second Language Vocabulary Acquisition*. Cambridge: Cambridge University Press, pp. 157–200.

Bahns, J., Burmeister, H. and Vogel, T. (1986), 'The pragmatics of formulas in L2 learner speech'. *Journal of Pragmatics*, 10, 693, 723.

Bahns, J. and Eldaw, M. (1993), 'Should we teach ESL students collocations?'. *System*, 21, (1), 101–14.

Bakhtin, M. (1986), *Speech Genres and other late essays*. Austin, TX: University of Texas Press.

Bardovi-Harlig, K. and Hartford, B. (1996), 'Input in an institutional setting'. *Studies in Second Language Acquisition*, 18, 171–88.

Biber, D., Conrad, S. and Cortes, V. (2004), 'Lexical bundles in university teaching and textbooks'. *Applied Linguistics*, 25, (3), 371–405.

Biskup, D. (1992), 'L1 influence on learners' renderings of English collocations: a Polish/German study', in P. Arnaud and H. Bejoint (eds), *Vocabulary and Applied Linguistics*. Basingstoke and London: Macmillan, pp. 85–93.

Bolinger, D. (1961), 'Syntactic blends and other matters'. *Language*, 37, 366–81.

Bolinger, D. (1976), 'Meaning and memory'. *Forum Linguisticum*, 1, 1–14.

Brinton, L. (1996), *Pragmatic Markers in English*. Berlin: Mouton de Gruyter.

Carter, R. (1998), *Vocabulary: Applied Linguistics Perspectives* (2nd edn). London: Routledge.

Carter, R. and McCarthy, M. (1995), 'Grammar and the spoken language'. *Applied Linguistics*, 16, 2, 141–58.

Carter, R. and McCarthy, M. (1997), *Exploring Spoken English*. Cambridge: Cambridge University Press.

Carter, R. and McCarthy, M. (2001), 'Size isn't everything: Spoken English, corpus and the classroom'. *TESOL Quarterly*, 35, 2, 337–40.

Cheng, W. and Warren, M. (1999), 'Facilitating a description of intercultural conversations: the Hong Kong Corpus of Conversational English.' *ICAME Journal* 23: 5–18.

Chomsky, N. (1965), *Aspects of the Theory of Syntax*. Cambridge, MA: MIT Press.

Cook, H. (2001), 'Particles', in A. Duranti (ed.), *Key Terms in Language and Culture*. Oxford: Blackwell, pp. 176–9.

Cook, V. (ed.) (2002), *Portraits of the L2–User*. Clevedon: Multilingual Matters.

Coulmas, F. (ed.) (1981), *Conversational Routine: Explorations in Standardized Communication Situations and Pre-patterned Speech*. Hague: Mouton Publishers.

Cowie, A. and Mackin, R. (eds) (1975), *Oxford Dictionary of Current Idiomatic English. Vol. 1*. London: Oxford University Press.

De Cock, S. (1998), 'A recurrent word combination approach to the study of formulae in the speech of native and non-native speakers of English'. *International Journal of Corpus Linguistics*, 3, (1), 59–80.

De Cock, S. (2000), 'Repetitive phrasal chunkiness and advanced EFL speech and writing', in C. Mair and M. Hundt (eds), *Corpus Linguistics and Linguistic Theory: Papers from ICAME 20 1999*. Amsterdam: Rodopi, pp. 51–68.

Dechert, H. and Lennon, P. (1989), 'Collocational blends of advanced learners: a preliminary analysis', in W. Oleksy (ed.), *Contrastive Pragmatics*. Amsterdam: John Benjamins, pp.131–68.

Edge, J. and Richards, K. (1998), ' "May I see your warrant please?": Justifying outcomes in qualitative research'. *Applied Linguistics*, 19, (3), 334–56.

Ellis, N. (1996), 'Sequencing in SLA: phonological memory, chunking and points of order'. *Studies in Second Language Acquisition*, 18, 91–126.

Erlich, K. and Wagner, J. (1995), *The Discourse of Business Negotiations*. Berlin: Mouton de Gruyter.

Erman, B. (1987), *Pragmatic Expressions in English. A study of 'you know' 'you see' and 'I mean' in face-to-face conversation*. Stockholm Studies in English 69. Stockholm: Almqvist and Wiksell.

Erman, B. and Warren, B. (2000), 'The idiom principle and the open choice principle'. *Text*, 20, 1, 29–62.

Firth, A. (1990), 'Lingua franca negotiations: towards an interactional approach'. *World Englishes*, 9, (3), 269–80.

Firth, A. (1996), 'The discursive accomplishment of normality. On lingua franca English and conversation analysis'. *Journal of Pragmatics*, 26, 237–59.

Fox, G. (1998), 'Using corpus data in the classroom', in B. Tomlinson (ed.), *Materials Development in Language Teaching*. Cambridge: Cambridge University Press, pp. 25–43.

Fromkin, V. (ed.) (1973), *Speech Errors as Linguistic Evidence*. The Hague: Mouton.

Gibbs, R. (1995), 'Idiomaticity and human cognition', in M. Everaert., E. van der Linden, A. Schenk and R. Schreuder (eds), *Idioms: Structural and Psychological Perspectives*. Hillsdale, NJ: Lawrence Erlbaum Associates, pp. 97–116.

Gramley, S. and Pätzold, K. (1992), *A Survey of Modern English*. Routledge.

Granger, S. (1998), 'Prefabricated patterns in advanced EFL writing: collocations and formulae', in A. Cowie (ed.), *Phraseology: theory, analysis and applications*. Oxford: Oxford University Press, pp. 145–60.

Haegaman, P. (2002), 'Foreigner talk in lingua franca business calls', in K. Knapp and C. Meierkord (eds), *Lingua Franca Communication*. Frankfurt: Peter Lang, pp. 109–34.

Hoey, M. (2005), *Lexical Priming*. London: Routledge.

Holmes J. (1984), 'Modifying illocutionary force'. *Journal of Pragmatics*, 8, 345–65.

Holmes, J. (1988), '*Sort of* in New Zealand women's and men's speech'. *Studia Linguistica*, 42, 85–121.

Hopper, P. (1979), 'Aspect and foregrounding in discourse,' in T. Givon (ed.), *Syntax and Semantics Volume 12: Discourse and Syntax*. New York: Academic Press, pp. 213–41.

Hopper, P. (1998), 'Emergent grammar', in M. Tomasello (ed.), *The New Psychology of Language*. Hillsdale, NJ: Lawrence Erlbaum Associates, pp. 155–75.

Irujo, S. (1986), 'Don't put your leg in your mouth: transfer in the acquisition of idioms in a foreign language'. *TESOL Quarterly*, 20, 287–304.

Jenkins, J. (2000), *The Phonology of English as an International Language*. Oxford: Oxford University Press.

Jenkins, J. (2005), 'Teaching pronunciation for English as a Lingua Franca: a sociopolitical perspective', in C. Gnutzmann and F. Intemann (eds), *The Globalisation of English and the English Language Classroom*. Tübingen: Gunter Narr Verlag, pp. 145–58.

Jespersen, O. (1894), *Progress in Language: with special reference to English*. New York: Macmillan.

Jespersen, O. (1904), *How to Teach a Foreign Language*. London: Allen and Unwin.

Kachru, B. (1985), 'Standards, codification and sociolinguistic realm: the English language in the outer circle', in R. Quirk and H. Widdowson (eds), *English in the World*. Cambridge: Cambridge University Press, pp. 11–30.

Kachru, B. (1991), 'Liberation linguistics and the Quirk concern'. *English Today*, 25, 3–13.

Knapp, K. (2002), 'The fading of the non-native speaker. Native speaker dominance in lingua franca situations', in E. Knapp and C. Meierkord (eds), *Lingua Franca Communication*. Frankfurt: Peter Lang, pp. 217–44.

Kövecses, Z. and Szabo, P. (1996), 'Idioms: a view from cognitive semantics'. *Applied Linguistics*, 17, (3), 326–54.

Krashen, S. (1981), *Second Language Acquisition and Second Language Learning*. Oxford: Pergamon.

Lesznyák, A. (2002), 'From chaos to the smallest common denominator: topic management in English lingua franca communication', in K. Knapp and C. Meierkord (eds), *Lingua Franca Communication*. Frankfurt: Peter Lang, pp. 163–94.

Lesznyák, A. (2004), *Communication in English as an International Lingua Franca: An Exploratory Case Study*. Norderstedt, Germany: Books on Demand.

Mair, C. (ed.) (2003), *The Politics of English as a World Language*. Amsterdam: Rodopi.

Mauranen, A. (2003), 'Academic English as a lingua franca – a corpus approach'. *TESOL Quarterly*, 37, 513–27.

McCarthy, M. (1988), 'Some vocabulary patterns in conversation,' in R. Carter and M. McCarthy, *Vocabulary and Language Teaching*. London: Longman, pp. 181–200.

McCarthy, M. (1998), *Spoken Language and Applied Linguistics*. Cambridge: Cambridge University Press.

McCarthy. M. (2003), 'Talking back: 'small' interactional responses in everyday conversation'. *Research on language and Social Interaction. Special Issue on Small Talk*, 36, (1), 33–63.

McCarthy, M. and Carter, R. (1994), *Language as Discourse*. London: Longman.

McCarthy, M. and Carter, R. (2002), 'This that and the other: multi-word clusters in spoken English as visible patterns of interaction'. *Teanga. Yearbook of the Irish Association for Applied Linguistics*, 21, 30–52.

Meierkord, C. (2005), 'Interaction across Englishes and their lexicon', in C. Gnutzmann and F. Intemann (eds), *The Globalisation of English and the English Language Classroom*. Tübingen: Gunter Narr Verlag, pp. 89–104.

Meierkord, C. (1998), 'Lingua franca English: characteristics of successful non-native-non-native-speaker' discourse'. *Erfurt Electronic Studies* (EESE) 1998. http://web-doc.sub.gwdg.de/edoc/ia/eese/eese.html.

Moon, R. (1994), 'The analysis of fixed expressions in text,' in M. Coulthard (ed.), *Advances in Written Discourse Analysis*. London: Routledge, pp. 117–35.

Moon, R. (1998), *Fixed Expressions and Idioms in English: A Corpus-Based Approach*. Oxford: The Clarendon Press.

Nattinger, J. (1980), 'A lexical phrase grammar for ESL'. *TESOL Quarterly*, 14, (3), 337–44.

Nattinger, J. and DeCarrico, J. (1992), *Lexical Phrases and Language Teaching*. Oxford: Oxford University Press.

Pölzl, U. (2003), 'Signalling cultural identity: the use of L1/Ln in ELF'. *Vienna English Working Papers*, 12, (2), 3–23.

Powell, M. (1992), 'Semantic/pragmatic regularities in informal lexis: British speakers in spontaneous conversational settings'. *Text*, 12, (1), 19–58.

Prodromou, L. (2005), 'You see, it's sort of tricky for the L2-user: idiomaticity in English as a Lingua franca'. (Unpublished Ph.D Thesis, University of Nottingham).

Quirk, R. (1990), 'Language varieties and standard language'. *English Today*, 21, 3–10.

Rampton, B. (1990), 'Displacing the "native-speaker"'. *ELT Journal*, 44, (2), 97–101.

Schiffrin, D. (1987), *Discourse Markers*. Cambridge: Cambridge University Press.

Schmitt, N., Dornyei, Z., Adolphs, S. and Durow, V. (2004), 'Knowledge and acquisition of formulaic sequences: a longitudinal study', in N. Schmitt (ed.), *Formulaic Sequences: Acquisition, Processing and Use*. Amsterdam: John Benjamin, pp. 55–86.

Schourup, L. C. (1985), *Common Discourse Particles in English Conversation*. Garland: New York.

Scott, M. (1996), *Wordsmith Tools: Manual*. Oxford: Oxford University Press.

Seidlhofer, B. (2001a), 'Towards making 'Euro-English' a linguistic reality'. *English Today*, 68, 14–16.

Seidlhofer, B. (2001b), 'Closing a conceptual gap: the case for a description of English as a lingua franca'. *International Journal of Applied Linguistics* 11, (2), 133–58.

Seidlhofer, B. (2002), 'The shape of things to come? Some basic questions about English as a lingua franca', in K. Knapp and C. Meierkord, *Lingua Franca Communication*. Frankfurt: Peter Lang, pp. 269–302.

Seidlhofer, B. (2004), 'Research perspectives on teaching English as a lingua franca'. *Annual Review of Applied Linguistics*, 24, 200–39.

Sinclair, J. (1985), 'Selected issues', in R. Quirk and H. Widdowson (eds) *English in the World*. Cambridge: Cambridge University Press, pp. 248–54.

Sinclair, J. (ed.) (1987), *Looking Up: An Account of the COBUILD Project in Lexical Computing*. London: Harper-Collins.

Sinclair, J. (1991), *Corpus, Concordance, Collocation*. Oxford: Oxford University Press.

Sinclair, J. (1996), 'The search for units of meaning'. *TEXTUS*, 9, (1), 75–106.

Sinclair, J. (2004), *Trust the Text: Language, Corpus and Discourse*. London: Routledge.

Skehan, P. (1998), *A Cognitive Approach to Language Learning*. Oxford: Oxford University Press.

Spöttl, C. and McCarthy, M. (2004), 'Comparing the knowledge of formulaic sequences across L1, L2, L3 and L4', in N. Schmitt (ed.), *Formulaic Sequences: Acquisition, Processing and Use*. Amsterdam: John Benjamin, pp. 191–225.

Stubbs, M. (2001), *Words and Phrases: Corpus studies of lexical semantics*. Oxford: Blackwell Publishers.

Thomas, J. (1983), 'Cross-cultural pragmatic failure'. *Applied Linguistics*, 4, 91–112.

Wagner, J. (1996), 'Foreign language acquisition through interaction – a critical review of research on conversational adjustments'. *Journal of Pragmatics*, 26, 215–35.

Weinert, R. (1995), 'The role of formulaic language in second language acquisition: a review'. *Applied Linguistics*, 16, (2), 180–205.

Widdowson, H. (1994), 'The ownership of English', *TESOL Quarterly*, 28, (2), 377–89.

Wray, A. (2000), 'Formulaic sequences in second language teaching: principle and practice'. *Applied Linguistics*, 21, (4), 463–89.

Wray, A. (2002), *Formulaic Language and the Lexicon*. Cambridge: Cambridge University Press.

Yorio, C.A. (1989), 'Idiomaticity as an indicator of second language proficiency', in K. Hyltenstam and L. Obler (eds), *Bilingualism across the Lifespan*. Cambridge: Cambridge University Press, pp. 55–69.

15 Perceptions of culture by British students learning French

Catherine von Knorring

1 Introduction

In the forward to his Pulitzer prize winning biography of *Adolf Hitler*, John Toland (1977: xi) writes: 'My book has no thesis'. Those five small words struck a liberating chord when I first came across them, and reminded me that research could also be an adventure into the unknown, a voyage of discovery. It was with this small phrase in mind that I set about exploring the question of culture and what culture might mean to my students of French at Leeds Metropolitan University.

I have been interested to observe that when talking of culture, the word itself seems to have a multitude of incarnations: anthropology, ethnography, sociology, sociolinguistics, language, psychology, the arts, and the list goes on! (Hofstede 1980; Agar 1996; Cronin 2000; Besemeres 2002; Phipps and Gonzalez 2004). My quest, however, has been to discover what young people today understand by the word and I was also interested in investigating whether there would be a difference in the notion of culture between a native language and an acquired language; that is to say, would students have a notion of French culture as 'high culture' since they would necessarily learn a certain amount about traditional French culture in the course of their A level studies? The overall purpose of my project was to gauge students' perceptions of culture in order better to prepare them for their year abroad.

My methodology was very simple. I asked a group of second year European Languages and Business students on two separate occasions to write what they understood first by 'English Culture' and a month later by 'French Culture'. In class, I wrote the instructions on the board; students were asked to write whatever came to mind and they had about half an hour to complete the task. These second year students all have an A level pass in French and have all, at some point in their young lives, visited the country. Many simply wrote a list of ideas that popped into their heads, others wrote one or two paragraphs, occasionally attempting to define culture in general.

I did not wish to contaminate their thinking with any notions I might have on the subject so they were taken somewhat by surprise, particularly on the first occasion when they had to write on English culture as it was a task given to them out of the blue. They no doubt copied from one another as they sought inspiration, and when it came to the second exercise on French culture, many of them were influenced by their lectures on contemporary French society, which had been running for a month. This was another reason for not presenting the task as homework or as something which they could look up; I was very interested in gleaning their opinions '*sur le vif*' so as to have as spontaneous a result as possible.

The findings were unexpected and are summarized below.

2 English and French culture as perceived by English students

2.1 *English culture (65 respondents)*

Food (58 responses) was the rather surprising top scorer defining English culture, though many respondents recognized that food plays a large part in all cultures. Repeated references were made to 'fish and chips', 'roast beef and Yorkshire pudding', 'steak and kidney pie', ' bangers and mash' and also to the tradition of a roast Sunday lunch (though hardly anyone referred to a cooked breakfast).

The timing of meals caused comment, with the English tending to eat earlier than the French; tea drinking was also repeatedly mentioned and there was a recognition that England has become more multi-cultural as far as food is concerned with a proliferation of Pizzerias, Chinese takeaways and so forth.

Less surprisingly the **Royal Family and tradition** came second (43 responses). Many students recognised that the influence of the Royal Family has dwindled over the years, but the institution is still in place and this aspect of historical permanence seemed important to many:

'English culture tends to be very traditional due to things such as the Royal Family which have been a major part of British culture for hundreds of years, although we place less importance on them now.'

Several respondents felt that the monarchy was 'respected worldwide' and 'renowned for good or bad reasons'.

Many references were made to a 'strong traditional culture'; one or two respondents perceived this as an England: 'Too set in its ways with many unnecessary procedures.'

Attitudes towards the **Family and a reserved attitude to life and relationships** (42 responses) was regarded as culturally defining by most respondents:

'English people have a tendency to be fairly reserved – stiff upper lip.'

Occasionally a note of scepticism was expressed:

'There are many stereotypes concerning the way British people live. Such ideas are that the British are boring and very conservative in the way we live.'

In addition, many respondents remarked that the English are thought to be polite. All of them recognized a difference between English family life and a supposed closeness of European family life.

Religion and the influence of the church (30 responses) proved to be the next most important and rather surprising definer of English culture. Linked to history and the monarchy was the role of religion, the Protestant church in particular:

'The Church of England introduced by the Royal family is a religion followed by a vast number of people and plays a large role in British life.'

Some defined English culture as specifically 'Protestant' as opposed to 'Catholic' and indicated that England had once been Roman and Catholic. Overall, there was a clear perception that English culture was 'influenced by the church'. This concern about Protestant roots is particularly interesting when one compares how the students defined French culture and the emphasis on religion when talking about France.

Pubs (27 responses) were seen by a large group of respondents as peculiar to English culture, not just for the beer, but for the socializing. The occasional dissenting voice was heard though:

'The British enjoy discovering life over a drink and a meal in the same way that the French do.'

But globally, the differences between English culture and Latin culture was seen as a taste for beer rather than wine, and an emphasis on drinking for pleasure.

A smaller indicator of culture was **art and architecture** (18 responses) which came in for a number of fleeting references in connection with history and religion. A number of respondents referred to history and then to 'art', 'museums', 'Buckingham Palace and the Houses of Parliament in Westminster'. Others elaborated:

'The many large aristocratic homes in many of the counties are also a large part of culture.'

Sport attracted some comment (15 responses); the national obsession with cricket, rugby and football was noted as a cultural particularity of the English, though respondents tended to simply list different sports rather than develop a reasoning for its importance:

'Sport has always played a large part in our culture and history, such as fox-hunting and cricket for example.'

The **performing arts** (14 responses) ranked in a surprisingly low position and respondents evoked a list of items which reflected a cultural component:

'Theatre, film, music, art' or 'dance, film, theatre, cinema'.

'Young people, particularly students, enjoy listening to a whole range of music: pop, rock, rave, heavy metal etc, and going to venues to hear it.'

But no musicans were mentioned by name, either classical or contemporary.

Another surprise was the rather low rating of **multi-culturalism and immigration** (13 responses) as contributors to English culture, though in general the comments made tended to be a little more expansive:

'Now in Britain with immigrants coming from ex-colonies such as Pakistan, there is a mixture of cultures, different dress, religion and morals.'

Few respondents commented on **education** (12 responses) and it tended to be briefly listed as a formative aspect of culture: 'the way we are educated'. Remarks such as: 'Schools 'not continental individual'' seemed to reinforce the formality perceived in English schools associated with uniform.

The **weather** (7 responses) rated a mention, occasionally expanded to:

'English weather is always thought of as being wet and windy.'

A similarly restrained number of respondents commented on **literature or language** (7 responses) as important to culture. The few times either was touched upon occurred in a list and no-one wrote of authors or reading, or different regional variations of language.

Along with English politeness came the inevitable references to **hooliganism and violence** (7 responses):

'The English are known for being polite although the "lager lout" image is well known throughout Europe.'

Another small group reflected upon English **attitudes towards Europe** (6 responses) as colouring cultural identity, stressing British reticence on the EU.

Some felt that differences were significant:

'The English tend to look out for one another more, perhaps this has something to do with England being a separate country from Europe but still at one with its fellow countries in the EU.'

These remarks generally reflected an openness towards Europe and at the same time an awareness of the students' own English identity.

There was in addition to these specific points (and others which only attracted a few responses) an attempt on the part of several students to define what they understood by culture in a general sense. More seemed to perceive differences between English and other cultures than similarities and the idea of culture being bound up with an individual way of life was endorsed by a majority of respondents:

> 'Culture is a way of life in which particular countries, counties or groups of people are used to living by. People are expected to live with this culture and grow up within it. Each country has its own individual culture.'

2.2 French culture (58 respondents)

Most respondents wrote their answers to this second survey in French, but some replies were in English (and I have translated the French into English). It was significant that the scores for all components of French culture were consistently lower than those for English culture, indeed only food scored more than 50 per cent. Perhaps students were less familiar with French culture and resorted to comparisons with English culture to define what they understand by French culture.

Food and wine (33 responses) as expected, came at the top of what most people considered an essential element of French culture. Whilst recognizing a certain hedonistic pleasure that the French undoubtedly find in eating, respondents also pointed out differences in eating habits:

> 'They eat differently to us. The food is different, some consider it more healthy.'

Overall, the stereotype of bread and cheese and wine and frogs' legs seems to have prevailed in most observations. Students seem aware of gastronomy, but one does not have the impression that they have actually experienced it.

The second most striking feature of French culture was **multi-culturalism, immigration and racism** (27 responses):

> 'France is a multi-cultural country which reflects a wide spectrum of influences. People come from all parts of the world: mostly from America, Europe, Africa and Asia, but also from several other countries.'

Many commented on problems of racism inherent in mixed societies. Whether respondents thought multi-culturalism in France similar or different to England they wrote about it in greater detail than other matters. Perhaps they were influenced by their lectures, or perhaps racism and immigration were in the news at the time.

The third most important element of French culture was **history, tradition and patriotism** (19 responses).

> 'France has a historical past with ideas and laws stemming from the Revolution, and these still exist today.'

A variety of points of view relating to history and tradition were expressed, similar to those for English culture, but with references to specific historical events like the Revolution or the Second World War. It is probable that students were prompted by the coursework they had covered over the previous month relating to French history and the development of modern France starting from the Revolution. This gave them an accuracy of information but did not, of course, account for the fact that they chose to dwell upon history and tradition as an important element of culture.

Education (10 responses) was the next influence on culture. Time spent at school and school rhythms seemed an important difference:

> 'From what I have seen French people work hard, their education system is much different to ours.'

Overall comments on education stress the differences in the systems, but without entering into specific detail. It is also apparent that some students had spent a little time in French schools, no doubt on school exchanges.

The **family** (10 responses) brought out contrasting views on difference, or similarity:

> 'I believe that there is a difference in the family unit between the two countries. France puts a greater emphasis on families – children tend to go to university during the week and come home for the weekend. The French also eat together more as a family sitting round a table at dinner time.'

Generally we can see that family life is seen as being closer than in England, with an emphasis on the family sharing meals, but no-one linked this to the social preoccupation with food in French life whether in or out of the home.

The **countryside** (10 responses), reflected a surprising number of respondents, who seemed aware of rural roots and the role they play in French life:

> 'French culture has developed from an agricultural population which worked the land; and in certain regions this way of life still exists.'

Of equal importance to the countryside, was **fashion** or 'la mode' (10 responses); in general this was just listed and rarely commented upon. Indeed, no-one mentioned a single couturier – no Dior, no Chanel!

A smaller percentage of respondents saw **architecture** (8 responses) as culturally relevant, with one or two people actually mentioning monuments by name:

> 'Other differences can be found in architectural design and ideas as the French are more inclined to experiment and try different things, for example the Centre Pompidou.'

A similar number of respondents mentioned **language** (8 responses):

'In a way, people are more formal and less friendly towards people they do not know. They distinguish between 'tu' and 'vous' for example, but in English there is only one form of address – 'you'.'

But no-one developed any more ideas other than to indicate formal and intimate forms of address, and no-one associated literature with the notion of language.

Europe (8 responses) and the relationship of France to Europe produced a few comments, notably on geographic location, and how this central position is useful for trade:

'France is at the heart of Europe.'

A certain Euro-enthusiasm was also observed:

'They are very European.'

Next on the list of cultural values was the mention of **class and hierarchy** (7 responses), which again was touched upon in most instances rather than developed:

'French culture is made up of all the different social classes.'

Definitions of what these respondents perceived as French culture in general were interesting:

'There are many different French cultures because of the immigrants who live there.'

A minority opinion felt that there were more cultural similarities than differences:

'French culture is more or less the same as English culture; traditional values are very important.'

But these voices were drowned out by those who saw difference; from those for whom difference seemed visceral, to those who were better able to identify what they felt was distinctive:

'English and French culture is very different. The law and traditions are different.'

French culture was also defined as a way of life, and as people:

'French culture is the people who live in France, their way of life.'

I was surprised by these results and interested in the way in which students interpreted culture as an essentially sociological and anthropological entity –

the way people live (Hofstede 1980). When they spoke of English culture this was clearly perceived as a way of life, with food, tradition and monarchy, and family life scoring the highest number of references. It was also intriguing to discover that nearly 50 per cent of respondents placed an emphasis on religion, yet surprisingly few perceived culture to be multi-cultural, and certainly 'high culture' was totally absent. No one mentioned Shakespeare by name, nor a single writer or artist. I expected a mention of specific pop groups, but naming names did not occur to anyone.

This view of culture was reflected in the descriptions of French culture, where culture was linked to society and behaviour in the broadest sense. The elements of English culture which were perceived as the most important were the same for French culture: food, history and tradition. French culture was essentially apprehended as similar to, or different from, a native culture. This is understandable given the age and experience of the respondents. For this group, however, the term has nothing whatever to do with intellectual life or the arts; no writers, no artists, not even a mention of a modern French pop group. Thus my own question as to whether students might have a different notion of French culture as 'high culture' received a clear answer.

If the title of the task set had been to write about France, or French society I do not think the answers would have been any different. The students in question are a lively group, who have decided to study language in a business context. These are young people who do not read books in English or in French, though many are well travelled. Their activities are social and sporty and they have deliberately chosen to study a language in a very practical way. This would, in part, explain their pragmatic interpretation of culture.

I discussed my findings with a group of French colleagues in Paris. They were dumbfounded and assured me that my students had no notion of what culture means. They acknowledged, however, that what culture might mean to them is not necessarily what it might mean to young people of 20, even in France! It became clear to me that it would be a very interesting exercise to find a group of undergraduates in a French University, also following a Business Studies course, and ask them the same question.

3 English and French culture as perceived by French students

I contacted Dr Andrew Rossiter of the Université de Franche Comté in Besançon, and he was kind enough to cooperate with the second phase of the project. He supplied the observations on English and French culture from a group of second year students studying on a Languages and Business degree programme in Besançon. All the students have visited the UK in the past so they had some experience upon which to draw.

The methodology was the same. Respondents had not been forewarned of the assignment so their observations are all spontaneous and uncontaminated by any notions from members of staff. When responding to English culture some students simply made a list of what came to mind, some wrote short paragraphs and others launched into a short essay. A small minority chose to reply in English. When writing about their own culture the vast majority wrote in paragraphs, some at length, and hardly any made use of lists.

The numbers taking part were smaller than for the British students' survey but nevertheless numerous enough (26) to give an interesting idea of what French students today understand by English and French culture.

3.1 French culture (26 respondents)

Unsurprisingly '**gastronomy**' (19 responses) was perceived as the most important element of French culture. I was amused to note that when these same students wrote about English culture they referred to food more often as '*food*' rather than the more glamorous '*gastronomy*!' Chauvinism lives!:

> 'To begin with, French culture can include "cuisine". That is to say, France has a number of local products which are envied by the rest of the world such as French wines, champagne and many other dishes which are only produced here and which are highly regarded all over the world.'

Most comments encompassed a certain hedonism, a pride in the quality of French food and wine, an awareness of the international reputation of French gastronomy and an ability to name chefs who are internationally famous. There was one observation, however, which warned of the dangers of stereotyping and pleaded for culture to be more than just wine and cheese:

> 'When you talk to English people about France, the first thing they say to you is "Oh France! – wine, cheese and bread." French culture is much more than just food.'

History and monuments (18 responses) rated the second highest number of references:

> 'French culture is the monuments like the Eiffel Tower, The Palace of Versailles and the castles on the Loire. These are things that every French person has a duty to know about. And let's not forget the Pyramid at the Louvre museum in Paris.'

For some students, history is a necessary element of culture in that culture evolves with the passage of time – we learn about culture from the past. Other respondents reveal an insight into the importance of history on culture and perceive that culture is marked by foreign influences, historical invasions; it is this diversity which contributes towards the richness of French culture. For all these students the wealth of French culture and the country's historical past is also a source of great pride which they do not hesitate to articulate.

The Arts (music, painting, cinema, sculpture, etc.) (13 responses) have been grouped together as this is what the respondents have done, and it became very difficult to disentangle the separate elements. Students were enthusiastic about the arts and several began by naming and identifying artists who have impressed them:

'Art is an important part of our country's culture. Rodin gives us a very special insight into sculpture; (a few years ago most of his work was exhibited on the Champs-Elysées.) But there is also poetry, music, cinema.'

The students reveal a sense of pride in the richness and reputation of French art. It is not only painting which inspires them: one student analyses the difference between French and English/American popular music and finds that French pop songs generally concentrate on the text whereas English or American songs seem to concentrate more on musical composition. Overall these students communicate a sense of confidence in high culture. They seem very proud of their own heritage and are excited by the developments in popular music and the cinema.

Language and literature (13 responses) stood *ex aequo* with the arts as a fundamental element of culture, reinforcing the overall impression that, for these students, culture is very much high culture. The wealth of French literature was restated by several students:

'Our literature is very rich and varied stretching from Ronsard to Sartre. Each literary genius has his 'father', his illustrious forbears. We have a very rich and poetic language (with multiple origins, Greek/Latin etc.)'

Geography and the regions (8 responses) was for some students the next most important element of culture:

'Because of its varied geography, France has a cultural heritage which is very diverse. You do not have the same customs in mountain regions as you do in coastal regions and so the culture is not the same.'

Where one lives, the language one speaks, the climate . . . all these will have an impact on one's regional culture. As the country is large, the diversity is great.

Notions of **cultural diversity and multi-culturalism** (7 responses) resonated with a smaller number of respondents. There were interesting variations of opinion as to the impact of multi-culturalism and a certain pride is expressed in the notion of 'a country of sanctuary'; however, an awareness of the difficulties this involves is also evident:

'French culture would like to reflect qualities of equality and solidarity between men, but certain political events daily cast a shadow on this rosy social vision of things. As a cosmopolitan country, France tries to absorb these differences, to appreciate everyone's cultural and technical contributions, (. . .) but I think that at the heart of our country there is much to be done to achieve an openness of mind, a more honest opening of frontiers, an openness towards "others".'

Overall, what is interesting about the students' comments is their political awareness, the expressions of pride in their country, and the idealism in some that acceptance and openness will enrich culture; yet they also reveal an underlying fear that tolerance of others is not quite so easy to achieve.

These, then, were the main elements of French culture which I was able to analyse as separate entities; but the students also made **general comments about French culture** which were mature and articulate.

For some, the essence of culture lies in difference from another culture, or the specificity of one's own culture. For others French culture is rich because of its ability to adapt:

'French culture is one of the richest and most complete cultures in the world. It is supple and adaptable and evolves through time and through history. It is a culture which is proud of its roots and defends these, whilst at the same time enriching itself with new elements. French culture is especially rich because it is open to everything that other cultures can bring to it, whilst simultaneously keeping its identity, its cultural roots.'

Other students were less effusive and more pragmatic and for some, knowledge was an inherent part of culture. The students underlined the importance of learning about general culture in a cross-cultural context. You will never understand a country unless you make an effort to learn something of its culture. All in all a very mature exhortation which another voice carried further:

'French culture is available to all. No one today can find a pretext for not being cultured – there are many opportunities for acquiring knowledge in France: libraries and universities make all sorts of areas more accessible to everyone, (e.g. theatre and opera) which in the past were reserved for an upper class.'

Finally, several students made references to general culture and French culture as a frame of mind, a way of life.

3.2 English culture (23 respondents)

Most students when they wrote about English culture did so in French. It was noticeable that students compiled more lists when speaking of English culture than they did when describing their own; obviously they were less familiar with the subject.

The monarchy and tradition (18 responses) came top of the list of elements that constitute English culture. For many students this seems quaint:

'English culture seems a little "old fashioned" as they still have a monarchy. So the country has an image of not evolving very much, though the monarchy is no longer relevant to the British political system. At the same time, because of this, the country has an image of honesty, and respect for traditions which many others have lost.'

The unsurprising observations about monarchy and traditions were closely followed by **language and literature** (17 responses) which scored highly as significant factors in English culture. There were a multitude of straight-forward references to language and/or literature, and one student felt strongly about the dominance of the English language:

'The hedgemonyhedgemonyhedgemony of the English language'.

One wishes he had expanded on this. Occasionally more developed observations were presented:

'Language is one of the main elements of English culture. It allows you to discover how the British think and reason. Knowledge of the origins of English and the history of the country is also part of culture.'

Other students speak specifically of writers and of their historical role in creating culture:

'Shakespeare is also one of the biggest representatives of English culture; I'm totally convinced that everybody knows the famous "to be or not to be" in Hamlet – Even if you are not very keen on literature, I'm sure you know that Shakespeare was an English writer.'

Shakespeare, indeed, was mentioned five times, and one student added to the list:

'Agatha Christie, Oscar Wilde.'

The respondents revealed a general knowledge of English literature through school books and syllabi no doubt; at the same time they also were sure that the study of language and literature is fundamental to culture. There is no other reason to explain why, for so many students, '*English language*' or '*English literature*' was first on their list.

History and monuments (15 responses) were mentioned both in a literary context and in association with traditions; more often the terms were simply listed as an important element of culture, a necessary ingredient which will enable a student to apprehend English culture. Brief comments were sometimes amplified by references, albeit in a rather stereotypical way, to monuments which the students have visited:

'When I think of English culture I immediately think of London, monuments such as Big Beng (*sic!*) with the Parliament.'

Food (14 responses) was the next most important ingredient of culture for these students. Many recognized an element of stereotyping, others did not:

'English culture means the food that I find horrible (except when you go to Indian restaurants).'

'Bad food', and 'English breakfast and tea time.'

Generally then the clichés about tea, fish and chips and bad food dominate, though one or two people did not seem to mind the puddings! These brief and not too revealing remarks about food were followed by more interesting observations on the **arts, (music, theatre, cinema, art)** (13 responses). There seemed to be a very positive view of popular English music as a power house of modernity:

> 'Today, English culture is made of music – it was the country of famous groups such as the Beatles, and nowadays Oasis, for instance.'

> 'The Beatles, Bonno (U2), The Spice Girls; Ken Loach 'Raining Stones', 'Ladybird, Ladybird'.'

Overall, these students seem knowledgeable about contemporary British cinema and music and one senses an enthusiasm for the arts in general.

Geography (12 responses) was the next most important element of English culture. References were on the whole very brief and referred to the geographical position of the country. Only two students commented on the island status of the UK:

> 'England represents an Island for us. You have to take a boat to get there. The system is quite different. You drive on the left, you count in miles and not a single measurement is the same as in France.'

One or two other respondents mentioned the capital and the misapprehension made by many travellers that London is England.

The world of **politics and social affairs** (12 responses) gave rise to comment, though most of it was brief:

> 'The Trade Unions – their powers; the Conservative Party (Thatcher, Major), the Labour Party (Blair)'.

Comments of this kind reflect the fact that these students are studying language on a Business Studies degree course. This would also account for the more stimulating observations on the state of the British **economy and its liberal roots** (10 responses) and its unexpected rating as an element of culture. Some offered elaborate explanations of culture and economics:

> 'In economics, English culture is very much influenced by the USA and the UK has a liberal tradition. The UK is the City, the hectic business world of bowler hatted gentlemen (. . .) as well as unemployment and industrial crises which are often a consequence of this ruthless liberalism.'

Fashion and the way people dress (7 responses) was noted; some were aware of the creativity of British fashion and a perceptive respondent noted the tolerance of the English with regard to dress and non-conformity:

'English culture may be something fun because you can see so many different clothes, there is no fashion, people are extravagant but the way they look seems to be respected, which is not the case in France.'

This tolerance of dress was complemented by students' perceptions that English culture is an **open, polite and tolerant** one (7 responses). From simple declarations like:

'Freedom', 'Politeness, good manners.'

To more developed opinions such as:

'The English are open and perhaps more tolerant (of other cultures, for example).'

Humour (6 responses) was seen by a number of students as a particuliarity of English culture but alas, no attempt was made to elaborate upon what respondents really meant:

'English humour is different from French humour.'

Frustratingly, this student did not explain the difference!

General statements about English culture were discerning. Many students perceived the acquisition of knowledge as the essence of culture:

'English culture is a knowledge of everything one knows or can learn about the country.'

Some students eloquently express a concept of all culture as an ongoing quest for knowledge in every area of life. They feel that this is a common thread between English and French culture; other students however attempted to define English culture as specifically all those elements of life which are true to one country and different from another:

'English culture is the specific way the English think and act. Each country has a different view of things and English culture is the English way of viewing the world; it is the way local people think, having and understanding the same sense of humour.'

Most students feel that it is difference which distinguishes one culture from another. They express the view that culture derives from a sense of history which has an impact upon the present:

'In my opinion the English culture, like the French, is proud and respectful of its past and of its actual life: it is a real culture – not like the American one which is too recent to be considered as a culture – because it has a past and because it is built on solid basis with the rules established for a long time.'

For a number of students culture is energetic and creative and sometimes ruthless:

'English culture' is a paradox as far as I am concerned: on the one hand it evokes a very vibrant world full of new ideas and on the other, it is a symbol of a liberal world which does not care for the weak.'

I was impressed by the maturity and the confidence of these responses. The graphic charts (see Appendix to this Chapter) on both English and French culture make it apparent that for the French students culture is predominantly high culture, that is to say culture as intellectual, artistic and social pursuits; they rated history, the Arts, language and literature as the most important elements. When defining culture in general these students were able to articulate very confidently exactly what they felt culture was, where it came from and how one went about acquiring it; for many respondents the citizen has an obligation to cultivate him/herself and nowadays, there are no excuses for not doing so as education, libraries and galleries are available to all. This no doubt reflects very much the influence of the French education system, in which, for example, philosophy is taught as a staple of the country's Baccalauréat, the school leaving certificate at the end of secondary education.

When speaking of French culture there was an overwhelming sense of pride in belonging to a nation which has such a rich culture, with deep historical roots and where the education system encourages one to learn about philosophers, writers and artists. They were clear in their apprehension of culture as something that is inherited from the past which needs to be protected; indeed some were fierce in their defence of French language, music and cinema against English and American attack. At the same time culture is something that evolves into the future. The categories of culture were in a sense more homogenous in that the majority of respondents viewed their own culture as high culture and there was very little deviation from this.

Not all opinions were uncritical; one student made it clear that French culture was perhaps only propaganda, that everyone was fed the same diet but the reality was a society overtaken by consumerism. There were also voices raised against racism and social inequality, and simultaneously a reiterated pride in France as the '*country of sanctuary*'; I also noted a political consciousness in references to French social solidarity and an awareness that some students recognized their culture as being communitarian rather than individualistic (Trompenaars and Hampden-Turner 1998).

When speaking of English culture, the French students seemed knowledgeable. They were able to mention history and to define its role in the evolution of culture; they spoke of Shakespeare and other authors, as well as commenting on the free market system, the monarchy, cinema and popular music; they expressed admiration for the creative force of British pop music and fashion, as well as mixed reactions to liberalism of the market economy and British euro-scepticism. It was disappointing that some ideas were not more fully explored, for example multi-culturalism. But the whole exercise was intended to encourage fast and spontaneous thinking, and of course was limited in time. It seems clear that these students perceived English culture essentially as high culture, perhaps because it is an acquired culture. It is something that they have learnt as they have been studying the language and in France, English tends to be studied in a traditional way, with an emphasis on language and literature, history, geography and institutions.

My colleagues last summer were therefore right in thinking that the French have very coherent ideas about culture, and that for them it falls more within the realm of intellectual pursuits and knowledge. Our British students perceived culture as the way people live and there was no reference at all to high culture. We therefore have a challenge to meet in preparing our students for their year abroad, and there are useful messages here for all language teachers. A great deal can be done to equip our students effectively, as it is obviously not enough to devote two or three sessions on the problems of student life and bureaucracy just before they leave. Whilst it is true that most people only learn from their own experiences, mostly from their own mistakes, we can attempt to bridge the cultural gap which our students will most certainly encounter. Through cultural awareness we can stimulate motivation for language learning; for example, through the use of art, contemporary literature and film in particular, as well as the linguistic grounding we offer, we can extend an exciting foretaste of France and we can strive to address the specific view of culture which the French embrace and which is quite different in England. For students unable to spend a year away, we can offer activities which will, to a small extent, replicate some of the learning which would go on in France.

Finally, I would conclude that the difference in perception between British and French students lies in the way language is taught in each country. For the past 25 years or so, Britain has been promoting language learning in school as acquiring skills which will enable learners to navigate the workplace and gain better employment. Alas, this very narrow and reductive view tends to crush both curiosity and motivation in students (Phipps and Gonzalez 2004). In France, language is taught relying on cultural awareness of the literature, art, geography and history of a country, and this broadens the learner's experience and enriches his/her knowledge. Language development is tremendously enhanced simply by reading in the target language yet many of our British students no longer read books. Encouraging them to read articles, newspapers and books can awaken their curiosity and they learn not just the words under their noses but ideas, points of view, notions which can challenge, stimulate and motivate them to expand their horizons.

References

Agar, M. H. (1996), *The Professional Stranger*, (2nd edn). San Diego: Academic Press Inc.

Besemeres, M. (2002), *Translating One's Self*. Berlin: Peter Lang.

Cronin, M. (2000), *Across the Lines*. Cork: Cork University Press.

Hofstede, G. (1980), *Culture's Consequences*. London: Sage.

Phipps, A. and Gonzalez, M. (2004), *Modern Languages: Learning and Teaching in an Intercultural Field*. London: Sage.

Toland, J. (1977), *Adolf Hitler*. New York: Ballantine Books.
Trompenaars, F. and Hampdon-Turner, C. (1998), *Riding the Waves of Culture*, (2nd edn). London: Nicholas Brealey Publishing.

Appendix

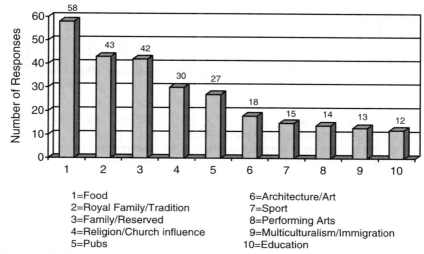

1=Food
2=Royal Family/Tradition
3=Family/Reserved
4=Religion/Church influence
5=Pubs

6=Architecture/Art
7=Sport
8=Performing Arts
9=Multiculturalism/Immigration
10=Education

Figure 15.1 English culture (1) LMU students

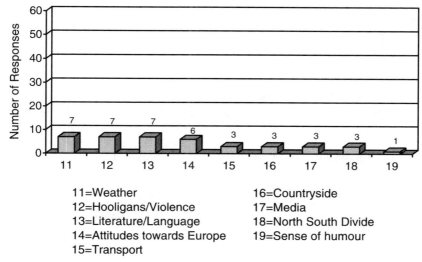

11=Weather
12=Hooligans/Violence
13=Literature/Language
14=Attitudes towards Europe
15=Transport

16=Countryside
17=Media
18=North South Divide
19=Sense of humour

Figure 15.2 English culture (2) LMU students

I am grateful to my colleague Isabel von Knorring, an industrial psychologist, in Tubingen for devising these charts.

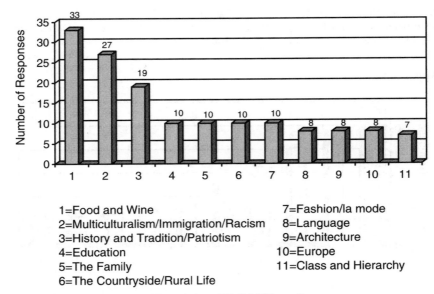

1=Food and Wine
2=Multiculturalism/Immigration/Racism
3=History and Tradition/Patriotism
4=Education
5=The Family
6=The Countryside/Rural Life

7=Fashion/la mode
8=Language
9=Architecture
10=Europe
11=Class and Hierarchy

Figure 15.3 La culture française (1) LMU students

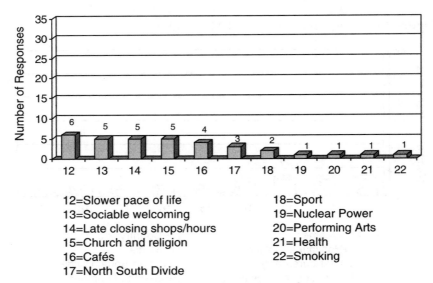

12=Slower pace of life
13=Sociable welcoming
14=Late closing shops/hours
15=Church and religion
16=Cafés
17=North South Divide

18=Sport
19=Nuclear Power
20=Performing Arts
21=Health
22=Smoking

Figure 15.4 La culture française (2) LMU students

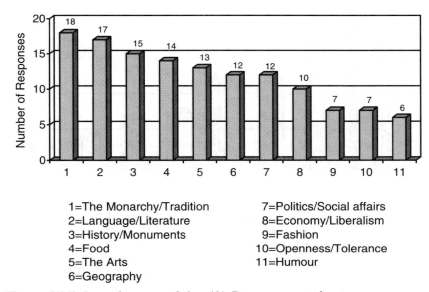

1=The Monarchy/Tradition   7=Politics/Social affairs
2=Language/Literature   8=Economy/Liberalism
3=History/Monuments   9=Fashion
4=Food   10=Openness/Tolerance
5=The Arts   11=Humour
6=Geography

Figure 15.5 La culture anglaise (1) Besançon students

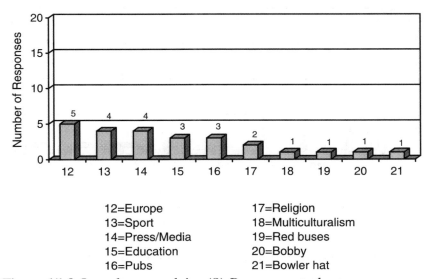

12=Europe   17=Religion
13=Sport   18=Multiculturalism
14=Press/Media   19=Red buses
15=Education   20=Bobby
16=Pubs   21=Bowler hat

Figure 15.6 La culture anglaise (2) Besançon students

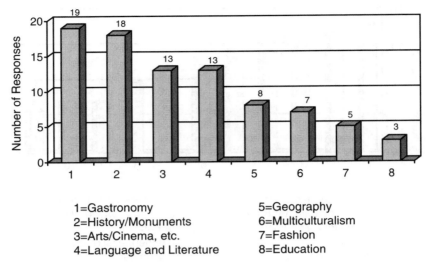

Figure 15.7 La culture française (1) Besançon students

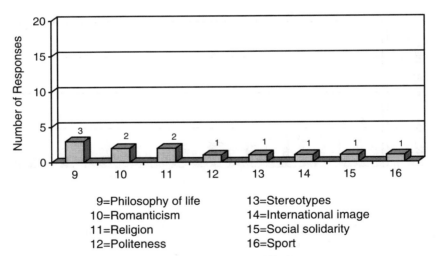

Figure 15.8 La culture française (2) Besançon students

16   A blind learner in EFL mainstream courses: A case study at the Lebanese American University

Nola Bacha

1 Introduction

Learners in academic EFL/ESL programmes need to acquire proficiency in listening, speaking, reading and writing skills in order to be able to communicate in the language for academic and/or professional purposes. In an academic university context, the focus of the present study, the learners of English as L2, need to acquire these skills successfully in order to cope with the studies in their chosen discipline (Jordan 1997; Kasper 2000; Bacha 2003). For a sighted person, this is all well and good; however, for the blind, coping with acquiring these skills in the regular classroom may be problematic as attention to their needs is often not given. The blind need special attention in having material read or taped for them and having access to special technology for written work. They also need more time for assignments and tests done in class under exam conditions. Conferencing time with their tutors is also very important for further clarification of material and work on assignments. Given these hurdles, many institutions are often not prepared to meet the problems and challenges, especially at the university level.

However, most educators are in agreement that blind students, despite their handicap and fears, should have the same educational opportunities as others (McLinden 1990; Blackburne 1994; Monahan *et al* 1996; Sack and Silberman 1998). Over the past century and a half, special educational services and schools around the world have been set up for the blind and have contributed to certain relative successes in developing the literacy levels of the blind, as well as giving them an education in both the arts and sciences (e.g. Lowenfeld *et al* 1969; Fletcher 1973). Alongside this work, educators have been recently claiming that serious consideration should be given to include blind students in regular mainstream classrooms where it is believed that they can learn alongside regular students if teachers are supported (Jobe, *et al* 1996; Thomas-Ozel 1998; Hayasaki and Moore 2002; Wall 2002).

At the university level, while some blind students have been included in regular classrooms, the work has been mainly in scientific subjects (Windelborn 1999; Bonicamp 2000). The teaching of English has been a challenge; but Seng (2005: 1) says, 'Of all the subjects teaching English to the blind is the easiest'. Having said that though, few university EFL/ESL programmes take on the challenge, though they have often been encouraged to (see Price 1993; Thomas-Ozel 1998, 2000, 2005; Kashdan *et al* 2005). Seng (2005: 2) says, 'Blind students may be visually impaired but their other senses are intact, so teachers of the blind should utilize the other senses'. Although visualization is an important facilitator of comprehension and learning, visually impaired learners are able to make use of visualization through the verbal descriptions of others and the use of tactile materials through objects, raised pictures and mounted material (Sacks and Silberman 1998; Thomas-Ozel 1998, 2000).

As an example of how the blind attempt to use their other senses as well as visualize their ideas, Jihad (a blind student at the Lebanese American University) drew two faces, one blind and the other normal (see below), with the help of the computer, as a visual aid for his oral report assignment in the Fundamentals of Oral Communication class (English 201). Jihad drew the blind face in comparison to the normal one with enlarged ears, nose, and hands in order to indicate to the class to whom he was delivering a speech on how the blind best learn that blind students depend a lot on hearing, smell and touch in their learning to make up for lack of sight. He also explained to the class that the blind can visualize things if they described for them and felt by themselves.

Nikolic (1987) comments that 'blind and visually impaired children can be taught to speak, read, and write foreign languages if the techniques and materials are adapted to capitalize on their strengths, including excellent memory and good hearing'. He goes on to say that although 'blindness . . . affects perception, [it] does not necessarily obstruct linguistic and verbal development' (p. 63). He also says:

> There is no specific method for teaching foreign languages to blind and visually impaired persons Rather, teachers should choose those characteristics of existing methods they think will work best with a student and that will help them engage in the learning process. . . . Furthermore, teachers must respect . . . (p. 65).

Eyes
Ears
Nose
Hands

'Normal' person   'Blind' person

Figure 16.1 Illustrations drawn by Jihad of 'normal' and 'blind' persons showing how blind people's sense of hearing, smell and touch increase as they rely on them more to communicate.

I believe that such an attempt was made with Jihad Kreem, the subject of the present study.

2 Jihad's personal background

Jihad Kreem, then a 25-year-old Lebanese man, the eldest of four children, told his story during an interview with the *Daily Star*, a newspaper in English printed and distributed in Lebanon (Ibrahim 1999). He told the reporter that at the age of about 11 he began to feel pain in his eyes and that the doctors diagnosed detachment of the retinas, after which he became completely blind. This did not stop Jihad from continuing his schooling. He attended the Lebanese School for the Blind in Baabda, Lebanon but moved later to Beirut, where he completed his secondary classes at the Achrafieh School for the Blind. He did well in school and after attending a computer-training session for the blind, he decided to continue his university education in computer science. He believes strongly in people following their dreams against all odds and said to the reporter, 'I want to encourage not only the blind, but every person with any form of disability to follow their dreams. All they really need is to believe in themselves'. He strongly believes that, 'It isn't we who have to change – it's society which has to change its attitude toward disabled people. I realize we're only a minority, but minorities also have rights'. Although there are increasing attempts to help the blind in Lebanon, the attitude towards the blind joining regular classes and including them in the workplace is in general not a positive one (Akiki *et al* 1999). Nevertheless, Jihad is one of the few disabled people in Lebanon who is now realizing his dream. With his parents' and teachers' support and above all his determination, Jihad has now graduated with a Bachelor Degree in Computer Science.

3 The beginning of Jihad's university life

On 6 October 1997 at 8:00 am, a young man walked into my office carrying a small machine (which I later found out to be a visio-braille computer) and a piece of paper that I later read to be a paragraph he had written about Lebanon a few days before in one of the remedial English courses at the university (see Appendix). He stood facing me, following my voice, and asked if I were the English teacher he had been assigned to. I had been informed that a student was being referred to me who needed attention, but it was only when I read the paragraph and looked up to tell him that it needed a rewrite for grammatical errors that I realized he was blind. After that, it was two years of hard but interesting work with Jihad.

Jihad is the first blind person to study at the Lebanese American University, Byblos Campus and the first blind person to major in computer science in Lebanon. Universities in Lebanon are normally not properly equipped to take on blind students, but Jihad was a very persistent person who believed in a dream that one day he would graduate from university and work in the community helping others. In fact, in his interview with the *Daily Star* Newspaper he recounted the work he was engaged in as the public-relations director for a Lebanese support group for the blind (Ibrahim 1999). There is very little follow up work done on the blind in Lebanon. However, according to Jihad, blind students who graduate from university, 70 to date, have extremely limited working conditions, the majority being unemployed. A few work in school or university libraries, as translators, while a few others work in banks, with none in any key positions (Kreem 1998).

4 Literature review

Thomas-Ozel (1998, 2000, 2005) who has worked with blind students in Turkey states (2005: 1):

> This area of ELT and Disability seems to be little covered in the literature in two respects. Firstly much evidence in education relates to primary and secondary levels, not post-compulsory education. Secondly, in the words of a British Council officer in Brazil, 'the ELT community still shows little interest in special education.'

She gives an account of the difficulties and successes faced by integrating a blind student in the Department of English at the Middle East Technical University (METU) in Ankara, Turkey with the aim that this small step '. . . will enable individuals in other institutions – without financial resources or managerial backing – to begin changes that will raise hope, and thus motivation' (Thomas-Ozel 2005: 1).

Kashdan *et al* (2005) describe the problems and possibilities of teaching English to blind or visually impaired immigrants and refugees in mainstream English as a Second Language programmes which indicate that this area needs more support from both institutions of higher learning and the community at large. They report on a joint venture between an immigrant and refugee English program and the St. James ESL Program in Seattle in which instruction and testing in EFL to the blind is adapted in '. . . [providing] three dimensional objects to exemplify graphics, [changing] some questions to eliminate visually oriented content, [rephrasing] items to make them relevant and appropriate, increase time allowances for completion and [pro-viding] accessible formats' (p. 17). The authors also draw on some research by Gardner (1993, 1994, 2001 cited in Kashdan *et al* 2005) who defined human intelligences (linguistic, logical-mathematical, spatial, musical, bodily-kinesthetic, interpersonal, intrapersonal, naturalist) that teachers should be aware of which could facilitate effective learning. These could be especially important for the blind in developing their functional literacy skills.

There are other universities that have begun to accept blind students on EFL courses. For example, the Xinhua News Agency (2002) reports that the Shanghai Teachers' University '[was] ready; to receive China's first blind college students'. The Deputy President of the university said that '. . .blind students were welcome to apply for the foreign languages department' and that 'with modern computer software that translated between Braille and English and blind people's good memories, foreign languages should be an ideal choice for them'.

Teaching blind students on mainstream EFL courses has been helped by technological developments. In addition to the Braille system, computers that convert Braille to print, websites, listening comprehension cassettes, electronic libraries and tactile materials are helpful aides for the blind (Bruton *et al* 1997; Wilder 1999; Hartz 2000; Medina 2002). It has also been helped by EFL methodologies that have been adapted for the blind (Nikolic 1987; Sacks and Silberman 1998; Thomas-Ozel 1998, 2000, 2005; Kashdan, *et al* 2005). These have been summarized by Nikolic (1987), who outlines methodologies that the research has investigated for teaching blind students Russian, German, French and English. Although this research focuses on pre-university, the methods are easily applicable to language study at tertiary levels and 'Thus it may be concluded that there are universal pedagogical and didactic principles and methodological criteria that should be respected in teaching foreign languages to blind and visually impaired students' (Nikolic 1987: 63). Perhaps one of the most important factors is motivation. Nikolic (1987) mentions that '. . . it is essential to know whether a language is taught as a compulsory school subject and whether there is an examination at the end of the course, which may motivate the students to learn better' (p. 63). Nikolic (1987) in surveying the literature in the field summarizes the elements that may contribute to the success of the blind in learning a foreign language. These appear below with some comments from myself and some from Nikolic:

(1) **The need for a monolingual environment:** This is not necessarily true. Blind people in Lebanon, just like sighted people, learn two foreign languages (French and English) in addition to their native language Arabic in elementary classes and often code switch in both social and academic settings.

(2) **Blind learners are adept at learning foreign languages:** Research indicates that the blind are highly motivated and enthusiastic, have excellent memories, deep concentration and good hearing, and this helps them in the L2 learning situation (Sacks and Silberman 1998; Thomas-Ozel 1998, 2005). In fact, Jihad showed all these qualities and could actually identify people through smell and sound that he had been introduced to previously. In class, he exhibited high mental concentration and even when films were shown, could remember some of the dialogues word for word.

(3) **Blindness does not hinder the learning of a foreign language:** Jespersen (1961 in Nikolic, 1987) stated that '. . . a language is learned by the sense of hearing, not by the sense of seeing'. Furthermore, some research concludes that blind students lack of success '. . . is probably the result of inadequate support from and encouragement by teachers. Thus, it may be said that although blindness and visual impairment affect perception,

they do not necessarily obstruct linguistic and verbal development' (Claudine 1976 in Nikolic 1987: 63). In Jihad's case, he was himself highly motivated and the staff at the university were supportive and tried their best to accommodate his needs.

(4) **Tactile stimuli are needed in the learning process:** It is obvious that the more all the senses are involved the better the learning environment and thus performance (Thomas-Ozel 1998; Kashdan *et al* 2005; Seng 2005). In Jihad's case, he would often use his sense of touch. But being at the university level where the emphasis was on textual elements rather than on objects, Jihad had to rely on his visio-braille computer to read and write, his concentration to follow oral instructions in class and his memory when listening to class lectures and taking notes.

(5) **Attention is needed to intonation, stress and rhythm:** This attention is noted by many language teachers, especially when responding to instructions and lectures. Blind people are more sensitive to these points in order to understand the attitude and pragmatic meanings of words said since they cannot see the facial gestures of the speakers to help them understand the underlying intended meanings. What Borisy (1931 in Nikolic 1987) said is still relevant to the blind learning a foreign language:

> . . . and yet I believe that, as a class, we are far better able to learn and appreciate languages than the majority of the seeing people. We are compelled to depend upon our ears as a means of instruction, whether practical or cultural. This is one of the strongest reasons advanced for our study of music, and rightly so, for it is through the ears that music enters the mind and calms or disturbs the soul. So, language study is essentially an ear science, just as music is. Men spoke long before they wrote, and they spoke to be heard (p. 63).

Certainly Jihad's sense of hearing was extremely heightened. He could quickly identify who was talking in class, what mood the teacher was in, and, of course, follow any instructions and the lecture better or just as good as any of the other students in the class, often explaining or clarifying to those around him.

Nikolic (1987) also summarized a few teaching/learning methods that may help in the learning process for blind students. Two methods that have proved successful, especially in the beginning stages of language learning, are the oral communicative method and the audio-visual and structural-global method (AVSG). Since the blind have heightened hearing skills, listening comprehension exercises where the student listens to something read or taped and then answers questions is useful because the student does not need to read or write. Using the second method (AVSG) after the oral method involves the student in responding in writing either through someone writing down what is said by the blind student or by using a computer of some sort. These two methods have been quite successful with blind students as they become involved in the learning process using all their senses (Thomas-Ozel 2005; Seng 2005).

Basically, the oral communicative method involves oral, audio and tactile instructional material. The students are exposed to listening comprehension exercises in which dialogues, role-playing, lectures and dramatization are used to develop aural/oral skills. For example, if a novel is assigned, one exercise is to summarize the main ideas of a chapter or two. The chapter(s) are read by another student and the blind learner then verbally summarizes the ideas. If a play is assigned, another student reads the lines and then the blind learner takes on a role and improvises the part if not everything is remembered. In developing note-taking skills, the blind student could use the visio-braille machine or computer to type the main ideas of a lecture.

The second method, the AVSG focuses on the learner's verbal involvement. Although the visual is a problem, learners rely on their memories and on aural and verbal skills in learning the language. What is different in this method is that more stress is placed on rhythm and intonation and Guberina (1972 in Nikolic 1987) used tactile materials such as raised pictures and real life objects, which proved a positive addition before students moved onto the textual approach involving reading and writing.

In the course of using the above two methods with the blind, suggestions have been made (Nikolic, 1987; Sacks and Silberman 1998; Kashdan *et al* 2005; Thomas-Cozel 2005) and are summarized below:

(1) **Instructional materials:** Basically, the materials that are most conducive to blind learners are audio material: cassettes, records and tapes. However, live voices are more effective as there is a personal and social contact with the students that supports and motivates the blind learner. Although blind students cannot make use of films in visual terms, through their heightened hearing skills, they can follow the dialogue and make use of it in any exercises given. Very importantly, they should not be made to feel 'inferior' to the other students, and, in fact, Jihad repeated the dialogues for some students who may have forgotten them in order to do the exercises based on the verbal message of the film. Of course, there are Braille books with raised pictures and diagrams and print that have been in use for many years. However, recently, a new technological breakthrough, the visio-braille device which can be attached to a computer, has allowed the blind person to feed information into the computer and to read and navigate the web. Jihad had one of these bought by his parents for $10,000 with which he used to take lecture notes, type his assignments, research papers and exams and read anything the teacher might have scanned for him from the class text books and readings. That is, he would type his assignments in Braille, but they would be converted into English script by the machine and vice versa. The machine is the size of a book, and so it was convenient for him to work on it as one would with a laptop.

(2) **Group work:** Engaging blind students in group work has proven to be beneficial for both them and the other students. Although in Lebanon group work in the foreign language classroom is still looked upon with caution by both teachers and students alike, activities that are geared to

helping those who are not fast learners and which capitalize on the stronger students have helped to create an atmosphere of team spirit and cooperation. Blind students can contribute with their speaking and listening skills and be helped with their writing and reading skills.

(3) **Teaching reading and writing:** Perhaps for the blind learner, these are the most difficult skills. The Braille system has helped many blind students to read and learn a language. However, it poses difficulties in its translation to the foreign language script. In English, it was noted that Jihad's spelling, punctuation, capitalization and spacing were problematic. In an interview with him (Kreem 1998), he explained that although he still visualized some of the English letters that he remembered before he became blind, he visualizes the Braille images of dots and thus when he types a word into his machine it is the Braille that he is typing, which does not always have the same one to one correspondence in spelling, punctuation, capitalization and spacing as the English script (see Jihad's writings in Appendix). However, since the mechanical aspect (spelling, punctuation, etc.) is given a lower evaluation grade than content and ideas to assess writing in the EFL programme at the Lebanese American University, this was not considered so problematic as long as the ideas were clear enough to be communicated. The difficulty that blind students had in translating from Braille to the alphabet was taken into consideration. What teachers should note, nevertheless, is that blind students do need more time to read whether it is Braille or material on the mini visio-braille device and more time to write their assignments (Kashdan *et al* 2005; Thomas-Ozel 2005).

5 The study

Jihad followed the regular course syllabi set out for all students; no special considerations were made in decreasing the work load. The EFL programme at the Lebanese American University consists of four English composition courses and one public speaking course. Students are placed into any one of the courses depending upon their English Entrance Exam scores administered by the university or their TOEFL scores. That is, if students score between 500–549 on the LAU EEE, they are placed in the remedial English course 009, which focuses on basic paragraph/essay writing and reading comprehension and vocabulary. The other courses are English 101 (essay writing), 102 (research writing), 201 (public speaking) and 202 (advanced argumentative writing). I was not Jihad's teacher for English 102, which he took during the summer 1998 session and thus that work is not included here. However, I did follow up on his work in the English 102 course, and the results were comparable to the other English courses. Being adept at using the computer, Jihad was able to access the internet and use many sources to support his topic in his research paper, which quite interestingly was on attitudes towards blind students at LAU.

Jihad's work in the other skills, listening, speaking and reading will be discussed only in passing as I have chosen writing as the focus in reporting Jihad's language learning experiences. Writing is considered important for a students' success in academic studies and perhaps the most difficult skill for EFL learners (Harklau 1994; Leki and Carson 1994; Bacha 2000). Also, the methods followed in helping Jihad acquire the language skills and specifically writing were mainly by having students read to him the required class material and comprehension questions after which he would write the answers on the visio-braille machine. One of the novels, *Like Water for Chocolate*, (Esquivel 1995) was actually taped for him. In essay writing, we would discuss the ideas he would like to write about and then he would draft the essays using his machine. Many hours of conferencing on the drafts would follow. In giving his speeches, we would conference on his speech written on the visio-braille machine and then he would review and revise the speech while I listened to him delivering it and using his self-made visual aid of the two faces. What was most useful was the step-by-step conferencing with Jihad on all tasks, especially at the beginning stages in the writing process from individual sentences to a group of sentences onto the paragraph and then a whole essay. The following sections are brief accounts of Jihad's English course experiences.

5.1 *English 009 – Remedial English 1 October 1997 – February 1998*

The first course Jihad was registered in was English 009. Basically, the tasks the class had to complete were two paragraph and two essay writing assignments done in class according to the process/product approach, reading comprehension, vocabulary and grammar exercises as set out in the required textbook and a final exam, which consisted of reading comprehension questions, vocabulary exercises and an essay. In order to show Jihad's progress, the first paragraph product, written in English 009, and the last essay written in the advanced English 202 class, (the latter after revisions were made), are given in the Appendix. It is clear that progress has been made not only in mechanics, but in sentence structure, vocabulary and the expression of ideas. The first paragraph deals with a concrete subject while the second, two courses later, deals with an abstract topic of justice which shows more complexity of ideas. The ESL Composition Profile by Jacobs *et al* (1981) was used to evaluate students' written work. This is a valid and reliable analytic scoring scale still used successfully in many EFL programmes in the USA and in many other countries (Hamp-Lyons 1991). The paragraph on *Lebanon* that Jihad wrote was discussed during a conference with Jihad according to the ESL Composition Profile (Jacobs *et al* 1981) and revisions recommended. The revised version was not included here since the second sample in the Appendix attests better to the writing development made.

As a result of his searching the internet, listening to students reading his assignments to him and his own curiosity in obtaining books for the blind, Jihad never failed to have ideas on the topics to write on in class. Through oral explanations, he was able to apply the organization of the paragraph and the three part organization of the essay in his own writing. Also, through extensive conference sessions with him and with some student volunteers in class and the university Learning Center, he was able to understand the errors he had made in his writing and to revise as much as possible in later drafts.

Although Jihad took much more time than the other students in class to complete the assignments, he understood all the instructions and actively participated in class discussions. He obtained a grade of 72 per cent as a final course grade with 75 per cent as the average class grade.

5.2 English 101 – English I – February 1998–June 1998

In the second of the Freshman English courses, written tasks were basically the writing of four essays and other summary and paraphrasing assignments as set out in the required textbook (Leki 1995). The most important writing assignment was the last, a researched essay for which students had to conduct a survey and carry out an interview with an expert. The results of the survey and the interview could be used as supporting material in the term paper. It is interesting that Jihad chose the topic of the attitudes of students towards blind people in the classroom, constructed a good survey and interviewed some students at the university, as well as people involved with helping the blind in the community. His findings confirmed those of others that people do not have very positive views towards blind students in regular mainstream classrooms.

Again, Jihad's heightened senses of listening and memory were assets in his understanding of the work to be done in the essays. He obtained 75 per cent for the final course grade with the average course grade being 78 per cent. Although Jihad had improved in supporting his ideas and sentence structure, spelling and other mechanical aspects remained problematic, a normal occurrence for blind people using two types of scripts, as was previously mentioned.

English 201 – Fundamentals of Oral Communication – October 1998–February 1999

Although the emphasis in this study is on the writing skill, a word concerning Jihad's oral communication is given briefly. The English 201 course is basically a public speaking one. In fact, it was the most popular of the four for Jihad, for he could use his oral/aural skills. The tasks in the course were to give four 5–7 minute speeches (informative, persuasive, debate and special occasion) on topics of students' choice. The final exam consisted of an impromptu speech and an evaluation of a written speech. Jihad's performance on all tasks was of comparable proficiency to those of his classmates'. In fact, he surpassed quite a number in class in his fluency, knowledge and confident presentation. Also, his acute listening skills gave him the added advantage to remember more than many of his colleagues and thus ask relevant and pointed questions once a speech had been delivered. It is ironic but interesting that Jihad used visuals to support the topic of his informative speech: the visio-braille device and how it is used by the blind, and the pictures of the two faces, one blind and the other normal to demonstrate the difference between the use of the various senses between the visually impaired and the sighted. Naturally, he did not have the ability to respond to the audience's feedback as far as facial expressions and gestures were concerned throughout the speech as a sighted person might have, but his topics were of so much interest and his verbal skills relatively fluent that the delivery of his speeches held the audience's attention quite well. He earned a grade of 85 per cent as a final course grade with 80 per cent as the average of the final course grade.

5.4 English 202 – Sophomore Rhetoric – February 1999–June 1999

Being an advanced English course, the teacher was skeptical whether Jihad would be able to cope with the writing demands of critique and argumentation based on the required text (Spack 1994). The tasks in the course were basically two written critiques and one persuasive essay. A great deal of reading was necessary on which the writing would be based. Jihad quite surprised the class and the teacher. He would listen for hours to volunteers reading to him the class reading assignments. He even had the whole novel, *Like Water for Chocolate* (Esqurvel 1995), audio-taped himself by a friend so that he could listen to it at his own convenience. The selected writing, the third draft of a persuasive essay (see Appendix) based on a few of the short stories and the novel assignments was in fact typed and assigned grades of 80 per cent and 85 per cent according to the ESL Composition Profile (Jacobs *et al* 1981) by two anonymous readers who did not know that this was Jihad's work. Although there are still mechanical errors, the value of the essay can not be denied on all the five levels of content, organization, vocabulary, language and mechanics. Of course, a lot of work had gone into the essay in the teaching/learning process, but the 'final' product was worth it. It is not uncommon, however, that many students in the class find critique and persuasive writing difficult, but studies have found them to be a very important and significant genres in both academic and professional contexts (Yeh 1998). Jihad's problem, as he mentioned himself, was mostly related to the time factor. Jihad earned an 80 per cent in this course with 78 per cent as the final average course grade.

6 Implications and conclusion

This study has reported a part of one blind students' experiences in four mainstream English courses focusing on paragraph and essay writing in three of the courses. Implications from this first case study for the teaching/learning of blind students in mainstream EFL classes at university level, LAU or any other, are far reaching. With teacher support, encouragement and conference time in a step-by-step approach, blind students can cope with the course work. I do not pretend to overlook the many hours and problems faced in having Jihad 'read' assignments and write and revise the paragraphs and essays. Also, I acknowledge the fact that there were different levels of success from fair to good in using various methods, such as having someone read many of the assignments to Jihad, having someone write down his answers to many language tasks, giving him more time to dwell on certain questions, etc. In addition, I admit that there are different motivation levels and abilities among blind students; Jihad had had a relatively good English background that others might not have. Also, not all students have Jihad's perseverance as the reader might have noted by now. However, this case study does indicate the possibility of including a blind learner in mainstream EFL classes.

Jihad completed his Bachelor of Science Degree in computer science at the Lebanese American University in June 2002. Not having sufficient funding, he was not able to continue onto the Masters Degree but hopes to one day. On Tuesday, 2 August 2005 at 10:00 am, I received a phone call; it was Jihad; how timely since I was editing this paper at the time. He wanted to visit. In ten minutes, a young man, slightly older and a little overweight, walked into my office and, although the office was a new one for him, he found his way to a chair and sat down. We chatted about old times and his work since leaving the university. He informed me that he had an 8:00–4:00 pm job in the Ministry of Social Affairs, Rights and Access Program and was responsible for networking. With the usual smile on his face, Jihad said he was very happy in his job, where everyone worked as a team, but was disappointed that two other blind female graduates were working on the switchboard. He wanted more attention given to the abilities of the blind. I asked about his visio-braille computer machine and he said that he was now in the process of having it repaired, but was using a software on a regular computer with sound. Jihad would never give up. Although the way has been hard, he has learned a lot and at the same has taught us a great deal.

Acknowledgement

Jihad Kreem's permission has been obtained to mention his name and to reprint his work. The author and Jihad welcome correspondence concerning any aspect of the article as well as any information that was not included here due to lack of space. Email: nbacha@lau.edu.lb

References

Akiki, E., Bacha, N., Kreem, J. and Rida, K. (1999), *Conference on the Rights of the Blind in the World*, organized by the Association of the Blind at University in Lebanon and in collaboration with the Lebanese American University.

Bacha, N. (2000), 'Academic writing in a multilingual context: A study of learner difficulties', *International Journal of Arabic-English Studies*, 2, 2, 239–68.

Bacha, N. (2003), 'English across academic and professional communities: a study of EFL learners' needs at the Lebanese American university'. *The Official Journal of the Association of American International Colleges and Universities*, 2, 16–62.

Blackburne, L. (1994), 'English advisers in revolt'. *Times Educational Supplement.* 4063,1

Bonicamp, J. M. (2000), 'Visual aides in teaching blind students mathematics'. *Journal of the Tennessee Academy of Science,* Jan–April, 33.

Bruton, A., Rosas, R. Nussbaum, M., Strasser, K. and Csaszar, F. (1997), 'Computer assisted mediation for blind children'. *Computers and Education,* 28, 4, 29.

Esquivel, L. (1995), *Like Water for Chocolate.* New York, Doubleday.

Fletcher, R.C. (ed.) (1973), 'The teaching of science and mathematics to the blind: report to the Viscount Nuffield Auxiliary Fund'. Worcester: England. http://www.technshare.org.uk/xpedio/groups/public/documnets/visugate/public_teachsci.

Hamp-Lyons, L. (ed.) (1991), *Assessing Second Language Writing in Academic Contexts.* Norwood, NJ: Ablex.

Harklau, L. (1994), 'ESL versus mainstream classes: contrasting L2 learning Environments'. *TESOL Quarterly,* 28, 1, 241–72.

Hartz, D. (2000), 'Literacy leaps as blind students embrace technology'. *English Journal,* 90, 2, 52.

Hayasaki, E. and Moore, S. (2002), 'L.A. to integrate disabled pupils'. *Los Angeles Times,* www.latimes.com.

Ibrahim, A. (1999), 'Navigating the Internet – Blind'. *Daily Star,* 1 October, 4.

Jacobs, H. J., Zinkgraf, S. A., Wormuth, D. R., Hartfiel, V. F. and Hughey, J. B. (1981), *Testing ESL Composition: A Practical Approach.* Rowley, MA: Newbury House.

Jobe, D., Rust, J. O. and Brissie, J. (1996), 'Teachers attitudes toward inclusion of students with disabilities into regular classrooms'. *Education,* 117, (1), 148–53.

Jordan, R. R. (1997), *English for Academic Purposes: A guide and Resource Book for Teachers.* Cambridge: Cambridge University Press.

Kashdan, S., Barnes, R. and Walsh, C. E. (2005), 'Teaching English as a new language to visually impaired and blind ESL students: problems and possibilities'. *American Foundation for the Blind.* www.//Section.asp?SectionID=44&TopicID=108&SubtopicID=32&DocumaentID=193.

Kasper, L. F. (2000), *Content-Based College ESL Instruction.* Mahwah, NJ: Lawrence Erlbaum Associates.

Kreem, J. (1998), *Personal Interview.* Lebanese American University.

Leki, I. (1995), *Academic Writing: Exploring Processes and Strategies.* New York: St. Martin's Press, Inc.

Leki, I. and Carson, J. (1994), 'Students perceptions of EAP writing instruction and writing needs across the disciplines'. *TESOL Quarterly,* 28, 1, 81–101.

Lowenfeld B., Abel, G. L. and Hatlen, P. H. (1969), *Blind Children Learn to Read.* Springfield, Ill: Charles C. Thomas Publisher.

McLinden, D. J. (1990), 'Beliefs about effective education among teachers of visually impaired Children'. *Journal of Visual Impairment and Blindness,* 84, 465–9.

Medina, J. (2002), 'Technology eases the way for the visually impaired'. *The New York Times,* B9(L), col 1.

Monahan, R. G., Marino, S. B., and Miller, R. (1996), 'Teacher attitudes toward inclusion: implications for teacher education in schools 2000'. *Education,* 117, 2, 316–20.

Nikolic, T. (1987), 'Teaching a foreign language in schools for blind and visually impaired Children'. *Journal of Visual Impairment & Blindness,* 62–6.

Price, V. (1993), 'The teaching of modern languages to visually impaired children'. *The British Journal of Visual Impairment,* 11, 3, 118–20.

Sacks, S. Z. and Silberman, R. K (eds) (1998), *Educating Students Who Have Visual Impairments with Other Disabilities*. Baltimore: Paul H. Brookes Publishing Co.

Seng, C. (2005), 'Teaching English to blind students'. *Teaching English – British Council Teaching English – Methodology*. www.teachingenglish.org.uk/think/methodology/blind.shtml.

Spack, R. (1994), *The International Story: An Anthology with Guidelines for Reading and Writing about Fiction*. New York: St. Martin's Press.

Thomas-Ozel, C. (1998), 'A student with special needs in my class?'. *Proceedings of the 5ᵗʰ METU EFL Convention*.

Thomas-Ozel, C. (2000), 'Beginners in the dark'. *Proceedings of the 6ᵗʰ METU EFL Convention*.

Thomas-Ozel, C. (2005), 'A special interest group (SIG) on disability'. www.dbe.metu.edu.tr/claire/claire_sol.htm.

Wall, R. (2002), 'Teachers' exposure to people with visual impairments and the effect on attitudes toward inclusion'. *Review*, 34, 111–19.

Wilder, S. (1999), 'Purdue web site helps blind students to learn'. *Ophthalmology Times*, 24, 5, 10.

Windelborn, A. F. (1999), 'Doing physics blind'. *The Physics Teacher*, 37, 6, 3666.

Xinhua News Agency (2002), 'Shanghai University ready for China's first blind students'. 1008183h2192.

Yeh, S. S. (1998), 'Empowering education: teaching argumentative writing to cultural minority middle-school students'. *Research in the Teaching of English*, 33, 1, 49–83.

Appendix – Written Work by Jihad Kreem

First Paragraph – Remedial English 009 – October 1997

I like spending my summer vacation en Lebanon because of its climate its social life and its nature.

Lebanon in summer has a fair weather a blue sea and a sun smiling the its summer guests.

Lebanese clubs restores their active life during summer they hold their sports festivals in this season, artistic ceremonies are held in summer too. The Lebanese migrates visit Lebanon during this season in addition to many other foreigner tourists.

Nature in Lebanon helps us enjoying this season, Especially in the country-side where we can find beautiful forests, fields, rivers, and springs.

Fair weather, the nature and the active social life makes Lebanon an enjoyable country specially in summer.

Extracts from Final Essay Class Assignment – Advanced English 202 – June 1999

Topic: Argue for or against the statement *Life is Unjust*

Introduction

Life is a gift from God. Since nothing can be contrived from its opponent, no one can accuse life of being unjust. Although injustice is frequently encountered, this is not due to life itself but to the way Man perceives it and lives it. Life is justice but the way many people lives it is not. Why? Simply, because life is the perfect donation from the Mighty. Man continuously attempts to reach the real faultlessness and justice of life. The way of living is closely related to the way he/she is brought up. This variability creates a kind of injustice. What is just for one is not for another. Around the years, the way of living has been perpetually changing. Nevertheless, once Man lives as life should be, justice will surround the world. Our lifestyles, therefore, are like stars rather than the sun or symbols in literature rather than the absolute wisdom.

Conclusion

Life is like water, it has its own cycle through which it rejects the contaminants to gain its purity. You can consider life as a cup of water. You can put it in the freezer and have fresh water, to use for your fruit juice or boil it and have it hot ready for your chocolate. On the other hand, you can mix it with salt and bitter it up. Many times we all make mistakes and accuse life of being unjust. We dye it with our unjust behaviors like water is dyed with ink.

Conclusions

Brian Tomlinson

Like most books on applied linguistics this book does not have a conclusion. However it does make some conclusions, not with the assertive conviction of proven theory but with the confidence of principled possibility. Too many books and articles on language acquisition conclude by stating that more research needs to be done before the findings of their research can be applied. My view is that much of what is dogmatically done in first and other language learning has never been validated by empirical research (e.g. unprepared reading aloud around the class; mechanical drilling, listening and repeating; following a presentation-practice-production approach). If there are indications from research and experience that something different might facilitate language acquisition and development, then it is worth trying it for real and finding out how valuable it is. After all there is not that much to lose.

Here are my own main conclusions taken from those theories, principles and procedures investigated in this book for which a strong case is made:

- Learners should be helped to achieve multi-dimensional mental representation when using language (i.e. helped to represent the language they are responding to and/or initiating through an interaction of sensory, motor, affective and cognitive activity). This can not only facilitate effective communication but can promote language acquisition and development too. See Chapters 1, 4, 5, 6, 7, 9, 10, 11.
- One of the most effective ways of helping learners/users to achieve effective multi-dimensional mental representation is to provide them with meaningful experience of potentially engaging written and spoken texts. See Chapters 1, 4, 5, 9, 10, 11.
- In order to develop communicative proficiency learners need opportunities not only to respond to comprehensible input but to produce outcome-orientated output. See Chapters 9, 10, 11, 12.
- Teachers can help learners achieve language acquisition and development by treating them as users of the language and interacting with them positively and communicatively. See Chapters 4, 5, 7, 13.

I would also strongly support action to:

- Apply what we know about the importance of phonological processing in learning to read in English as an L1 to the teaching of reading in English as an L2, rather than just assuming that learners will be able to transfer their reading skills from their L1 (Chapter 1).
- Make use of research findings to experiment with different ways of facilitating transfer from L2 to L1 reading skills to help those millions of children who have to learn to read in a foreign language (Chapter 2).
- Make use of both dual route and single mechanism theories to develop strategies which could facilitate the acquisition of the simple past in English (Chapter 3).
- Introduce visual and auditory imaging activities in the early stages of language learning courses and materials (Chapters 4 and 5).
- Make more use of research on private speech to find out more about the acquisition process and, in particular, why and how the learner syllabus differs from the teacher syllabus (Chapter 6).
- Train language teachers to develop interactional skills which will enable them to help learners achieve positive affect (Chapter 7).
- Help language learners to become more aware of the existence and validity of varieties of the language they are learning and to develop the ability to interact with speakers of those varieties (Chapter 8).
- Develop materials through which teachers can use recasts in meaning focused activities to facilitate acquisition through varied repetition and the establishment of salience (Chapters 9 and 10).
- Make much more use of the potential of stories, not only on children's courses but on those for adults as well (Chapter 11).
- Develop language learning courses which start with an emphasis on meaningful comprehension but go on to put greater focus on meaningful production (Chapter 12).
- Make use of corpus data to develop courses which help L2 learners to respond to and make use of idiomaticity (Chapter 14).
- Increase learners' awareness of both the cultures of the target language and of their own cultures (Chapter 15).
- Help handicapped learners to acquire languages on mainstream courses (Chapter 16).

Perhaps the most pervasive message from many of the chapters in this book is the need for more action research. Applied linguistics needs to pay more respect to action research and funding bodies need to give more funding to action research on language learning rather than to 'academic' projects which measure in laboratory conditions only what is measurable or what is already known. And most of all we, as teachers and researchers, need to do action research whenever we can, not to attempt to confirm hypotheses but to try out informed hunches in order to find out more about how to make use of them to contribute positively to our learners' acquisition, development and education.

Index